D1453737

Before *Lawrence v. Texas*

Jack and Doris Smothers Series in Texas History, Life, and Culture

Before *Lawrence v. Texas*

The Making of a Queer Social Movement

WESLEY G. PHELPS

University of Texas Press

AUSTIN

Publication of this work was made possible in part by support from the J. E. Smothers, Sr., Memorial Foundation and the National Endowment for the Humanities.

Requests for permission to reproduce material from this work should be sent to:
    Permissions
    University of Texas Press
    P.O. Box 7819
    Austin, TX 78713-7819
    utpress.utexas.edu/rp-form

∞ The paper used in this book meets the minimum requirements of ANSI/NISO Z39.48-1992 (R1997) (Permanence of Paper).

Cataloging-in-Publication Data is available from the Library of Congress.

ISBN 978-1-4773-2232-1 (cloth)
ISBN 978-1-4773-2665-7 (PDF)
ISBN 978-1-4773-2666-4 (ePub)

doi:10.7560/322321

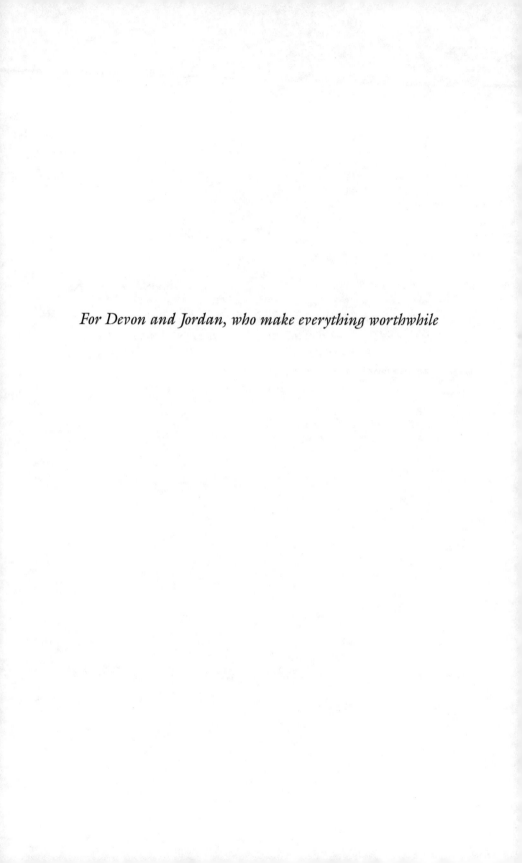

For Devon and Jordan, who make everything worthwhile

I am very aware of the fact that we may lose the decision. Long after the debate and arguments of this case, I hope to say we brought something to Texas and a better understanding of gay people. You have to look at the long term, not the short term in this case.

BAKER V. WADE PLAINTIFF DONALD F. BAKER, 1986

CONTENTS

Before *Lawrence v. Texas*

Before *Lawrence v. Texas*

On June 26, 2003, as Pride Month celebrations took place across the country, the United States Supreme Court delivered an opinion that invalidated the latest iteration of the Texas sodomy law, which made it illegal to engage in oral or anal sex with a person of the same sex, even within the privacy of one's own home. Named after John Lawrence, who was arrested by police in his apartment for allegedly having sex with Tyron Garner, *Lawrence v. Texas* marked a critical turning point in the movement for queer equality. Writing for the majority, Justice Anthony Kennedy concluded that the Texas law violated the privacy protections afforded by the due process clauses of the Fifth and Fourteenth Amendments. Lawrence and Garner, Kennedy wrote, "are entitled to respect for their private lives. The State cannot demean their existence or control their destiny by making their private sexual conduct a crime." What made the opinion in *Lawrence v. Texas* even more remarkable was that in order to strike down the Texas sodomy law based on a constitutional right to privacy, the justices had to overturn one of their own recent decisions. In 1986, the justices had upheld Georgia's sodomy law in *Bowers v. Hardwick*, ruling that the state's interest in promoting morality justified prohibiting certain private sexual activities between consenting adults. Further, the court had ruled that there was no fundamental constitutional right to engage in same-sex sexual activities that had to be respected by any state. Reversing course less than two decades later, Justice Kennedy's statement that the *Bowers* decision "was not correct when it was decided, and it is not correct today" was quite extraordinary.[1]

The immediate effect of *Lawrence v. Texas* was to invalidate discriminatory sodomy laws in Texas and thirteen additional states. The Supreme Court's action also signaled the arrival of a wave of renewed efforts to guarantee equality for queer citizens, setting the stage for an expansive recognition of rights in the post-*Lawrence* era. In 2010, the US Congress repealed the military policy of Don't Ask, Don't Tell, which since the early 1990s had allowed gays and lesbians to serve in the armed forces only if they remained in the closet. The new policy allowed them to serve openly for the first time in US history. In 2013, the Supreme Court nullified a portion of the Defense of Marriage Act, which since 1996 had defined marriage as between one man and one woman, legalized discrimination against gays and lesbians in the dispersal of federal benefits, and allowed states to refuse to recognize same-sex marriages performed in other states. The Supreme Court's action in *United States v. Windsor* struck down the withholding of federal benefits from same-sex spouses, opening the door for the federal government to extend recognition to same-sex marriages. Two years later, the high court ruled in *Obergefell v. Hodges* that marriage was a fundamental constitutional right that could not be denied to same-sex couples by any state. According to the ruling, every state must validate same-sex marriages using the same procedures as those used for opposite-sex marriages. In June 2020, the Supreme Court surprised many observers by ruling that the Civil Rights Act of 1964 protected gay, lesbian, bisexual, and transgender workers from being fired for their sexual orientation or gender expression. Before the decision in *Bostock v. Clayton County, Georgia*, it was legal to fire an employee for these reasons in more than half of the states in the nation. Activists have also achieved dozens of local victories in their quest for equality as individual states and municipalities across the country moved to protect their queer citizens from discrimination, harassment, and violence. Critics often point out that the consequences of these victories are limited and usually confined to those who are able and willing to assimilate into mainstream culture. There is some validity to this view, and there is no doubt that the quest for freedom and equality remains unfinished. The last two decades have nevertheless witnessed remarkable changes in American society when it comes to recognizing the inherent worth and dignity of queer individuals, and millions of Americans have felt these changes in their daily lives.[2]

Helping make these recent gains for queer equality possible has been the eradication of state sodomy laws. In the absence of *Lawrence v. Texas*, such victories would have been unthinkable. As long as their sexual relationships were outlawed, queer Americans wore a stigma of criminality, and the likelihood that a group viewed as serial lawbreakers might successfully assert their rights and gain equal treatment seemed implausible. Why would officials protect their employment rights, opponents might ask, when they would not protect the rights of other criminals like murderers and rapists? Why would same-sex couples be allowed to marry or adopt children if they were admitted criminals? How could Congress allow criminals to serve in the US military? Why would the federal government extend benefits to people who were labeled criminals in many states? As long as sodomy laws remained in state criminal codes, it was difficult to argue for fair and equitable treatment. *Lawrence v. Texas* was momentous because it changed the terms of the debate about citizenship rights, thereby laying the groundwork for an impressive array of subsequent actions to guarantee equality for queer Americans.

The successful outcome of *Lawrence v. Texas* depended on individuals willing to pursue the litigation and risk their lives and livelihoods and on multiple organizations willing to provide the necessary resources. At the center of the case were John Lawrence and Tyron Garner, working-class gay men arrested near Houston in 1998 for allegedly violating the homosexual conduct law, although as the legal scholar Dale Carpenter has shown, the two men most likely were not having sex. On its face, the Texas sodomy statute prohibited certain conduct, but the arrest and prosecution of Lawrence and Garner when they likely had not engaged in the proscribed sexual acts revealed that the law could be used against queer Texans regardless of whether they actually committed a violation. As John Lawrence said multiple times in the aftermath of his arrest, "We were arrested for being gay." Once police charged Lawrence and Garner with violating the homosexual conduct law, several local and national gay and lesbian organizations provided legal and financial support. The willingness of Lawrence and Garner to take a reluctant step into the spotlight and the commitment of organizations to fight for equality delivered the 2003 victory in *Lawrence v. Texas*.[3]

This landmark achievement in the battle against the nation's remaining sodomy laws did not, however, materialize out of thin air when police officers arrested Lawrence and Garner in 1998, nor did *Lawrence v. Texas* launch an expansionary era of queer equality on its own. While *Lawrence* marked a pivotal moment, the case should be viewed as the culmination of a social and legal revolution that had been building for nearly three decades rather than a sudden or unexpected development. Although legal challenges to Texas sodomy laws began in the mid-nineteenth century, it was during the late 1960s that activists organized constitutional challenges to such laws and began achieving partial victories in both state and federal courts. These pre-*Lawrence* legal challenges to various iterations of the Texas sodomy law between the late 1960s and the late 1990s are critical for understanding the deep historical roots of the recent gains of the queer civil rights movement. By providing a necessary blueprint for the personal sacrifice, adaptable legal strategy, and robust organizational support required to launch a successful legal challenge to the Texas sodomy law, the cases documented in this book made possible the Supreme Court victory in 2003 and were therefore equally important to achieving the subsequent gains in the struggle for equality.[4]

This book aims to apply the tools and insights of social history to a study of law and politics. Focusing the lens on grassroots activists and organizations reveals that legal reform and constitutional change often arise from the bottom up. As the legal scholar David Cole has argued, constitutional reforms are not solely the result of high-minded legal theories and augustly robed justices pontificating on various interpretive philosophies for reading the nation's founding documents. Rather, lasting constitutional change stems from below as grassroots activists and organizations make demands using the court system. "To focus on federal judges and courtroom lawyers," Cole writes, "is to miss much of the story—and probably the most important part. Look behind any significant judicial development of constitutional law, and you will nearly always find sustained advocacy by multiple groups of citizens, usually over many years and in a wide array of venues." As they struggled to eradicate discriminatory Texas sodomy laws, the activists and organizations documented in this book set forth their own visions of justice and equality, and occasionally their visions carried the day. Yet even in their failures, they insisted their voices be heard, demonstrating the critical role ordinary citizens play in a thriving democracy.[5]

Early Challenges

For about as long as the state of Texas had a sodomy law there were individuals willing to challenge its legitimacy in a court of law. The criminal codes of the republic and early statehood periods relied heavily on English common law but surprisingly had nothing to say about same-sex sexual behavior. That changed in 1860 when state legislators added the first sodomy law to the penal code, codifying the common law phrasing of the crime against nature that prohibited all nonprocreative sexual activities and usually included oral and anal sex between members of the same or opposite sex and sex with animals. "If any person shall commit with mankind or beast," the 1860 statute read, "the abominable and detestable crime against nature, he shall be deemed guilty of sodomy, and on conviction thereof, he shall be punished by confinement in the penitentiary for not less than five nor more than fifteen years."[6]

The vague language borrowed from the common law proved to be problematic for prosecutors, and Texas judges found it difficult to discern precisely what the new statute prohibited. In 1869, law enforcement officials arrested W. Fennell in Guadalupe County near Seguin and charged him with committing sodomy with another man. After a trial court returned a verdict of guilty and sentenced him to prison, Fennell appealed his case to the Texas Supreme Court, arguing that the language of the statute did not define an actual crime clearly enough to allow for prosecution. In a three-to-two decision, the justices agreed and overturned the conviction. "The crime against nature is wholly undefined by the criminal code," Justice Livingston Lindsay wrote in the majority opinion, "and, therefore, according to its express injunction, is not punishable." Four years later, police officers in McLennan County near Waco arrested Jeff Frazier and charged him with the same crime. On appeal, state supreme court justices reached a similar conclusion in *Frazier v. State* and overturned the conviction. Relying on *Fennell v. State*, Justice Wesley Ogden wrote that "we must hold that there is no such offense known to our law as the one charged in the indictment." Because the penal code required that crimes be explicitly defined, the state sodomy law became unenforceable.[7]

State legislators remedied this problem when they revised the penal code in 1879. Leaving the language of the sodomy statute unchanged, legislators removed the requirement that crimes must be defined in explicit terms. This freed judges and prosecutors to apply the common law definition of the crime against nature to a range of sexual activities they wished to prohibit, as Parker County resident Edward Bergen soon discovered. In 1883, law enforcement officials arrested Bergen near Weatherford, charging him with sodomy and setting his bail at $1,000. Bergen filed a motion alleging excessive bail and unjustified detainment because, as the state supreme court had ruled in *Fennell* and *Frazier*, the statute under which he was charged did not explicitly define a crime. When the trial judge dismissed his motion, Bergen appealed to the newly created Texas Court of Criminal Appeals. The appellate judges disagreed and determined that state legislators had "materially altered" the penal code to allow for the use of the common law in determining the meaning of individual statutes. "We are of the opinion," the judges ruled, "that 'sodomy,' which is the 'abominable and detestable crime against nature' known to the common law, is . . . made an offense, with a penalty affixed thereto in compliance with" the code's requirements. The appellate court upheld the lower court's dismissal of Bergen's appeal, and as a result, Bergen remained in the Parker County jail until his trial date. With a slight modification to the criminal code, state legislators made the Texas sodomy law enforceable throughout the state.[8]

Yet new questions about the applicability of the law arose in state appellate courts during the late nineteenth century. In 1889, Galveston police arrested Charles Medis and Ed Hill for allegedly engaging in anal sex with Milton Werner. Although the court record is sparse because, according to the trial transcript, "the details of the transaction involved in this prosecution are too foul and disgusting to be recorded even in a report of judicial proceedings," it is probable that officers also arrested Werner and that he became a witness for the state in return for a more lenient sentence. During the trial, two additional witnesses testified that they had seen Medis and Werner having sex. Hill, according to the witnesses, was lying nearby reading a newspaper and waiting patiently "to be served next." Werner confirmed this sequence of events for the jury, admitting that he had been a willing participant in the day's activities. In fact, when the unnamed witnesses accused the men of engaging in sodomy, Werner replied that he "did not care a d—n," according to court records. The jury found Medis and Hill guilty and sentenced them to ten years in prison. On appeal, Medis and Hill argued that since Werner was a willing participant, the jury should have been instructed that his testimony required corroboration, as an accomplice cannot serve as a witness against co-conspirators unless that testimony is confirmed by other witnesses. The unnamed witnesses presumably corroborated Werner's testimony, but the appellate judge overturned the convictions because the trial judge did not explicitly instruct the jury that corroboration was necessary. *Medis v. State* established the precedent that if two consensual partners engaged in prohibited sexual conduct, the testimony of one could not be used against the other unless at least one additional nonparticipating witness provided corroboration.[9]

A few years later, a state appeals court heard a case in which judges considered precisely what activities the sodomy law prohibited. Although the case involved a man's sexual abuse of a young girl rather than consensual sex between two members of the same sex, *Prindle v. State* is significant because it set a precedent for the next fifty years and determined a significant limitation in how the law could be applied to consensual sexual activities between adults. In 1892, police officers in Wichita County near Wichita Falls arrested Charlie Prindle after discovering that he had coerced a minor to engage in oral sex. In the absence of a specific statute against the sexual abuse of children, a trial court convicted Prindle of violating the sodomy law and sentenced him to five years in prison. Early the following year, the

Court of Criminal Appeals overturned Prindle's conviction, ruling that the statute referenced a common law definition of sodomy that did not include oral sex. "However vile and detestable the act proved may be, and is," the appellate judges ruled, "it can constitute no offense, because not contemplated by the statute, and is not embraced in the crime of sodomy." The appellate judges noted that for the crime of sodomy to be committed, "the act must be in that part where sodomy is usually committed," presumably the anus. Leaving unaddressed the clear limitation of a penal code that had no statute prohibiting child abuse, the court's decision in *Prindle v. State* established that the state sodomy law did not prohibit oral sex, even for same-sex partners.[10]

Texas appellate judges also had to determine whether the sodomy statute prohibited anal sex between members of the opposite sex, including married couples. In 1896, law enforcement officials arrested Alex Lewis in DeWitt County in rural South Texas and charged him with violating the sodomy law by engaging in anal sex with a woman. A trial court found Lewis guilty and sentenced him to fifteen years in prison, although like many similar cases, the specifics of the case remain unknown because, as the appellate judges noted, "the details are revolting, and not necessary to be stated." On appeal, Lewis argued that the crime of sodomy only applied to two men who engaged in anal sex but not to a man who engaged in anal sex with a woman. In contrast to *Medis* and *Prindle*, this time appellate judges upheld Lewis's conviction. In the phrase, "If any person shall commit with mankind . . . the abominable and detestable crime against nature," the word *mankind*, according to the appellate judges, also included women. Because "the appellant copulated with a woman by penetrating her fundament or anus with his penis," the appeals court ordered Lewis to remain in prison to serve out his sentence. *Lewis v. State* established that the sodomy law could be used to prosecute both same-sex and opposite-sex couples engaging in anal sex.[11]

By the turn of the twentieth century, Texas courts had determined that the sodomy law was enforceable, that a willing participant's testimony must be corroborated, and that anal sex between members of the same or opposite sex fell within the legal definition of sodomy. Yet the question of whether the statute prohibited oral sex continued to plague judges. In 1906, police arrested Jim Mitchell and B. Hammon in Jefferson County near Beaumont for engaging in oral sex with each other. After a trial court sentenced them to five years in prison, the Court of Criminal Appeals overturned the conviction and set the men free. Citing *Prindle v. State*, the appellate judge reiterated that the state sodomy law did not prohibit oral sex. Three years later, law enforcement officials arrested Arthur Harvey in Hill County near Hillsboro and claimed he had violated the sodomy law by performing oral sex on a woman. After the trial court sentenced him to five years in prison, the Court of Criminal Appeals reversed the conviction, asserting that even though "the charge is too horrible to contemplate, and too revolting to discuss," the fact remained that oral sex did not meet the definition of sodomy. Yet Judge William F. Ramsey hastened to add, "We think that some legislation should be enacted covering these unnatural crimes."[12]

The state legislature did not heed Judge Ramsey's request. While revising the penal code in 1911 and in 1925, legislators left the language of the sodomy law unchanged. When the question came before an appellate court in 1926, judges concluded that the legislature intended to exclude oral sex in the statute. That year, police officers arrested Juan Muñoz in Webb County near the border town of Laredo after they alleged he engaged in oral sex with another person whose sex remained unidentified. A trial court convicted Muñoz of violating the sodomy law and sentenced him to five years in prison. As they had done in similar cases since 1893, appellate judges overturned Muñoz's conviction on the grounds that not only did the statute exclude a prohibition on oral sex, but the state legislature had twice failed to add oral sex to the definition of sodomy. "The undisputed evidence," Judge Frank Lee Hawkins wrote in his opinion in *Muñoz v. State*, "shows that appellant performed the disgusting, abominable and nauseating act of using his mouth upon the person of one Meyers." Yet "however vile and detestable the act may have been," Hawkins concluded, "it does not come within the definition of 'sodomy' as known to the common law and adopted by the legislative enactment in our State." During the first few decades of the twentieth century, appellate judges continued to wrestle with the limitations of a statute that did not include a prohibition on oral sex, and state legislators seemed to be in no rush to change the law in response to this judicial frustration.[13]

While overhauling the criminal code in 1943, legislators rewrote the sodomy law to make it both more expansive and more specific. In addition to outlawing sex with animals and intercourse between adults and minors, Article 524 of the revised penal code made criminals out of anyone having "carnal copulation . . . in the opening of the body, except sexual parts, with another human being . . . or whoever shall use his mouth on the sexual parts of another human being for the purpose of having carnal copulation."

The new statute removed all uncertainty; both oral and anal sex were now prohibited, and the offense could be committed by either same-sex or opposite-sex partners, married or unmarried. The crime carried felony charges, and the punishment included a prison sentence between two and fifteen years.[14]

The first significant challenge to Article 524 occurred in 1945 after police arrested Bernard Furstonburg in Tarrant County near Fort Worth and charged him with engaging in oral sex with "a young girl." A trial court found him guilty and ordered him to serve the maximum allowable sentence of fifteen years in prison. While this case may have involved the sexual abuse of a child, the question Furstonburg raised in his appeal forced appellate judges to rule more broadly on the language of Article 524. Furstonburg argued that the law was so vague, particularly in its use of the phrase "carnal copulation," that it could not be enforced. The term could be applied to a mere handshake or kiss, Furstonburg asserted, and therefore did not define a legitimate crime. Judge Harry Graves dispensed with this characterization and upheld the conviction. Comparing Article 524 with its predecessor law, the appellate judge noted that the legislature intended to prohibit both oral and anal sex, which the trial court had convicted the defendant of committing. As for the language of the statute, Judge Graves pointed out that the "term 'carnal copulation' is used interchangeably with the term 'sexual intercourse,' and such phrase appears in the denunciation of the crime of sodomy in a majority of the states of the Union." Two years later the Court of Criminal Appeals upheld a similar conviction of Antonio Medrano, whom police had arrested in Bexar County near San Antonio. After entering a plea of guilty, Medrano appealed his prison sentence. Although the appellate judge found that it was "not necessary to set out the revolting facts" of the case, he upheld Medrano's sentence because it fell within the range specified in the statute. It seemed that the days of successfully challenging the legitimacy of the Texas sodomy law were coming to an end.[15]

Appellate judges consistently upheld sodomy convictions and even expanded the reach of the law during the following two decades. In 1956, Coyce Blankenship allegedly engaged in oral sex with another man in a Dallas jail cell. A trial court found him guilty of violating Article 524 and sentenced him to five years in prison. Blankenship appealed, arguing that he was drunk at the time and did not have any memory of the event, but appellate judge William Morrison upheld the conviction. The following year, a Houston police officer arrested William Jones and Wilford Beckham after he claimed to have witnessed the two men engaging in anal sex in a parked car. During the trial, the prosecuting attorney forced Jones to admit that he had previously served a prison sentence for a drug conviction. "Is that where you learned to do this sort of thing?" the attorney asked Jones, an exchange the trial judge instructed the jury to disregard. In his appeal, Jones argued that the trial judge should have ordered a mistrial because of the harassing question. Judge Morrison, who had ruled in the *Blankenship* case the previous year, disagreed and upheld Jones's conviction.[16]

In 1958, law enforcement officials arrested Donald Sinclair in an Amarillo theater for allegedly engaging in oral sex with another man. During the trial, the arresting officer testified that he had seen Sinclair enter the theater and sit next to a man named Lewis. A few minutes later, according to the officer, Sinclair's head "was moving and bobbing" near Lewis's lap. A jury convicted Sinclair of violating Article 524. On appeal, Sinclair pointed out that prosecutors had failed to prove he had actually taken Lewis's penis into his mouth, arguing that the law required physical penetration. Appellate judge Kenneth Woodley disagreed, noting that the statute only stipulated that the crime involved using the mouth of one person on the sexual parts of another. By upholding Sinclair's conviction, Judge Woodley set a precedent that penetration was not required to convict an individual of violating the sodomy statute. Two years later, Lubbock police officers arrested Delmer Shipp for allegedly having anal sex with another man inside a park restroom. A trial court convicted Shipp and sentenced him to two years in prison even though arresting officers had not witnessed anal penetration. Shipp appealed his conviction, arguing that it was based on insufficient evidence. In his opinion, appellate judge William Morrison, who had heard his fair share of sodomy cases, highlighted many of the details of the case because it was the evidence itself that was in question. "The facts will have to be stated more fully than we would normally do," Morrison reluctantly admitted. The two arresting officers had reported that they saw Shipp standing directly behind another man named Pelton, who had his pants pulled down and was bending over. "Be sure and get it hard because it's no good . . . unless it is hard," officers remembered Pelton saying. According to the officers, Shipp replied that it was "hard enough." After watching for several seconds, the two officers burst into the restroom, at which time they reported that they saw Shipp's erect penis and Pelton's anus, which "was red and looked like it was turned wrong side out," one officer remembered. While neither officer could confirm that anal penetration had occurred, both agreed that bodily contact had taken place. That satisfied Judge Morrison, who upheld Shipp's conviction and concluded that it was not necessary for arresting officers to witness anal penetration firsthand in order to charge someone with violating Article 524. Combined with Judge Woodley's decision in the *Sinclair* case, by the late 1950s it had become much easier for police to secure convictions and for judges to uphold sentences for violations of the sodomy statute. The judicial uncertainty of the late nineteenth and early twentieth centuries gave way to a law that could be used with impunity.[17]

Before *Lawrence v. Texas*

This book begins during the middle of the twentieth century when significant developments shaped both the evolution of the Texas sodomy law and legal challenges against it. During the 1940s and 1950s, the sex researcher Alfred Kinsey published his two volumes on male and female sexuality, and several of his conclusions affected sodomy laws in the United States and around the world. Kinsey discovered, for example, that the prevalence of same-sex sexual activity among Americans was much higher than most thought, and he recommended the eradication of laws that criminalized this type of sexual behavior. In 1951, the American Law Institute (ALI) published its "Model Penal Code," a blueprint for state legislatures to update, systematize, and modernize their criminal statutes. One of ALI's recommendations was to repeal laws criminalizing private sexual behavior between consenting adults, including same-sex sexual activity. In 1961, Illinois became the first state to repeal its sodomy law, but by the early 1970s, few other states had followed its lead.

The effects of these developments on the Texas penal code are the subject of chapter 1. In 1965, state legislators mandated the first major revision of the penal code in more than a century. Initially using the Model Penal Code as a guide, including its recommendation to eliminate laws regulating private sexual behavior between consenting adults, legislators soon discovered that political considerations eroded any plans to liberalize sex laws. Complicating matters further were several legal challenges to the current sodomy law, the most important of which was *Buchanan v. Batchelor*. Dallas police officers arrested Alvin Buchanan twice in 1969 for allegedly having sex in public restrooms. Paired with a married couple who admitted to engaging in prohibited sexual behavior, Buchanan launched the first constitutional challenge to the state sodomy law. A federal district court found Article 524 to be overly broad and therefore unconstitutional, but only because the law invaded the privacy of the married couple. Although Buchanan did not achieve the victory he sought in the courts, state legislators took notice, and his case helped lay the groundwork for subsequent constitutional challenges. Rather than simply deleting Article 524 from the code, however, legislators instead replaced it with a new statute that criminalized oral and anal sex only if engaged in by individuals of the same sex. Taking effect in January 1974, Section 21.06 of the new state penal code, known as the homosexual conduct law, singled out queer Texans and punished them for engaging in sexual behavior that was completely legal for opposite-sex couples.

In chapter 2, I explore the myriad ways 21.06 operated on the ground across the state. The new homosexual conduct law not only labeled as criminals those who engaged in same-sex sexual activity, but it also justified rampant discrimination, harassment, and even violence against them. Although rarely enforced in a private setting, the new sodomy law legitimated the denial of first-class citizenship to queer individuals. During an era of liberation in many parts of the country, a new wave of repression in Texas sent them searching for ways to protect themselves. In chapter 3, I look at how queer Texans began organizing to assert their rights during the 1970s. By the end of the decade, many activists decided to make a concerted effort to challenge 21.06, which they rightly viewed as the primary culprit justifying their oppression.

In 1979, Dallas resident and gay activist Don Baker filed suit in federal court claiming that the new homosexual conduct law violated his constitutional rights. The case, *Baker v. Wade*, the subject of chapter 4, marked a critical turning point both in the emerging movement to overturn the state's discriminatory law and in the rising struggle for equality. Building on the foundation of *Buchanan v. Batchelor*, Baker's case was the first organized and financially supported attempt to challenge the legality of the state sodomy law. *Baker v. Wade* also marked the first time a federal judge struck down a sodomy statute based on the constitutional rights of gay and lesbian individuals. The victory in federal court, however, was not the endpoint many activists wanted, and the appeals process turned out to be an even lengthier ordeal requiring the prolonged commitment of local activists. Another complication was the existential threat posed by the AIDS crisis, which began claiming lives during the appeals process and proved easily exploitable by defenders of the homosexual conduct law. After a period of legal wrangling, a federal appellate court reinstated 21.06, and the

Supreme Court affirmed that decision by refusing to hear the case in 1986. *Baker v. Wade* nevertheless helped establish the necessary groundwork for the eventual victory in the Supreme Court in *Lawrence v. Texas* and was a significant development in the longer struggle for queer equality.

After the loss in *Baker v. Wade* and the Supreme Court's 1986 decision in *Bowers v. Hardwick* upholding a similar sodomy law in Georgia, activists seeking to overturn remaining state sodomy laws made the tactical decision to focus on state-level cases. In chapter 5, I investigate the response of Texas activists to this challenge. In 1989, Houston resident and lesbian activist Linda Morales and four additional plaintiffs filed suit in a Texas civil court and claimed that the homosexual conduct law violated several provisions of the state constitution, including the right to privacy, equal protection, and gender equality. The case, *Morales v. Texas*, further developed the legal arguments that would eventually prove successful in eliminating the statute. A district and appellate court agreed that the sodomy law violated the Texas Constitution, but the state's supreme court overturned the ruling in 1994 and reinstated 21.06. Around the same time, Oklahoma native and Texas transplant Mica England sued the Dallas Police Department when they refused to hire her because she admitted to being a lesbian on her application. *England v. City of Dallas* seemed to be a more promising case, but it hit a roadblock on its way to the Texas Supreme Court and thus never received a ruling applicable to the entire state. Like *Morales v. Texas*, however, England's case continued to advance the legal strategy that would eventually prove successful in the highest court in the land.

In light of the many legal challenges to the Texas sodomy law before 2003, it is clear that *Lawrence v. Texas* did not appear out of nowhere. In the book's conclusion, I reinterpret the Supreme Court's *Lawrence* decision with this longer history in mind. While legal developments outside the state were important, by the time police officers arrested John Lawrence and Tyron Garner near Houston in 1998, more than two decades of grassroots mobilization, legal precedent, and organizational momentum in Texas played an equally significant role in making possible their momentous victory over the nation's remaining laws that justified open and blatant discrimination against queer Americans. Only by viewing *Lawrence v. Texas* in this new light does it become possible to understand just how central the fight against discriminatory sodomy laws was to the broader struggle for queer equality.

Because this study places queer political and legal activism at the center of the analysis, it by necessity focuses its lens on Texas cities. Historians are beginning to uncover the experiences of rural gays and lesbians and to investigate how they contributed to the emergence of queer identities. Yet most rural queer life, as this scholarship is showing, was essentially apolitical. "Rural individuals who engaged in same-sex sexual or gender diverse practices," the historians Pippa Holloway and Elizabeth Catte wrote in a recent survey of the field, "were less likely to consider themselves part of a queer community and often did not participate in the political organization and struggles for change that dominate archival records." Rather than intentionally neglecting the lives of rural queer Texans, this book places the emphasis on a political and legal movement and consequently foregrounds urban activists who helped create the organizational and financial support to launch effective challenges to the state sodomy law.[18]

The iterations of the state sodomy law that this book documents, particularly Article 524 and Section 21.06, disproportionately affected Texans who operated outside the bounds of heteronormativity. This included not only lesbian, gay, and bisexual Texans, but transgender individuals whose sexual partners, in the eyes of the state, shared their sexual anatomy. The sodomy statute also applied to Texans who had sex with members of the same sex but who never identified as lesbian, gay, bisexual, or transgender. When specific persons or source materials furnish identity terms, I employ those labels. To be as inclusive as possible more generally about the many Texans whose lives were affected by the sodomy law, I use the label "queer" in an effort to include the state's rich diversity of nonheteronormative experiences and identities. The use of "queer" in this way is not without its limitations. "Queer" acknowledges that personal lives and sexual and gender identities were complex and often fluid, but some of the activists who appear in this book reject it as a label for themselves. To avoid the common pitfalls of bisexual and transgender erasure, however, I hope the advantages of using a wide-ranging queer umbrella to include the many thousands of Texans affected by the state sodomy law outweigh any shortcomings of painting with too broad a brush.

This book offers a new framework for understanding the pre-*Lawrence* legal challenges to Texas sodomy laws as critical to the late twentieth- and early twenty-first-century struggle for queer equality. Viewed in this way, *Lawrence v. Texas* was not a sudden explosion setting off a chain reaction of victories but instead was a raging fire fueled by the burning embers of several decades of citizen activism that continues to sustain efforts to expand the meaning of equality in American society today. A diverse lineup of organizations and individuals from all walks of life fought and sacrificed for the expansion of political and legal equality for queer Americans over the past several decades. The battles documented in this book, complete with both celebratory achievements and crushing setbacks, illuminate the centrality of grassroots activism in bringing about constitutional change and keeping the ideals of democracy alive. The focused activism of the individuals featured in these pages played a determinative role in producing the recent gains, and they accomplished these triumphs through the tried-and-true tactics of organizing, mobilizing, and agitating. In our current political climate, where the rights of queer Americans are under attack, it is imperative to acknowledge that these recent victories did not come out of nowhere. Many activists dedicated significant portions of their lives to the struggle for queer equality, and it remains this type of committed activism that will not only gain additional victories for the cause but also protect what has already been won.

CHAPTER 1

Buchanan v. Batchelor and the Evolution of the Texas Sodomy Statute, 1965–1974

The Penal Code of Texas, as it now exists, . . . is a hodgepodge of inconsistencies, inequities, and penalties which have no basis in reason or common sense.
BEXAR COUNTY GRAND JURY FOREMAN RALPH G. LANGLEY, 1966

Regardless of the outcome, there will be many suits filed in the future which will continue to demonstrate the reluctance of the homosexual to accept second-class citizenship.
BUCHANAN V. BATCHELOR ATTORNEY HENRY MCCLUSKEY JR., 1970

On February 20, 1973, members of the Texas Senate witnessed something in the Austin capitol they had undoubtedly never seen in their political careers. Appearing before the Senate Subcommittee on Criminal Matters, three openly gay men offered their testimony in opposition to a proposed new sodomy statute. Section 21.06, later dubbed the homosexual conduct law, made it a crime for two members of the same sex to engage in any activity in which one participant's genitals came into contact with the other person's mouth or anus. While Article 524, the previous sodomy statute, had outlawed oral and anal sex for all Texans in general terms since 1860 and in explicit terms since 1943, 21.06 would target only same-sex partners. The Austin activist Troy Stokes questioned the claim of many legislators that the statute would protect society from danger. When he had sex with another man, he told the committee, "I don't see how in the world I harm myself or you." Fellow activist Frank Stovall argued that gay and lesbian Texans should be afforded the same control over their bodies that the US Supreme Court's recent decision in *Roe v. Wade*, a Texas abortion case decided less than a month prior, recognized for women. The proposed sodomy law, Stovall said, would violate the rights of gay and lesbian citizens the same way the state's now invalidated abortion law violated women's right to make private decisions about their own bodies. Dennis Milam echoed Stokes and Stovall, pleading with members of the committee to withhold their approval of a sodomy law that would discriminate against approximately 500,000 Texans "whose love, affection, and sexuality is their only crime." Senators listened quietly to the three men before adjourning their hearings, but it remained unclear whether the testimony of Stokes, Stovall, and Milam had changed anyone's mind about the wisdom of including the homosexual conduct law in the state's criminal code.[1]

The 1973 Senate committee hearings capped off a nine-year effort to modernize the criminal laws of Texas. In 1965, the legislature appointed a special committee to perform an overhaul of the state's criminal code, the first such effort in more than a century. Chaired by Page Keeton, dean of the University of Texas School of Law, the penal code revision committee initially found inspiration in several recent developments in the fields of science and law, particularly the publication of the Model Penal Code by the American Law Institute (ALI) in 1962 that called for the decriminalization of all private consensual sexual activities between adults. Ultimately, however, the committee's effort to eliminate the sodomy statute fell prey to state politics. By the time it finally passed in 1973 and was enacted the following year, the new criminal code included Section 21.06, which made all oral-genital and anal-genital contact between members of the same sex a Class C misdemeanor, punishable by a fine of up to $200. Despite the seemingly light penalty, particularly when compared to Article 524's prison sentence of two to ten years, many observers understood that 21.06, like its predecessor statute, would serve as a basis for a range of discrimination, harassment, and violence against queer Texans. The work of legal reformers like those associated with ALI had profound effects on American life and law, but legislators in a majority of US states, including Texas, displayed a stubborn resistance to change laws criminalizing sexual behavior they deemed to be sinful, destructive, or worse. Yet the harmful effects of Article 524 and the potential consequences of 21.06 provoked a handful of Texans to challenge these laws by appealing to the US Constitution. *Buchanan v. Batchelor*, the most significant of these cases, produced lasting consequences for both the shaping of 21.06 and the subsequent legal battle against it. Disorganized, poorly funded, and ultimately unsuccessful, the *Buchanan* litigation nevertheless helped chart the way forward for queer Texans battling for legal equality in their state.[2]

The Model Penal Code and Keeton's Committee

When members of the American Law Institute, a group the legal scholar William Eskridge has called "the grand assembly of law reform, a collection of America's most eminent lawyers, judges, and academics," came together in 1951 to craft a model penal code, they sought to bring order and modernization to the nation's cacophony of disorganized and archaic state criminal codes. Like most Americans, ALI members were familiar with the sex researcher Alfred Kinsey and his two monumental works, *Sexual Behavior in the Human Male* (1948) and *Sexual Behavior in the Human Female* (1953). Kinsey discovered that among his research participants, many sexual behaviors condemned by society, including same-sex sexual activity, were actually in common practice. He also introduced a way of thinking about sexual orientation as a spectrum of attraction and behavior rather than as distinct categories of homosexual and heterosexual. Known as the Kinsey Scale, this new paradigm posited a numbered continuum where 0 represented exclusively heterosexual, 6 represented exclusively homosexual, and 1 through 5 represented some degree of attraction to both sexes. Based on his research, Kinsey concluded that the vast majority of individuals fell somewhere in the middle of the scale.[3]

Kinsey's work initially affected legal reform efforts in Britain, where a committee headed by University of Reading vice chancellor John Wolfenden successfully persuaded the British government to decriminalize same-sex sexual activity in 1967. In the United States, Kinsey's research most directly influenced ALI members as they assembled during the 1950s to streamline US law. Completed in May 1962, the Model Penal Code (MPC) was a strikingly comprehensive reimagining of American law. Article 213 on sexual offenses, for example, called for significant changes in existing laws regulating private adult sexual conduct in all fifty states. The MPC retained and even strengthened penalties for rape, sexual assault, sexual abuse of children and minors, and public sex. Yet the code's authors, after much negotiation and accommodation, recommended removing penalties for adults engaging privately in "deviate sexual intercourse," which the code defined as "sexual intercourse per os or per anum between human beings who are not husband and wife." According to the MPC, penalties for such offenses should be imposed only if coercion were involved.[4]

During a symposium sponsored by the *Columbia Law Review* in 1963, University of Pennsylvania law professor Louis Schwartz, who headed the subcommittee that drafted the MPC's section on sexual offenses, explained their justification for decriminalizing private consensual sexual activities between adults. "The Model Penal Code," Schwartz explained, "does not penalize the sexual sins, fornication, adultery, sodomy or other illicit sexual activity not involving violence or imposition upon children, mental incompetents, wards, or other dependents," based on the idea that "private morality be immune from secular regulation." Citing Kinsey's studies, Schwartz noted that what he termed "sexual derelictions" were in common practice and difficult to control with statutory law. Forbidding same-sex sexual activity seemed especially problematic. "The decision against penalizing deviate sexuality," Schwartz explained, "is rested not merely on the idea of immunity from regulation of private morality, but on a consideration of practical difficulties and evils in attempting to use the penal law in this way. . . . Capricious selection of a few cases for prosecution, among millions of infractions, is unfair and chiefly benefits extortioners and seekers of private revenge." Despite this seemingly enlightened view of the harmful effects of sodomy laws, Schwartz also adopted the opinion of many health professionals that homosexuality was a mental illness. The American Psychiatric Association (APA), for example, officially categorized gay and lesbian individuals as mentally ill until 1973. Yet Schwartz used this view as additional support for decriminalizing private sexual behavior because, as he saw it, criminalizing same-sex sexual activity "prevents some deviates from seeking psychiatric aid." Schwartz recognized that many state legislators around the country would be resistant to decriminalizing what they considered "deviate" sex, even between consenting adults in private, but he warned that failure to eradicate such laws would eventually provoke constitutional challenges.[5]

Schwartz's prediction proved to be accurate in Texas. As Keeton and his twenty-seven-member State Bar Committee on Revision of the Penal Code began convening in 1965, they discovered what a monumental task lay ahead of them. As Keeton later noted, the state's criminal laws were woefully outdated. As Texas transitioned from an agricultural and rural state to an industrialized and urban one, further modernized by two world wars, its criminal code, as Keeton stated, had "not kept pace." Confusing and unnecessary duplication permeated the current code, as did a spirit of overcriminalization and irrational and contradictory distinctions. A person stealing six bushels of oranges, for example, faced up to ten years in prison. A person stealing an entire truckload of watermelons, however, would only receive a $100 fine. Stealing a horse could earn a person ten years in the penitentiary, but murder without malice could only get someone five years in prison. Breaking a gumball machine in a gas station carried a longer jail sentence than breaking into a car. Keeton and the rest of the committee sought to correct these inconsistencies while modernizing the state's criminal laws.[6]

The MPC initially proved useful to the committee. As Keeton explained,

"The Model Penal Code proposals may be modified or rejected, but they cannot be ignored." Early indications suggested that the committee might follow the code's advice to eliminate laws like Article 524. In January 1966, committee member Judge J. Frank Wilson told the *Dallas Morning News* that he believed his colleagues would support deleting prohibitions on private consensual adult sexual activity. Wilson maintained that homosexuality was a mental illness and therefore should not be punished through the criminal code. "My opinion is that it's a shame to send these perverts down to the penitentiary," he said. "I think they ought to be in hospitals." The following month, Joe Estes, chief judge of the federal district court for the Northern District of Texas, wrote to Keeton's committee to suggest eliminating all laws criminalizing "sex deviation between consenting adults." Austin district attorney Tom Blackwell, while not going as far as Estes, at least agreed that prison should not be a punishment for engaging in same-sex sexual activity, writing to the committee that people prosecuted for violating the law should be allowed to check into a psychiatric hospital in lieu of confinement.[7]

In the fall of 1966, Keeton's committee formed the Sexual Offenses subcommittee under the direction of University of Texas law professor Joel Finer to consider how the new penal code would treat sexual crimes. Finer presented his report to the full revision committee during a two-day meeting in Austin in April 1967. Closely mirroring the MPC, Finer's report defined "deviate sexual intercourse" as "any act involving the sex organ of one person and the mouth or anus of the other with the intent (for the purpose) of arousing or gratifying the sexual desires of any person." While it is unclear what situation Finer and his subcommittee had in mind where a person might engage in this activity without the intent of sexual gratification, the definition nonetheless contrasted "deviate" sexual behavior with "ordinary" sexual intercourse, which "occurs upon any penetration of the female sex organ by the male sex organ." Like the MPC, adults engaging in "deviate sexual intercourse" would only be subject to legal punishment if force were involved or if one or more participants were unable to express consent. In effect, Finer's report called for eliminating Article 524 and decriminalizing consensual same-sex sexual activity between adults in private. Members of the revision committee seemed to agree, as the meeting minutes showed no indication that anyone expressed concern about that portion of the sexual offenses section.[8]

The following year, with Finer on a leave of absence, Keeton traveled to Dallas to meet with representatives of the Circle of Friends, the city's first gay rights group, founded by Phil Johnson in 1965. As Johnson reported in the organization's newsletter, the group's letter-writing campaign had convinced Keeton to eliminate Article 524 from the revised penal code, and Keeton wanted Johnson's group to know that he would keep his promise. In a draft of the Sexual Offenses subcommittee's final report, Keeton recommended "that acts of deviate sexual intercourse between consenting adults in private no longer be criminal, and that the law reach only nonconsensual or public acts." In the new code, Keeton explained, "consensual acts of heterosexual or homosexual cunnilingus, fellatio or anal intercourse, although perhaps immoral, would not be criminal." Keeton noted that he and the members of the subcommittee found none of the most common reasons given for preserving a prohibition on private sex acts between adults to be persuasive, particularly the argument that decriminalizing same-sex sexual activity would relay a message of societal approval and produce a spike in the number of people engaging in it. Citing Kinsey's research, Keeton pointed out that 60 percent of married couples already admitted to engaging in oral sex, which was illegal under Article 524. As for same-sex sexual activity, Keeton noted that "homosexuality is viewed as a mental disease by most experts, and it is hardly likely that mental illness will become more widespread as a result of legalizing the practice." Keeton noted that a majority of people would continue to find same-sex sexual relationships "repulsive" and that it remained unlikely decriminalization would result in an increase in same-sex sexual behavior "among people of normal psychological makeup." He also reasoned that prison was not an effective deterrent for gay and lesbian individuals, as incarcerating them "is very much like throwing Br'er Rabbit in the briar patch," suggesting that being locked inside a penitentiary would be a reward instead of a punishment, particularly for gay men. Yet Keeton also thought the threat of imprisonment might deter many gay and lesbian individuals from seeking the psychiatric assistance they needed.[9]

Beyond reflecting contemporary stereotypes about the mental health of gay and lesbian individuals, the chairman also pondered the extent to which criminal laws should be used to enforce morality. "If, indeed, ours is a free society," he wrote, echoing the MPC, "the inescapable conclusion is that it is not the function of our government to attempt to establish an extensive code of morality through the use of the criminal law." Keeton also worried that laws regulating private adult sexual behavior might violate constitutional guarantees of privacy and protections against cruel and unusual punishment. Such laws were "in opposition to the basic right of men to be free in society," Keeton wrote. He also pointed out that Article 524 was "very difficult to enforce, rarely enforced, and subject to discrimination in enforcement," opening up the possibility of blackmail and a general disrespect for the law. "When all factors are weighed," Keeton concluded, "I believe that 'deviate' sexual acts between consenting adults in private should not be the subject of penal sanctions." Keeton admitted, however, that decriminalizing private consensual same-sex sexual activity between adults would "undoubtedly give rise to more controversy than any [other] section."[10]

The Committee's Second Thoughts

Keeton's concern grew stronger when members of the revision committee met in Austin in June 1968 to discuss the report on sexual offenses. Only nine of the twenty-seven committee members attended, giving this small group enormous power over the future of Texas laws regulating sexual behavior. Although no one on the committee had yet raised any concerns over the proposal, several members used this meeting to oppose "legalizing homosexuality." Bexar County district attorney James E. Barlow was the most outspoken in the group, exclaiming that if the prohibition on same-sex sexual activity were eliminated, "you would have every deviate in the United States coming to Texas." Barlow "didn't want to open Texas to homosexuals by legalizing it." San Antonio judge Archie Brown agreed but was not as certain about punishment because, repeating a sentiment Keeton had expressed in his report, "sending a homosexual to prison is more like a reward than a punishment." Harris County district attorney Carol Vance stated that Chicago police had uncovered evidence of "colonies of homosexuals in hotels" in the city, presumably as a result of the decision of the Illinois legislature to repeal its sodomy statute in 1961. Vance opposed eliminating laws like Article 524 on moral grounds but agreed with Brown that perhaps the punishment should be reduced. Law Enforcement Advisory Committee member Glen Conner agreed, reporting that he had spoken with police officers around the state and that they nearly unanimously wanted same-sex sexual activity outlawed, primarily because it was, according to officers, "so destructive of moral fiber and so insidious—especially regarding the young." Yet committee members unanimously supported one significant change to Article 524; they did not want engagement in what they termed "heterosexual deviate sexual intercourse" to be a crime.

This was a remarkable development. While every committee member in attendance favored decriminalizing all private consensual sexual activities between opposite-sex couples, many of them also supported outlawing certain sexual behaviors between same-sex partners. The sex of the partners would become the determining factor when judging the legality of the behavior.[11]

Before making a final decision, committee members asked the consulting psychologist George Parker to weigh in on the matter. Parker, perhaps somewhat weary of the unscientific nature of the preceding conversation, could provide no professional justification for any law criminalizing same-sex sexual behavior. He attempted to counter two of the main arguments that seemed to support such laws. First, Parker acknowledged that many people viewed this type of sexual activity as sinful and unnatural, but he maintained that these personal opinions were insufficient to criminalize the behavior. Second, Parker stated that some individuals, including several members of the committee, believed that removing criminal sanctions against same-sex sexual activity "is going to lead to a massive breakdown of moral fiber and we will be surrounded by male homosexuals because a lot of the youngsters are going to be 'turned on' by this." Yet Parker had been unable to uncover any evidence to support this potentiality. He pointed out that there had been similar fears about the legalization of pornographic books and magazines. The justification for laws against pornography, Parker noted, was "that if youngsters see these things it will turn them into raging sexual monsters and we'll really have our hands full." Yet the recent decriminalization of pornographic literature in Denmark seemed to offer some counterevidence. After an initial surge in sales, the consumption of pornography had tapered off and even dropped below its pre-decriminalization level, and fears of a wave of "sexual monsters" rampaging through the Danish streets never materialized. Parker encouraged the members of the revision committee to differentiate between personal opinions and evidence-based knowledge. "We can talk about how we feel about it but there are no data to back anyone up," he concluded.[12]

Parker's professional advice, no matter how scientifically grounded, was no match for political considerations. Several committee members worried about their reputations should they appear to condone homosexuality by eliminating laws against it. Judge Brown wondered aloud how a "representative from [rural] Polk County could go back home and explain why he endorsed homosexuality." They were also concerned about the fate of their proposal in the state legislature if they took such action. Many legislators, committee members feared, might oppose a revised code if Article 524 were not preserved in some way. Committee member Newton Gresham suggested that if the absence of Article 524 raised too many eyebrows, they should prepare an alternative statute designating same-sex sexual activity a misdemeanor carrying a three-to-twelve-month prison sentence. If decriminalization threatened the fate of the entire code, Gresham reasoned, the alternative statute could be used as a bargaining chip. The rest of the committee agreed, and they drafted language that made private same-sex sexual acts a gross misdemeanor. Others remained unsatisfied with this compromise, and committee member Hume Cofer, an Austin trial lawyer, urged the committee to go ahead and add the alternative statute to the official draft to be presented to the legislature. His motion narrowly passed in a 5–4 vote. Despite the MPC's recommendation to eliminate archaic sodomy laws, the lack of evidence to support the efficacy of such laws, and the extensive research conducted by Joel Finer and the Sexual Offenses subcommittee, a portion of the full revision committee, in a bare majority vote, decided not to risk the appearance of condoning homosexuality by eliminating Article 524. Yet it was even worse than that. While Article 524 theoretically applied to all Texans, the new statute targeted only queer individuals in its application. As the legal scholar Dale Carpenter has argued, this action was "unprecedented in Texas history" because the new homosexual conduct law "represented an *expansion* of the types of acts historically prohibited under sodomy laws . . . [and] also represented a *narrowing* of the class of people historically covered, since now the law applied only to same-sex couples." The result could hardly have been more discriminatory toward queer Texans.[13]

A few years later, recent Southern Methodist University law school graduate Randy Von Beitel interviewed eight of the nine penal code revision committee members who were present for this meeting. Perhaps unsurprisingly, he discovered that those committee members who favored decriminalization believed that laws such as Article 524 violated an individual's personal privacy and represented a form of government overreach. Further, the decriminalization proponents thought that eradicating these types of laws would result in less social discrimination against gay and lesbian Texans and therefore might improve their mental health and well-being. The reasons given by those committee members who favored continued criminalization, however, were more surprising. Only one committee member told Von Beitel that he believed a sodomy statute would reduce the frequency of private same-sex sexual activity. Instead, nearly all of the pro-criminalization committee members reported that it was the possibility of an increase in the number of minors engaging in same-sex sexual activity and a potential rise in other related crimes such as public sex and adult sex with minors that motivated their decision to retain the prohibition. Von Beitel, as well as many of the pro-decriminalization committee members, labeled these fears unfounded, particularly since there was no evidence that the law affected the incidence of same-sex sexual activity among young people and since sex in public and sex between adults and minors would remain felonies in the revised code. The other significant reason pro-criminalization committee members gave for their support of the statute was an assumption that the removal of prohibitions on same-sex sexual activity might increase the visibility of the gay and lesbian subculture and might even provoke gay and lesbian Texans to begin demanding equal rights. Further, they worried that it would be more difficult for employers to discriminate against gay and lesbian Texans if there were no laws against their sexual behavior. "A desire to keep gay people in their place (separate and unequal)," Von Beitel reported, "became quite clear. . . . Several of the Committee members expressed the view that while it was one thing for two homosexually-oriented persons to live together in private, it was quite another for that same pair to kiss in public or be shown on television, flaunting their homosexual orientation."[14]

Most committee members—even those who favored decriminalization—worried that removing a criminal sanction for same-sex sexual activity might doom the revised code entirely. As Chairman Keeton had warned when the Sexual Offenses subcommittee delivered its recommendation, removing Article 524 from the criminal code without offering a punitive replacement would be controversial, particularly among state legislators required to explain their support of a revised code to their constituents. Even those committee members who supported decriminalization were concerned that their action might force many legislators, in an effort not to appear to condone homosexuality, to oppose the revised code entirely for fear their action might encourage more Texans to engage in same-sex sexual behavior. "The fear was that an illusion of moral imprimatur," Von Beitel noted, "would cause those people who are on the borderline between heterosexuality and homosexuality (or as one member of the committee put it 'are on the fence') to come down on the homosexual side of the 'fence,' thereby resulting in more homosexually-oriented persons." Political considerations seemed to take priority for most committee members, and they proved to be determinative in the decision to include the homosexual conduct law in the revised penal code.[15]

Buchanan v. Batchelor

Less than one year after this fateful committee meeting, a groundbreaking federal judicial decision involving Texas's sodomy law reshaped the debate over revising the criminal code. In February 1969, vice officers from the Dallas Police Department arrested thirty-seven-year-old Alvin Buchanan in a public restroom in Reverchon Park for allegedly engaging in oral sex with another man. Two months later, officers arrested Buchanan in a downtown department store restroom for allegedly committing the same offense. Dallas County prosecutors charged him with violating Article 524, and after a brief trial in May, state district judge Ed Gossett sentenced Buchanan to five years in jail.[16]

Representing Buchanan during his trial was twenty-six-year-old Dallas native and Baylor University Law School graduate Henry McCluskey Jr., who had a keen interest in using his position to advance a variety of social justice causes. In September 1969, for example, a local Dallas physician referred Norma McCorvey to McCluskey when McCorvey indicated that she wanted to terminate her pregnancy. One of McCluskey's specialties was adoption law, and since Texas banned abortions, the physician thought adoption would be the best solution. McCluskey, however, viewed McCorvey's situation through the lens of constitutional protections, particularly in light of recent US Supreme Court decisions regarding personal privacy. Recognizing that the Texas abortion law violated these new precedents, McCluskey referred McCorvey to his childhood friend and fellow lawyer Linda Coffee, who in turn consulted with attorney Sarah Weddington. The case resulted in the landmark Supreme Court decision *Roe v. Wade* in 1973, which recognized a woman's right to an abortion based on constitutional privacy protections.[17]

McCluskey was also a gay man, and he often accepted cases from queer clients that other attorneys refused to handle. He believed that Buchanan's case presented an opportunity to challenge the constitutionality of Article 524. Initially, Buchanan and McCluskey targeted police tactics in their federal lawsuit, arguing that the Dallas vice squad's unlawful surveillance of public restrooms violated Buchanan's constitutional protections against unreasonable searches and guarantees of due process and equal protection. Because Dallas police officers often concealed themselves in the attics, air ducts, and walls of public restrooms and other gay meeting places in order to catch gay men in the act, Buchanan asserted in his brief, it was impossible for "homosexuals to be treated as their heterosexual equals." Yet after consulting with Linda Coffee, McCluskey and Buchanan decided to attempt to bring down the sodomy law itself by relying on constitutional protections of personal privacy. In 1965, the US Supreme Court ruled in *Griswold v. Connecticut*, a case that affirmed the right of a married couple to make their own private decision about using contraception, that the Constitution offered multiple protections against invasions of personal privacy, particularly in the Fifth, Ninth, and Fourteenth Amendments. The problem for McCluskey was that vice squad officers had arrested Buchanan in a public restroom on both occasions. McCluskey needed to find a way to appeal to *Griswold*'s privacy precedent despite the public nature of Buchanan's arrests.[18]

A month after Buchanan's second arrest, McCluskey developed a strategy that combined the *Griswold* precedent with a challenge to police misconduct. On May 26, 1969, Buchanan and McCluskey filed their case in federal district court. The named defendants were Dallas police chief Charles Batchelor, two vice squad officers, and Dallas County district attorney Henry Wade, whose name would achieve national recognition in 1973 when he became the defendant in *Roe v. Wade*. To broaden the constitutional attack on Article 524, McCluskey expanded the number of plaintiffs. Michael and Jannet Gibson joined Buchanan to represent married couples who feared being prosecuted under the sodomy law. Also joining the plaintiffs was Travis Strickland, a gay man who represented other gay and lesbian Texans who had never been arrested but nonetheless feared prosecution because they violated Article 524 in the privacy of their own homes.[19]

In November 1969, a federal panel from the northern judicial district of Texas, composed of judges Sarah T. Hughes, Irving Goldberg, and William M. Taylor, heard oral arguments in *Buchanan v. Batchelor*. McCluskey argued that the state of Texas "has no right to dictate the private sex practices of consenting adults." In addition to the right of privacy, McCluskey argued that the law violated the equal protection clause of the Fourteenth Amendment. Article 524 "denies homosexuals their right to be treated as their heterosexual equals," he told the judges. At the same time, McCluskey realized that the judges were most likely to respond favorably to the argument that Article 524 violated the constitutional rights of married couples like the Gibsons. Even the assistant state attorney general agreed that it would be problematic if a married person ever challenged the validity of the law, although to his recollection none ever had. Dallas County assistant district attorney John Tolle confirmed that no heterosexual couple had ever complained about the law to his office. Judge Goldberg concurred that the state sodomy law might run into trouble if a married couple ever did challenge it, perhaps even indicating which way he might rule on Buchanan's case. Article 524, he noted, was potentially "an unconstitutional statute which no one is going to come in and ask to declare it unconstitutional." Yet there in his courtroom were four plaintiffs making that very argument.[20]

On January 21, 1970, Judge Sarah T. Hughes, expressing the panel's unanimous decision, did what no other federal court had ever done and struck down a state sodomy law on constitutional grounds. As McCluskey had predicted, however, the judges relied specifically on how the law affected private sex acts between married couples. Hughes dismissed Buchanan's request to have his two convictions overturned, pointing out that his actions had been conducted in public places. Hughes also wrote that the question of police surveillance tactics would have to be handled by a different court. The only question for the federal panel was whether Article 524 violated the US Constitution, and for that the judges concerned themselves primarily with how the law might affect Michael and Jannet Gibson.[21]

While the panel recognized that the *Griswold* precedent had thus far only protected private sexual relations between married adults and did not apply to same-sex sexual behavior or public sex, the judges were troubled by how the Texas sodomy law attempted to outlaw a long list of sexual behaviors with a single statute. Article 524 prohibited all adult consensual oral and anal sex, whether between same-sex or opposite-sex partners, whether between married or unmarried couples, or whether public or private. Some of these prohibitions were appropriate, the court reasoned, but some were not. "The State has regulated sexual relations by the passage of laws prohibiting what it considers immoral acts, such as adultery and fornication," Hughes wrote, "and we believe that it has that right with reference to sodomy." A prohibition on sodomy, however, must not unnecessarily reach into other areas where it might violate the rights and freedoms guaranteed by the Constitution. "Sodomy is not an act which has the approval of the majority of the people. In fact such conduct is probably offensive to the vast majority," Hughes wrote, in direct conflict with what the sex researcher Alfred Kinsey had discovered more than two decades earlier, "but such opinion is not sufficient reason for the State to encroach upon the liberty of married persons in their private conduct." Even though there was no evidence that a married couple had ever been charged with Article 524, Hughes argued that married couples all over the state who engaged in oral or anal sex were at risk of punishment for their private sexual behavior. Hughes pointed out that this was not simply a hypothetical risk, since law enforcement officials regularly enforced the statute. The Dallas Police Department, for example, reported that its officers made 451 sodomy arrests between 1963 and 1969. Hughes wrote that the rate of arrests, combined with "a [Dallas County] District Attorney [Henry Wade] who takes pride in the manner in which he has enforced the law," illustrated clearly that the Gibsons and other married couples faced "a real threat of prosecution." Because of this, the federal judges found that the Texas sodomy law violated constitutional protections of privacy. "Article 524 is void on its face," Hughes wrote, "for unconstitutional overbreadth insofar as it reaches the private, consensual acts of married couples." Even though the court recognized a state's right to regulate what it viewed as immoral sexual behavior, Hughes's opinion struck down the entire sodomy law as unconstitutional because of its effect on married couples.[22]

Even though it was far from an affirmation of queer equality, the federal panel's decision was a qualified victory for anyone interested in keeping the state out of the bedrooms of consenting adults. Yet by leaving open the possibility of revising the state sodomy law to exempt married couples from its reach, Hughes's opinion raised the prospect of a statute even more injurious to queer Texans. Two days after Hughes issued the court's ruling, the *Dallas Morning News* published an editorial suggesting that very solution. The newspaper's editors worried that the invalidation of Article 524 "will not be good because the perverted mind is not prevented from preying on minors or others in public places." The editorial noted a general slide into social degeneration, as evidenced by *Buchanan* and several recent judicial rulings on pornography. "Filth, smut, permissiveness and sexual perversion will be encouraged. . . . Immorality has been given additional legal status—if not a semblance of respectability." Editors urged law enforcement officials and state legislators to work together to write "a state statute that will give the decent some sense of protection."[23]

Rather than waiting for the legislature to act, the Dallas City Council enacted a new ordinance to replace Article 524 within its jurisdiction. Council members defined sodomy as oral or anal sex conducted in public, and the new law prohibited this behavior, and the solicitation of these acts, only if conducted in public. Violating this new law would be a misdemeanor with a maximum penalty of a $100–$200 fine. Curiously, the new city law did not criminalize private consensual sexual behavior, including same-sex sexual activities, nor did it seem to outlaw solicitation for private

Figure 1.1. Judge Sarah T. Hughes served as a federal judge on the US District Court for the Northern District of Texas from 1961 to 1982 and wrote the decision in *Buchanan v. Batchelor* that invalidated Article 524 on constitutional grounds.

same-sex sexual encounters. In their attempt to replace the state sodomy law, the Dallas City Council, as the *Los Angeles Advocate* later stated, may have passed "America's first city 'consenting adult' law." In the legislature, however, there was movement in a different direction. After the *Buchanan* decision, Representative Joe Golman of Dallas urged Governor Preston Smith to call a special session of the legislature to consider the state's rising crime rate, and one of his goals was to replace Article 524. Mirroring the penal code revision committee, Golman's proposed statute made oral and anal sex a felony but exempted married couples from the prohibition if they consented to engage in the behavior in private. Golman reasoned that his proposal was necessary to "protect the public against homosexual rape," failing to explain how the criminalization of private consensual sexual behavior between adults had anything to do with rape.[24]

While members of the Dallas City Council and the Texas Legislature debated differing ways of replacing Article 524, Alvin Buchanan remained confined in a Dallas jail cell. Despite Judge Hughes's opinion in *Buchanan v. Batchelor*, Judge Ed Gossett refused to release him, reaffirmed his five-year sentence, and even lashed out at the federal court's opinion. "This court," he proclaimed, "is not going to release a confessed and convicted homosexual until and unless compelled to do so," indicating that the three-judge panel's ruling was insufficient to alter his sentencing. Gossett disagreed with the federal court's decision in stark terms. "The (federal) opinion should be reversed or at least modified or restricted," he wrote, "to save society from the flood of perverts which the said opinion would turn loose upon us." Gossett was firm in his conviction that gay and lesbian Texans belonged in prison or some other form of confinement. "Whether sodomy and homosexuality be a crime or a disease," he stated, "the confessed practitioners thereof should be isolated from the society upon which they prey." Gossett also framed Buchanan's case in relation to national concerns about a rising crime rate, evidenced just two years prior with the election of the "law and order" presidential candidate Richard M. Nixon. Like Nixon and many of his supporters, Gossett placed most of the blame for increased crime on federal judges. The recent "liberal decisions of the federal courts," he wrote, "are aiding and abetting the crime wave from which we suffer." The Dallas judge saw the invalidation of Article 524 as part of this troubling descent into lawlessness.[25]

Judge Gossett's effort to connect the decision in *Buchanan v. Batchelor* to the law and order politics of the early 1970s touched off a lively debate among readers of the *Dallas Morning News*. "Keep up the good work,

Judge Gossett," one reader wrote, "and you have the support of the great silent majority that is beginning to make itself heard." Another wrote, "If more of our state judges will stand up and be counted on such matters we may be able to reverse the dangerous trend toward government by court edict." Dallas resident B. R. Tilford applauded Gossett on his willingness to stand "for the right" in his refusal to follow the decision of the federal court. "They are trying to legalize homosexuality, adultery, and the use of drugs," Tilford exclaimed. "I just would not be a bit surprised if they tried to legalize murder next." Richardson resident Wes Drawbaugh agreed, exasperated that there had been "too much demand for the civil rights of criminals." Dallas resident Larry Campbell, however, praised the federal court's decision striking down Article 524. "We can certainly thank our lucky stars for the federal courts," he wrote. "They review these Victorian laws written in an age of darkness, enforced in a state of ignorance and persecution and rightfully deem them void. . . . Judge Gossett would do well to liberalize his medieval views to conform with modern society, and learn to respect individual rights, as well as federal court decrees." The federal court's decision in *Buchanan v. Batchelor* and Judge Gossett's defiant resistance to it illustrated how the question of decriminalizing same-sex sexual behavior intersected with both local and national politics, much the same way it had during the penal code revision committee's debates about how to replace Article 524 in the new state criminal code.[26]

Dallas County district attorney Henry Wade agreed with Judge Gossett's vehement denunciation of the federal court's decision. Near the end of February 1970, Wade announced that he would appeal the *Buchanan* decision to the US Supreme Court. Wade contended that Michael and Jannet Gibson, the married couple who intervened in Buchanan's case, had no legal standing to become plaintiffs since they had never been prosecuted for violating Article 524. Judge Hughes had ruled that the Gibsons had reason to fear prosecution since they admitted to engaging in the prohibited sexual conduct and there was ample evidence that local authorities enforced the law. Wade disputed this evidence, but his argument that the Gibsons lacked standing faced a setback two months later when he discovered that the Dallas County district attorney's office had indeed prosecuted a married couple for violating Article 524 in 1961. The trial ended in a hung jury, but the arrest and prosecution suggested that the Gibsons, and indeed every married couple in Texas who admitted to engaging in oral or anal sex, faced a legitimate threat of prosecution, as Hughes had concluded in her opinion.[27]

For Wade, this revelation simply necessitated a slight adjustment in his argument. "The crime of sodomy," he wrote in his appeal, "like the crimes of murder, incest and narcotic abuse, must not be protected merely because it is performed behind the marital door." Because of *Griswold*, which established privacy as a fundamental constitutional right, Wade needed to show how the prohibition of private consensual oral or anal sex between married partners advanced a state goal compelling enough to outweigh the privacy rights of the individuals involved. "Sodomy in marriage often leads to revulsion and divorce," Wade argued. "Many women have taken the witness stand in divorce cases and testified as grounds for divorce that they were forced to submit to unnatural sex acts." Since marital rape was not yet recognized in the state's criminal justice system, the woman in Wade's scenario could not accuse her husband of forcible sexual assault. Wade contended that a sodomy statute might be her only protection. If the state could not outlaw sodomy within marriage, Wade also wondered how many other crimes married couples would be allowed to commit. "Will we draw the line," he asked, "when our narcotics statutes are attacked by a married couple who believe that if they smoke pot or peyote, they'll have a more meaningful relationship? Or do we allow this in the name of marital privacy and draw the line at murder committed in the privacy of a bedroom during a lover's quarrel? Or do we allow this conduct also?" Wade worried that decriminalizing private oral and anal sex between consenting adults would "be tantamount to opening Pandora's box."[28]

While the US Supreme Court considered whether to hear the case, Buchanan continued to sit in jail, unable to afford the $2,500 bail. To make matters worse, Buchanan suffered deplorable treatment while in custody. "Prisoner life is not easy," he wrote in a letter to the *Los Angeles Advocate* in April 1970. Buchanan reported that all known gay men were segregated together in one cell, clarifying that this was not done for the protection of gay prisoners. "Sometimes I have been beaten by other prisoners and threatened by jail guards," he confessed. "Sometimes they bring horny heterosexuals to our cell to get their rocks off." Yet this was not even the full extent of his suffering. "Some of the things I am forced to do while I am in jail," he wrote, "are unspeakable." While some members of the penal code revision committee speculated that confinement in a jail or a prison would be a reward instead of a punishment for gay men, Buchanan's experiences revealed a much more disturbing reality.[29]

Buchanan also lamented the lack of support he was receiving from gay and lesbian organizations in his home state, writing to the *Los Angeles*

Advocate in April 1970 that these groups "have refused repeatedly to help me." By rejecting an offer to plea down to a lesser charge and preserve some of his anonymity, Buchanan had taken the risk of becoming the public face challenging the state sodomy law, helping hundreds of similarly situated individuals in the process. "Yet," he wrote, "these same people have failed to give me one dime for the freedom that I have purchased for them." After some prodding and a change in organizational leadership, members of Dallas's Circle of Friends managed to provide some support, although their efforts to raise funds from a few national organizations such as the National Legal Defense Fund and the Homosexual Law Reform Society proved unsuccessful. Nevertheless, newly elected Circle of Friends president Paul Russell did put McCluskey in touch with national gay rights activist Frank Kameny, who helped write Buchanan's cross appeal to the Supreme Court. Kameny was the US Army veteran and Harvard University–trained astronomer who was fired from his job with the federal Army Map Service in 1957 when his superiors learned he was gay. In 1960, he filed the first lawsuit on behalf of gay and lesbian civil rights to reach the Supreme Court. Although he lost that case, Kameny went on to create the Mattachine Society of Washington, DC, one of the country's earliest gay and lesbian advocacy groups, and assisted numerous individuals in filing their own discrimination lawsuits.[30]

In their cross appeal, McCluskey and Kameny attempted to expand the scope of Buchanan's case to keep alive the possibility that the Supreme Court might recognize the privacy rights of gay and lesbian citizens. The danger was that if the Supreme Court simply affirmed Judge Hughes's opinion, legislators in Texas and other states could simply write new laws exempting married couples, as Representative Golman was already suggesting. "What we want to do," McCluskey told an interviewer, "is to broaden the basis of the appeal so that with a favorable ruling, any single person, any homosexual, in any one of these states with anti-sodomy statutes would have a solid legal basis for challenging those statutes in Federal Court." In other words, McCluskey and Kameny wanted to convince the court that gay and lesbian citizens enjoyed constitutional privacy rights, and they emphasized the importance of having long-term goals in the struggle for equality. "Regardless of the outcome," McCluskey stated, "there will be many suits filed in the future which will continue to demonstrate the reluctance of the homosexual to accept second-class citizenship."[31]

In response to Buchanan's complaint about the lack of help from gay and lesbian groups, Dallas Circle of Friends president Paul Russell persuaded two national organizations—the North American Conference of Homophile Organizations (NACHO) and the American Civil Liberties Union (ACLU)—to assist in the case. Although unable to provide financial contributions, their vocal support and legal expertise brought national attention and sharpened McCluskey and Kameny's constitutional arguments. NACHO leaders filed an amicus brief with the high court in which they pointed out that Buchanan's case was "the first time in the history of the United States that any successful attack on the sodomy statutes has ever been made in any court on constitutional grounds." The brief urged the justices to uphold the lower court's decision and eradicate the remaining sodomy statutes in forty-eight states. "If the United States Supreme Court reverses this decision and upholds the constitutionality of this statute of Texas," NACHO leaders wrote, "the cause of law reform all over the United States will have been set back for our lifetime." Because the moment was so critical, NACHO leaders pleaded with gay and lesbian rights organizations across the country to contribute to its success. NACHO leaders concluded their brief by pondering "whether the [gay and lesbian] movement has any inkling of what is at stake." Editors at the *Los Angeles Advocate* certainly recognized the importance of *Buchanan v. Batchelor*. In a headline that month they proclaimed, "Dallas Sodomy Case Is Now Most Important One Ever."[32]

Buchanan and McCluskey did not achieve the outcome they hoped for in the Supreme Court. In an eight-to-one decision in March 1971, the high court justices vacated the federal panel's decision. The eight justices in the majority based their decision not on their view of the constitutionality of Article 524 but on a question of federalism, citing a recent case, *Younger v. Harris*, which limited the ability of federal district courts to rule on the constitutionality of state laws. In the case from California, John Harris, a member of the radical student group the Progressive Labor Party, appealed his conviction for violating the state's Criminal Syndicalism Act, claiming the law violated his First and Fourteenth Amendment rights of free speech and due process of law. A California federal district court ruled in Harris's favor, but the Supreme Court overturned the ruling, remarking that federal courts may only rule on the constitutionality of state criminal laws in very special circumstances. "The possible unconstitutionality of a statute 'on its face,'" the justices wrote, "does not in itself justify an injunction against good-faith attempts to enforce it." By citing *Younger v. Harris*, the high court ruled in *Buchanan v. Batchelor* that the three-judge federal panel lacked the authority to decide the constitutionality of Texas's

Article 524. The *Dallas Morning News* reporter Saralee Tiede noted that the Supreme Court's decision in *Younger*, *Buchanan*, and a number of other cases illustrated just how much the high court "has recently become strict in its 'hands-off' policy for federal courts." Article 524 emerged from its first federal legal challenge wholly intact, yet the Supreme Court had refrained from ruling on the statute's constitutionality and instead affirmed the law by asserting that its legitimacy was none of the federal judiciary's business.[33]

Thrilled with the Supreme Court's ruling, Dallas County district attorney Henry Wade announced that his office would commence prosecuting violators of Article 524 with gusto. "Until a final ruling is made on its constitutionality," Wade told the *Advocate*, "I intend to enforce the law." Within a few months, Wade reported that he had filed sodomy charges against thirty offenders. Dallas vice squad officers were also back out on the beat. The unit sergeant designated seven officers to arrest violators of the sodomy and pornography statutes, although he admitted that his officers had never stopped arresting people for violating Article 524. To circumvent Judge Hughes's opinion, officers had been charging alleged offenders with different laws, such as obscene conduct. With the Supreme Court's ruling, however, law enforcement officials were free to arrest and prosecute suspected violators of Article 524 to their heart's content.[34]

Once the Supreme Court reinstated Article 524, Alvin Buchanan's appeal of his two convictions proceeded. Since their constitutional challenge to the statute had failed to persuade the Supreme Court, Buchanan and McCluskey adjusted their strategy to focus solely on illegal police tactics. In their brief filed the following summer in the Court of Criminal Appeals, they argued that Dallas vice squad officers violated Buchanan's Fourth Amendment rights by invading the privacy of a restroom stall, rendering the evidence used against him inadmissible. In July 1971, Judge Leon Douglas agreed, but he added a significant qualification. "What people seek to preserve as private," Douglas wrote in his opinion, "even in areas accessible to the public, may be constitutionally protected as the Fourth Amendment protects people, not places." Judge Douglas concurred that a bathroom stall, even though available for public use, constituted a private space and that persons who used such a stall "are entitled to the modicum of privacy its design affords." For its occupant to expect a reasonable level of privacy, however, the stall in question required a door. This reasoning was both good and bad news for Buchanan. The Sears restroom where police arrested him provided a locking door on each stall. Judge Douglas overturned that conviction, ruling that police officers had violated Buchanan's right to privacy on that occasion. In the Reverchon Park restrooms, however, there were no doors on any of the stalls. In that instance, Judge Douglas concluded, Buchanan had no reasonable expectation of privacy, and he affirmed Buchanan's conviction under Article 524 and his sentence of five years in prison.[35]

While *Buchanan v. Batchelor* was problematic because it involved public sex, the case nevertheless was an important milestone on the road to the eradication of state sodomy laws. Judge Sarah T. Hughes's opinion marked the first time a federal court struck down a sodomy law on constitutional grounds. Despite its limited reach, the ruling helped lay the groundwork for using constitutional privacy protections to dismantle discriminatory sodomy laws. Second, and most important, Judge Douglas's opinion in Buchanan's appeal essentially rendered Article 524 enforceable only if applied to public sex. By asserting that Dallas police officers violated Buchanan's privacy rights by peering into a closed bathroom stall, Douglas foreclosed law enforcement's ability to arrest anyone for violating the sodomy law in private, which of course included the privacy of the home. It stood to reason that if two individuals—of the same or opposite sex—were arrested for engaging in oral or anal sex in private, they would be able to cite Judge Douglas's opinion and similarly argue that police officers had illegally obtained evidence against them in violation of their constitutional right to privacy. While opponents of the state sodomy law might not have recognized the significance of Douglas's ruling, it represented a step toward a judicial recognition of the rights of all Texans, including the state's queer citizens.

Constitutional Considerations

Buchanan v. Batchelor significantly affected the ongoing effort to revise the Texas penal code. In March 1970, two months after Judge Hughes delivered the judicial panel's opinion striking down Article 524, Page Keeton issued a report to his fellow penal code revision committee members exploring the recent developments in constitutional law regarding privacy. Keeton pointed to recent Supreme Court cases like *Griswold*, which protected the right of married couples to seek advice on contraception from their physicians, and *Stanley v. Georgia*, which protected the right of individuals to possess pornographic materials in their own homes. The high court based both rulings on constitutional protections of privacy. Keeton pointed out that Judge Hughes relied on these privacy precedents to strike down Texas's current sodomy statute. "The future development of this concept," Keeton concluded, "may well substantially limit the power of the state to control a person's acts in private which are not harmful to others." The committee chairman undoubtedly intended to persuade members of the committee who continued to support criminalizing private consensual sexual activity among adults that their efforts might raise troubling constitutional questions.[36]

By the spring of 1970, however, Keeton was pessimistic that he would be able to convince a sufficient number of committee members to decriminalize same-sex sexual behavior in the new code. Eliminating the state sodomy law was also something Keeton was increasingly reluctant to fight for, especially since he wanted the committee's proposal ready to present to the state legislature the following year. Keeton's lugubrious outlook became evident in April when the Dallas Young Adult Institute held a conference titled "The Homosexual and Society" that brought together "professional people to study homosexuality," as the *Dallas Morning News* phrased it. The conference included sessions on religion, the military, mental health, education, and the law. Accepting an invitation to speak, Keeton told conference-goers that it was unlikely Judge Hughes's opinion in *Buchanan v. Batchelor* would stand without a challenge, remarking that he doubted a higher court would "strike out the whole sodomy statute." As for his committee, Keeton similarly held out little hope that the Texas sodomy law would become a relic of the past. "I doubt seriously that the Legislature will ever eliminate homosexuality as an offense," he told his audience, echoing concerns on his committee that a proposed new criminal code without a prohibition on same-sex sexual activity would be unlikely to receive approval from the legislature. The best that opponents of Article 524 could hope for, he stated, was a possible reclassification of the crime of sodomy from a felony to a misdemeanor that would carry a one-year prison sentence instead of a two-to-fifteen-year sentence. This message must have been little consolation for anyone interested in advancing the citizenship rights of queer Texans, particularly since Keeton doubted that either the legislature or the courts were going to provide fruitful avenues for advancing equality in the state.[37]

During the following summer, Keeton's original recommendation to decriminalize all private consensual sexual behavior between adults, including between same-sex partners, got a surprising boost from a group of experts at Sam Houston State University, which housed the premiere criminal justice program in the state. In June 1970, Professor Roland A. Brinkley and his colleagues at the university's Institute of Contemporary Corrections published a report titled "The Laws Against Homosexuality." In their view, private morality should not be governed by criminal law. In a survey of state sodomy laws, authors of the report discovered that most statutes were vague and that penalties were "harsh and unjust." For gay and lesbian individuals, sodomy laws often left them vulnerable to police harassment and entrapment. Brinkley and his colleagues concluded by recommending the repeal of all laws regulating private morality, including sexual behavior. "Each individual has and should develop his own moral standards," they wrote. "The legal structures of the United States cannot impose a standardized code of moral behavior for its members." Further, the report called for the recognition that gay and lesbian individuals constituted a minority group deserving of equal rights. "It appears strange, as the problem is viewed objectively," the report's authors wrote, "that at a period of American history when the government is fighting for the ultimate annihilation of discriminatory practices against any minority, so very few measures are being taken in behalf of the homosexual group." For all these reasons, Brinkley and his criminal justice colleagues encouraged the penal code revision committee to follow the recommendation of the Model Penal Code and eliminate all laws regulating the private consensual sexual behavior of adults in the state of Texas.[38]

The Sam Houston State University report seemed to have little effect on the revision committee or the state legislature. Despite some committee support to eliminate the sodomy law, the final draft of the new code included a sexual offenses section that remained essentially unchanged since the critical 1968 meeting when committee members narrowly voted to preserve the prohibition on private same-sex sexual activity between adults. The committee's proposal labeled this type of sexual behavior a Class A misdemeanor that carried a one-year prison sentence. The phrasing Keeton used to describe this section of the revised code, however, could have been interpreted in multiple ways. The committee chair wrote that acts previously criminalized, such as fornication, seduction, adultery, and private consensual oral or anal sex between adults of the opposite sex, would not be outlawed in the revised penal code. "These offenses are rarely prosecuted today," Keeton stated, "but more importantly the committee believes the state has insufficient interest in the consensual sexual conduct of adults in private to justify subjecting that conduct to the criminal law." Keeton could have left it there, allowing readers to draw their own conclusions about the absence of same-sex sexual conduct in the list of decriminalized acts. Yet he elected instead to point out the omission, writing in parentheses, "An exception is homosexual conduct between consenting adults in private, which the proposed code continues as an offense." Perhaps Keeton intended his phrasing to highlight the inconsistency of retaining a prohibition on same-sex sexual conduct but decriminalizing a long list of other sexual behaviors. Keeton had been a proponent of following the MPC's recommendation to eliminate laws against private consensual sexual behavior between adults, and perhaps this was another effort to persuade members of the legislature to do just that. Another way readers might have interpreted Keeton's explanation was as a reassurance that despite relaxing many laws regulating sex, same-sex sexual behavior would continue to be criminalized. The political future of the proposed criminal code had been a significant consideration during the 1968 committee meeting, and Keeton may have simply been pointing out to legislators that they could vote in support of the proposal without appearing to condone same-sex sexual behavior. Either way, the revised penal code, at this point the product of more than five years of labor by Keeton's committee, was now open to public comment and criticism, both of which it received in abundance.[39]

Public Debate

As its 1971 session opened in January, members of the Texas Legislature prepared to debate the committee's proposal. Yet before legislators began their work, the court of public opinion offered its thoughts. The Dallas Chamber of Commerce passed a resolution in January praising the committee for producing a proposal that would "make the law easier to understand, faster to administer, and, thus, more useful in combating crime." The loudest voices during the early months of 1971, however, came from critics of the proposal. Dallas County district attorney Henry Wade stated his opposition to the revised code early and often. In February, Wade encouraged the legislature to delay consideration of the proposal until its 1973 session to allow for more deliberation, and he especially wanted to allow time for law enforcement officials to amend what he saw as wrongheaded attempts to create new defenses for criminals and shorter penalties for lawbreakers. Wade wrote hundreds of letters to local police chiefs, state criminal judges, and members of the legislature, suggesting that the revision committee had operated "under a cloak of secrecy" and that their proposal was "detrimental to effective law enforcement." Of particular concern to Wade were the changes Keeton's committee made to sexual offenses. The district attorney lamented that the committee had reclassified homosexual conduct as a misdemeanor that now only carried a one-year jail term. Wade argued that this change, combined with others for which the committee recommended abbreviated sentencing, revealed a desire to liberalize the state code and hamstring efforts to preserve law and order.[40]

Several organizations followed Wade's lead. In February, the North Texas Police Chiefs Association (NTPCA) condemned many of the proposed changes to the criminal code and echoed Wade's call for a two-year delay in the state legislature. NTPCA spokesperson Forrest Keene, police chief in the Dallas suburb of University Park, stated that Keeton's committee was attempting to strike "a death blow to law enforcement" and charged that the committee's members wanted to rush their new penal code through the legislature before anyone had sufficient time to study its contents. "Let's make sure that the representatives have an opportunity to see what the study committee is proposing," Keene told the *Dallas Morning News*. Two weeks later, members of the Dallas City Council passed a similar resolution echoing demands for a delay in the legislature "to allow a more intensive study of the proposed changes and their effect upon law enforcement by those responsible for law enforcement." Even Texas attorney general Crawford Martin added his voice to the growing chorus calling for the legislature to delay its consideration of the new penal code. By late February, Wade was routinely referring to the reform proposal as a "monstrosity," and support was growing for his proposal to delay legislative consideration until the 1973 session and to give law enforcement officials a larger role in determining its contents.[41]

Members of Keeton's committee knew that elected legislators would be sensitive to the growing opposition to the proposal. In response to the critics, several committee members attempted to defend their work. Seth Searcy, executive director of the project, defended the proposal during an event in Dallas in late February. "I can't imagine anyone faulting the Legislature for haste," he told his audience, pointing out that the penal code was long overdue for an update. Yet Searcy would not apologize for the committee's efforts to lessen some penalties to reduce the number of incarcerated Texans. The committee had a "preference for non-custodial disposition of defendants," he said. On March 1, the revision committee charged their critics with misrepresentation in the way they focused on "a few emotion-charged issues—the numbers game in sentencing, marihuana [*sic*] possession, the insanity defense, homosexual conduct—and ignored most of the truly significant changes proposed." Committee members argued that the real reason law enforcement officials opposed changes to the penal code was because they wanted "the widest possible discretion in applying the criminal law—to arrest or not to arrest under broadly drawn statutes, to charge or not to charge a particular offense, to determine guilt and punishment in advance of trial through plea bargaining, and generally to expedite the wholesale processing of alleged offenders by every possible means." Revision committee members, on the other hand, were attempting to make the law more transparent and law enforcement officials more accountable. "This is the philosophy of government by law," they wrote, "and not by men." In response to the accusation that the committee had operated in secrecy, committee members reminded critics that one hundred organizations and individuals had been involved in drafting the new penal code and that at least a dozen of those participants had been from the law enforcement community, including a representative from Wade's office. As for calls for the legislature to delay consideration of the proposal until 1973, committee members argued that postponing legislative action would only serve the interests of law enforcement and would unnecessarily delay reforms that were needed as soon as possible. "A new penal code merits the closest study, by proponent and opponent alike," committee members concluded, "and the proposed code's sponsors will do everything in their power to ensure the code receives this attention."[42]

In March 1971, state legislators created a joint House-Senate committee to study the proposed code and to hold public hearings on its various components. Since law enforcement officials had voiced the loudest opposition, joint committee members decided to hear from their representatives first. Harris County district attorney Carol Vance, who had served as a member of the revision committee, appeared in Austin on March 1 and tried to stake out a middle ground. Vance agreed with proponents that in an ideal world, the legislature would vote on the new criminal code by the end of its current session. He argued that realistically, however, legislators needed more time to study the proposal and that perhaps the 1973 session would be a more reasonable target for a full vote. At the same time, Vance stated that the proposal represented "a more logical compilation of statutes than that under which we currently labor." Vance proceeded to explicate many of the various sections of the proposed code, paying particular attention to how it would affect law enforcement. He was pleased that the committee removed forcible oral and anal sex from Article 524, placing the crimes in sections on rape and sexual abuse where they were more clearly defined and appropriately punished. Vance also pointed out that Section 21.06 retained a prohibition on "homosexual conduct," rendering illegal any private oral or anal sex between members of the same sex. This was an improvement over the current code, according to Vance, because Article 524 had prohibited this behavior between opposite-sex partners as well, including married couples. The federal court's decision in *Buchanan v. Batchelor*, Vance noted, had invalidated the law for this very reason. As Vance was speaking, the justices of the US Supreme Court were preparing to uphold Article 524, but their opinion rested not on the legitimacy of the law but rather on the court's view of the proper role of federal courts in determining the constitutionality of state statutes. The constitutionality of Article 524, therefore, was still an open question. In the revised penal code, Vance believed, 21.06 would withstand constitutional scrutiny in a way that Article 524 had not.[43]

Two weeks later, Keeton appeared before the joint committee to urge legislators to approve his committee's proposal during the current legislative session. He told legislators that their proposal represented a "comprehensive codification of the general principles of criminal law," a feat they accomplished by producing a simplified yet thorough code. He also denied that the proposal hampered law enforcement efforts. The revised code, Keeton emphasized, included "many new tools to aid law enforcement." He also repeated his warning that to delay consideration of the new code for two years might sink the entire proposal. Central Texas representative James E. Nugent, co-chair of the joint legislative committee, assured Keeton that while it was possible a new criminal code might not be enacted quickly, the full legislature would pass a version of his committee's proposal during the current session. "I believe you'll see a penal code pass this session of the Legislature," he stated. "I think the effective date may be put off in order for prosecutors and defense lawyers to become fully acquainted with the provisions." While Keeton and other revision committee members may have taken some solace in this proclamation, it did nothing to diminish Henry Wade's confidence that a two-year delay was both necessary and likely. "We don't feel it can be corrected in a few days," Wade told the *Dallas Morning News.* "We will participate in any meetings to change it, but I will still ask for a postponement until the next session. By then, we'll have time for lawyers and law enforcement to go over it line by line by line." Wade made no secret of the kinds of changes he wanted to see in a revised proposal. "You can't amend the liberal philosophy of it by making a few changes," he said, indicating that he would only support a new criminal code if it appeared fundamentally different from the current proposal.[44]

The battle in the legislature reaffirmed Keeton's conviction that it would be nearly impossible to remove prohibitions on same-sex sexual activity in the revised code. During an interview with the *Advocate*, Keeton explained the political implications involved in his committee's work, particularly during the 1968 meeting where members voted to include Section 21.06 in the final draft. "There was substantial sentiment on the [drafting] committee that homosexual conduct is not the sort that can be dealt with in a satisfactory way through the criminal law," he stated. "But the view of the committee was that public sentiment at this time would not permit outright sanction." Keeton wanted the legislature to pass his committee's proposal during its current session, and he was not willing to push on the issue of equal rights for gay and lesbian Texans for fear it would hurt the proposal's chances of passage. While he stated that Section 21.06 was an improvement over Article 524 because a conviction would result in less time in jail, Keeton ultimately had to admit that county jails remained dangerous places for gay men regardless of the length of sentence.[45]

In their condemnation of the proposed code, some public figures pointed directly to the sexual offenses section. Henry Wade nearly always listed sexual offenses in his attacks on the reduced sentences in the revised code. The Dallas district attorney agreed with retaining a prohibition on same-sex sexual activities, evidenced by his robust defense of Article 524 during *Buchanan v. Batchelor*. Yet by including the sexual offenses chapter in his critique, Wade undoubtedly thought a one-year jail sentence for violating the new sodomy law was insufficiently severe. Other opposition voices pushed this argument even further. Perhaps no one attacked Keeton and his committee with more vitriol than retired state district judge A. R. Stout, who when he retired from the bench in rural Ellis County after thirty-two years was the longest-serving judge in state history. In April 1971, Stout began circulating a pamphlet titled "The Proposed Keeton Code Et Al Should Be Defeated," in which he referred to Keeton as "the Harvard College man" and the committee's proposal as "radical" and "Socialistic." Stout wondered if the proposed criminal code "had been written in the State Penitentiary by a committee composed of convicts, social workers and bleeding hearts, with Earl Warren as its chairman," although he later concluded that the proposal was the work of "longhaired men and shorthaired women, ... fuzzy law clerks and instructors [who] have their pot almost with impunity." Stout's main charge was that Keeton and his committee had written a new criminal code completely from scratch. Perhaps Keeton, Stout wrote, thought the Texas penal code needed different sorts of legal models, "perhaps some tribal code of Indians, or one dictated by legal queers, libertarians, Socialists, criminal lawyers or a combination thereof." Stout was aghast that the proposal "abolishes two of the TEN COMMANDMENTS by providing that adultery and fornication (or 'covetness'), no matter how flagrant or repeated, are no longer offenses under any kind of Texas law." He similarly lamented reduced criminal penalties, particularly for "depravity." When he finally got around to critiquing the individual components of the proposal, Stout began with the section on sexual offenses. Admitting that in the revised code no "appreciation is shown for homosexuals," he nevertheless charged that "great leniency is shown, for they are subject to the maximum penalty of a $1,000 fine and one year in jail."[46]

Through these public attacks, opponents of the proposed criminal code succeeded in convincing a majority of state legislators to agree to a two-year delay. "Henry Wade has demagogued a good piece of legislation to death," one member of Keeton's committee said. At the end of May, legislative joint committee co-chair Nugent stated that while the proposal was "basically sound and many of the revisions it makes are urgently needed," it had aroused too much opposition to get it through the full legislature during its current session. Texans would have to wait at least two more years for a new penal code. During those two years, legal developments continued to have an effect on the future of the revised criminal code. As Wade helped delay legislative consideration of the new penal code, the US Supreme Court upheld Article 524 in *Buchanan v. Batchelor*, and Texas courts followed suit. By the time the legislature convened again in January 1973, the uncertainty about the constitutionality of the state's sodomy law had been cleared up and any remaining chance of eliminating the prohibition on same-sex sexual activity in the revised code seemed lost.[47]

More Legal Challenges

Several cases challenging the state sodomy law fell apart as a result of *Buchanan v. Batchelor*. In Galveston, police officers arrested William D. Everette for violating Article 524, and a jury sentenced him to two years in prison in 1970. Everette appealed his conviction the following year, citing the federal court's recent decision in *Buchanan v. Batchelor* and arguing that the state sodomy law was "unconstitutional on its face in that it violates, through its overly broad provisions, the right of privacy and fundamental personal liberties protected under the First Amendment to the United States Constitution." In April 1971, as the legislature made its decision to delay consideration of a new criminal code until its next biennial session, the Texas Court of Criminal Appeals denied Everette's appeal, citing the Supreme Court's *Buchanan* ruling and its own recent decision in *Pruett v. State*, in which it had upheld Article 524 even before the Supreme Court had affirmed the law. Everette had to serve out his two-year prison sentence.[48]

A few months later, in a case known as *Dawson v. Vance*, constitutional arguments against the sodomy statute met a similar roadblock in a federal court. In April 1970, Houston police officers arrested James Dawson and charged him with violating Article 524. There did not yet exist an organized movement for gay and lesbian equality in Houston, but had there been one, activists most likely would have avoided becoming involved in the case, since police charged Dawson with having sex with minors. In fact, if the state had been operating under the revised criminal code, police would have charged Dawson with statutory rape. Article 524, however, made no distinctions in its prohibition of oral and anal sex if it occurred between same-sex or opposite-sex partners, if it was consensual or forcible, or if it occurred between two adults, two minors, or an adult and a minor. The crime, according to Article 524, was the specific sexual act of oral or anal sex.[49]

Houston's ACLU chapter saw Dawson's case as an opportunity to challenge the constitutionality of Article 524, as McCluskey and Buchanan had done in Dallas earlier in the year, so long as they could separate their constitutional arguments from the specific facts of Dawson's alleged crime. Attorney Ben Levy, who had been one of the founding members of the city's ACLU chapter in 1957, encouraged Dawson to appeal his case in federal district court, hoping for an affirmation of Judge Hughes's opinion in *Buchanan v. Batchelor*. Employing a strategy similar to McCluskey's, Levy recruited a married couple to join Dawson in his lawsuit. Donald and Jan Snell agreed to intervene in the case to represent all married couples in Texas who engaged in oral or anal sex, which they admitted they often did, and who feared prosecution under Article 524. During the initial trial, federal district judge Allen Hannay upheld Dawson's conviction, which contradicted Judge Hughes's opinion in *Buchanan v. Batchelor*. Because there was a conflict between two federal district courts, Dawson, the Snells, and Levy appealed to a three-judge federal appellate panel. While awaiting their day in court, however, the US Supreme Court overturned Hughes's invalidation of Article 524, ruling that federal courts must refrain from considering the constitutionality of state criminal statutes except under extraordinary circumstances. As a result, *Dawson v. Vance* was sent back down to Judge Hannay's court for a final decision.[50]

Judge Hannay used the opportunity not only to dismiss the appeal but also to push beyond the boundaries of Dawson's specific crime by issuing a full opinion upholding the constitutionality of Article 524 and condemning the sexual acts it proscribed. Citing the book of Genesis, Hannay wrote, "Sodomy . . . is an act of immemorial anathema both at common law, wherein it was punishable by death, . . . and in ancient times." Thus, Hannay saw no reason to limit a state's authority to prohibit it. "Sodomy is, therefore, in the general sense a crime the control of which is clearly within the reserved and police powers of the several states," he wrote. As for the privacy rights of the Snells in light of *Griswold v. Connecticut*, Hannay asserted that the state sodomy law had never been used to prosecute a married couple. In Hannay's view, Article 524 only prohibited a small number of sex acts among criminals. "The statute is addressed to sufficiently narrow and limited forms of human libidinal aberration," he wrote. "At common law and by sovereign legislative mandate the proscribed conduct is felonious and involves moral turpitude." Article 524, according to the judge, withstood constitutional scrutiny because it did not threaten the privacy rights of married Texans, and Hannay dismissed Dawson's appeal and ordered him to remain in prison. Like *Buchanan v. Batchelor*, *Dawson v. Vance* showed that any legal challenges to the state sodomy law would run up against both judicial distaste toward gay sex and the waning likelihood that federal courts would strike down state statutes on constitutional grounds.[51]

In the Legislature

By the time the legislature reconvened for its 1973 session, the state Court of Criminal Appeals had reaffirmed the constitutionality of Article 524 in a handful of additional cases. Judge Sarah T. Hughes's opinion that Article 524 was overly broad nevertheless convinced many penal code reformers that the sodomy law needed to be replaced with a more specific and targeted statute. During the summer of 1972, Keeton's committee worked with law enforcement officials and prosecutors from around the state to draft a compromise proposal. In October, Keeton presented this revised proposal to the legislature in the hopes it would be taken up immediately when the new session began in January.[52]

The revised proposal included Section 21.06, which outlawed oral-genital and anal-genital contact only if performed by two or more people of the same sex, although committee members reduced the crime from a Class A to a Class B misdemeanor and designated a penalty of less than one year in jail. This was perhaps surprising to some observers, considering how resistant Henry Wade and others were to the idea of leniency in sentencing. Nevertheless, the Dallas County district attorney, who had been the most outspoken critic of the work of Keeton and his committee two years earlier and had been credited with sinking the proposal during the 1971 legislative session, announced that he was satisfied with the compromise proposal, possibly the result of having won a concession on harsher penalties for drug crimes. Wade still "felt the revision was probably unnecessary," the *Dallas Morning News* reported in March 1973, "but if one is adopted, the latest revision is probably preferable to the previous version." Officials with the Texas District and County Attorneys Association and the Texas Criminal Defense Lawyers Association also voiced their support of the compromise proposal. Eight years after Keeton and his committee began their work, it seemed their proposal would finally receive the full consideration of the legislature.[53]

In February 1973, the Texas Senate's Subcommittee on Criminal Matters opened hearings on the proposal. In contrast to the brief hearings during the 1971 session, this subcommittee dedicated a substantial amount of time to discussing the code's sexual offenses chapter, and more than a few witnesses raised objections to criminalizing same-sex sexual behavior. Frank Maloney of the Texas Criminal Defense Lawyers Association went on record opposed to 21.06, pointing out that despite the fact that the entire section on sexual offenses had a guiding principle of decriminalizing all private consensual sexual activities between adults, the revision committee had inexplicably retained a prohibition on private consensual sexual activities between adults of the same sex. "Realizing the facts of life," he stated, "I don't really think it has any place in this code . . . [and] should be deleted." If legislators were concerned about public sex, rape, or sex with minors, Maloney reminded them that other chapters in the sexual offenses section covered those crimes. There was no need, he testified, to retain 21.06, explaining that "there is little harm in removing this last vestige of using the criminal law to enforce controversial religious and moral sentiment." Harris County district attorney Carol Vance countered that the committee had reduced homosexual conduct from a felony to a Class B misdemeanor, which he believed to be sufficiently fair to everyone in the state. Maloney disagreed. "The evil of Sec. 21.06," he responded, "is . . . that it diverts law-enforcement effort from serious anti-social conduct and subjects otherwise upstanding and respectable citizens to reputation-destroying publicity on the occasion of an arrest." Despite the disagreement over prohibiting same-sex sexual activity, no member of the Criminal Matters subcommittee posed any follow-up questions about 21.06, perhaps having already made up their minds about the fate of the proposed homosexual conduct law.[54]

The Senate hearings also provided an opportunity for several gay rights advocates to voice their opinions on the proposed sodomy law, likely the first time any openly gay man spoke before a legislative committee in Texas. Troy Stokes, a leader of the Gay Liberation Front at the University of Texas at Austin, told the committee that there was no persuasive justification, such as harm to the individual or to society, for including Article 524 in the current code, and similarly he saw no compelling reason to include 21.06 in the new code. "The reason I am against 21.06 is it isn't harmful, as far as I can tell," Stokes told members of the subcommittee. "When I engage in that kind of conduct, I don't see how in the world I harm myself or you." Stokes recognized the potential for harm if force were involved or if the activity occurred in public, but he pointed out that other sections of the code prohibited those types of crimes. Dennis Milam, chief spokesperson of the newly created National Organization for the Repeal of Sodomy Laws, argued that 21.06 would discriminate against a significant minority that, according to his conservative estimate based on sex researcher Alfred Kinsey's studies, included more than 500,000 gay and lesbian Texans. "The state of Texas has no place in the bedrooms of its citizens and no right in selectively harassing and discriminating against women and men whose love, affection, and sexuality is their only crime," he told the committee. "We who are America's homosexual millions, and the tens of millions of heterosexual relatives, friends, and supporters of us," Milam concluded, "demand and ask you for the right to seek sexual and affectional self-determination" by deleting 21.06 from the proposed criminal code.[55]

James W. Burfeind, a Socialist Workers Party candidate for the Austin City Council, registered his opposition to 21.06 by calling the proposed law "reactionary" and charging that it would "threaten with arrest a large section of the Texas population for living normal lives." Citing Kinsey's studies, Burfeind argued that 37 percent of Texans currently engaged in sexual activities that would land them in jail. "No one has the right to dictate to human beings what kinds of sexual acts between them are morally accept-able," he reasoned. Instead of targeting gays and lesbians with a new crim-inal statute that would punish them for the people they loved, Burfeind ar-gued that the state of Texas should instead protect the rights and dignity of its gay and lesbian citizens. Frank Stovall, a member of the Young Socialist Alliance and a gay man, framed his opposition to 21.06 on the evolving social and legal understanding of privacy and the sanctity of the body. Citing the US Supreme Court's recent abortion rights decision in *Roe v. Wade*, Stovall argued that the same reasoning should be applied to the privacy rights of gay men and lesbians to control their own bodies. "It is a basic human right of every individual in this society to control his or her own body without any legal interference," he stated. "The flimsy ground on which the sodomy laws are based, . . . that of posing a threat to the moral peace of the commu-nity, are [*sic*] a mere fabrication and have no logical basis." Stovall agreed with Stokes that the alleged "crime" of oral-genital or anal-genital contact between members of the same sex caused no harm to anyone and produced no victims. Without harm or a victim, Stovall concluded, there should be no crime. Discriminatory sodomy laws, according to Stovall, simply "force gay people to relegate what could be meaningful relationships to the ur-gent secrecy of a public restroom or cheap motel." Worse, sodomy laws perpetuated false myths about gay and lesbian individuals, encouraging "repression and discrimination, legally and socially, in jobs, housing, and all other aspects of life in this society." With no questions from state legis-lators, the Senate subcommittee concluded its consideration of the sexual offenses section of the proposed criminal code.[56]

The debate over 21.06 continued beyond legislative chambers. In March 1973, George Beto, the recently retired director of the Texas Department of Corrections, spoke at Southern Methodist University in Dallas and was op-timistic about the prospect for change. He predicted that if discriminatory sodomy laws were not eradicated, at least the penalties for these victimless crimes would be reduced. That same month, David Morris, a graduate stu-dent at the University of Texas at Austin and, along with Dennis Milam, a founder of the National Organization for the Repeal of Sodomy Laws, wrote an essay for the *Texas Observer* in which he took aim at the proposed homosexual conduct law. The injustice of a law that specifically targeted certain citizens for their consensual private sexual behavior, according to Morris, was most evident in the way it would force gay and lesbian Tex-ans to live in fear of prosecution. "It does violence to the person to have intimate aspects of life the subject of any criminal statute at all," he wrote.

"Whether consciously or not, every homosexual lives with the constant threat of going to jail and of being thus officially and publicly drummed out of the ranks of the fully human." Morris reminded readers that laws against public sex, rape, and sex with minors were in other parts of the criminal code. Why, he asked, was it still necessary to prohibit same-sex sexual activity conducted in private between consenting adults? "The only conceivable need for 21.06," he wrote, "is to insure the reign of law and order in the bedrooms of homosexuals." Despite the obvious perniciousness of the proposed sodomy law, Morris held out little hope the legislature would eliminate 21.06, primarily because of the absence of a gay and lesbian liberation movement in Texas. "Gay liberation in Texas has barely gotten off the less hidebound campuses where it began," he wrote. Without the type of pressure that an organized movement for gay and lesbian equality could place on state legislators, Morris worried that a sodomy law would remain part of the state's penal code for quite some time.[57]

Both Morris's and Beto's predictions proved accurate as the state legislature continued to debate the proposal. By May 1973, the Senate Subcommittee on Criminal Matters had voted to approve the code and allow it to advance through the legislative channels, at which time the House Jurisprudence Committee initiated hearings. Although there remained some dispute between prosecutors and defense attorneys on the appropriate severity of criminal penalties throughout the code, both sides managed to keep alive the spirit of compromise to send the proposal to the full legislature for a vote. It was during these final discussions that legislators decided to reduce homosexual conduct to a Class C misdemeanor with a maximum penalty of a $200 fine and no jail time, perhaps part of a compromise that stiffened penalties for another crime. Late in the month, both the House and the Senate approved the proposal and sent it to Governor Dolph Briscoe, who signed it into law in June. The new Texas penal code would take effect on January 1, 1974.[58]

A New Sodomy Statute

After nearly a decade of work, Texas finally had a criminal code written during the twentieth century that brought coherence to what had been a disorganized collection of laws and regulations. In many ways, the new code followed the lead of the MPC by streamlining the state's laws and modernizing penalties. Authors of the MPC had also recommended that states eliminate laws criminalizing private sexual behavior between consenting adults. Initially, members of the revision committee agreed, recommending that Article 524 be eliminated and replaced with laws that only criminalized sexual behavior if it occurred in public, involved force, or qualified as abuse. Yet that effort soon fell prey to political considerations, as members of the committee worried about legislators having to explain to their constituents why they supported decriminalizing same-sex sexual behavior. Many committee members feared that their entire proposal might be endangered if they pushed too hard on this single issue. The state of Texas also saw the first constitutional challenge to its sodomy law while Keeton's committee conducted its work, which affected the legislative debates over the new code. *Buchanan v. Batchelor* marked the first time a federal court struck down a state sodomy statute on constitutional grounds. Poorly funded and without a concerted organizational force behind it, Buchanan's litigation nonetheless helped chart a path forward for queer activists who wanted to use the judicial system to advance their quest for equality. Yet the narrowness of the federal panel's decision, applying only to married opposite-sex sexual partners, as well as the US Supreme Court's decision to overturn the ruling, emboldened the Texas Legislature to include a new version of the sodomy law in its revised criminal code. The result was a statute that criminalized individuals who engaged in oral-genital or anal-genital sexual contact, but unlike Article 524 that had applied to all Texans, Section 21.06 of the new code applied only to citizens who engaged in these activities with someone of the same sex. The other significant modification of Article 524 could be found in the penalty for violating the law, as under the old code a violation was a felony that carried a two-to-ten-year prison sentence, whereas under the new code it was a Class C misdemeanor that carried a $200 fine.

Many observers, including many members of the revision committee and the state legislature, undoubtedly believed that the reduction in the penalty for violating the sodomy law represented a more just and humane way of punishing queer Texans for their sexual behavior. Keeton, for example, thought 21.06, while not a perfect solution, was an improvement over Article 524. Yet while violators would no longer be sent to the penitentiary, the sodomy law nevertheless remained pernicious precisely because opposite-sex partners were now exempt from punishment. Whereas Article 524 had applied to all Texans, 21.06 singled out queer individuals for an unequal application of the law and would now treat them differently from everyone else in the state. It should have come as no surprise, then, that the new sodomy law provided a legal justification for discrimination in a wide range of areas, including employment, housing, family law, and police harassment. Members of the revision committee and the state legislature created a more concise and modern state criminal code between 1965 and 1974, but they ultimately contributed to the ostracizing of a significant minority of Texans and the rendering of them as second-class citizens, making them vulnerable to a range of unequal treatment. Over the following few years, it became evident just how unequal queer Texans had become as a result of 21.06.

CHAPTER 2

The Texas Homosexual Conduct Law in Action, 1974–1982

21.06 serves as the cornerstone of an all-pervasive system of oppression against gay people.
ATTORNEY AND LEGAL SCHOLAR RANDY VON BEITEL, 1974

I was terminated not because of any poor job performance or anything related to my job, but simply because I am gay.
FORT WORTH HILTON HOTEL EMPLOYEE HAROLD WRIGHT, 1975

In 1974, as the new homosexual conduct statute took effect across the state of Texas, Mary Jo Risher and Ann Foreman settled into a new four-bedroom townhouse in Garland, a working-class suburb of Dallas. Risher, a nurse, and Foreman, a bank auditor, also had living with them their children from previous marriages. Risher had two sons aged nine and seventeen, and Foreman had a ten-year-old daughter. The blended family had the full support of Foreman's ex-husband and his new wife, both of whom had an amicable relationship with the two women and their children. When Risher's ex-husband, Douglas, learned about the women's relationship from their older son, however, his reaction was anything but supportive. He filed a motion asking the county family court to remove the children from Mary Jo's home and award custody to him because his ex-wife was a lesbian and therefore, by his estimation, an unfit mother. In October 1975, Judge Oswin Chrisman agreed to reopen the Rishers' child custody case and to place the new evidence about Mary Jo's sexual orientation before a jury. Dallas newspapers reported that this was the first instance in the nation when a jury would consider whether a parent's sexual orientation alone could be used to determine child custody, and the case created national headlines and set an unfortunate judicial precedent. During the trial, Mary Jo Risher faced questions about her parenting abilities, probes into her sexual proclivities, and repeated queries about whether she and Foreman engaged in sexual acts in front of the children. Since the oldest Risher son was now seventeen, he could choose where he wanted to live, and Mary Jo had to hear his decision during the court proceedings. He opted to live with Douglas, stating that he felt "more at ease" living with his father and that he was "ashamed of the way she is" after being harassed by his school peers for having a mother who was a lesbian. "It's a more suitable environment," he said about his father's home, "because it's a man and wife instead of two women or two men together."[1]

The question before the jury was where the Rishers' nine-year-old son would live. During her tearful testimony, Mary Jo asserted that she could "be a homosexual and be proven as a fit mother also." The three psychologists who served as expert witnesses disagreed on that point. Two of them testified that the nine-year-old boy seemed to be well adjusted and thriving while living with his mother and their blended family. More important, the boy told psychologists that he wanted to continue living there. The third psychologist, however, told the jury that Mary Jo had used poor judgment with her son, including allowing him to attend educational programs at the local YWCA and even permitting him to wear a YWCA T-shirt and unisex blue jeans handed down from Foreman's daughter. According to this psychologist, the boy would be better off living with his father. In his closing arguments, Douglas Risher's lawyer stated that leaving the younger son in the custody of his lesbian mother would make him "a guinea pig of somebody's social experiment," and he pleaded with members of the jury to send the boy to the "fine Christian family atmosphere" of his father's home. After a week of testimony, Judge Chrisman instructed the jury to consider whether the revelation of Mary Jo's sexual orientation had created "such a material and substantial change of conditions" that the boy should be removed from his mother's home and placed permanently with his father.[2]

A local celebrity was also involved in the trial. Former Dallas Cowboys offensive lineman Tony Liscio, who had played for nine years under the legendary coach Tom Landry and helped the Cowboys win Super Bowl VI in 1972, served as the jury foreman. Recently retired, Liscio had begun making a post-Cowboys name for himself as a Dallas real estate developer and community volunteer. Liscio recalled that when deliberations began, it was "the lifestyle of a lesbian that most of the jurors were concerned about." With the jury's attention diverted from Mary Jo Risher's actual parenting abilities, it was perhaps predictable that jurors would award custody to Douglas Risher. Only Liscio and one other juror voted to allow the nine-year-old to remain with his mother, believing they had been provided insufficient evidence to revoke her custody rights. Two days before Christmas, after deliberating for five hours, the jury stripped Mary Jo of her custody rights and sent her youngest son to live with his father. Distraught after the

Figure 2.1. Mary Jo Risher is consoled by her mother and attorney Frank Stenger after a jury revoked custody of her son because of her sexual orientation.

reading of the verdict, Mary Jo Risher broke down in tears before being led out of the courtroom by her attorney, her sons taken away from her simply because of her sexual orientation.[3]

Mary Jo Risher's experience was emblematic of a fierce backlash against the increased visibility of gays and lesbians in many parts of the country during the 1970s. From singer Anita Bryant's campaign to overturn Miami's city ordinance protecting the employment rights of gay and lesbian workers to California state senator John Briggs's proposal to remove all gay and lesbian teachers from public schools, opponents of queer equality mobilized in the immediate post-Stonewall years to block additional civil rights victories. In addition to this renewed wave of oppression, the new Texas homosexual conduct law inflicted specific harm on queer individuals throughout the state. There was widespread oppression before the state legislature enacted a new criminal code in 1974, but the adoption of 21.06 represented a critical point of departure. Never before had a statute regulating sexuality been so clearly aimed at a specific segment of the state's population. By prohibiting certain types of sexual contact only when performed by two individuals of the same sex, the legislature created a separate class of citizens, marked by their same-sex relationships, upon whom to target the statute. In the years immediately following the Stonewall uprising of 1969 and in the midst of an era of gay and lesbian liberation, 21.06 fueled a renewed wave of harassment, discrimination, and violence against queer Texans. This legal subjugation took many forms, including police raids of gay and lesbian business establishments; a curtailment of the rights of free speech and assembly; incidents of violence and arson based on hatred; and open and blatant discrimination in employment, housing, child custody, public accommodations, public assistance, immigration, and other areas of life. Yet it was precisely this new wave of inequity that provoked activists across the state to develop creative ways to resist their own oppression, ranging from launching protective patrols in their neighborhoods and filing official complaints about police mistreatment to political lobbying in support of equal rights ordinances and litigation challenging the legal status quo. Queer activists came to understand that the homosexual conduct law lay at the heart of their unequal treatment, and they began to transform their scattered resistance efforts into a targeted attack on the legitimacy of 21.06. Their refusal to accept the new law's damaging consequences proved to be a significant milestone on the path to an organized movement to eradicate 21.06 from the lives of all Texans.[4]

Police Harassment

One of the most visible consequences of the enactment of 21.06 was increased police harassment of queer Texans, particularly in bars, dance clubs, and other social gathering places. In August 1974, just a few months after the new homosexual conduct law took effect, the Dallas Police Department announced that it had hired four new investigators in a recently beefed-up vice control division. Assistant Chief Donald Steele told the *Dallas Morning News* that officers "intend to enforce the law, all over the city. . . . We are going to enforce liquor violations, pornography laws, homosexual violations, gambling and prostitution laws." To achieve this purpose, he outfitted the vice control division with two lieutenants, four sergeants, and fifteen investigators, and these officers found plenty to do. In the early morning hours of March 15, 1975, they raided the Old Plantation, a thriving gay discotheque in the heart of the city. Like many dance clubs, the Old Plantation occasionally remained open after 2:00 a.m., when Texas law required that it stop serving alcohol, and allowed customers to continue dancing and drinking nonalcoholic beverages like coffee. After clearing the club, officers arrested the Old Plantation's general manager, a bartender, and a door attendant and charged them with allowing public dancing after 2:00 a.m. Dallas had a rarely enforced municipal ordinance, passed in 1952, which prohibited public dancing between 2:00 a.m. and 2:00 p.m. Although prosecutors ultimately dropped the charge, officers physically assaulted the bartender, Ricky Carroll, during the raid, ramming his head into a banister outside the club and causing a laceration that required six stitches. This was the first major gay bar raid by DPD's newly revamped vice control division, and it set the tone for subsequent harassment of gay and lesbian establishments.[5]

The following August, officers raided Club Dallas, a gay nightclub and bathhouse near downtown, arresting fourteen customers. Police charged most with public lewdness or indecent exposure, but prosecutors ultimately dropped those charges because it was not clear whether Club Dallas was a public or a private establishment. Despite the uncertainty, one year later officers again raided Club Dallas, arresting four men and charging them with violating the new homosexual conduct law. Club Dallas owners fought these charges, arguing that they operated a private establishment that required members to pay dues and sign a statement upon entry affirming that they would "not be offended by anything that goes on inside." Undercover vice officers had paid these dues and signed the statement and therefore, according to club owners, had not completed the membership requirements in good faith. The charges, they argued, should be dropped because the evidence officers obtained was invalid. Officers retorted that simply charging customers an admission fee did not necessarily make the establishment private. Yet 21.06 prohibited even private acts of same-sex sexual activity, meaning officers could have entered Club Dallas on reasonable suspicion that criminal activity was taking place inside. That was how deleterious the homosexual conduct law was in its effects on the lives of queer Texans. Even after a judge ruled that Club Dallas was a private establishment, thereby invalidating any criminal charges of public lewdness, officers continued to arrest customers for violating 21.06. DPD's chief vice officer, D. L. Burgess, announced in the wake of the raid that in addition to making the arrests, his officers had obtained a map identifying twenty-three additional gay and lesbian establishments in Dallas. "We're going to see a lot more of these arrests coming up soon," Burgess predicted. The journalist Henry Tatum, writing in the *Dallas Morning News* just after the 1976 raid, stated that "the arrests at the Club Dallas last week served notice that stepped-up enforcement of the state laws against homosexuality has begun." Periodic raids of Club Dallas continued for the next two years, during which police often accused customers of violating 21.06.[6]

More often, Dallas police officers arrested gay men for allegedly violating Section 21.07, the public lewdness law. Because the new penal code singled out gay men and lesbians as criminals, police officers often believed they were justified in applying laws like 21.07 in a discriminatory fashion. Most observers agreed that police rarely arrested opposite-sex couples for public lewdness, even in the city's adult entertainment bars. Yet same-sex couples who engaged in public dancing, hugging, or kissing always risked arrest for violating 21.07. In a study of police records for the year 1979, for example, only one of the 110 prosecutions for public lewdness was against a woman. One reader of the gay and lesbian publication *This Week in Texas* (*TWT*) even suggested that queer Texans try to educate the nongay population about the unfairness of 21.07. "The next time you see a straight couple exchanging a caress in public, deep kissing, playfully touching each other's lower extremities, or even dancing too closely," he wrote, "hand them a card" informing them that they are breaking the law. Perhaps then they would recognize the ways that 21.06 unjustly rendered all gay and lesbian Texans criminals, susceptible to an inequitable application of other laws. This unjust enforcement was put on full display in October 1979 during a police raid of the Village Station, a new gay and lesbian dance club that had just recently opened in Dallas's Oak Lawn neighborhood, when officers arrested ten customers for public lewdness.[7]

Gays and lesbians in Dallas also suffered their share of police harassment and violence outside bars and nightclubs. In June 1979, Southern Methodist University student Doug Greeson and his friend, identified as John S., walked out of the Fraternity House, a small gay bar in Oak Lawn, and got into John's vehicle. Greeson and John exchanged a brief kiss before starting the car to head home for the evening. It was then that DPD officer William Miller rushed to John's car, flashed his badge, and ordered, "Get out of here, you stinking fags!" When Greeson responded that they had every right to be there, Miller hit him in the face with his fist before striking him repeatedly in the back of the head with his baton. The beating continued outside of the car, and when it was over, Greeson required six stitches in his head. Officer Miller charged both men with public lewdness and Greeson with assaulting a police officer. Despite the fact that John S. witnessed this beating, a Dallas judge ultimately convicted Greeson of assault on a police officer, willing to believe Officer Miller's version of events against that of two gay men. As a result, Greeson became a convicted felon, lost his right to vote, and could not leave the city without consulting his probation officer. The following October, two men were having a conversation in a park in Oak Lawn when a pair of officers arrested them for public lewdness. One of the men protested that they had not been doing anything illegal and in fact had not even been touching, merely having a conversation. According to the man arrested, one of the officers responded, "You should plead innocent; it's your word against ours." Police also began zealously enforcing minor ordinances in Oak Lawn, such as parking and jaywalking, in an effort to harass gays and lesbians. In all these instances, individuals targeted by DPD officers reported being disrespected, verbally abused, or physically assaulted. The situation had gotten so dire by February 1980 that an unknown person spray-painted "Stop Police Harassment" in giant letters on the side of Oak Lawn's Village Station nightclub.[8]

Police harassment in Dallas also helped provoke a wave of violence against gays and lesbians in the city, particularly in the Oak Lawn neighborhood. In July 1979, M. R. Williams wrote to *TWT* to report several incidents he had witnessed, including large groups of teenagers who traveled to the neighborhood to start fights with residents and bar-goers. Many groups stationed themselves outside of popular gay and lesbian bars, waiting to attack anyone who walked out. Williams had also witnessed a group of men driving past a crowded gay and lesbian bar, shouting obscenities and epithets, and finally firing three gunshots into a parked car. The mere presence of 21.06 in the penal code rendered queer citizens criminals, subject to harassment from police and violence from other citizens.[9]

The tense relationship with police was similar in Galveston and Houston. In the summer of 1976, municipal police officers and Texas Alcoholic

Figure 2.2. Graffiti appeared on the side of Village Station in Dallas in February 1980 amid increased police harassment.

Beverage Control agents raided a Fourth of July party at the Kon-Tiki Bath Club in Galveston, arresting thirty-nine people and charging them with indecent exposure and homosexual conduct. Kon-Tiki manager Charles Jernigan reported that officers treated patrons harshly, slamming bodies against the wall before throwing them to the ground to handcuff them. In the aftermath of previous such raids, most of those arrested quietly pleaded guilty and paid their fines so as not to attract attention. This time, however, eleven of the individuals arrested at the Kon-Tiki decided to fight their charges in court. The following August, Edward Ashworth went on trial for indecent exposure, "a random charge drummed up by local police on the night of the raid," according to a court observer with *TWT*. Ashworth's attorneys demonstrated the inconsistencies in the testimony of law enforcement officers. The judge recognized "that the two officers didn't have a leg to stand on," *TWT* reported, "and, after 55 minutes of a rather amusing trial, found the defendant not guilty on charges of indecent exposure." Police dropped most of the other charges after it became clear they rested on equally faulty police testimony. Yet despite the victories for these defendants, the raid at the Kon-Tiki signaled a renewed effort to target gay and lesbian establishments and potentially drive them out of business. Meanwhile, reports began increasing across the state of police arresting gay bar-goers simply for dancing together.[10]

Soon after the Kon-Tiki raid in Galveston, Houston police intensified their harassment of gay and lesbian establishments. On July 16, officers arrested thirty-six people at the Exile, a popular downtown gay bar, and charged most with public intoxication, although multiple witnesses reported that many of those arrested were not even drinking alcohol that night. Subsequent police surveillance and harassment forced the Exile to close its doors. During the same weekend, Houston police arrested two men at Tangiers, a gay nightspot in west Houston, charging them with lewd dancing. Owners of the Venture-N in midtown Houston also reported an increased police presence in their bar. In late July, the owners of Tooter's Restaurant, a twenty-four-hour eatery and popular gathering place for many queer Houstonians, complained that police officers had targeted their business for harassment. According to Tooter's co-owner Lisa Thompson, Officer H. C. Burks had proclaimed that it was his own personal mission to close down the restaurant. On one particularly busy morning that month, Burks stopped Thompson's son and business partner Norman Thompson in the restaurant's parking lot on the pretext of a drug deal in the area. After refusing to move their cruisers and creating a traffic jam in the Tooter's parking lot, officers arrested Lisa and Norman, charging them with "interfering with the law." One witness concluded "that there was no motive for the action of the policemen except that of harassment."[11]

As in Dallas, the increase in police harassment coincided with a rise in violent crime against gay and lesbian Houstonians. In November 1976, the activist Ray Hill lamented the recent spike in reports of gay men and lesbians being attacked on the streets of the city, including several unsolved beatings and murders in the Montrose area. "Gay people have traditionally been prime targets for 'acceptable' violence," he wrote in *TWT*. "In many social environments it is OK to 'beat up queens.' It is frequently considered the red-blooded American thing for males to do." Yet Hill offered an additional explanation for the victimization of so many gays and lesbians. "Only the grossly unobservant would fail to recognize that one factor present this year, but not present in previous years, is the very active anti-gay propaganda effort given priority by the Houston Police Department." When HPD officers used 21.06 as a justification to raid a bar or harass gays and lesbians on the street, their actions sent a message to the rest of the city that this segment of the population could be treated as criminals or worse.

Renewed police activity struck at the heart of gay and lesbian Houston, and Hill predicted that the attacks on gay businesses and meeting places would continue unabated. "I do expect continued . . . assault on the bars to make it increasingly expensive to be in these businesses," he wrote in *TWT* in March 1977. That seemed to be the point of the raids, as Officer Burks's statement about closing down Tooter's Restaurant made clear. It proved difficult to administer a profitable business enterprise in the face of unrelenting police harassment. The result would be a steady erosion of a sense of community. "Over a period of time we will have fewer and fewer institutions," Hill concluded, making the gay and lesbian community less cohesive and more vulnerable to attack.[12]

A few months later, Houston police officers raided Levi's Lounge, one of the most popular gay bars and dance clubs in the city, and arrested twelve people, including Levi's manager, Bob Jones. Jones reported that during the raid he and another person "were brutally attacked and beaten by members of the HPD Vice Squad," after which both men were arrested and "jailed and held without bond or any charges being pressed against us for 13 hours, before the trumped up charge of 'Interfering with a Police Officer' was placed against us." Officers raided Levi's again days later and arrested twelve people. During this second raid, Jones noted that officers "promised to return again and again until they ran us out of business," saying that this was exactly what police had done to the Exile. Sure enough, Levi's closed its doors for good in August. According to Jones, this was to protect patrons from continued harassment, but owners undoubtedly suffered financial distress because of the raids.[13]

During the first weekend of January 1978, officers launched a string of raids across Houston, arresting several people at popular gay and lesbian nightclubs such as Uncle Charlie's, the Midnite Sun, and the Silver Bullet, charging most with public intoxication. The biggest raid of the weekend occurred at the Old Plantation's Houston location, the largest gay and lesbian club in the city. At 1:15 a.m. on Saturday, six police cruisers pulled up in front of the nightclub, and officers quickly moved in to block all the club's exits to hold the nearly five hundred patrons inside. As officers herded people to the front exits, they picked out and charged several customers with public intoxication and one bartender with serving an intoxicated person. Bob Saulter, who worked as an advertising manager for a weekly news publication catering to the city's gay and lesbian community, was one of those arrested for allegedly being intoxicated in public, even though he had only begun drinking his second beer when officers arrived that night.

At one point during the arrest, an officer put his hand between Saulter's legs and asked, "How do you like this? Are you getting excited, huh, pretty boy?" He also reported that officers belittled and assaulted bar patrons and grabbed several by the throat. Ten days later, officers raided the Locker, a leather bar in the heart of the Montrose neighborhood. Patrons reported that twenty HPD officers stormed inside near midnight, some armed with shotguns and semiautomatic rifles, and arrested eight people, most for not being able to produce a valid form of identification. Police harassment of gay and lesbian establishments had become so commonplace by this time that a reporter for a local newspaper wrote that the Locker "was subjected to one of the increasingly frequent raids by officers of the Houston Police Department." In March 1978, officers raided the Venture-N and the Old Surf's Up Lounge, charging patrons with public intoxication and bartenders with allowing intoxicated persons to remain on the premises. By this time, observers began to notice a pattern. Each of these police raids netted thirteen arrests, "the exact number who can fit in a [police] paddy wagon," one of the arrested individuals remarked. Rather than serving the needs of the community or protecting public safety, many HPD officers were intent on harassing queer citizens, making it difficult to operate a business catering to those citizens, and even shutting down gay and lesbian establishments.[14]

As Ray Hill had argued when the police raids began to increase in 1976, this kind of visible police harassment fomented a rise in other kinds of violence directed at gays and lesbians. During the summer of 1979, several Montrose residents noticed an increase in property damage, including smashed windows and slashed tires on their vehicles. Many also had either witnessed or been a victim to random beatings on the streets of their neighborhood, usually by roving gangs of teenagers. *TWT* editors reported in August that a great number of readers had written over the summer "who have been accosted, beaten, maced, robbed and shot at by a passing motorist" in Montrose. By the end of the summer, there were ten unsolved murders in the neighborhood.[15]

Police harassment in Houston increased during the following few years. Perhaps nothing better illustrated this than a series of raids on Mary's Lounge in the heart of Montrose. Mary's was more than a bar; it was a cultural center, a rallying location, and a political organizing site in addition to a place for the city's gays and lesbians to have fun. As Ray Hill remembered, "I found everything an activist could want [at Mary's]: creative artists and writers, people with connections all over the advertising industry and GLBT folk aplenty yearning to be equal and free, not to mention a few very good-looking men ready to invest their energy into having a good time." It was therefore quite a blow to the community when police raided Mary's during a Halloween party in October 1979. Eight officers, accompanied for some inexplicable reason by a police dog, entered the bar and began placing patrons in handcuffs. They arrested bartender Andy Mills and charged him with assault because he attempted to use the bar's public address system to announce the presence of police officers. Police charged Betty Matthews, a familiar face at Mary's, with possession of a deadly weapon and assault. The deadly weapon, according to police, was a studded bracelet she wore around her ankle. As in previous raids, officers were abusive, even causing Matthews to suffer a leg injury requiring hospitalization. Three months later, officers raided Mary's again, arresting seven patrons for public intoxication and injuring one person in the process.[16]

The largest raid on Mary's, the timing of which sent a clear message to Houston's queer community, occurred during the early morning hours of June 20, 1980, on the eve of the city's Pride celebrations. Around midnight, fifteen officers entered Mary's and ordered all of the approximately ninety patrons up against the walls of the bar. Many later reported that officers "were shoving people against the wall" and "selected at random" certain individuals for arrest, focusing specifically on "people who looked different, those without shirts or in leather." Officers then began loading bar patrons into two police vans, overcrowding one of them with at least thirty people. "We were shoved in like cattle," remembered one of the arrestees. "There was no ventilation. Those things seal like refrigerators, and after ten minutes breathing started getting difficult." Police charged most with public intoxication, but they also charged Mary's owner, Jim Farmer; manager Andy Mills; and several bartenders with serving intoxicated individuals. Farmer, who was one of that year's grand marshals in the city's Pride parade, stated that police officers used "gestapo tactics" during the raid. Yet in the end, prosecutors managed to secure only three convictions among the sixty-one individuals arrested, illustrating that the police used these raids not to enforce the law but to harass, intimidate, and threaten the city's gay and lesbian citizens and business owners.[17]

Many queer Houstonians also experienced police harassment and even deadly violence outside the city's bars. On the night of June 28, 1980, just one week after the most recent Mary's raid, off-duty officer Kevin McCoy shot and killed twenty-seven-year-old Fred Páez, a beloved gay activist who dreamed of becoming a police officer himself. According to McCoy,

Páez approached the off-duty officer, then working as an overnight security guard at a downtown warehouse, and suggested that McCoy and his co-worker, another off-duty HPD officer, join him on the side of the building for a sexual encounter. Once the three men reached the side of the building, according to the two officers, Páez began touching McCoy around his groin area. At that point, McCoy reported that he identified himself as a police officer, drew his gun from its holster, pushed Páez against a parked car, and attempted to place handcuffs on him. It was then, according to the two officers, that Páez was somehow able to accomplish the unbelievable feat of reaching back over his head and shoulders to take the gun from McCoy. During the scuffle, McCoy said, the gun accidentally fired, and a bullet struck Páez in the back of the head. Páez died less than an hour later at a local hospital.[18]

After a brief investigation, HPD's homicide division accepted Officer McCoy's version of events and concluded that Páez had been killed by an accidental firearm discharge while attempting to resist arrest. Gay and lesbian activists conducted their own investigation, during which a firearms expert testified that the type of gun McCoy carried could not have fired accidentally because it was equipped with no fewer than three safety devices.

Figure 2.3. A crowd gathered in Houston to protest the police murder of Fred Páez in 1980.

Investigators also discovered that McCoy and his co-worker were probably intoxicated that night. More damning were the bloody fingerprints investigators found on several empty beer cans, evidence that the officers continued drinking even after McCoy shot Páez. Questions also remained about the nature of Páez's interactions with the officers, as he had worked closely with HPD as a law enforcement incident investigator for gay and lesbian Houstonians and as a deputy constable. Multiple friends testified that Páez never cruised the streets of Houston looking for sexual partners and that as someone who counseled others about how to deescalate interactions with police, it would have been completely out of character for him to initiate a conflict. With such evidence mounting, in October 1980 a Harris County grand jury voted to indict Officer McCoy for negligent homicide. The following year, however, a jury unsurprisingly acquitted McCoy, and the officer returned to his job.[19]

Conflicts between police and queer Houstonians were not often fatal, but even if no one ended up dead, confrontations always had the potential to turn violent. Montrose resident David Reneau and his roommate Cheree, an African American drag performer, found this out one night in September 1980. As they walked from one bar to another, several undercover HPD officers surrounded them, yelling that they were looking for someone named Johnson. Since the officers were not in uniform, Reneau and Cheree thought they were being mugged and attempted to defend themselves. One officer responded by pinning Reneau to the ground and pointing a gun at his head while the others savagely beat Cheree "into a bloody pulp," as Reneau remembered. A few passersby saw what was happening and tried to help, only to be thrown to the ground and beaten themselves. Officers arrested twelve people "simply for being gay and in the area," Reneau asserted. The situation did not improve when the group arrived at the city jail. According to Reneau, officers continued to assault the men, particularly Cheree, who, as a Black gay man, was "humiliated as I've never seen anyone done before," he said. Cheree's "face was beaten and swollen to the point of non-recognition and some of his hair was pulled out," Reneau reported. "He was called names and obscenities (as we all were) that are too vile to print. The mildest of which was 'god-damned n——r faggot, cocksucking drag queen.'" In a clear case of mistaken identity, Houston police officers continued to terrorize and brutalize this group of gay men *TWT* editors dubbed the "unlucky dozen." Yet this was not the result of a run of bad luck. Rather, it was part of an intentional campaign of harassment, intimidation, and violence. As Reneau rightly warned, "Cheree could have easily become the next Fred Paez."[20]

In San Antonio, queer citizens experienced similar harassment and violence, albeit from a different source. San Antonio was a military town, housing four military bases and several additional federal Defense Department installations. Base policies reflected a desire to keep military personnel out of trouble, specifically by preventing young recruits from frequenting San Antonio establishments where alleged criminal activity took place. This effort gave rise to an off-limits list, an index of local establishments that military personnel were prohibited from frequenting, which included houses of prostitution and bars where fights were common. Beginning in late 1973, the off-limits list also included San Antonio's gay and lesbian bars and nightclubs. Although military officials never formally explained this change, the state legislature's passage of 21.06 likely influenced the military's decision to get ahead of the law's enactment and forbid its personnel from patronizing establishments now seen as havens for criminals.[21]

The change in the military's off-limits policy gave rise to a series of military police (MP) raids, as officers insisted on conducting searches for violators. The largest and most popular establishment to appear on the off-limits list was the San Antonio Country, a thriving gay and lesbian dance club located in the heart of downtown close to the Alamo. It made sense, therefore, that the most sweeping military police raid, and the one that received the most attention, occurred at the Country. On the night of December 23, 1973, just one week before the new state penal code took effect, MP officers arrived at the Country to search for military personnel who might be there, an activity they had been engaging in several times per week since the nightclub opened the previous April. During the raid, one MP reported that a bar patron shoved him, prompting the MP in charge of the raid to call in city police. Within minutes, nearly fifty officers arrived with several paddy wagons and began indiscriminately arresting customers and placing them in the vehicles. When San Antonio Country co-owner Gene Elder inquired as to why police were arresting his customers, several officers threatened him with their batons and ordered him to stay out of the way. Although officers only arrested three people that night, they sent a clear message that changing laws and military policies would usher in a new reality of oppression for San Antonio's queer community.[22]

For their final issue of 1980, *TWT* editors compiled a list of the most significant news stories of the year, finding that harassment and violence against gays and lesbians topped the list. This could have been true, in fact, for every year since 1974, when the new state criminal code went into effect. "It is unfortunate that half of the top ten stories of the year are of violence and harassment within the gay community," editors wrote, "but without a doubt, *TWT News* observes that violence has been the most continuous story of the year." They noted that police officers across the state continued to raid gay and lesbian bars and nightclubs, harass gay and lesbian citizens in their neighborhoods, and unfairly target gay men for violating the public lewdness law. Violent groups of men, including some law enforcement officials, persisted in harassing and attacking gays and lesbians, occasionally even killing them in cold blood. It seemed a new era had dawned for queer Texans, who faced a renewed and systematic effort by police to harass and intimidate them and by fellow citizens to threaten them. At the heart of this wave of oppression was the new homosexual conduct law.[23]

Arson

In addition to the direct harassment, threats, intimidation, and violence queer Texans faced in the mid- and late 1970s, a string of arsons also destroyed multiple gay- and lesbian-owned establishments. There was a troubling history to these kinds of arsons in the region. Across the border in Louisiana in June 1973, an arsonist had set fire to the Up Stairs Lounge in New Orleans, a working-class gay and lesbian bar in the French Quarter. Thirty-two people died, making it the deadliest mass murder of gays and lesbians in the country's history until the 2016 mass shooting at the Pulse Nightclub in Orlando, Florida. The perpetrator ignited the fire near the front door, trapping the crowd of bar patrons inside. Those who were small enough to fit through the barred windows jumped from the second story to the pavement below, but flames quickly consumed those who could not escape. Law enforcement investigators never identified a suspect.[24]

Although mainstream news outlets in New Orleans ignored the Up Stairs Lounge tragedy, gay and lesbian publications reported on the fire, and many queer Texans undoubtedly knew about it. This must have made it all the more frightening the following year when arsonists began targeting gay and lesbian bars in Houston and Dallas. On March 3, 1974, an arsonist set fire to the Farmhouse Club, one of Houston's largest gay and lesbian nightclubs that sat on the western edge of Montrose, completely destroying the building. Fire investigators found two gasoline cans near the rubble that had been used to ignite the fire. Luckily no one was injured or killed, since the Farmhouse Club was undergoing a remodeling project. Club owners offered a $5,000 reward for information about a suspect, but the Houston Fire Department failed to track down any leads. In August

1975, fire struck Odds & Ends, a gay and lesbian dance club near downtown, burning the two-story building to the ground. Arson investigators reported that the fire was a professional "saturation job," meaning someone had used flammable liquid inside the club to ignite the blaze. There were also several occupied apartments above Odds & Ends, but thankfully all six residents were able to flee before the fire consumed the building and an explosion ripped apart the walls, presumably from a ruptured natural gas line. "It looked like someone tried to kill us," Odds & Ends owner Jim Backer stated. While those responsible for the fire did not succeed in killing anyone, they did manage to destroy the nightclub.[25]

The following few years saw arsons increase. In 1976, arsonists set fires at Club Houston and Dirty Sally's Second Sun, popular nightclubs in the city. Between October 1977 and February 1978, arsonists hit the Silver Bullet Saloon in Montrose on three separate occasions, and the last one completely destroyed the building. Owner Dan Roberts struggled with insurance company red tape for a year in order to rebuild, but an arsonist struck a fourth time in March 1979 and again destroyed the building. Roberts could not help but wonder if the steady police harassment gays and lesbians had experienced since 1974 was related to the destruction of his business. "We don't have any real enemies," Roberts stated to a local gay and lesbian newspaper. "And we haven't had any real threats. The only threat against the bar that I know of was from Houston police officers who said they would close the bar one way or the other." If not the police, Roberts said, then perhaps the fires were part of an anti-gay hate campaign. "We're the last minority group to hate," he stated. In March 1978, two weeks after the third fire that destroyed the Silver Bullet, an arsonist struck Mary's Lounge, one of the most popular gay and lesbian bars in Houston, by breaking its natural gas meter and setting it ablaze. All fifty patrons were able to escape the building with no injuries. The editors of Houston's gay and lesbian weekly *LXIX* theorized that the arsons were part of a hate campaign. "If this theory is true," they wrote, "it is certainly frightening. It reveals a very dangerous kind of homophobia on the loose in the area. If the anti-Gay force behind it all is as vicious as it would appear in this case, we have certainly not seen the last fire."[26]

Houston's queer community had not seen its last fire. Two months later, an arsonist struck Old Surf's Up Lounge near downtown. In addition to battling the blaze, emergency responders transported bar owner Donald Banning to the hospital, and friends later reported that he was in critical condition with burns on 95 percent of his body. Investigators discovered empty gasoline cans at the scene but once again had no leads on who might be responsible. In January 1979, an arsonist set fire to Club Houston, causing extensive property damage but luckily no injuries. The following June, an arsonist struck the Silver Phoenix, a club built to replace the Silver Bullet that had burned down the previous year, but bartenders quickly extinguished it. Unsatisfied, the arsonist returned a few hours later, setting a second fire and causing extensive damage. In August, an arsonist fire-bombed the Midtowne Spa, which had a large gay and lesbian clientele, and triggered the emergency sprinklers, causing massive water damage. The following weekend, an arsonist once again targeted the Silver Phoenix, this time setting three separate fires in a matter of two days.[27]

Gay and lesbian establishments in Dallas also suffered from a string of arsons during the mid- and late 1970s. In January 1976, an arsonist burned down the Oak Lawn construction site for what was to become the Old Plantation, billed as the city's newest and largest gay and lesbian dance club. It was nearly a total loss for the club's owners, who ultimately decided to build elsewhere under stricter security. Investigators concluded that it was a professional arson and that the fire had gotten so hot that it melted the steel beams of the structure. In October 1977, an arsonist targeted Dimensions III, a popular gay disco in the city, causing extensive damage. Nearly two hundred customers were in the building at the time, but everyone managed to get out safely. In October 1979, an arsonist burned down Mom's Meatball Cafe in Oak Lawn, a popular restaurant among the neighborhood's gay and lesbian residents. The fire occurred after the restaurant had closed for the night, so there were no injuries reported. As with most of the other arsons that occurred in Houston and Dallas, investigators had no leads on potential suspects.[28]

Discrimination

In addition to police harassment, bar raids, street violence, and arsons, queer Texans faced other types of discrimination in their lives, all of which were justified by the fact that the new homosexual conduct law labeled them criminals. For example, employers could fire or refuse to hire queer individuals based solely on their sexual orientation. Unless a local ordinance prohibited it, it was legal to discriminate against employees in this way, and in the late 1970s, only the city of Austin had a nondiscrimination ordinance that protected them. As a result, employment discrimination against queer

Texans was rampant across the state. In August 1974, after 21.06 had been in effect for less than one year, the owners of the Fort Worth Hilton hotel terminated the employment of Harold Wright after learning he was gay. Wright was a student at Texas Christian University and a gay activist. "I was terminated not because of any poor job performance or anything related to my job," Wright told a local gay and lesbian newspaper, "but simply because I am gay." A similar firing occurred in May 1975 when supervisors with the Dallas Department of Streets and Sanitation dismissed a man identified as "Dennis Doe" after discovering he was gay. Soon after, officials with the city's Water Utilities department passed over Steve Childers, who had worked for the department for six years, for a promotion because of his sexual orientation, and the police department followed that up by refusing to hire Childers for a position in their evidence room for the same reason. During his interview with DPD, Childers mentioned that he was a deacon in the Metropolitan Community Church of Dallas, which had a particular outreach to the city's gay and lesbian community. In a common conflation of homosexuality and pedophilia, hiring officials reasoned that they could not trust Childers in this position because officers stored confiscated child pornography in the evidence room. In Houston that same summer, the Harris County treasury department fired assistant treasurer Gary Van Ooteghem when he notified his superiors that he was gay and intended to continue his activism for gay and lesbian equality. Van Ooteghem's termination came just days after the county treasurer referred to the assistant treasurer as "the best accountant I've ever seen in local government." In the mid-1970s, employers across the state indicated they were willing to dismiss gay and lesbian employees not because of their job performance but solely based on their sexual orientation.[29]

Teaching school seemed to be an especially sensitive profession for gay and lesbian Texans because many believed gays and lesbians preyed on children or tried to recruit them to their side of the Kinsey Scale. Ollie Adamson, a French teacher at Newman Smith High School in Carrollton, a suburb north of Dallas, found this out in May 1978 when she allegedly voiced a pro-gay argument during a class discussion, although Adamson said she had only told her class that she believed "very strongly about individual choice being one of our basic rights." Nevertheless, school administrators demanded that Adamson immediately sign a letter of resignation. In September 1979, Bill Nelson, a teacher and coach at Dallas's W. T. White High School, attended a gay and lesbian rights rally over Labor Day weekend in Oak Lawn. A week later, when a photograph of him at the rally appeared in *TWT*, school district officials reprimanded Nelson for presenting himself as a gay man in such a public fashion. The following month, Dallas police arrested North Mesquite High School guidance counselor Robert Sego in a restroom at Northpark Mall in Dallas on suspicion of public lewdness. Since the court had not set a trial date, possibly because prosecutors were contemplating dropping the charge because of police entrapment, Sego returned to his job and hoped to keep the arrest quiet. A North Mesquite parent, however, alerted a reporter at the *Mesquite Daily News*, who published the story a few days later. Before school officials could fire him, Sego traveled to his grandfather's grave site in West Texas and shot himself. A few months after Sego's tragic death, state legislators took inspiration from the failed Briggs Initiative in California the previous year and contemplated a bill to bar gay and lesbian citizens from teaching in any of the state's public schools.[30]

Queer Texans also faced discrimination in housing. Houston and Austin activists attempted to persuade city council members to approve housing protections for gays and lesbians in their cities, but both efforts failed. In February 1975, as the Houston City Council debated a new fair housing ordinance, gay, lesbian, and transgender activists appeared at city hall to advocate for increased protections. When the council instead passed a law offering protections only based on race, color, sex, religion, and national origin, categories already protected by federal law, activists were outraged. Transgender activist Anne Mayes accused council members of being "guilty of the grossest kind of discrimination—discrimination by omission." In August 1977, Austin City Council members adopted a fair housing law that, as in Houston, failed to protect gay, lesbian, and transgender individuals. The following year, the Austin Human Relations Committee, an advisory group on minority matters, conducted a survey of housing discrimination in the city and found that more than 75 percent of gay and lesbian respondents reported being discriminated against when looking for housing in Austin. The report's authors concluded that "in terms of legal protection in their search for housing, . . . [gays and lesbians] are the most despised minority of all." Yet it took several more years before officials in Austin or in any other Texas city considered adding sexual orientation or gender identity or expression to their fair housing laws. Hanging over all these discussions was the fact that the state's new homosexual conduct law labeled queer Texans criminals, making it difficult to persuade elected officials to support nondiscrimination ordinances.[31]

Discrimination also appeared in the administration of public assistance, as Gene Leggett discovered when he attempted to enroll in the food stamp program at San Antonio's Department of Public Welfare. In July 1974, Leggett, fired from his position as a Methodist minister because he was gay, applied for food stamp assistance and agreed to a home inspection as part of the application process. Yet welfare officials denied the application before Leggett even knew a home visit had occurred. The inspector assigned to Leggett's case reported that he had been to Leggett's apartment the previous week and, even though he had not spoken to Leggett or been inside his apartment, had collected all the information he needed to complete his report. It seemed that the inspector had spoken with Leggett's landlord and a few neighbors and had ascertained that Leggett was gay, which presumably meant he was a consistent violator of the homosexual conduct law. Leggett expressed skepticism about the inspector's ability to judge his worthiness for financial assistance based on conversations with other people, but the inspector insisted that he knew "what was going on there." When Leggett pressed him for a more thorough explanation, the inspector finally blurted, "You're living with that man as husband and wife!" Leggett vowed to appeal the decision, but in the meantime, he would not have access to food stamp benefits.[32]

During the early 1970s, many gay and lesbian college students across the nation began forming support organizations on their campuses, and in Texas many of them also felt the sting of discrimination based on state laws. In 1970, when Article 524 was still in effect, a small group of students at the University of Texas at Austin created the group Gay Liberation and attempted to register with university administrators. Assistant Dean of Students Erwin Price disappointed the students by rejecting their application, forbidding them from using university facilities and from circulating printed material around campus. In 1976, after the new homosexual conduct law had been in effect more than two years, a group of students at Texas A&M University created Gay Student Services and applied for university recognition. Founding member Sherri Skinner explained to university administrators that the group would provide referral services for professional counseling, education for the university community on the realities of gay and lesbian life, speakers to classes and organizations wishing to know more about gay and lesbian students, and a forum for exchanging ideas about the problems gay people faced on campus. Vice President for Student Affairs John Koldus rejected their application, asserting that since 21.06 rendered homosexual conduct illegal in Texas, the university could not officially support an organization likely to "incite, promote, and result" in same-sex sexual activity. Koldus also concluded that the stated purpose of Gay Student Services was not "consistent with the philosophies and goals" of the university.[33]

In response to the growing assertiveness of gay and lesbian students at the state's two largest universities, several legislators attempted to prohibit these groups from ever being recognized as official student organizations. During its 1977 session, the legislature considered a bill that would have prohibited any student organization on a state-supported university campus from receiving funding or privileges if it welcomed gay and lesbian members. When that bill failed to pass, legislators introduced an amendment to an appropriations bill that required universities to be vigilant in preventing the formation of student groups that promoted "illegal activities," and it passed. Since oral-genital and anal-genital sexual contact between members of the same sex was illegal under the recently revised penal code, university administrators could use this requirement as a justification to continue denying recognition to campus organizations that included gay and lesbian students.[34]

Gay, lesbian, and transgender immigrants to the United States also suffered from decades of discrimination based on perceptions of criminality and mental illness. The federal government is responsible for administering national immigration policy, and questions of inclusion and exclusion have dominated policy debates since the nineteenth century. Between the 1880s and the 1920s, a majority of the members of Congress supported efforts to exclude racial and ethnic groups such as Southern and Eastern Europeans and immigrants from Asia. During the same period, Congress also passed laws barring immigrants who engaged in same-sex sexual activities. As early as 1891, US immigration laws included a provision to exclude immigrants who had committed a crime of "moral turpitude." Revisions to immigration laws between the 1930s and the 1950s strengthened these exclusions and allowed immigrants to be deported if they committed such crimes within five years of entering the country. Immigration and Naturalization Service (INS) officials raised concern, however, about their ability to determine an immigrant's sexual orientation, even with a medical examination performed by the Public Health Service (PHS). PHS examiners suggested that a more effective way of weeding out gay and lesbian immigrants would be to use existing measures for psychopathic personality, which could be broadened to include same-sex sexual activity or attraction. INS administrators agreed and began categorizing gay and lesbian individuals as psychopathic personalities, making any admission to or evidence of same-sex attraction grounds for exclusion. Over time, the label of "psychopathic personality" became a euphemism for homosexuality in immigration law. In their 1965 revision, Congress replaced the label of "psychopathic personality" with the term "sexual deviate," but both terms applied to the same thing. As the historian Margot Canaday has argued, both labels were "strategically ambiguous" to allow INS officials a maximum level of power to exclude particular immigrants, especially when evidence supporting a decision of exclusion was weak.[35]

Vague labels for queer immigrants meant that state laws such as 21.06 could have detrimental consequences, particularly once immigrants had lived in the country for a period of time and wished to apply to become naturalized citizens. Such was the case for Richard Longstaff, a British citizen who came to the United States in November 1965. Longstaff had spent three years in the Royal Air Force between the ages of seventeen and twenty, and it was then that he discovered he was gay, a secret he had to keep hidden for fear of being kicked out of the military. Around 1960, Longstaff entered into a relationship with Ian Thompson, who was completing his PhD, and a few years later Thompson received a job offer from the University of Oklahoma. Longstaff accompanied Thompson to the United States, although the relationship soon ended. Because he was able to obtain a green card, Longstaff worked for Braniff Airways in Oklahoma City, and the company soon transferred him to their headquarters at Love Field airport in Dallas. Yet Longstaff had bigger dreams, and in 1971 he had raised enough capital to open the Union Jack, a men's clothing store first located near Southern Methodist University. In 1972, he moved to the Oak Lawn neighborhood on Cedar Springs, in what was becoming Dallas's gayborhood, where he sold trendy clothing to a mostly gay male clientele until 2014. His business was so successful, in fact, that he was able to open a second Union Jack in Houston in 1974.[36]

In the fall of 1975, Longstaff helped initiate a voter registration drive in Oak Lawn. As an immigrant with a green card, Longstaff enjoyed many rights and privileges in the United States, but not the right to vote. Inspired by the experience, he decided to apply to become a naturalized citizen. Longstaff remembered his January 1977 INS interview as more of an interrogation than an interview. When INS examiner James Curry arrived at the question of whether Longstaff was "a homosexual," Longstaff followed his initial reflex to deny it. Curry asked a few more questions but soon returned to Longstaff's sexual orientation, and Longstaff again denied being gay. Longstaff remembered sensing that Curry was already in

Figure 2.4. Dallas business owners Bill Nelson (*left*) and Richard Longstaff (*right*).

possession of personal information on him. He knew that INS officials had conducted a criminal background check, but he had never been arrested for any crime. He did remember that once, however, he had gone to a party in Dallas that included mostly gay and lesbian attendees and that police were seen recording license plate numbers outside. He could only assume that officers had recorded his license plate number and had kept the information on file. Curry came back to the question a third time, this time shouting it at Longstaff. "Are you a homosexual?" Longstaff remembered him yelling. "You know what I mean. . . . Gay!" Longstaff knew that being dishonest could sink his bid for citizenship and might possibly result in his deportation, so he decided to come clean. "Well, I've had some homosexual experiences," he told Curry, but he refused to go into detail about his private sex life. Two months later, INS officials summoned Longstaff back for a second interview, during which he was similarly honest yet vague in his answers. After debating the merits of Longstaff's application for more than a year, by early 1979 INS officials still could not decide the appropriate determination in the case. One of the examiners recommended denying the application because Longstaff was gay, while the other examiner recommended processing the application because, although he admitted to being gay, Longstaff had nonetheless "established good moral character, notwithstanding his homosexuality." Unable to reach a satisfactory conclusion, the local INS office referred Longstaff's case to a federal judge for a final decision.[37]

On March 9, 1979, Longstaff appeared before Judge Joe Estes of the United States District Court for the Northern District of Texas. As an appointee of President Dwight D. Eisenhower in 1955, Estes was not known for his open-minded views on human sexuality. Longstaff remembered the intimidating atmosphere of the federal courtroom, with its high ceilings and elevated judge's bench, and described it as "scary" and "imperious." Judge Estes "was way up high there and I was down here and looking up," Longstaff remembered, an overwhelming situation further worsened by the fact that Longstaff had no attorney to represent him. Judge Estes took a few minutes to read over Longstaff's naturalization application before arriving at the substance of the conflict. "We want to know if you're homosexual," he blurted out. When Longstaff admitted that he had "had some homosexual experiences," Estes immediately banged his gavel and proclaimed, "Application denied." In his written opinion, Estes cited what he perceived as Longstaff's "lack of candor" during his first INS interview and his failure "to discharge his burden of proof establishing good moral character." Yet the primary reason Judge Estes denied Longstaff's application was Longstaff's admission that he had engaged in sexual conduct in violation of state law. Despite the fact that the federal government set national immigration policy, 21.06 became a roadblock on Longstaff's journey to become a United States citizen.[38]

The homosexual conduct law also provided a rationale for denigrating queer Texans in popular culture. During the 1960s, the city of Dallas created their own film review board to issue parental warnings about movies screening in the city's theaters. Local elected officials considered the national ratings board too permissive, and they hoped their own board would provide viewers with more accurate warnings about the content of films. In December 1976, the Dallas Motion Picture Review Board added the new label of "P" for perversion, which would alert potential viewers to any instances of "masochism, homosexuality, necrophilia," or any other sexual activities the reviewers deemed to be perverse. Equating same-sex sexual activity with pedophilia had long been a trope used to demean gays and lesbians, but the city's film review board now equated it with violent sex and sex with dead people. The board continued to use the label "P" until 1993, when it created a new rating for movies that included scenes of same-sex sexual activity. The new warning label was "DS" for "deviant sex," hardly an improvement in the way the board perceived gay and lesbian relationships. In February 1977, the *Fort Worth Star-Telegram* printed a cartoon that depicted gays and lesbians as criminals alongside child molesters, kidnappers, pornographers, and drug dealers. In April 1979, local television station KXTV Channel 39 aired a documentary produced by a local televangelist named James Robison titled *The End of Outrage*, which juxtaposed members of the gay and lesbian rights movement alongside images of prostitutes, abused children, drug addicts, and murderers. Because 21.06 criminalized all gay and lesbian citizens in the state, it was easy for anti-gay forces to lump them together with other groups of lawbreakers, thereby belittling their attempts to gain equality with their fellow citizens.[39]

Section 21.06 also threatened access to public accommodations. During the fall of 1976, several self-proclaimed guardians of public virtue in Houston banded together to form the Committee on Community Standards (CCS), an organization dedicated to "cracking down on the filth in our community." They began by launching a movement to rid convenience stores of explicit magazines like *Penthouse* and *Hustler*, but near the end of the year, CCS activists gradually shifted their attention to public places that attracted a gay and lesbian clientele. At that time, CCS organizers initiated a petition drive to gather 50,000 signatures demanding strict police enforcement of the homosexual conduct law. What was even more alarming for gay and lesbian Houstonians, though, was the CCS's effort to persuade state legislators to place strict limits on where queer Texans could congregate and what sorts of activities they could engage in while in those environs. In February 1977, CCS activists convinced state senator Walter Mengden to introduce a bill to prohibit same-sex dancing in any establishment that sold alcohol to the public. When that bill failed to garner enough support, CCS members changed tactics. During the 1979 session, they supported a bill that would deny a state liquor license to bars or nightclubs that allowed same-sex dancing or drag shows, a simple change of semantics they hoped would persuade more legislators to support the bill. The previous year, two gay men and two lesbians in Austin discovered what a bill like that would mean if passed, as they were kicked out of the Cabaret Club inside the Driskill Hotel near the state capitol because they were dancing together, despite the fact that the Austin City Council had recently approved a public accommodations ordinance that protected gays and lesbians. By the summer of 1979, there were so many complaints in Houston of discrimination against gays and lesbians in public accommodations that several local activists launched a drive to document and record all the cases. With 21.06 in the criminal code, it seemed that businesses open to the public could freely treat queer Texans as second-class citizens.[40]

Centering 21.06

Between 1974 and 1982, it became clear just how severe the consequences of 21.06 were for queer Texans. The homosexual conduct law affected nearly every area of their lives, from the safety of their homes and meeting places to the security of their jobs and the protection of their children. In myriad ways, 21.06 justified the harassment, violence, and discrimination they faced. For the police officers who raided their bars and nightclubs, the toughs who attacked them on the streets of their neighborhoods, the arsonists who set fire to their homes and businesses, the employers who refused to hire or promote them, the landlords who refused to rent to them, the judges and juries who denied them custody of their children, the public assistance administrators who refused to treat them equally, the university administrators who denied them the right to assemble, the immigration officials who refused to allow them to become US citizens, and the producers of popular culture who humiliated them by depicting them as deviant social outcasts and lumping them together with other criminals, the homosexual conduct law served as a rationale for denying queer Texans the rights and freedoms of first-class citizenship. Unwilling to accept second-class status, however, many queer Texans came together during the late 1970s to contest their unjust treatment, and in the process, they helped lay the groundwork for challenging the homosexual conduct law itself.

CHAPTER 3

Resisting the Effects of the Texas Homosexual Conduct Law, 1974–1982

I believe that I can be a homosexual and be approved as a fit mother also. . . . I promised my son I would never stop, never give up until I had exhausted every avenue to get him back.
NURSE AND MOTHER MARY JO RISHER, 1976

If we are quiet for too long, bad things begin to happen. Maybe if we're noisy for long enough, good things will begin to happen.
HOUSTON GAY ACTIVIST RAY HILL, 1976

In December 1974, Southern Methodist University law student Randy Von Beitel penned an essay for the Dallas–Fort Worth publication *Community News* in which he attempted to explain the significance of the state's recently enacted criminal code. Of all the new laws affecting gays and lesbians in the state, he singled out 21.06 as "the most pernicious." Although he predicted that few Texans would face convictions for their private sexual activities, he nevertheless asserted that gay and lesbian Texans "are daily affected by Section 21.06 in myriad ways," as the new statute "serves as the cornerstone of an all-pervasive system of oppression against gay people." Von Beitel argued that because the new law prohibited sexual activities between members of the same sex, it "rather effectively precludes recovery in a lawsuit seeking relief from discrimination on the basis of sexual orientation in housing or employment. It also makes the entry and naturalization of gay aliens difficult, if not impossible, as well as making marriage, adoption and child custody proceedings unduly complicated for gay citizens." By branding all gay and lesbian Texans criminals, 21.06 created an image of them as "bad people," Von Beitel wrote, "and we certainly don't want bad people teaching our children, working beside us, or heaven forbid, living next to us. It is this type of thinking in society which makes it difficult to get a jury to convict in an assault case where the victim is gay . . . [and] makes a gay person hide that fact from friends, family and employers." Yet Von Beitel lamented that too few gays and lesbians recognized the need to eliminate 21.06 from the penal code in order to advance the cause of gay and lesbian equality.[1]

During the following few years, however, several queer Texans took aim at the effects of 21.06, if not at the statute itself, once the harassment, violence, and discrimination touched their lives. Facing the realities of police harassment and violence and the wide range of discrimination leveled against them because of the homosexual conduct law, some began to resist these efforts to marginalize and oppress them. Over time, these activists convinced more queer Texans that 21.06 lay at the root of their unfair treatment.

Organized Resistance

Many queer activists came together to create organizations to resist their own oppression and discovered a new strength in numbers that propelled them to assert their rights and to demand fair treatment. In 1974, activists from around the state gathered in Fort Worth for the first "Texas Gay Conference" and heard national speakers like Barbara Gittings and Frank Kameny. Inspired by the event, several attendees created the Texas Gay Task Force (TGTF), a lobbying and education group that sought legislative repeal of 21.06. In Galveston, where police raided the Kon-Tiki Bath Club in 1976 and arrested several customers, the newly created Galveston Gay Society sponsored several benefit events to pay the legal fees of those charged with criminal activity. In San Antonio, where military policies prohibited service men and women from frequenting gay and lesbian establishments and where military police often raided gay and lesbian bars, a few business owners and community leaders pushed back against those policies. The city's recently formed Gay Community Services created a legal defense fund to help those individuals who had been arrested, and the San Antonio chapter of the American Civil Liberties Union (ACLU) provided legal assistance. In 1974, Gene Elder, co-owner of the San Antonio Country, where there had been a major military and civilian police raid in December 1973, filed a complaint with military officials protesting the use of raids and requesting the easing of restrictions on military personnel. Surprisingly, military officials agreed to engage in these sweeps of gay bars only with the permission of owners and to review their off-limits list for possible revision. As Elder remarked, these responses from military officials "have brought about long-range effects which should improve the quality of life of the community as a whole."[2]

Harassment and discrimination in Houston provoked the formation of the city's most active and enduring gay and lesbian political organization. In 1975, activists Pokey Anderson, Ray Hill, Rev. Bob Falls, and Jerry Miller announced the creation of the Houston Gay Political Caucus (HGPC). Determined to improve the lives of their fellow gay and lesbian Houstonians, HGPC members sought to change the face of city politics. Much of that drive came from Robert "Mort" Schwab, a Miami native who became the first chair of the HGPC board. After earning a PhD in international relations at Emory University in Atlanta, Schwab moved to Houston in 1974 to begin law school at the University of Houston just six months after 21.06 took effect. Despite advice from his professors to avoid distractions, Schwab discovered a fondness for the direct engagement of gay political activism. "The intellectual challenge of this activity," he remembered, "countered the sterile artificial competitive existence of law school." As HGPC chair, Schwab oversaw the launching of a voter registration drive, a system for screening local political candidates, and a program to endorse local candidates who supported gay and lesbian civil rights—all of which he accomplished in two years before leaving the organization to devote his attention to eliminating 21.06 from the state penal code.[3]

As raids of gay and lesbian bars and bookstores increased in 1976, HGPC leaders scored a meeting with Mayor Fred Hofheinz to express their concerns. The mayor vowed to end police harassment, although that turned out to be an empty promise. In response, HGPC activists took it upon themselves to protect queer Houstonians from the police, which included creating a harassment hotline and circulating a flyer with instructions about how to respond to a raid. In August, HGPC leaders met with police officials, but this meeting was another disappointment, as it became clear that officers were unconcerned with the problems of gay and lesbian citizens. Nevertheless, as the activist Ray Hill pointed out, "at least the lines of communication are open, whether official action is stirred or not." More important was the fact that Houston's gay and lesbian activists were beginning to stir action themselves. "If we are quiet for too long, bad things begin to happen," Hill stated. "Maybe if we're noisy for long enough, good things will begin to happen." He encouraged his fellow gay and lesbian Houstonians to "literally tie up city hall phone lines complaining" when police raided gay and lesbian businesses and made needless arrests. "Those arrested should demand the jury trials they are entitled to," he continued, "and then sue for redress for any excessive police action." In January 1977, HGPC leaders began collecting affidavits from individuals who had been treated harshly by police during raids and assisted with lawsuits against

Figure 3.1. The activist Ray Hill speaking at Houston's "Town Meeting I" in 1978.

individual police officers. The following year, several HGPC members teamed up with gay and lesbian business owners to create the Houston Human Rights League with the mission of protecting these businesses and their customers from abuses of police power.[4]

In Dallas, queer individuals similarly created their own organizations to respond to police harassment and the increasing number of raids. In June 1976, Dallas activists traveled to Houston to attend the "Texas Gay Conference III" hosted by the Texas Gay Task Force, and it was there they met several HGPC leaders and became inspired to create a similar organization in Dallas. Within a few weeks, they had created the Dallas Gay Political Caucus (DGPC) and the Dallas Alliance for Individual Rights (DAIR). "We're tired of paying first-class taxes and being treated like second-class citizens," Metropolitan Community Church of Dallas pastor James Harris stated upon announcing the formation of DAIR after a police raid at Club Dallas. "They [the police] thought we were going to cower in a corner like we've always done," but Harris vowed that this time would be different. By January 1977, DAIR, in cooperation with gay and lesbian business owners, DGPC activists, and members of the city's ACLU chapter, had raised more than $12,000 to help defend individuals arrested during bar raids in the city, and in 1978, they used some of the funds to hire King Solomon,

Figure 3.2. Dallas Gay Political Caucus officers (*from left*) Don Baker, Dick Peeples, Louise Young, Steve Wilkins, and Jerry Ward in 1977.

a prominent Dallas civil rights attorney, to defend the four men arrested at Club Dallas. Solomon was able to persuade a judge to dismiss all the cases, and the club's owners even filed a federal civil rights lawsuit against the Dallas Police Department seeking $200,000 in lost revenue. DAIR also ran one of their own candidates for a city council seat who promised to change the way the city's police officers interacted with gay and lesbian citizens.[5]

Operation Documentation

In Houston and Dallas, gay and lesbian activists launched a new initiative in 1979 to record discriminatory and abusive interactions with police officers. Titled Operation Documentation, the goal was to build a database of evidence to use when defending individuals who had been arrested or when registering complaints with local officials. Within five months, HGPC members collected more than one hundred stories of police abuse, brutality, and harassment against queer citizens. When a federal civil rights

Figure 3.3. Advertisement for a fundraiser hosted by the Dallas Gay Political Caucus in 1977 to benefit Miami's gay and lesbian community in their battle to preserve the city's nondiscrimination ordinance.

commission visited Houston that same month as part of a nationwide investigation into police brutality and civil rights violations committed against people of color, HGPC activists saw an opportunity to bring their evidence to an audience beyond Houston. To help persuade commission members to hear their testimony, HGPC activists organized a rally at city hall, where more than one thousand people showed up to lend their support. Attendees heard a diverse array of speakers that day, including HGPC president Steve Shiflett, activist Ray Hill, the Hispanic Coalition's Ishmael Reyes, and US Congressman Mickey Leland. Members of the federal civil rights commission responded by calling Shiflett, HGPC vice president Larry Bagneris, and transgender activist Phyllis Frye to testify, and the Houston activists used the data collected through Operation Documentation to present a vivid illustration of the problem in their city. According to a reporter with *This Week in Texas* (*TWT*), their appearance before the commission was an unparalleled success. "The commission of eight people from the Justice Department," he wrote, "were not only impressed by the professional manner in which the cases had been documented, but were also appalled that Houston gays were able to assemble so many cases of gay harassment in so little a time span of five months. Contrary to the mayor, the city council, and the HPD, the US Civil Rights Commission admits that a severe problem does exist." After the commission recommended that city officials take steps to solve the problem, Houston mayor Jim McConn appointed a twenty-one-member police advisory committee tasked with improving police-community relations in the city, and he named Patricia O'Kane, a lesbian lawyer, as one of its members. Operation Documentation was a bit slower getting off the ground in Dallas, but by early 1980, DGPC and DAIR activists had collected dozens of similar reports and forwarded them to the federal civil rights commission. The evidence they collected also forced Dallas political officials to respond. In January, Dallas assistant city attorney and chief prosecutor David Rosen appeared at a DGPC meeting to clarify how to file official complaints of police misconduct. By the beginning of the 1980s, gay and lesbian activists in Houston and Dallas had discovered the power of using documented evidence to force changes in the way police officers treated them.[6]

Fighting Criminal Charges

During the late 1970s, many gay men began to contest criminal charges more openly. Police officers across the state disproportionately targeted gay men in their enforcement of Section 21.07 of the penal code, the public lewdness statute, while rarely arresting opposite-sex couples who engaged in similar public behavior. It is not difficult to understand the reason behind this discrepancy in enforcement, as 21.06 already predetermined that gay men were criminals and habitual lawbreakers, and it was easier to win convictions against gay men. When arrested for such an offense, many closeted individuals tended to plead guilty, pay a fine, and keep a low profile. As more gays and lesbians broke free of their closets of secrecy, however, more were willing to accept the publicity associated with fighting criminal charges. The more gay and lesbian Texans pleaded not guilty and filed complaints about police mistreatment, activists reasoned, the less willing police officers would be to abuse their power. This was the mindset of Houston gay newspaper publisher Henry McClurg when officers arrested him on charges of public intoxication and assault on a police officer. On May 29, 1979, McClurg was leaving Numbers Disco in the heart of the Montrose neighborhood when two officers approached him and told him to follow them to their police car. Offering no explanation, the officers frisked McClurg and placed him inside the car. McClurg informed the officers that he was the publisher of the *Montrose Star* and that he intended to report his experiences in the newspaper in the coming days so that everyone would know "what happens to gay people when they're taken to jail," he recalled saying. "I'll tell you what we do with faggots," McClurg remembered the officer responding. "They don't always make it to jail." He reported that the arresting officer threatened to "treat you like we treated Torres," a reference to the beating and drowning of Joe Campos Torres at the hands of Houston police officers in 1977. Upon arriving at the city jail, McClurg reported that officers threw him to the ground, breaking his left index finger and giving him bruises on his knees and shoulders. The verbal abuse continued inside the jail, where officers called him a "faggot" more than twelve times and threatened to allow another inmate to rape him in a private cell.[7]

The next morning, McClurg pleaded not guilty and filed an official complaint about his treatment to the police department; the US Commission on Civil Rights, which was then meeting in Houston; the city councilperson who represented Montrose; and the mayor of Houston. When his hearing date arrived in July, the two arresting officers failed to appear in court, perhaps cognizant of the flimsy evidence they had to prove McClurg was guilty of the charges. The two officers again failed to attend the trial two weeks later, and as a result, the judge dismissed the case and dropped the charges against McClurg. In a summation of his case that he published in the *Montrose Star*,

McClurg encouraged others in his position to take a similar course of action. "If you're ever the victim of abuse by police—speak up," he instructed his readers. "Say something about it. Say it to the courts, say it to the politicians, say it to the media. . . . And if everybody (or nearly everybody) who found themselves in this same position would do the same thing—we'd see this situation of rampant abuse by police (especially at City Jail) virtually dry up." Not only would these actions expose the blatant harassment and false arrests plaguing queer citizens, but complaints to the right people also had the potential to spark internal investigations of the officers involved, possibly diminishing the number of police officers willing to engage in this type of harassment and brutality. Perhaps inspired by McClurg, in September 1980, twelve of the men arrested during the police raid on Mary's Lounge the previous summer pleaded not guilty, and eleven of them had the charges against them dropped because of their willingness to face a trial.[8]

Dallas gays and lesbians also fought criminal charges during the late 1970s. After the October 1979 police raid on Village Station, during which officers arrested ten customers for allegedly engaging in public lewdness, eight arrestees pleaded not guilty and faced public trials. Many hoped they could prove that police officers lied about what they saw in the dance club. For the first two defendants to go before a judge, the gamble paid off. When the six arresting officers took the stand, the cross-examination by defense attorney and Dallas gay activist Don Maison demonstrated that the officers could not even agree on which of them wrote the arrest report or on the internal layout of the dance club. Finding the police testimony unpersuasive, county criminal district judge Chuck Miller acquitted the two defendants. At that point, however, Dallas County district attorney Henry Wade, angered by the possibility that none of the arrests would result in convictions, dropped the charges against the six remaining defendants and refiled them under judges he believed were more likely to return convictions. This was a practice known as forum shopping, and it was of suspect legality and ethics. To defend his action, Wade accused Judge Miller of being biased against the city's vice squad officers. After an investigation, Wade finally agreed to allow the county clerk to assign cases to judges randomly. The district attorney got the results he wanted, however, as Judge Ben Ellis and Judge John Orvis found the remaining six defendants guilty of violating the public lewdness statute, sentencing most of them to one year of probation and a small fine.[9]

The case of Richard Schwiderski was illustrative of what many gay and lesbian defendants had to face in a court of law. Dallas police officers had

Figure 3.4. A young man greets customers at the entrance to Village Station in Dallas in the late 1970s.

arrested Schwiderski, a Braniff Airlines flight attendant, during the raid on Village Station in October and charged him with public lewdness for allegedly allowing another man "to touch his genitals, with the intent to arouse and gratify the sexual desire of the defendant." Schwiderski's attorney, Don Maison, argued in court that statute 21.07, the public lewdness law, only applied to the person performing the inappropriate touching and not to the person being touched. When this argument failed to gain traction before Judge Orvis, Maison and Schwiderski attempted to show that on the night of the arrest, Schwiderski and his partner were simply dancing together rather than engaging in any sort of lewd behavior. Maison called to the stand two professional dancers—a man and a woman—to demonstrate "the rock," the particular type of disco dancing Schwiderski was doing on the night of the arrest. Judge Orvis allowed the demonstration only on the condition that the dancers do it silently with no music, warning the two witnesses that if they engaged in lewd behavior in the courtroom, they would be arrested. Apparently, the judge did not consider the dance demonstration lewd, for there were no arrests in court that day, but that did not stop prosecuting attorney Bob Phillips from describing the dancers and Schwiderski's character witnesses as "a parade of perverts." This sort of denigration of queer Texans had become commonplace. During a previous trial of another Village Station defendant, Assistant District Attorney Winfield Scott had attacked gays and lesbians in the courtroom in his closing argument, telling the judge that the defendant's witnesses "are nothing more than perverts engaged in repulsive, disgusting, outrageous obscene behavior in public." Judge Orvis agreed and found Schwiderski guilty of violating the state's public lewdness statute, a conviction that an appellate judge later overturned. Despite the convictions of six of the eight men arrested during the Village Station raid, the fact that there were trials at all showed an increased willingness of some members of the Dallas gay and lesbian community to risk their own privacy and safety to begin challenging police harassment.[10]

In 1980, gay and lesbian bar-goers in San Antonio began reporting that despite fewer military police (MP) raids enforcing the off-limits policy, harassment now came from city police officers. On April 23, officers raided the popular gay and lesbian dance club Sunset Boulevard and jailed eight patrons on charges of public intoxication, though witnesses reported that few if any were actually intoxicated. "One [arrested] customer had not even had a drink," Sunset Boulevard owner Steve Hutchinson told a *TWT* reporter. Finding inspiration in the way Gene Elder had responded to MP raids at the San Antonio Country in 1974, Hutchinson helped secure bail for those arrested and pledged to pay for their legal defenses. "I want to show our customers and the gay community," he said, "that we will not allow city authorities to intimidate gays in their own bars." The following month, Hutchinson filed a misconduct complaint against the arresting officers and demanded a personal meeting with police officials, a request the police department surprisingly granted. During the resulting conference with San Antonio police chief Robert Hueck, vice squad officer Jimmy Despres, and city attorney Jane Macon, Hutchinson sought assurances that the department would end its policy of harassment against gay and lesbian businesses. Chief Hueck readily agreed, admitting that two of his officers were "making visits too often and they would be restricted to one visit weekly unless called by the club." The chief also admitted that the department had lost control of one of its vice officers who had harassed Sunset Boulevard patrons every day for three weeks in April because his gay brother was a bar regular. The officer, according to Hueck, had been carrying out a "personal vendetta" by targeting Sunset Boulevard. Whatever the source of the harassment may have been, obtaining a public guarantee from Chief Hueck to lay off gay and lesbian establishments was a victory for Hutchinson and San Antonio's queer community. The chief and city attorney also agreed to drop the public intoxication charges against the Sunset Boulevard patrons arrested during the raid.[11]

A more ambiguous consequence of fighting public lewdness charges originated in Texas appellate courts when judges modified the accepted interpretation of the homosexual conduct law by blurring the lines between deviate sexual contact and deviate sexual intercourse. On May 4, 1979, Dallas police officers arrested Charles Donoho at the Locker, a popular gay bar and dance club, and charged him with engaging in deviate sexual intercourse in a public place. During the trial, the arresting officer testified that while he watched Donoho dance with a man named James Roberson, "Donoho got down on his knees and placed his mouth against the genital area of Roberson who stood there moving back and forth." If accurate, this behavior would have been cause to convict Donoho of public lewdness for engaging in public sexual contact. The charge against Donoho, however, was that he committed deviate sexual intercourse in public, making his case significant in how judges might rule in subsequent 21.06 cases. A jury convicted Donoho, fining him $250 and sentencing him to one year of probation. In his appeal, Donoho argued that if deviate sexual intercourse did not require penetration, it at least should involve skin-to-skin contact, or as Donoho phrased it, "flesh being placed upon flesh." The definition of sexual contact included a broader range of touching, and a state appellate court had recently ruled that contact through clothing constituted an offense. Yet in Donoho's case, appellate judge Charles Bleil, rather than instruct the trial court to consider a charge of public sexual contact, stretched the meaning of deviate sexual intercourse to uphold Donoho's conviction. Deviate sexual intercourse, according to Judge Bleil, did not require skin-to-skin contact, as such a strict definition might enable a defendant to fight the charge if he wore a condom while engaging in oral or anal sex. In his 1982 decision, Judge Bleil concluded that "if the legislature intended to require that there be flesh-to-flesh contact or penetration for the offense of deviate sexual intercourse to be committed, it could have so provided." This appellate decision substantially expanded the list of behaviors for which queer Texans could be prosecuted.[12]

Street Patrols

In addition to resisting police harassment, many queer Texans also sought to protect themselves from street violence. Whereas the frequency of police raids indicated a problem of overpolicing, the violence many gays and lesbians faced indicated a problem of underpolicing as well, as officers often failed to protect them. In 1979, Houston activists attempted to solve this problem by creating their own security force, the Montrose Patrol. According to the supervisor Elaine Bonilla, the patrol placed officers on the streets of the neighborhood to assist anyone who needed their help. All volunteer officers, easily recognizable by their identification cards and armbands, would undergo a two-month training period before being certified to patrol the streets. The new security organization started paying dividends quickly, and violence in Montrose began to decline after its peak during the summer of 1979. In September of that year, a group of five teenagers robbed a gay man at knifepoint as he was leaving a Montrose dance club. The man reported the teens' license plate number to the Montrose Patrol help line, and one week later a Montrose Patrol officer noticed the same car driving suspiciously in the neighborhood. Upon notifying the Houston Police Department, officers arrested the teenagers after finding stolen wallets in the vehicle, complete with the driver's licenses of their victims. Around the same time, a car full of adults approached a gay man in Montrose and began shouting at him. One of the car's occupants pointed a handgun at him and yelled, "Bang bang, queer!" After the man called the Montrose Patrol help line and reported the incident, patrol officers located the car and notified Houston police, who arrested the men in the car. "In both simultaneous events," *TWT* reported, "seven people (2 adults and 5 juveniles) were apprehended in just 28 minutes. . . . The HPD said they couldn't have made the arrests without the assistance of the Montrose Patrol. . . . The MP and the HPD are working together to make Montrose safer." Not only did the Montrose Patrol make the neighborhood more secure, it also served to build a more cooperative relationship between Houston's queer citizens and the police.[13]

Challenging Discrimination

Several gay and lesbian Texans also stood up for their employment rights during the mid- and late 1970s. Despite the existence of the homosexual conduct law that provided a justification for employers to terminate or refuse to hire gay or lesbian workers, some employees nonetheless pointed out the unfairness of doing so. In May 1975, a gay man identified as Dennis Doe filed a federal lawsuit against Dallas's Department of Streets and

Sanitation for firing him after he was arrested during one of the police raids on Club Dallas. Doe argued that since police had ultimately not charged him with any crime, he should be allowed to keep his job regardless of his sexual orientation. Unfortunately for Doe, the court disagreed, but similar legal challenges followed that ended more successfully. When the owners of the Fort Worth Hilton hotel fired Harold Wright because they discovered he was gay, Wright filed a federal discrimination lawsuit and lodged a complaint with the Equal Employment Opportunity Commission (EEOC), alleging that his firing violated Title VII of the Civil Rights Act of 1964 that prohibited discrimination on the basis of sex. Nearly one year later, the hotel's owners reached an out-of-court settlement with Wright in which they agreed to rehire him, pay him nearly one year's worth of missed wages, offer a formal apology for his termination, and issue a new policy statement to their hotel managers instructing them not to discriminate on the basis of sexual orientation. In December 1978, Gary Van Ooteghem, whom the Harris County treasurer had fired for being gay, received a similarly surprising result when a federal district court ordered the county to reinstate Van Ooteghem and pay him lost wages. The following year, the Carrollton-Farmers Branch school board allowed high school French teacher Ollie Adamson to rescind her letter of resignation, which she had written and signed under pressure from school administrators after they forced her to admit she was a lesbian. After Adamson appeared before the board to recount the incident, board members voted three-to-two to allow her to keep her job.[14]

Some gay and lesbian Texans challenged housing discrimination during the late 1970s. Austin's 1977 fair housing ordinance, for example, failed to include sexual orientation on its list of protected classes despite overwhelming evidence that gays and lesbians suffered greatly when looking for housing in the city. In 1981, as the Austin City Council debated a new housing ordinance, gays and lesbians mobilized their resources more effectively. Under the leadership of political action chair Donna Johnson and women's chair Ellen Rayfield, the Austin Lesbian and Gay Political Caucus (ALGPC) rallied supporters to attend the six-hour city council meeting during which the housing ordinance debate took place. According to the ALGPC newsletter, at least thirteen busloads of people carrying Bibles and singing religious hymns packed the council chambers and "charged that the extension of protection to the 'queers and fairies,' as one put it, would lead to, among other things, rampant sex in the public parks, an unprecedented rise in child molestation, the legalization of homosexuality, and a general deterioration of the country's moral fiber." A majority of the council disagreed and approved a new fair housing ordinance in February 1982 that protected gays and lesbians in their search for housing, making Austin the first city in Texas with such protections.[15]

As a result of the willingness of several individuals to resist discrimination, the city of Austin also led the way in protecting the rights of gay and lesbian Texans in public accommodations. When managers forcibly removed two gay men and two lesbians from a dance club inside the city's Driskill Hotel in 1978, the two couples immediately filed a complaint with the Austin Human Relations Committee. This marked the first time anyone had filed an official complaint against any business in the city for discriminating on the basis of sexual orientation, and the city attorney followed up by filing charges against the hotel's dance club for violating the city's public accommodations ordinance. During a trial the following year, a six-member Austin jury found the dance club guilty and fined its owners $200. Many observers, including an attorney with Gay Rights Advocates in San Francisco who traveled to Austin to help with the case, noted that this victory would serve as an important precedent for subsequent challenges to discriminatory practices. In the words of a *TWT* reporter, "the Austin jury said that gays do have rights!"[16]

Former Methodist minister Gene Leggett used the opportunity presented by his experience with San Antonio's Department of Public Welfare in 1974 to challenge discrimination against gays and lesbians in the allocation of public assistance. When welfare officials denied his application for food stamp assistance after an inspector discovered he was gay, Leggett demanded that a different inspector visit his home to complete the application process. Specifically, Leggett requested someone "who was not prejudiced against gay people." A few days later, a new inspector visited and "was quite pleasant to me," Leggett reported. The inspector concluded that Leggett's home was in full compliance, and later that afternoon officials granted his request for food stamp assistance. A supervisor also informed Leggett that the initial inspector would be counseled as to how to conduct himself in a nondiscriminatory manner. "Many times we gay people suffer intimidation from straight people," Leggett concluded about the experience, "who, by innuendo, suggest that we are engaged in activities so horrible that basic rights available to other people should be denied to us." By refusing to accept this type of discrimination, Leggett helped change the atmosphere at the San Antonio Department of Public Welfare and undoubtedly inspired other victims of discrimination to resist unfair treatment.[17]

Some gay and lesbian Texans pushed back against discrimination based on 21.06 using popular culture. When the *Fort Worth Star-Telegram* printed a cartoon equating gays and lesbians with child molesters and drug dealers in 1977, a group of more than sixty protesters showed up at the newspaper's office demanding an apology and a retraction. Two years later, when local televangelist James Robison sponsored the airing of a television documentary that equated gays and lesbians with dangerous criminals, activists in Dallas were ready to fight back. After the documentary aired, Robison delivered a televised sermon in which he stated that the murders of San Francisco supervisor Harvey Milk and mayor George Moscone, as well as the Jim Jones tragedy, whose People's Temple had connections to the city, were evidence of God's wrath on a city that so openly welcomed gays and lesbians. He told viewers that the movement for gay and lesbian equality was "despicable and perversion of the highest order" and asserted that numerous police officers could attest that gay men tried to recruit children so they could murder them. DAIR and DGPC members complained to the station manager and demanded equal airtime. According to the Fairness Doctrine, which the Federal Communications Commission (FCC) had adopted in 1949, broadcasters must allow equal time to competing views of controversial topics. WFAA-TV station manager Dave Lane granted the request and even decided to cancel Robison's television program, stating that "our religious programs should not deal with such matters." Although WFAA-TV eventually reinstated Robison's program, it was under an agreement that the televangelist not attack gays and lesbians on the air.[18]

Lobbying and Litigation

Many gay and lesbian Texans used political lobbying to resist oppression. In 1979, the Texas Gay Task Force (TGTF), which had formed during the first "Texas Gay Conference" in 1974, opened a new office in Austin and hired Bettie Naylor as a full-time lobbyist. According to TGTF leaders, the new office near the state capitol would serve "as a place where legislators could hear from their gay constituents; to help legislators find ways to support and work with gay rights advocates; and, most importantly, to educate lawmakers about gays and attempt to dispel the various myths they might have regarding gays." With a $20,000 budget, Naylor and her staff helped defeat bills put forward during the 1979 legislative session to ban gay and lesbian student groups at state-funded universities and to deny liquor licenses to establishments that allowed drag performances or same-sex dancing. Naylor and her staff also pressured legislators to remove discriminatory language in occupational licensing bills and supported a measure that provided funding for domestic violence shelters that employed outreach programs to gays and lesbians. The TGTF also supported funding a study of child sexual abuse and pornography, and researchers ultimately concluded that most perpetrators of these crimes were heterosexual male family members of their victims, which bolstered Naylor's effort "to foil attempts to target gays as the scapegoats in floor debate on pornography and child sexual abuse legislation," as she stated it. Naylor even discovered that a few legislators supported repealing the homosexual conduct law, which TGTF activists rightly viewed as the basis of discrimination against gays and lesbians in Texas. While unable to get a repeal bill to the floor, the fact that thirty House members and six senators supported eliminating 21.06 was a step in that direction. At the end of the 1979 legislative session, Naylor declared victory. "We put forth a professional effort which caused the state's lawmakers to begin questioning some of their ill-conceived myths about us," she stated at the conclusion of the session. "They didn't have their greatest fears come true . . . dykes on bikes racing through the Capitol halls and queens in flowing garb strutting in and out of the guarded 'men only' stations." She was confident that through education about gay and lesbian Texans, a majority of lawmakers could be persuaded not only to repeal the discriminatory homosexual conduct law but also to pass a bill explicitly protecting the rights of gays and lesbians throughout the state.[19]

Gay and lesbian Texans also relied on litigation to challenge the harassment, discrimination, and violence they faced during the mid- and late 1970s. Although individual results were mixed, activists discovered that obtaining a fair hearing and receiving an equitable administration of justice was at least possible in courtrooms across the state. Most important, these early cases helped lay the groundwork for more robust constitutional challenges to the homosexual conduct law during the following two decades. Ken Cyr's lawsuit against the Fort Worth Police Department produced a partial victory. Cyr was a twenty-two-year-old gay activist in June 1974 when he helped stage the state's first "Texas Gay Conference" in Fort Worth. As president of the Awareness, Unity and Research Association (AURA), a gay and lesbian rights organization he had created the previous year, Cyr spent most of the 1970s establishing contacts with like-minded activists across the state. As a result, he and his co-organizers, which included members of the Daughters of Bilitis and the Dallas Circle of

Friends, attracted a large turnout for the first "Texas Gay Conference." The Fort Worth Police Department also took notice. While conference-goers listened to speakers such as national gay and lesbian rights activists Barbara Gittings and Frank Kameny, several of the city's police officers were busy recording the license plate numbers of attendees. Not only did officers place the information in their surveillance files, they also turned it over to the local newspapers for publication. Thankfully, the local press had ceased printing the names and addresses of gays and lesbians arrested in the city, and they promptly discarded the information. Cyr nevertheless worried about what the police department would do with this list of conference attendees. Although Cyr and other gay and lesbian activists expressed their outrage, the Fort Worth city attorney told them the police had not broken any laws in their surveillance of the event, and a police spokesperson told the press that his officers would continue to obtain identifying information at any gathering in the city they wished.[20]

After the "Texas Gay Conference," Cyr and other activists noticed an increased police presence around gay bars and nightclubs, including several officers who were recording vehicle license plate numbers in the parking lots. Fed up with this level of surveillance, and against the counsel of other gay and lesbian rights leaders in the city who were pessimistic about the odds for success, Cyr filed a federal lawsuit against the Fort Worth Police Department in February 1975, charging officers with illegal surveillance and harassment of the city's gay and lesbian population. Cyr asked the judge to issue an injunction against the police department to prohibit its officers from continuing their surveillance activities and to order the department to destroy its current files on gay and lesbian citizens. The next day, Texas Christian University fired Cyr from his position as a post office clerk, necessitating Cyr's relocation to Houston for financial reasons. After the move, Cyr and his partner Charles Gillis opened Wilde 'n' Stein Book Shop in 1978, which became a cultural institution in Montrose until it closed in 1986. Despite the economic dislocation caused by his case, however, Cyr remained undeterred. As he and his attorney stated in their court brief, the case "is not, as defendants suggest, brought to redress a single instance when defendants recorded license plate numbers of cars belonging to members of the plaintiff class. Instead, this action is brought to enjoin a continuing and pervasive pattern of harassment and surveillance carried on by defendants which infringes not only on plaintiffs' rights of privacy, but also has a chilling effect upon plaintiffs' first amendment rights of association."[21]

In March 1978, United States district judge Eldon Mahon ruled in Cyr's favor, making the decision, along with Judge Sarah T. Hughes's initial ruling in *Buchanan v. Batchelor*, one of the earliest legal triumphs for queer Texans in federal court, even if they were only partial victories. In his written opinion, Mahon ruled that the Fort Worth Police Department's surveillance activities violated the constitutional rights of gays and lesbians in the city. As requested by Cyr and his attorney, Mahon forbade the police department from continuing their surveillance operations in the absence of clear probable cause to believe that criminal activities were taking place. The judge also instructed police officials to destroy all files they had collected on gay and lesbian citizens that were not directly related to an ongoing criminal prosecution and prohibited them from keeping any such files in the future. Yet Mahon also included in his ruling a troubling statement that tempered the victory. Representatives of the Fort Worth Police Department had argued that gay and lesbian individuals could not also be law-abiding citizens, as the state's homosexual conduct law rendered all of them criminals. Instead of remarking on the constitutionality of 21.06, perhaps because Cyr had not raised a specific challenge to the law, Mahon affirmed this view of the homosexual conduct law. If police proved that the individuals they were surveilling did in fact engage in illegal homosexual activities, their tactics might be legal and acceptable. In this particular case, the police had not met this burden of proof. As Judge Mahon noted, non-gay individuals also attended the "Texas Gay Conference" and occasionally frequented gay and lesbian bars, as did queer individuals who did not engage in the precise same-sex activities proscribed by 21.06. Yet Mahon left open the possibility that police surveillance and harassment of gay and lesbian individuals could be justified under a different set of circumstances. While Cyr's legal challenge to police harassment marked a step forward in the movement for equality, it was not a total victory.[22]

Gay and lesbian students at Texas A&M University used the court system to achieve another partial victory for equality in the state. After Vice President for Student Affairs John Koldus refused to recognize Gay Student Services (GSS) in 1976, denying the gay and lesbian student organization the use of university facilities or the ability to distribute literature on campus, founder Sherri Skinner and other GSS members filed a lawsuit in federal district court demanding that university administrators treat their organization the same as other student groups. *Gay Student Services v. Texas A&M University* marked the first time that a gay and lesbian student organization sued a Texas university for official recognition under the shadow of the state's homosexual conduct law. By the time they filed their suit in February 1977, the A&M students could rely on several recent cases to bolster their constitutional argument. Students and their attorneys relied on the right to freedom of association found in the First and Fourteenth Amendments. Freedom of association, the students' legal brief pointed out, could only be denied under specific circumstances. Citing a 1972 case in which the US Supreme Court had ruled that administrators at Central Connecticut State College must recognize a campus chapter of Students for a Democratic Society (SDS), GSS members argued that university administrators' disagreement with the group's purposes was insufficient to deny recognition. Students also cited several cases in which federal judges ruled universities must extend recognition to gay and lesbian organizations despite administrators' personal beliefs about homosexuality. Although the A&M students lost their case at the district level, a three-judge panel of the Fifth Circuit Court of Appeals in New Orleans agreed with GSS in 1984 and overturned the lower court's ruling, ordering university administrators to extend to the organization the full rights and privileges enjoyed by any other registered campus group. Quoting the earlier US Supreme Court decision in the case involving an SDS chapter, the panel stated that a "mere disagreement of the [university] President with the group's philosophy affords no reason to deny it recognition. . . . The College, acting here as the instrumentality of the State, may not restrict speech or association simply because it finds the views expressed by any group to be abhorrent." After an eight-year battle, Texas A&M University, under court order, finally recognized its first gay and lesbian student organization later that year.[23]

Like Ken Cyr's case against the Fort Worth Police Department, *Gay Student Services v. Texas A&M University* was a qualified success. One of the university's arguments was that they could not extend official recognition to GSS because to do so would encourage unlawful activity on campus, referring to their view that the mere existence of GSS would lead to illegal same-sex sexual activity. The federal panel refrained from commenting on the constitutionality of the homosexual conduct law and instead focused its attention on whether there was evidence to indicate that GSS members encouraged illegal activity. The judges ultimately ruled that the mere speculation that members of a group might engage in illegal activity was insufficient to deny First Amendment protections of speech and assembly, particularly when there was no evidence that any member of GSS engaged in or advocated engagement in criminal behavior. Once again, a federal court left open the possibility that some infringement on the constitutional rights of gay and lesbian citizens might be justifiable if it could be proved that they violated 21.06. *Gay Student Services v. Texas A&M University* was a victory for gay and lesbian students across the state, as members of several other organizations followed the lead of GSS and sued their universities for official recognition. Yet it was also a reminder that as long as the homosexual conduct law was on the books, queer Texans would be forced to settle for these kinds of limited victories.[24]

Even litigation that failed to yield victories demonstrated a new willingness of gay and lesbian plaintiffs to challenge discrimination in court. When the Dallas Water Utilities department refused to grant a promotion to twenty-four-year-old Steve Childers because he was gay and the Dallas Police Department (DPD) declined to hire him for a position in the evidence room for the same reason, Childers fought back. First, he filed a complaint with the Dallas Civil Service Board. He pointed out that his supervisors in the water department had never questioned his job performance until a photograph of him marching in a Gay Pride parade appeared in a local newspaper. Similarly, during his interview with DPD for a position in the evidence room, his interviewer expressed no concern about his ability to perform the job duties adequately until Childers mentioned that he was a member of a local church that welcomed gays and lesbians. In response, DPD sergeant H. J. Wages told the board that his department could not legally hire Childers because the police code of conduct required all employees to uphold the state penal code. Wages argued that because Childers admitted to being a gay man, there was little likelihood that he adhered to the homosexual conduct law in his private life. After considering the testimony, members of the Civil Service Board ruled against Childers, concluding without elaboration that he had not provided enough compelling evidence to show a clear case of discrimination.[25]

Childers saw himself as part of "a movement to guarantee equal employment opportunity for homosexuals," he told a *Dallas Morning News* reporter, and he was unwilling to let the issue drop. In April 1976, despite having relocated out of state, Childers filed a lawsuit against DPD in Judge Robert Porter's US District Court for the Northern District of Texas. After several postponements, in March 1980, Childers finally had his day in court. As a working-class gay man, Childers lacked the resources to hire a team of attorneys to prosecute his case. Financed by Dallas's ACLU chapter and donations from the city's gay and lesbian community, and represented by ACLU attorney Fred Time, Childers testified before Judge Porter that he had a stellar employment record with the city of Dallas, reading directly from overwhelmingly positive reviews of his job performance in his personnel file. Yet, according to Childers, when DPD property room supervisor Tom Lochenmeyer interviewed Childers for the position in 1974, the conversation quickly shifted from job performance to sexual orientation. "He assumed, correctly so, that I am gay," Childers testified. Lochenmeyer responded that "there are a lot of cops who like to bust fags," Childers remembered, adding that any gay DPD employee "would have to have a high tolerance for jokes." More important, Lochenmeyer told Childers that he could not hire a gay man to work for the police department, even if that man were qualified for the job. These facts were undisputed. The question before the court was whether Lochenmeyer and other hiring officials had violated Childers's constitutional rights. Childers and his attorney argued that the police department had violated Childers's First Amendment rights of free speech and association, as well as his Ninth and Fourteenth Amendment rights of procedural due process. Dallas assistant city attorney Joe Werner countered that the police department was justified in its actions because of 21.06. "Childers was not hired . . . because he indicated in his employment interviews he was a habitual law-violator," Werner told Judge Porter, alluding to his contention that Childers "engaged in relationships that violated state law against homosexual conduct." As long as the state criminalized queer Texans, DPD hiring officials seemed to have plenty of backing in their refusal to hire them.[26]

On March 30, 1981, nearly six years after DPD supervisors refused to hire Childers because he was gay, Judge Porter ruled that the police department was justified in its decision. While he recognized that Childers had been "a satisfactory and in some respects a superior employee," and that when he took the civil service test for the position with the police department he "made the highest score of anyone who took that examination," Judge Porter still did not think police officials had violated any of Childers's constitutional rights. In his opinion, Porter wrote that the First Amendment right of free association was not absolute and that in the case of public employment, situations might arise when the interests of a public employer might outweigh the constitutional rights of public employees. Such was the case with DPD, a public employer that, according to Judge Porter, had met its burden of proof by showing that its refusal to hire Childers was required for the efficient operation of the organization. Because Childers gave no indication that he would be discreet about his sexual orientation, the federal judge thought the entire police department would suffer "ridicule and embarrassment" if it hired him. Porter also agreed with hiring officials that Childers, as a gay man, might not be trustworthy when it came to handling certain types of police evidence, such as seized gay pornography. Finally, Judge Porter believed that the mere presence of Childers in the department would destabilize its work environment, as Childers would undoubtedly be subject to harassment from his co-workers. For all these reasons, Porter ruled that because the police department had successfully provided legitimate reasons for its refusal to hire Childers, it had not violated his constitutional right to freedom of association.[27]

Mary Jo Risher also decided to use the court system to challenge the discrimination she faced in her son's custody hearing and was similarly disappointed. When a Dallas jury took her son away from her in December 1975 because she was a lesbian, Risher enlisted the help of the Dallas chapter of the National Organization for Women (NOW), whose board of directors passed a resolution in support of her case during the trial, asserting that "an individual's affectional or sexual preference is not a valid basis on which to deny or abridge full legal rights." Although there had been some tension within NOW on the issue of sexual orientation, Martha Dickey, a representative from Dallas on the NOW national board of directors, saw Risher's case as a clear incident of discrimination. "She's discriminated against and she's a woman," Dickey said, "so it is a feminist issue" as well as a lesbian rights issue. "I don't think if she was a heterosexual they would be calling the custody into question," she told the *Dallas Morning News*. Several Dallas-area gay and lesbian organizations joined together with NOW for a series of fundraisers in early 1976 to help Risher pay for her appeal. The national press picked up the story, and news of Risher's custody decision and her subsequent appeal appeared on the pages of the *New York Times* and *People* magazine. Risher and her partner, Ann Foreman, also embarked on a nationwide speaking tour to raise funds for the appeal.[28]

In a Dallas appellate court in December 1976, Frank Stenger, Risher's attorney, known for his legal activism on behalf of gay and lesbian Texans, argued that the jury in the original hearing had been prejudiced against his client. He argued that "sexual preference alone has no relationship [to] a person's ability to raise his or her child, and the jury verdict was based solely on Mrs. Risher's lesbianism." Those arguments fell on deaf ears, as the three-judge appeals panel ultimately ruled that Risher failed to meet the filing deadline for the appeal and therefore the appellate court had no jurisdiction to rule in the case. Risher and Stenger then appealed to the Texas Supreme Court, hoping for a more favorable outcome, but they were again disappointed when the state's highest court refused to hear the appeal. Risher never regained custody of her son.[29]

Richard Longstaff's immigration case resulted in an equally disappointing outcome. After federal district judge Joe Estes denied Longstaff's application for citizenship in March 1979, the British immigrant decided to pursue his case in the Fifth Circuit Court of Appeals in New Orleans, charging that policies of the Immigration and Naturalization Service (INS) were discriminatory against gays and lesbians. During the initial hearing, INS officials from the Dallas office, represented by two attorneys from the US Department of Justice, argued that Longstaff had admitted during his two interviews to having sexual relationships with other men, which was a violation of 21.06. This admission, according to the INS brief, proved that Longstaff had failed to establish "good moral character . . . as a prerequisite to naturalization." The state's homosexual conduct law was key, as INS officials defined breaking that law as a crime of moral turpitude. "Applicant's admitted acts of homosexuality have been made criminal by the Texas legislature," the INS brief continued, "and as a result his conduct cannot be acceptable under the 'community standards' test for good moral character." Longstaff and his attorney countered that the Dallas business owner had never been arrested or convicted of violating 21.06 and, even if he had, the state homosexual conduct law, as a Class C misdemeanor, did not represent a crime of moral turpitude. While the appeals court considered the case, in September 1979 INS officials in Washington eliminated their policy that denied entry to gay and lesbian immigrants and discontinued several deportation efforts against gays and lesbians already in the country. Longstaff believed this to be a good sign for his case, but those hopes were quickly dashed. In October 1980, the Fifth Circuit upheld Judge Estes's ruling against Longstaff, agreeing with INS officials that Longstaff had failed to establish good moral character.[30]

The good news for Longstaff was that the appellate judges also ruled that he could reapply for citizenship. The bad news, however, was that INS officials discovered a new way to deny his application. Starting anew in late 1981, Longstaff completed the lengthy INS application and endured another interview by an INS official, complete with all the questions about his private sex life. This time, Longstaff told the interviewer that he had been gay since birth, that he had violated 21.06 many times, and that he had engaged in sex with other men in England before coming to the United States. In January 1982, the inspector recommended denying the application both because Longstaff had failed to establish evidence of good moral character by admitting to violating the state homosexual conduct law and because he was not eligible to enter the country when he arrived in the United States nearly two decades prior. When Longstaff first entered the country in 1965, he had answered no to a question on the immigration application asking if he had "ever been afflicted with psychopathic personality." At the time, this label applied to all gay and lesbian individuals. As a result, INS officials concluded that Longstaff had been ineligible to enter the country and was therefore barred from becoming a naturalized citizen. Judge Estes agreed and denied Longstaff's application a second time, ruling that Longstaff had illegally entered the country in 1965 and, because he admitted to violating 21.06, had not established good moral character since his arrival. The following year, the Fifth Circuit affirmed the decision, as did the US Supreme Court. Although INS officials briefly threatened to initiate deportation proceedings against him, they ultimately decided not to follow through. As of this writing, Longstaff still lives in the United States and is a resident of Florida, but INS officials have persisted in their refusal to allow him to become a naturalized US citizen.[31]

Challenging 21.06

By the end of the 1970s, many queer Texans had reached the conclusion that the homosexual conduct law was at the root of their unequal status. By that time, several had begun to challenge various manifestations of that inequality, made possible by the willingness of individuals to accept the risk of speaking out and the proliferation of organizations dedicated to achieving equality. Queer Texans relied on a variety of tactics to contest their unequal treatment, such as fighting criminal charges, organizing neighborhood security patrols, demanding equal opportunities in employment and housing, lobbying to prevent anti-gay bills from passing the state legislature, and using litigation to resist discrimination. Some of these efforts were more successful than others, but all of them demonstrated the necessity of acting to protect the lives and livelihoods of queer people in the state. No one, however, had yet offered a direct challenge to the legality of 21.06. That changed in 1979 when Don Baker, a Dallas schoolteacher and graduate student, teamed up with the newly formed Texas Human Rights Foundation to question the constitutionality of the homosexual conduct law. The decision to confront the validity of 21.06, which persuaded a federal court for the first time in history to recognize that queer citizens also enjoyed the constitutional rights of privacy and equal protection, helped clear a path to the eventual elimination of the law not only from the Texas penal code but from the criminal codes of all other states where sodomy laws remained.

CHAPTER 4

Baker v. Wade, 1975–1986

I shall begin today to join in the celebration we have awaited for so many years. For not only are we celebrating the decision, we are celebrating ourselves, our friends, a fair and responsive judicial system, and the great and on-going experiment known as American Democracy—a concept which holds as its highest single precept the sovereign citadel of the individual human heart and mind.
BAKER V. WADE PLAINTIFF DONALD F. BAKER, 1982

Winning this case in Texas on Constitutional grounds may well pave the way to success in gay civil rights battles across the country.
NATIONAL GAY TASK FORCE EXECUTIVE DIRECTOR LUCIA VALESKA, 1982

In 1965, before there were any serious challenges to the constitutionality of the state sodomy statute, Texas native Donald F. Baker graduated from W. H. Adamson High School in the Dallas neighborhood of Oak Cliff. Baker had been born in 1947 into what he described as "a very stable and religious family." His grandfather was a "hellfire and brimstone" Pentecostal preacher, as Baker's sister Maggie Watt remembered, and as a child, Baker was a committed participant in his Central Tabernacle Church. When he reached adolescence, Baker perceived a growing sense of alienation from his family's religious tradition when he discovered that he was sexually attracted to other boys his age. Baker's emerging sense of sexual identity sparked an intense crisis because, according to a later recollection, he had internalized the message that "queers were bad." In an attempt at self-preservation, he tried to convince himself that he was not one of them. "I had heard all about the queers and faggots in junior and senior high school," Baker remembered, "but could never bring myself to identify with something so negative." Yet even more difficult times lay ahead as he accepted his high school diploma. Baker later described the seven post–high school years of his life as "the worst agony and hell I had ever experienced."[1]

Baker attended East Texas State University (now Texas A&M University at Commerce) from 1965 to 1967, where he began conducting research on homosexuality. In the process, he learned that same-sex sexual conduct was considered not only "sinful" and "wrong" but also "criminal" due to the existence of Article 524 in the state criminal code. He often sought out church prayer lines begging to be delivered from the curse of his sexual orientation. After two years at East Texas State, he transferred to the University of Texas at Austin to complete his degree in education and, according to him, try out a school that had "good football." In November 1967, Baker had a chance encounter that forced him to confront his sexual longings. While watching a televised football game in the student union during a break from his shift at the campus bookstore, he noticed a fellow student standing near him with a look on his face Baker interpreted as "erotic." The two men walked into the restroom together, but Baker found himself too anxious and guilt-ridden to return the man's affections. Baker remembered being "overwhelmed with fear and disgust," believing himself to be a "dirty, nasty thing." "I went through a long crying session," Baker remembered, and hoped he "could just go to church and ask God to cure me. . . . For two weeks I couldn't go out, I was so afraid I had a disease and somebody could catch it." In May 1968, in a futile effort to "run away from what he was," Baker enlisted in the United States Navy.[2]

Stationed in Germany and Guam from 1968 to 1972, Baker served as a communications technician and was honorably discharged after four years of service with an excellent record. Yet he still "agonized over what he was" and knew that if he was indeed gay, he "wouldn't have a job, his family would reject him, and he would burn in hell." Upon returning home to Dallas in 1972, Baker remembered being troubled by a "terrible fear" that his family would discover his secret. After just two weeks at home, he packed his belongings and moved to Massachusetts. The change of environment, however, did not ease his suffering. Even though he had not had a single sexual encounter, his attraction to other men caused his personal shame to be so overwhelming that he considered taking his own life. To take his mind off the battles raging inside him, Baker enrolled at the Cortland branch of the State University of New York to complete his education degree.[3]

While finishing his degree, Baker reached a critical turning point. One day while working his part-time job in the student union building at nearby Cornell University in Ithaca, he noticed a meeting announcement for a gay student organization. Baker remembered that he was so full of uncertainty that he roamed around the campus for an hour before he worked up the nerve to enter the building where the meeting was taking place. Even after he went inside, he remained hidden on a balcony where he remained invisible to the participants below. Peering down, Baker witnessed something he never thought possible. This was the first time he "had ever seen other human beings that he knew were homosexual, too, but who were not ashamed of that fact." According to Baker, this moment launched his own coming-out process. He became acquainted with others who identified as gay and "learned that they were not monsters." Baker also began studying the history, sociology, and theology of human sexuality, satisfying himself that he was not abnormal. As Baker remembered, this moment "was like I had awakened from a seven-year dream." His religious faith, in particular, proved to be central to Baker's acceptance of himself as gay. As he remembered, he "re-examined the Bible and satisfied himself that he could be a devout Christian as well as a homosexual." This was a transformative development in Baker's life. "True peace," he stated, "came only when I realized my self worth and that God loved me as I was." In 1975, after graduating with his education degree, Baker moved back to Dallas, confidently came out to his family, and obtained a teaching job with the Dallas Independent School District.[4]

By the time Baker returned to Dallas, Texas's new homosexual conduct law had been in effect for a full year and branded the returning Texas native a criminal, whether Baker realized it or not. Section 21.06, in effect since 1974, prohibited all oral-genital and anal-genital sexual contact between members of the same sex. During the mid- and late 1970s, the new law resulted in increased harassment, discrimination, and violence against queer Texans, prompting some to resist this new wave of oppression. Baker soon became a central figure in this resistance movement as he engaged in a momentous legal battle not only to eliminate a pernicious law but to help advance the cause of queer equality by attacking the very foundation of legal discrimination against them. Although the emerging AIDS crisis changed the terms of the debate and the case ultimately failed at the appellate level, *Baker v. Wade* was the most significant challenge to the state's sodomy law during the twentieth century. Despite its failure to eradicate 21.06 permanently, Baker's case advanced and refined several potentially successful constitutional arguments and helped pave the way toward a final victory two decades later, laying the groundwork for a flurry of civil rights victories in the state of Texas and nationwide.[5]

Assembling the Legal Team

Although *Baker v. Wade* became associated with the city of Dallas, primarily because Baker lived there and the city's activists provided critical support for the litigation, its genesis can be traced to gay activism in Houston. When Mort Schwab stepped down as board chair of the Houston Gay Political Caucus (HGPC) in 1977 to commit his energies to eradicating 21.06, he created the Texas Human Rights Foundation (THRF) to launch a challenge to the homosexual conduct law in the courts. The following year, Schwab reached out to Dallas attorney Dick Peeples, who became the treasurer of the organization. Peeples had been active in the Dallas Gay Political Caucus (DGPC) since its creation in 1976 and suggested adding two fellow lawyers from the DGPC—Lee Taft and Mike Anglin—who became president and vice president of the THRF Board of Trustees. The next task was to develop a legal strategy for attacking the homosexual conduct law. There were many questions to answer about how a successful challenge should proceed. Should the case be litigated in state or federal courts? Should a plaintiff be found who had actually been arrested for violating 21.06, or would seeking a declaratory judgment striking down the law be preferable? Should the constitutional argument against the law be based on privacy, due process, equal protection, or a combination of all three? Because there were so many uncertainties, the THRF board gathered input from attorneys with experience litigating civil rights cases.[6]

J. Patrick Wiseman, an Austin attorney who had represented gay and lesbian Texas A&M students in their fight to obtain university recognition of their organization, presented Schwab with a strategy memo for attacking 21.06 in February 1978. According to Wiseman, any constitutional challenge should by necessity argue that 21.06 violates an individual's right to privacy. Citing the landmark decision in *Roe v. Wade* (1973), Wiseman highlighted the Supreme Court's recognition of "certain areas or zones of privacy" based on the due process guarantees of the US Constitution, particularly those found in the Fourteenth Amendment. These privacy rights extended beyond a "physical zone of privacy" to "the privacy interests of the individual in making certain kinds of decisions." Federal judicial precedent had established that the Constitution protected private sexual conduct between consenting adults. The problem, Wiseman wrote, was that these privacy protections "are not absolute." There could exist certain state interests that are so compelling that they might justify intrusions into an

Figure 4.1. Robert "Mort" Schwab, founder of the Texas Human Rights Foundation.

individual's privacy. It was clear, according to Wiseman, that "an individual has a right to be free from unjustified intrusion into personal decisions related to marriage, . . . procreation, . . . contraception, . . . family relationships, . . . and child-rearing and education." Yet it remained an open question whether the newly articulated constitutional right protected the private sexual conduct of same-sex couples. The Supreme Court's recent decision in *Doe v. Commonwealth's Attorney* (1976), which let stand a lower court decision that upheld the constitutionality of a similar law in Virginia, was perhaps not as troubling as it first seemed. In that case, the lower federal court had ruled that the right to privacy only applied to married couples. Wiseman pointed out that the decision failed to align with the Supreme Court's own opinion in *Eisenstadt v. Baird* (1972), which extended the Court's privacy decision in *Griswold v. Connecticut* (1965) to nonmarried couples. What was cause for even more optimism was that the *Doe* decision did not seem to be binding because it had already been undermined by *Carey v. Population Services International* (1977). In that case, Supreme Court justices ruled that the court had not yet determined whether the Constitution prohibited laws regulating the private sexual conduct of adults. For Wiseman, this meant that the Supreme Court "seems to invite a fresh challenge on the homosexual conduct ban." Texas seemed to be an ideal location to launch a new attack because of the partial success in *Buchanan v. Batchelor* in 1970. According to Wiseman, *Buchanan* was encouraging because, despite its limited precedential weight, it revealed "a willingness on the part of Texas judges to favorably dispose of such a case." The educational value of a new challenge to the homosexual conduct law would also enhance its impact, as the case would shed light on the struggle for gay and lesbian rights. "And you will remember," Wiseman stated, "that while the early [African American] civil rights cases generally found cool reception in Federal Courts, the public education that those cases produced made passage of the 1964 Civil Rights Act acceptable politically." Based on his legal analysis, Wiseman estimated a new court challenge to 21.06 would have about a 50 percent chance of success.[7]

A few months later, Dallas-based civil rights and personal injury trial lawyer James C. Barber provided Schwab and the THRF trustees with an additional strategy memo. Originally from the small West Texas town of Colorado City, Barber was a 1965 graduate of the University of Texas Law School and had moved to Dallas in 1969. Barber had a decade of trial court experience and had just represented Ken Cyr in his successful case against the Fort Worth Police Department earlier in the year. Barber agreed with Wiseman that the homosexual conduct law violated the constitutional right to privacy, and he was hopeful that a federal judge could be persuaded to recognize privacy as a fundamental right for same-sex couples. Barber also believed that 21.06 violated the equal protection and due process clauses of the Fourteenth Amendment because the state of Texas placed queer individuals into a separate category based on sexual orientation and applied the law unequally to that particular group. This was not necessarily unusual, as state legislatures across the country frequently passed laws affecting one particular group more directly than others. Under normal circumstances, a state must demonstrate that a reasonable relationship exists between the particular law and a legitimate interest of the state. In these cases, a court would use what is known as rational basis scrutiny, which is the least stringent degree of scrutiny and rarely results in an overturned law because the burden is placed on the challenger to prove the absence of a rational relationship between the law and a state interest. If, however, a state enacts a law that creates what is known as a suspect class of individuals, such as one based on immutable characteristics like race, a court may apply strict scrutiny to determine the constitutionality of that particular law. In that case, the burden is placed on the state to show a compelling interest that is furthered by the law and to persuade the court that the unequal application of the law is necessary to pursue that interest. Since this is the most exacting level of judicial scrutiny, most laws reviewed in this way do not survive. Barber thought the homosexual conduct law could potentially be overturned if a court used rational basis scrutiny, but he was more hopeful he could persuade a judge to use strict scrutiny. "It should and could be argued," Barber wrote, "that homosexuality is a fixed and immutable condition, which a person has no control over, and it is an unjust and unfair penalty on persons of homosexual orientation to penalize homosexual acts." The heart of the constitutional violation, according to Barber, was that "the law clearly discriminates between homosexuals and heterosexuals . . . and this irrational categorization could not be supported in my opinion by any compelling state interest." Finally, Barber argued that 21.06 violated the establishment clause of the First Amendment because sodomy statutes were, by their very nature, based on a Judeo-Christian code of morality. As for an effective legal tactic, Barber urged the THRF board to locate a gay rights organization to file suit in a federal district court in Texas and ask for a declaratory judgment that would deem the law unconstitutional, which would put an end to successful convictions and eliminate the need for an individual to serve as a plaintiff in the case. "It is my feeling," Barber concluded, "that if an appropriate and thorough attack were made on the statute through the form of declaratory judgment action, in the proper court, that the chances for success would be about 55–45."[8]

Locating a Plaintiff

In September 1978, Schwab and THRF trustees, impressed by both attorneys' thorough legal analysis, hired Barber as lead attorney for their legal challenge to 21.06 and retained Wiseman as a legal consultant on the case. During the intervening month between when he wrote his proposal and when Schwab hired him, Barber changed his mind about including a named plaintiff in the case. Now recognizing that the issue of standing might become a problem in the absence of a specific individual or group of individuals who could show imminent harm from the law, Barber and members of THRF set out to find a suitable plaintiff. Initially, Barber preferred candidates who could emphasize similarities between same-sex and opposite-sex couples, as a judge might find it difficult to deny a constitutional right to privacy when presented with a relationship that resembled a marriage. The ideal plaintiffs for a case challenging 21.06 would be "a gay couple who has been together several years," as Barber phrased it. After a year of searching unsuccessfully for a couple willing to take this risk, during the summer of

1979, THRF trustees attempted to convince British immigrant and Dallas business owner Richard Longstaff to add a constitutional attack on 21.06 to his pending citizenship appeal. Barber consulted with Longstaff's attorney, but both men ultimately agreed that a federal immigration case was not the most effective way to challenge the constitutionality of a state law. In July, there was a brief glimmer of hope as a couple tentatively volunteered to become plaintiffs, but by August they had, according to THRF board president Peeples, "expressed reservations" and were thus eliminated from the list. Nearly two years after conceiving the idea to challenge 21.06 through the courts, Schwab and THRF activists still lacked a plaintiff to pursue the case.[9]

While Barber and THRF leaders searched for the perfect plaintiff, Don Baker returned to Dallas and settled into his new position as a language arts teacher and football coach at Daniel Webster Elementary School in Oak Cliff, the same neighborhood in which he had grown up. Although not yet an outspoken activist for gay and lesbian rights, Baker joined the DGPC board in 1977 under a pseudonym and began making connections with like-minded people in the city. Yet he also yearned to be more open about his sexual orientation in order to live a more authentic life. His opportunity came in October 1977 when the US Supreme Court upheld the constitutionality of a Seattle school board policy requiring the immediate termination of any gay or lesbian teacher in the district. When the high court's ruling became a national story, members of the Dallas news media investigated their own school district's employment policies. In response to their queries, Dallas Independent School District (DISD) Superintendent Nolan Estes clarified that his district's policy, though unwritten, was firm. "Anybody that is a known homosexual and is so identified," he told the *Dallas Morning News*, "would be asked to resign by me." During another interview, Estes stated, "We're not going to have our young people exposed to that. . . . I don't know of any parent who wants his child taught by a homosexual." Alarmed by these statements, Baker remembered that he "took Estes' threat very personally and very seriously." Wishing to take a stand yet not ready to single himself out, Baker contacted *Dallas Morning News* reporter Eric Miller as a confidential source to provide some insight into what it was like to be a gay teacher in the district. Using the pseudonym "John," Baker told Miller that based on the work of the sex researcher Alfred Kinsey, it was likely that approximately 10 percent of DISD teachers, or roughly seven hundred individuals, were gay or lesbian. Attempting to counter the widespread ignorance and rampant myths about gays and lesbians, Baker explained that people like him did not base their entire lives on sex. "There is this myth that gay people want to be in the sack 24 hours a day," he told Miller. "That's simply not true. Sex plays no greater portion of our lives than it does with any heterosexual person."[10]

DISD school board member Harryette Ehrhardt, who later earned the nickname "Fairy Godmother of Texas" for her advocacy of gay and lesbian equality during her career as a state legislator, also found Estes's comments troubling. She feared the superintendent's proclamation might mean that "a Spanish Inquisition [was] getting ready to happen," and that gay and lesbian teachers would now live in fear of being discovered and terminated. She researched everything she could find on gay and lesbian issues in the field of education and contacted a colleague in Dallas who specialized in counseling services for gay and lesbian clients. Once word got around that a member of the school board was taking an interest in gay and lesbian teachers, DGPC leaders set up a meeting between Ehrhardt, the DGPC board, and key individuals in the gay and lesbian community to discuss Superintendent Estes's proclamation.[11]

This meeting presented a dilemma for Baker. While he was aware of the dangers he would face if he revealed his identity as the gay teacher who had spoken to members of the Dallas news media, he also recognized the significance of the moment. The rest of the DGPC board, however, insisted his identity remain secret—even in this private meeting with Ehrhardt—so as to protect his job. Reluctantly, Baker agreed to an arrangement that had all the makings of an improvisational comedy sketch. During the meeting in the Oak Lawn apartment of DGPC president Steve Wilkins, Baker sat on a chair in a closet adjacent to the living room where DGPC board members discussed Estes's statement with Ehrhardt and fellow DISD board member Robert Medrano. Although Ehrhardt and the rest of the meeting participants knew that the gay teacher who had spoken to the Dallas media was there and encouraged him to participate as much as possible, it proved too difficult to include him in the conversation. Finally, after about thirty minutes, Baker threw caution to the wind. "As the meeting progressed," he remembered, "I became more and more irate and restless. . . . How, in good faith, could I sit back and not be honest about myself and not discuss the issues I so deeply believed in? I had just completed a very painful seven-year coming-out experience. It was one of those life-changing events, one in which my self-acceptance had created an evangelistic fervor to get involved in the cause for lesbian and gay civil rights. It burned too deeply within me to merely sit on the sidelines and listen to what others thought needed to be done. Enough was enough!" As Ehrhardt remembered, Baker "stormed out and he said, 'I'm not staying in here any longer. My name's Don Baker and I'm the DISD teacher. . . . And I'm coming out! And I'm not hiding anymore!'" For the second time in his life, Don Baker had come out of the closet.[12]

After the meeting, Ehrhardt and Medrano agreed to meet with DISD board members to promote a resolution protecting the employment rights of gay and lesbian teachers. Although unsuccessful, the board did make it clear to the superintendent that only the board had the authority to hire and fire teachers. In direct contradiction to Estes's proclamation, board members also guaranteed that there would be no "Spanish Inquisition" and that gay and lesbian teachers would not be fired simply because of their sexual orientation. Baker was ecstatic and praised the leadership exhibited by Ehrhardt and Medrano. "This was one of those 'cornerstone' events," Baker remembered, "upon which an emerging gay community could build an identity and establish a solid rapport with others, ensuring that lesbian and gay interests were considered in all aspects of city government."[13]

The showdown with DISD was critical in Baker's evolution as a committed activist willing to take significant risks to advance the cause of equality. Even though he took a semipublic stance, Baker was not yet comfortable with the idea of public activism. He later stated that he "lived in fear" of being fired if anyone ever learned of his sexual orientation, no matter what the school board promised. His experience brought him some attention, but he was not yet in the public eye. As late as 1977, Baker was still using his middle name, Floyd, when he granted interviews with the local press. That changed in 1979, however, when Baker temporarily resigned his position at Webster Elementary School to accept a fellowship in the graduate program in education at Southern Methodist University in Dallas. No longer worried about losing his job, Baker was now free to become a more public and committed activist, including taking a more active role in leading the DGPC.[14]

From the beginning of his tenure as vice president and later president of the DGPC, whose board later changed the name of the organization to the Dallas Gay Alliance (DGA), Baker believed that challenging the constitutionality of 21.06 should be their top priority. In 1979, he got the opportunity to put his words into action. One night in September, Baker ran into THRF vice president Mike Anglin at the Roundup Saloon, a Dallas gay bar and country and western dance club. The two men had known each other since the mid-1960s when they were students at East Texas State University in Commerce. Over a few beers, Anglin began explaining that, like the DGA, the THRF was determined to attack the homosexual conduct

Figure 4.2. Don Baker at the National March on Washington for Lesbian and Gay Rights in 1979.

law in the courts. What they needed was a plaintiff for the case. "I wanted to know if through his contacts at the DGA," Anglin remembered, "if he knew of someone that was presentable, articulate, immediately likable, because we had this whole press thing that we were going to have to worry about, too. We wanted someone that could articulate, talk about, educate about why this makes sense." While explaining that the THRF board had secured Jim Barber as the litigating attorney and outlining the basics of their legal strategy, Anglin came to a sudden realization. "The more I described it to him," Anglin recalled, "I realized I was looking at him. I said, 'Don, you're the guy.' He said, 'You're not serious.' I said, 'You're exactly the guy. You should be the plaintiff in this.'" After a bit more persuasion, and perhaps a few more beers, Baker agreed.[15]

Filing the Case

With all the pieces in place, the twentieth century's most significant legal challenge to the Texas homosexual conduct law was ready to proceed. In

November 1979, Baker, Barber, and members of the THRF board filed suit in Judge William Taylor's United States District Court for the Northern District of Texas in Dallas, claiming that 21.06 violated the constitutional rights of gay men and lesbians. The defendants in the lawsuit were Dallas County district attorney Henry Wade and Dallas city attorney Lee Holt, who would represent all other district and city attorneys in the state. In his complaint, Baker stated that he was a "practicing homosexual, who regularly engages in private homosexual acts and will do so in the future, and who is constantly in fear of criminal prosecution under the statute in question." Additionally, Baker stated that 21.06 put him at risk of losing his job as a public school teacher, his apartment, and his friends and business associates due to the stigma of a potential conviction. According to Baker's suit, the homosexual conduct law "violates plaintiff's fundamental right to privacy to control his body in personal relationships, in the privacy of his own home" without a significant state interest to justify the intrusion. Further, Baker and his legal team argued that the law violated the equal protection guarantees of the Fourteenth Amendment because it classified citizens on the basis of sex and sexual orientation. "Under this statute," the complaint stated, "a female can engage in 'deviate sexual intercourse' with a male, but a male, because he is male, may not. Conversely, a male can engage in 'deviate sexual intercourse' with a female, but a female, because she is female, may not. . . . 'Deviate sexual intercourse' is illegal under the statute only if engaged in with 'another individual of the same sex.' The statute thereby treats heterosexuals and homosexuals differently." Baker and his team asserted that the state had the authority to classify on the basis of sex and sexual orientation only if there were a legitimate interest furthered by the classification. Yet Baker and his legal team could find no such state interest that was at least rationally related to the classification of gay and lesbian Texans into a separate category. Finally, Baker's legal complaint argued that 21.06 violated the establishment and free exercise of religion clauses of the First Amendment because the law was "based solely on religious objections to homosexual conduct, without any clear secular purpose." Baker asked the court to issue a declaratory judgment striking down the homosexual conduct law as unconstitutional.[16]

To coincide with their litigation, Baker and his legal team aimed to educate the public about how 21.06 violated the rights of queer citizens. During a press conference announcing the lawsuit, Baker stated that the law "declares that homosexuals are criminals, and is used to poison society's concept of decent and otherwise law-abiding men and women." He asserted a moral obligation to counter the myths about gay men and lesbians. "I knew when people spoke of homosexuals," Baker said, "they thought of degenerates, perverts, all the negative things. But that's not true. It would be completely morally wrong for me to allow this kind of lie to continue in this society." Baker also wanted to offer hope for people like him to come to terms with their own sexual orientation. After sharing some of his own life story, including the turmoil he endured trying to reconcile his religious faith with his sexuality, Baker stated, "I was literally born again. I was able to break through all this, but many gay people still live with the sense of self-hate I once felt." Laws like 21.06, he argued, perpetuated cultural messages that gays and lesbians were incapable of leading productive lives. "The law insinuates in many people's minds," Baker stated, "that homosexuals are criminals. The law intimidates us." Although Baker recognized that the homosexual conduct law contributed to widespread discrimination against gay and lesbian citizens in multiple areas of their lives, he found that employment discrimination was the most harmful. Baker stated that he and his legal team had seen "documented evidence that persons are dismissed from their jobs because . . . an employer doesn't want a criminal hanging around," perhaps referencing Steve Childers's experience with the Dallas Police Department, Gary Van Ooteghem's run-in with Harris County, or the many other cases of gay and lesbian Texans who were refused employment because of the statute. By categorizing all gay and lesbian individuals as criminals, Baker concluded, 21.06 justified a host of discriminatory actions against them.[17]

By the time Baker's case went to trial, Judge Taylor had retired from the bench. To replace him, in late 1979 President Jimmy Carter appointed Jerry Buchmeyer, a 1957 University of Texas law school graduate and partner at the Dallas firm Thompson and Knight. Barber was pleased with this change, as he had argued several cases before Buchmeyer and knew him to be "no-nonsense, but sympathetic" to civil rights for gays and lesbians. Baker offered his testimony on the first day of the trial in June 1981, recounting his troubled experience coming to terms with his sexual orientation. Describing himself as "pretty much a middle-of-the-road, typical Dallas man," he told Buchmeyer about his religious upbringing, his feelings of shame related to his sexual longings, his torturous years in the navy, his fear of the consequences of being branded a criminal, and finally his acceptance of his sexual orientation. On the witness stand, Baker admitted that he had violated 21.06 on multiple occasions, would continue to do so, and disagreed strongly with the constitutionality of a law that criminalized all gays and lesbians, but only gays and lesbians, for their private and intimate relations. Baker also pointed out that the stigma placed upon gay and lesbian Texans as a result of the homosexual conduct law encouraged additional forms of discrimination, such as police harassment, employment and housing discrimination, and denials of child custody in divorce proceedings. He told the court that while he was a teacher in Dallas schools, he often feared the loss of his job if anyone found out about his sexual orientation.[18]

Baker's legal team also assembled an impressive group of experts to testify about the harmful consequences of the homosexual conduct law and the absence of a persuasive justification for its existence. University of Houston sociologist William Simon, who had been a researcher at the Alfred Kinsey Institute at Indiana University before moving to Texas, testified bluntly, "Homosexual behavior is not something that can be controlled by law." Simon argued that 21.06 endangered gay and lesbian citizens by making them "victims of assaults, robbery and blackmail." Judd Marmor, a Los Angeles–based psychiatrist and expert on human sexuality, reminded the court that the American Psychiatric Association no longer classified homosexuality as a mental illness and that a person's sexual orientation was not a personal choice. "Homosexuality in and of itself," Marmor testified, "does not constitute a psychological disorder. People do not choose to be homosexual." According to Marmor, more than twenty states had already repealed their sodomy laws. "I don't think there have been any adverse side effects" as a result of those legal changes, he told Judge Buchmeyer. Southern Methodist University's religion scholar Victor Furnish also testified in support of overturning the law. Earlier that year, Furnish had published *The Moral Teaching of Paul*, which included a chapter devoted to Paul's writings regarding homosexuality. During the trial, Furnish reiterated his book's conclusion that nothing in Paul's surviving writings concerned sexual relationships between consenting adults of the same sex. "Like many of his contemporaries," Furnish testified, Paul "presumed that all homosexual practice was the most extreme form of heterosexual lust, and that it always involved the sexual exploitation of one person by another." What Paul expressly condemned, according to Furnish, was the kind of sexual exploitation he believed he saw in the Greek practice of pederasty and in the sexual relationships between masters and slaves. Furnish argued that Paul would have had no knowledge about modern conceptions of human sexuality or of same-sex relationships as they existed in the twentieth century. "Paul was not alluding to the type of homosexual conduct we are discussing in this courtroom," Furnish concluded.[19]

The defendants attempted to show how the homosexual conduct law operated within the constitutional guarantees of privacy and equal protection. During the 1960s and 1970s, the US Supreme Court had issued several opinions, most notably in *Griswold v. Connecticut* (1965) and *Roe v. Wade* (1973), in which the justices recognized privacy regarding intimate personal decisions related to sex, contraception, and abortion as a fundamental right protected by the Constitution. These decisions stipulated that any state intrusion into these zones of privacy must be related to a compelling state interest. With regard to constitutional guarantees of equal protection, a federal New York appellate court had ruled in 1980 in *New York v. Onofre* that a state law prohibiting oral and anal sex between unmarried couples but not married couples violated the equal protection clause of the Fourteenth Amendment because the state had not offered any rational explanation for the discriminatory treatment. In Baker's case, the defendants argued that 21.06 protected the decency, morality, and welfare of society and was therefore justified in its intrusion into the private lives of queer Texans. In their oral testimony delivered via deposition, however, neither Dallas County district attorney Henry Wade nor Dallas city attorney Lee Holt explained precisely how those state objectives were achieved with this particular statute. Although Barber provided Wade and Holt with ample opportunities to explain a justification for the law's intrusion into the private sex lives of adult Texans and to defend the targeting of the statute at queer individuals, both men failed. The following was an exchange during Barber's questioning of Wade that illustrated the district attorney's difficulty finding a way to justify the statute:

> Barber: Can you explain to me how this law furthers the state interest of *decency*, if any, by prohibiting private homosexual conduct but permitting private heterosexual conduct that constitutes deviate sexual conduct, as defined by the statute?
> Wade: No.
> Barber: You also indicate . . . that one of the purposes of this law is to further the *welfare of society*. And what I'd like to know is what kind of societal welfare is furthered by a law that intrudes into the bedroom of consenting sexual adults?
> Wade: I don't know of any. There may be some.
> Barber: And I take it since you don't know of any, you don't know how it's furthered by the statute?
> Wade: No.

Barber: Do you know how this statute furthers the *welfare of society* by prohibiting homosexual sodomy but permitting heterosexual sodomy?
Wade: No . . .
Barber: How does this law further *morality* of society by prohibiting private homosexual sodomy but permitting private heterosexual sodomy?
Wade: I don't really know . . .
Barber: Doesn't the statute . . . permit private sodomy by heterosexuals but not homosexuals?
Wade: I wouldn't even know that, but I'm taking your word for it.
Barber: Assume it does.
Wade: Yeah.
Barber: What rational basis is there for that classification, if you know of any?
Wade: I don't know of any.[20]

Wade's uninspired defense of the homosexual conduct law was surprising given his vigorous apologia for Article 524 during *Buchanan v. Batchelor* in 1969. Dallas city attorney Lee Holt fared little better and refused to comment on the constitutionality of 21.06. "We have the duty," Holt told the court, "to enforce the law until such time as a court relieves us of that responsibility . . . and it's not for me to set myself up as a constitutional authority on every law that the legislature has passed." When Barber pressed Holt on the question of whether the state had a legitimate interest to justify the law's differential treatment based on sexual orientation, the city attorney claimed to have no knowledge of the state legislature's intentions when they created the classification.

Barber: Do you know of any rational basis for the prohibition of private homosexual conduct by homosexuals but the absence of that prohibition in regard to heterosexuals in this law?
Holt: I would be relying on the courts to tell me about a rational basis after evidence has been produced and the opportunity to adjudicate it. Then we'd rely on that . . .
Barber: I'm asking you, as one of the defendants in this case, if you know of any rational basis for this classification in this statute?
Holt: I have no knowledge of what may have motivated the legislature to adopt this law.[21]

If Wade and Holt were unable to articulate a compelling defense of 21.06, the state's legal team did attempt to use expert testimony to defend the statute. Dr. James Grigson, a psychiatrist who had once been a member of the faculty at Southwestern Medical School in Dallas, was no stranger to Texas courtrooms. He had earned the moniker "Dr. Death" from his critics because of the many times he had served as a witness in death penalty cases. Grigson had testified in all twenty-two of Dallas County's capital murder trials between 1973 and 1979. After conducting an interview with each defendant, he concluded that all of them continued to pose a danger to the community and would likely commit violent crimes in the future. All but one of those trials ended in a sentence of death. In 1977, a United States district judge ruled that Grigson had failed to warn defendants that these interviews could be used as evidence in court. In 1981, the US Supreme Court agreed and overturned the death penalty conviction of one of those defendants. As a result, the American Psychiatric Association censured Grigson for his unethical conduct.[22]

In Baker's case, Grigson testified that gay and lesbian individuals were "less stable and have more pathological, emotional, mental illnesses than the general public as a whole." Defiantly opposed to his profession's decision to discontinue classifying homosexuality as a mental illness, Grigson stated, "I think that homosexuality is an illness and a disease and certainly that homosexual behavior is deviant behavior." Whereas neither Wade nor Holt could come up with a legitimate state interest furthered by the homosexual conduct statute, Grigson testified that 21.06 "is a reflection of general society's attitude. It is in keeping with the normal biological drive." Repeal of the law, on the other hand, "can lead to confusion in the individual. If you are raised in one concept and you are confronted with another concept, it can lead to confusion. It would be like telling a child that someone with a broken leg is normal, whereas the child is normally taught that something is wrong with the leg." Grigson also expressed concern that eliminating the homosexual conduct law might discourage gays and lesbians from seeking the professional care he thought they needed. Pointing out that he had treated between forty and fifty homosexuals during his career, Grigson stated, "If you repeal the law, there will be less anxiety in the homosexual community and fewer will seek help and a cure." During Barber's cross-examination of Grigson, however, the discredited psychiatrist was unable to point to any recently published studies reflecting his belief that homosexuality remained a mental illness or to any other professional psychiatrist who shared his view that homosexuality should remain criminalized, illustrating to Judge Buchmeyer just what an outlier Grigson had become within his own profession.[23]

In their post-trial briefs, Wade and Holt attempted to make up for their lackluster defense of 21.06 by pointing out the vulnerabilities in Baker's case. The defense argued that a federal courtroom was not the proper venue for Baker to challenge the law. Since Baker had never been charged with violating the homosexual conduct law, they argued, he should seek repeal through the state legislature. Wade pointed out that no federal court had ever recognized same-sex sexual activity as a fundamental right or viewed gays and lesbians as a protected class worthy of equal protection. Wade and Holt agreed that even if 21.06 did invade the privacy of citizens, the state of Texas was justified in this action because the law was rationally related to promoting "the health, safety, and welfare of its people," as Wade put it, or to "protecting the welfare of young people and in preserving decency and morality," as Holt stated. Baker and his legal team countered that because both Wade and Holt testified that they would prosecute 21.06, Baker possessed a realistic fear of prosecution severe enough to settle the question of standing. Baker also pointed out that his case raised legal questions that remained unanswered at the federal level, particularly the question of whether gays and lesbians should be shielded by the equal protection clause of the Fourteenth Amendment. Finally, Baker and his attorneys found Wade and Holt's argument for the existence of a compelling state interest furthered by 21.06 to be unpersuasive.[24]

Judge Buchmeyer's Decision

On August 17, 1982, three years after Baker filed suit, Judge Buchmeyer issued his ruling. On the right to privacy, Buchmeyer agreed with Baker and his legal team that 21.06 violated the US Constitution. The federal judge viewed privacy as a fundamental right enjoyed by all Americans regardless of sexual orientation. "It is clear," Buchmeyer wrote, "that the right of privacy protects decisions concerning marriage, procreation, contraception, abortion, and family relationships—and that any government regulation upon such fundamental rights may be justified only by a compelling state interest and must be narrowly drawn to express only the legitimate state interests at stake." Yet it remained an open question whether the right to privacy extended to consensual sexual activity. "Does the right of privacy extend to private sexual behavior between consenting adults?" Buchmeyer asked. While the Supreme Court had skirted this question in several recent cases, Buchmeyer offered an answer. "Every individual," Buchmeyer stated in his opinion, "has the right to be free from undue interference by the state in important and intimate personal matters," including whether to engage in private sexual conduct with another consenting adult. "This is true whether it is a husband and wife choosing to engage in oral or anal sex in the privacy of their bedroom—or whether it is an unmarried male and female privately engaging in extramarital sexual relations of their own choice. And, it is equally true as to a homosexual choosing to engage in sodomy in private with a consenting adult of the same sex. The right of privacy, therefore, does extend to private sexual conduct between consenting adults (whether heterosexual or homosexual)—and any regulation of this fundamental right must be justified by a compelling state interest," something the state had failed to demonstrate.[25]

Buchmeyer similarly ruled on the question of equal protection. Because the state had not shown a legitimate interest in applying 21.06 only to gays and lesbians, the judge ruled the statute violated the equal protection clause of the Fourteenth Amendment. Using the rational basis test, and therefore avoiding the question of whether sexual orientation was a suspect classification requiring strict scrutiny, Buchmeyer found the state's explanation for why the law disproportionately affected gay and lesbian Texans unpersuasive. "The evidence in this case," Buchmeyer stated, "established that none of the interests claimed by defendants . . . were furthered by 21.06. . . . Indeed, the defendant Wade conceded this: he testified that he knew of no rational basis for the discrimination in 21.06 between homosexual sodomy and heterosexual sodomy. . . . Therefore, 21.06 is invalid because it violates the plaintiff's right to equal protection." Buchmeyer's opinion could not have been stated any more clearly. "This statute," he concluded, "makes criminals out of more than 700,000 individuals in Texas who are homosexuals . . . and who engage in private sexual conduct with other consenting adults. This is prohibited by the constitutional right of privacy (as well as equal protection of the law)—because, if it were not, the state would have the same power to intrude into the private lives and bedrooms of heterosexuals, and regulate the intimate sexual relationships of married couples and single males and females. . . . The right of privacy does extend to private sexual conduct between consenting adults—whether husband and wife, unmarried males and females, or homosexuals—and the right of equal protection condemns a state statute which (like 21.06) prohibits homosexual sodomy, but not heterosexual sodomy, without any rational basis."[26]

The ruling in *Baker v. Wade* sparked widespread celebrations among queer Texans, especially in Dallas, where a poster appeared the following day proclaiming the arrival of "Gayteenth." This was a not-so-subtle reference to Juneteenth, an annual celebration of June 19, 1865, when enslaved people of African descent in Texas received the news that the Civil War was over and they were now free. During a post-decision press conference held in the Grenelefe Hotel in Dallas, Don Baker stated that Buchmeyer's ruling was "the Texas gay community's Magna Carta, Declaration of Independence and Emancipation Proclamation all rolled into one." "I hope that people understand the emotional importance of this," Baker said. "While the decision addresses the sexual aspect, it also affirms that gay people are entitled to the same basic human rights as other American citizens." Citizenship was a dominant theme in Baker's thoughts, as it was during the trial itself. "This is the greatest thing that ever could have happened to gay rights," Baker proclaimed. "They are now recognized on a federal level. Now it will challenge the negative thoughts of any legislators who have never thought of us as citizens." THRF president Mort Schwab agreed that the implications of Buchmeyer's decision for the citizenship rights of gay and lesbian Americans were enormous, calling the ruling "a landmark decision and a great day in the civil rights movement." *Baker v. Wade*, according to Schwab, was part of a string of court victories that were "establishing a legal precedent for the equality and human dignity of gay women and men." "I think it's time to recognize," Schwab told the press, "that the days of homosexuals being treated as second-class citizens in Texas are over."[27]

One of Baker's most important goals in pursuing his case was to educate the public, including the queer public, about the worth and dignity of queer individuals. Buchmeyer's decision gave Baker hope that this message was getting through. "I want gay people in Texas to understand," Baker stated in the wake of the ruling, "that this is their victory—that they should internalize this and feel good about themselves." Baker undoubtedly felt gratified in the days following his victory when he began receiving feedback from individuals in Dallas's gay and lesbian community. Wade Moore, a twenty-two-year-old from Richardson, wrote to Baker to tell him that "what you are doing is great. I imagine that this is taking a lot of courage for you to do and I admire you for it." Steven Engwall wrote that Baker was undoubtedly going to experience "some unmitigated hell" as a result of his public activism, but he implored him to keep in mind that there were "thousands of us who believe in what you are doing and bear you in the highest esteem." Similarly, Steve Parker wrote to assure Baker that "there are thousands of gay Texans that will be forever grateful for this achievement." "We have never met," Ric Huett wrote from Fort Worth, "however, my lover, Tim, and I realize that your lengthy litigation was not merely for

TMT NEWS staff photo

GAYTEENTH
AUG. 17, 1982

TEXAS HOMOSEXUAL CONDUCT LAW

RULED UNCONSTITUTIONAL

Figure 4.3. Poster proclaiming "Gayteenth" in the wake of Judge Jerry Buchmeyer's decision on August 17, 1982, to strike down Section 21.06 on constitutional grounds. Don Baker raises his arms in victory.

your benefit, but for 'us all.'. . . Thanks for your determination in spite of great opposition, discouragement and perhaps even profound danger and peril. Again, congratulations on our victory!" Charles B. Woodard wrote to remind Baker not to "forget that you have made a difference; perhaps not legislatively yet, but you have helped shape public opinion in a positive way and I believe that public opinion is more powerful than a law." Two men identified only as Sonny and Gary sent a telegram that simply read, "We are indebted to you. You have validated our existence." Throughout three years of litigation, Baker stressed that his case, in addition to eliminating a discriminatory law, should also be an exercise in public education, particularly for queer individuals who had internalized the message that they were nothing more than criminals who practiced deviant sex acts. These letters revealed the immense power of Baker's attempt to remove that stigma.[28]

The impact of Buchmeyer's decision extended beyond the state of Texas. Abby Rubenfeld, an attorney with the American Civil Liberties Union in Tennessee and soon to become managing attorney for the Lambda Legal Defense and Education Fund in New York City, wrote a letter of congratulations to Schwab. In the letter, Rubenfeld thanked Schwab for the legal precedent he established with the case. "Both the Tennessee Gay Coalition for Human Rights and the ACLU of Tennessee," Rubenfeld told Schwab, "are considering various attacks on the Tennessee 'Crime Against Nature' statute this year, and the information from your case will provide invaluable insight." Lucia Valeska, executive director of the National Gay Task Force, issued a formal statement in which she praised Buchmeyer's ruling, noting that it marked the first time a federal court had issued such a ruling against a state sodomy law. She also pointed out that the case made Texas the twenty-sixth state nationwide to decriminalize same-sex sexual activity, surpassing an important halfway point on the way to a nationwide victory. "Until now, the battle to revoke sodomy statutes has not received systematic national focus," Valeska told the *Dallas Morning News*. "But that will follow from this decision. A national strategy will emerge."[29]

Even as he celebrated Buchmeyer's decision, Baker was already looking forward to the next stage in the movement for gay and lesbian equality. "This single ruling has not accomplished what is known as the 'gay cause,'" he stated during a post-decision press conference. "In reality it has just begun. Now it is the responsibility of every gay woman and man in the state to work toward a better understanding about homosexuality and about gay people in general. We cannot depend upon a judicial ruling to

A federal judge has just declared an odious Texas law unconstitutional.

In celebration, this bar will offer Two for One all day today.

Bye-bye, 21.06 !!

Figure 4.4. Dallas Gay Alliance poster celebrating Judge Jerry Buchmeyer's decision to strike down Section 21.06 in 1982.

change the hearts and minds of people." Yet even as Baker attempted to forge ahead, nagging questions hung over the celebrations of Buchmeyer's decision. Would the state of Texas appeal the ruling? If so, what was the risk of seeing this monumental achievement overturned and 21.06 reinstated? One week after the ruling, *This Week in Texas* (*TWT*) reported that Texas attorney general Mark White was receiving letters and telephone calls urging him to appeal the decision. The *Dallas Morning News* editorial page also urged White to appeal, stating that the death of the homosexual conduct law would result in "the 'normalization' of a practice deeply opposed by society." Many gay and lesbian activists felt secure in the victory, since most gay political organizations had supported White, and the attorney general was up for reelection just a few months later. What Baker and other activists perhaps could not have anticipated was that the appeal, when it did come, would be complicated by state-level election politics, an ambitious West Texas district attorney, and the emergence of a new and terrifying disease that struck at the heart of queer communities all over the world.[30]

Changing Circumstances

When Buchmeyer struck down the homosexual conduct law in 1982, Ray Hill was the most recognizable leader in Houston's gay and lesbian community and well on his way to earning his future moniker, "Mayor of Montrose." An outspoken advocate for queer equality since the late 1960s, by the early 1980s Hill was active with the HGPC as a political organizer and strategist. One of his organizing tactics was to visit neighborhood bars in Montrose, which, as many historians have shown, often served as queer community-building sites. One afternoon in December 1981, Hill was visiting one of these establishments when Michael "Mac" McAdory, a well-known local bar manager and recent recipient of Houston's "Mr. Gay Pride" crown, appeared distraught and said that he needed to discuss something urgent with Hill in the restroom. Upon finding some privacy, McAdory removed his pants to reveal, as Hill remembered, "angry-looking, swollen places, kind of like an exaggerated strawberry rash, some of them the size of a half-dollar, some of them even a little larger." Neither McAdory nor Hill had ever seen anything like it. McAdory admitted that he had avoided seeing a doctor because he was afraid of what he might find out, so Hill accompanied him to the office of a general practitioner in the area. A biopsy revealed that McAdory was suffering from Kaposi sarcoma (KS), an extremely rare type of skin cancer usually seen in elderly patients. All three men were dumbfounded. How could a young and otherwise healthy person be suffering from a disease like this?[31]

Across town in Houston's Texas Medical Center, Dr. Peter Mansell, a newly hired oncologist and epidemiologist at the MD Anderson Hospital and Tumor Institute, had for several months noticed an increase in the number of gay male patients with compromised immune systems that made them susceptible to opportunistic infections. Mansell was aware that the Centers for Disease Control (CDC) in Atlanta had reported that since January 1980 more than one hundred gay men, mostly in New York City and Los Angeles, had been diagnosed with either KS or Pneumocystis carinii pneumonia (PCP), another disease rarely seen in young and healthy individuals. Most shocking, nearly half of these men had died from their infections. Seemingly the only link between patients was that they were all gay men. Theories abounded as to what was causing the often fatal immunological disease and how it spread, but medical professionals deduced that it must be some sort of blood-borne pathogen that weakened the immune system to the point of total failure and that an exchange of bodily fluids was likely how it spread. By the end of 1981, the death toll had reached 234. The following year, CDC researchers identified the causative agent as a virus and labeled the illness it caused as AIDS, or acquired immune deficiency syndrome, alerting the public that it could be transmitted through sexual contact, blood transfusions, and sharing hypodermic needles with an infected person. Scientists eventually typed the specific virus and named it the human immunodeficiency virus, or HIV. Mansell was particularly concerned about this newly identified pathogen given the frequency of blood transfusions received by his MD Anderson patients following cancer surgeries and chemotherapy. Together with his associate Dr. Guy Newell, a cancer prevention specialist, Mansell began treating people with AIDS at MD Anderson Hospital and launched an education drive in Montrose to alert the gay and lesbian community to the dangers of this new disease. On March 9, 1982, Houston resident Clint Moncrief, a Montrose small business owner, became the first person in Texas to die from KS brought on by AIDS. By the end of the year, four additional gay men from Houston, Dallas, and San Antonio had died from either KS or PCP as a result of the new disease. The AIDS crisis had arrived.[32]

As AIDS began to dominate the news, the Texas political landscape was in a period of transformation. During the 1970s and 1980s, conservative

Republicans began to replace moderate and conservative Democrats as the dominant force in state politics. Amid this rightward shift, many moderate Democrats tempered their progressive leanings and even adopted conservative positions, particularly with regard to social issues. In 1978, the oil industry executive Bill Clements won the governor's race, making him the first Republican governor of Texas since Reconstruction. Many Democrats held on to top elected positions, though, including Houston newspaper publisher Bill Hobby as lieutenant governor and Houston lawyer Mark White as attorney general. White, in particular, found himself in a precarious position, as he had his sights set on the governor's office. The 1980 presidential election was alarming for Democrats like White because the Republican candidate, Ronald Reagan, carried Texas with 56 percent of the state's popular vote. As the historian Randolph B. Campbell phrased it, the 1980 election vividly illustrated to Texans "that their state's influence in Washington increasingly operated through the Republican rather than the Democratic Party." By 1982, although support for President Reagan remained strong, a slight recession threatened to wipe out the gains in Texas's booming economy, and many voters blamed Clements and, by extension, the Republican Party. Mark White saw an opportunity and launched his campaign for governor with a strategy of appealing to African Americans and Mexican Americans without alienating too many of the state's conservative voters.[33]

Openly reaching out to potential gay and lesbian supporters was not something any statewide candidate had attempted before, and White proceeded cautiously. When Buchmeyer issued his opinion in *Baker v. Wade* in August 1982, it was the attorney general's responsibility to decide whether to appeal the decision. White knew that gay and lesbian Texans had organized politically by the early 1980s and that they could potentially become a base of support for the state's Democratic Party. Yet he also was aware of a possible backlash if he were to take a stand against 21.06, a law many Texans continued to support. In September and October, White quietly campaigned among gay and lesbian Texans and told many supporters that he opposed the idea of regulating the private sexual behavior of consenting adults. HGPC leaders thought this meant he would allow the homosexual conduct law to die by not appealing Buchmeyer's decision, so they endorsed White in the governor's race and mobilized voters in support of his candidacy. It therefore came as a surprise on November 1, the day before Texas voters went to the polls, when White notified the Fifth Circuit Court of Appeals in New Orleans of his intention to appeal the decision in *Baker v. Wade.* HGPC officials demanded an explanation, and White held a secret meeting with them, explaining that as attorney general he was oath-bound to defend the constitutionality of all state laws. While some activists felt betrayed, most HGPC leaders saw this meeting as a victory; it was the first time a gubernatorial candidate had ever met with a gay or lesbian group in the state's history. Nevertheless, many activists worried about the future of Buchmeyer's ruling. Would the newly elected Democratic attorney general, Dallas lawyer Jim Mattox, continue White's appeal in the Fifth Circuit? As the political landscape in Texas was changing, many opponents of 21.06 feared their victory might be endangered by Democrats who faced a largely conservative electorate.[34]

A lesser known but equally significant political figure in the fate of Baker's case was a young and ambitious district attorney in the West Texas meat industry town of Amarillo. Potter County district attorney Danny Hill (no relation to Houston activist Ray Hill) had served two terms as a state representative in Austin before being elected DA as a Democrat in 1980 in his home county, where residents voted overwhelmingly for Reagan in the presidential race. In August 1982, Hill was in Dallas campaigning for Mark White in the governor's race when he picked up a newspaper to discover that Buchmeyer had issued a decision in *Baker v. Wade.* "It irritated me," he later remembered. "I didn't feel one federal judge who is not elected and who answers to no one should have the final say on any Texas statute." With the attorney general busy with his gubernatorial campaign, Hill took it upon himself to file an appeal on the grounds that he, as a district attorney, was a member of the defendant class and therefore had a right to intervene in the case. After the election, once White had filed his intent to appeal with the Fifth Circuit Court, Hill withdrew to allow the attorney general to handle the case. Yet Hill made it clear to the new attorney general that he would be monitoring the case closely and was willing to revive his appeal if Mattox failed to defend 21.06 in court.[35]

These three developments—the emergence of the AIDS crisis, the changing nature of Texas politics, and the opportunism of Danny Hill—came together between 1982 and 1986 to determine the outcome of *Baker v. Wade.* Advocates of 21.06 used the prevailing fear of AIDS to argue that sodomy prohibitions were necessary to protect public health. As conservative Republicans continued to make inroads in what had been a solidly Democratic state since the previous century, many Democrats tried to appeal to voters by adopting more conservative positions, particularly on issues concerning women, racial minorities, and gays and lesbians.

This changing political landscape made it more difficult for opponents of 21.06 to determine who their allies were among the state's public officials. Heightening that uncertainty was whether Danny Hill, theoretically one of the defendants in the case, had sufficient standing to pursue an appeal even if the new attorney general decided to abstain from challenging Buchmeyer's ruling and to allow 21.06 to become unenforceable. Ultimately these three factors contributed to a lengthy appeal that resulted in the reinstatement of the homosexual conduct law.

The State's Appeal

In January 1983, many Texans focused their attention on newly inaugurated attorney general Jim Mattox for indications about whether he would continue to pursue the state's appeal in *Baker v. Wade*. Mattox was a political ally of Mark White, now the governor, but the new attorney general signaled during his first days in office that he was rethinking White's decision to appeal. On March 9, Mattox made it official, notifying the Fifth Circuit that the state would accept Buchmeyer's decision to strike down the homosexual conduct law. A spokesperson from Mattox's office told the *Houston Post* that the attorney general was unable to determine any justification for "the statutory intrusion into something that has been classified as private conduct" and that he believed that continuing the appeal would not serve the interests of the state of Texas. "[The case] has been seriously, seriously reviewed," Mattox's spokesperson announced, "and the trial court record just is inadequate to sustain the statute as presently drafted in the books. . . . There was just nothing whatsoever to support the legitimacy of the statute." Gay and lesbian rights advocates across the state praised Mattox's decision, which Baker called "a great victory for all the gay men and women in this state." HGPC president Larry Bagneris agreed. "No longer is there a rule on the book that we are criminals," he stated. "We are legal citizens of the state of Texas." While the language of 21.06 remained in the penal code, Mattox's decision to drop the state's appeal and allow Buchmeyer's decision to stand meant Texans could no longer be prosecuted and convicted for violating the statute.[36]

As he had promised, Amarillo district attorney Danny Hill revived his own appeal when he received news of Mattox's decision. In addition to suing the attorney general in state court in an attempt to force him to defend 21.06, Hill served notice to the judges of the Fifth Circuit that as a member of the defendant class, he intended to pursue an appeal on behalf of the state of Texas. Hill also lined up financial contributors to support the litigation, the most important of which was a group known as Dallas Doctors Against AIDS (DDAA). Despite its name, the individuals who created DDAA included one medical physician, one dentist, and a handful of lawyers. The new organization claimed that its mission was to educate the public about cutting-edge scientific research on AIDS, but DDAA's primary goal was to reinstate the homosexual conduct law. DDAA members assured Hill that they could bolster his case for the preservation of 21.06 by linking same-sex sexual activity with the spread of AIDS. DDAA vice president Clem Mueller, an internist, told the *Dallas Morning News* that his organization stemmed from "a strong desire to protect the community. . . . We thought that before [the appeals court] legalized sodomy they should be aware of AIDS." Dallas attorney and DDAA secretary-treasurer Donovan Campbell agreed. "There is a high incidence of AIDS in homosexual males," he told members of the press, "and that needs to be brought out to the judges."[37]

Baker's legal team recognized the potentially dangerous consequences of allowing the fear and misinformation associated with the emerging AIDS epidemic to encroach upon the constitutional debate about 21.06, and they successfully persuaded the Fifth Circuit appellate judges to deny DDAA's motion to file an amicus brief. "I am sorry that these gentlemen are so misinformed on the issue they would use their profession as a front for an effort to keep gay men and women victimized by such laws," Baker told a reporter from the *Dallas Times Herald*. "Gay people are the victims, not the producers of this disease." DGA vice president Bill Nelson echoed Baker's sentiment about Hill and DDAA, stating that he wished "they would put their energy into encouraging the development of a cure instead of prejudiced and bigoted statements about homosexuality." THRF founder Mort Schwab delivered the message that activists must keep up hope: "The homophobes with their bigot bucks will not succeed. The gay community will actively resist attempts to take back this victory from us." Yet as the AIDS crisis continued to make national headlines, it proved difficult to prevent the subject from intruding into the debate about the future of the homosexual conduct law.[38]

Ceverha's Bill

In addition to reviving Danny Hill's appeal, DDAA members also sought to craft legislation even more severe than 21.06. In early April 1983, as the

Fifth Circuit deliberated about whether to allow Hill's appeal to proceed, William Bundren, attorney for both Hill and DDAA, assisted Republican state representative Bill Ceverha, from the north Dallas suburb of Richardson, in drafting a new statute targeting queer Texans. House Bill 2138 aimed to define the only acceptable form of sexual contact as genital penetration between a man and a woman. Whereas 21.06 had defined deviate sexual intercourse to be oral-genital and anal-genital sexual contact, HB 2138 added to that definition "the penetration by one person of the genitals or the anus of another person with any portion of the body (including, by way of example, but not limitation, a finger, hand or foot)." In addition, the new law would prohibit oral-anal contact and the "touching by one person of the anus, breast, or any part of the genitals of another person with the intent or purpose of arousing or gratifying the sexual desire of any person." Similar to 21.06, the new law made it a crime to engage in any of these acts only if performed with a member of the same sex. House Bill 2138 would greatly enlarge the breadth of the Texas sodomy law to include contact that had never been outlawed by 21.06 while retaining the discriminatory targeting of the law only at queer Texans. The penalties for violating the new law were more severe than those for the previous statute, ranging from a Class A misdemeanor to a second-degree felony. A conviction, therefore, had the potential to carry a prison sentence of between two and ten years and thousands of dollars in fines.[39]

Members of the House Criminal Jurisprudence Committee held hearings on Ceverha's bill the following month. To support the proposal, Ceverha solicited testimony from Mike Thomas, an officer with DPD's vice control division. Amid frequent gasps and occasional laughter, Thomas described the orgies he had witnessed at the Club Baths of Dallas on Swiss Avenue, the sex he saw in public places like Reverchon Park and department store restrooms, the lewd dancing he endured at various gay bars, and the glory holes he discovered in adult theaters and bookstores in the city. He claimed to have arrested approximately twelve hundred individuals engaged in these types of activities and charged them with public lewdness. Increasing the shock value of his testimony, Thomas presented the most outrageous sexual activity as the norm among gay and lesbian individuals. "The last time I was in the [Club Baths of Dallas]," he told the committee, "I observed a white male about 35 years of age, wearing a leather collar with spikes in it, leather chaps, and a leather leash crawling on his hands and knees while another patron struck his buttocks with a leather whip." Thomas testified that he and his fellow vice squad officers had seen even more revolting behavior in public restrooms in Dallas. "One of our officers," he said, "observed a man on one occasion at the Northpark [Mall] restroom masturbate at a urinal and then go into a stall and lick the inside of a toilet bowl and drink water from it." Most shocking to Thomas, however, were the activities he witnessed at adult theaters, bookstores, and arcades. After seeing the use of glory holes, Thomas was troubled by the anonymity of these encounters. "There are seldom introductions or an exchange of words," he lamented. Near the end of his testimony, Thomas apologized to the committee for the graphic nature of his remarks but maintained that his detailed descriptions were necessary because "few normal people are aware of the offenses committed by homosexuals[,] and the filth in some of the places they frequent is sickening and much of it is indescribable." Thomas desired to shed light on this seedy underside of Dallas gay life for those committee members unfamiliar with it and who would likely never experience anything quite like it. "A normal citizen," Thomas concluded, "has no concept of what it is like to slip and slide across a semen-stained vinyl floor."[40]

Houston representative Debra Danburg invited several witnesses to testify against Ceverha's proposal, including Don Baker. "I would say the 'American way of life,'" Baker told the committee, "has to do with the idea that our government is an institution that allows individuals to discover, attain and affirm their ultimate human worth and value while also allowing them the freedom to establish their own moral code." Discriminatory pieces of legislation like Ceverha's bill, according to Baker, "are conceived in ignorance and nurtured by myths and misunderstandings." Baker explained to the committee that being gay or lesbian was more psychologically complex than simply a propensity to engage in certain sexual acts. "Orientation involves emotional, psychological and erotic attraction between members of the same gender," he testified. "'The act' is only a manifestation of this state of being." To challenge Thomas's generalizations, Baker pointed out that the vast majority of gay and lesbian Texans supported laws prohibiting public sex. "Like most heterosexuals," Baker stated, "most gay people abhor public display of intimate sexual conduct." The insinuation that most gay and lesbian individuals participated in the kinds of activities that Thomas described was simply a diversion from the real issue at hand. "What [the debate] really boils down to," Baker concluded, "is the age-old struggle of enlightenment vs. ignorance, bondage vs. freedom, tolerance vs. bigotry and prejudice." Baker also pleaded with gays and lesbians across the state to contact their representatives and urge them to resist this insidious proposal.[41]

The testimony provided by Baker and other opponents to Ceverha's bill and the resulting groundswell of opposition persuaded a majority of the committee members of the inadvisability of House Bill 2138, and the proposal died at the close of the 1983 legislative session in May. Gay and lesbian activists must have been gratified that they were able to mobilize so effectively to block this type of discriminatory legislation. Richland College math professor Allan Calkin, a Dallas area political strategist, told the *Dallas Fort Worth Gay News* that the city's gay and lesbian community should be largely credited with preventing Ceverha's bill from reaching the floor of the Texas House of Representatives. Alongside this sense of accomplishment, however, lurked a parallel and perhaps more important lesson. The introduction of House Bill 2138, the support it received from several legislators and well-funded organizations like DDAA, and the provocative testimony offered by its supporters all illustrated that activists like Baker must remain vigilant in their efforts to bring about queer equality. The fight over House Bill 2138 showed how easily opponents could use the issue of AIDS to attack the movement. "I would stress that there is a dark cloud on the horizon," Baker warned during the committee hearings, "and if we think, at all, that this bill is just a *faux pas*, we are gravely mistaken. This is a very serious matter, and these people are gathering a tremendous amount of support from right-wing religious organizations and congregations in the Dallas area."[42]

New Challenges

On August 17, 1983, gay and lesbian activists and their supporters gathered for a rally at Dallas's Reverchon Park to mark the one-year anniversary of Buchmeyer's decision. While a spirit of victory permeated the event, Danny Hill's ongoing appeal, with its ample funding and legal assistance from DDAA, cast a shadow over the otherwise festive mood. Many of the speakers prodded the crowd to recognize the potential impermanence of Buchmeyer's decision and to continue the battle for queer equality. DGA president Mike Stewart praised Buchmeyer because he "affirmed what we have known for a long time—that it's okay to be gay in Texas." Yet he recognized that the fight was far from over. Just as his organization had been instrumental in supporting the case, Stewart assured those gathered that the DGA would continue to "play a vital role, a leadership role, in securing and defending the rights of gay men and lesbians" throughout the appeals process. TGTF lobbyist Bettie Naylor was a bit more circumspect. Though she portrayed the demise of 21.06 as something worthy of celebrating, Naylor cautioned against taking the victory for granted. As a warning, Naylor reminded her audience about the fate of the Equal Rights Amendment, a cause for which she had devoted much of her energy during the previous decade. "When the population was able to consider the proposition on its own merits," Naylor argued, "it whizzed through the legislature, but it was only when the merchants of fear began to oppose the ERA and achieve a foothold, did it fail to pass." Baker continued heralding the remarkable victory of Buchmeyer's decision while remaining focused on the future. Baker reminded the crowd that 21.06 had been the basis of discrimination against gay and lesbian Texans "because we were perceived as people habitually involved in criminal activities." The invalidation of this discriminatory law was therefore a revolutionary achievement for gay and lesbian citizens in the state. "This is our day," Baker told the crowd. "The Irish have St. Patrick's Day, the Italians have Columbus Day. August 17th is ours." This is precisely what made staying vigilant in the appeals process imperative. "I hope you understand," Baker stated, "that this is not the culminating activity. The door's been open[ed], but we've got to go through it." Countering the ignorance and myths about gay and lesbian individuals should take priority, according to Baker, because they continued to be "the reasons we suffer the problems we do."[43]

As Baker and other activists focused on preserving their victory and countering DDAA and Hill's politicization of AIDS, the disease struck close to home. In May 1983, THRF founder Mort Schwab announced that he had been diagnosed with AIDS earlier that year. Granting an interview with the *Dallas Fort Worth Gay News*, Schwab hoped to use his experience as a way to educate the public, much as he was doing with *Baker v. Wade*. In contrast to the lurid way gays and lesbians had been portrayed during the committee hearings on House Bill 2138, Schwab described his own life. "I have led a very conservative lifestyle . . . [and] have had a conservative number of sexual partners. . . . I have never been to the bookstore, hardly ever been to the baths, and have avoided group sex." Schwab speculated that it had been during a single sexual encounter that he had acquired the disease, and he wanted others to know that it could also happen to them. He warned that if public health agencies continued to neglect AIDS, the crisis would turn into a widespread epidemic. Schwab urged gay and lesbian organizations to use their resources to demand increased funding for AIDS research and for outreach programs to help those already afflicted. These were going to be added responsibilities, according to Schwab, as the activist community still needed to focus on winning the case against 21.06.[44]

Schwab's health deteriorated during the subsequent few months. In September, he gave an interview to the *Houston Post* about living with AIDS in which he was much more direct about the effect the health crisis could have on the gay and lesbian community. "I agree with gay leaders who say this is the greatest threat to the gay movement that's occurred," he stated. "But just as the Anita Bryant incident was turned around and was made into a very positive thing about the community and the damage was contained, this can be too. But how many thousands of people are going to die first?" Schwab's time came the following December when he died at the age of thirty-six, the forty-fourth person to die from complications of AIDS in Texas. During a packed memorial service the following month at the Rothko Chapel in Houston, Baker delivered a eulogy that recognized Schwab's important contributions to the movement for gay and lesbian equality. "His ingenious creativity and dedication to abolish 21.06," Baker said, "made him a person all lesbians and gay men in this state will always honor and respect." Above everything else, Baker told the crowd that Schwab should be "admired for . . . his willingness to dedicate his total life for the cause of justice and freedom." Houston City Council member George Greanias, who represented the Montrose neighborhood and had become a champion of gay and lesbian rights in the city, told the crowd that "we will remember [Schwab] long after this service has ended, because he conducted his life as a testament to his beliefs. . . . His death, however sorrowing to us, does not mark the end of our steady, sure progress." Thomas J. Coleman, who had taken the reins as the THRF's executive director when Schwab's health began to decline the previous year, committed the organization Schwab had created to continuing the battle he had started. "Although Schwab is no longer with us," Coleman proclaimed, "the struggles for human rights will continue through the Texas Human Rights Foundation." *Baker v. Wade* remained central to the struggle to remove the criminal stigma from the lives of queer Texans and to allow them to enjoy all the privileges of first-class citizenship.[45]

As 1984 dawned, Coleman was ready to hit the ground running as a tribute to everything Schwab had accomplished. "The loss of [Schwab] set us back because he served so many roles," Coleman told the *Dallas Fort Worth Gay News* a week after Schwab's death. "He had experience and guts and made our cause public. We have to keep it going." This persistence was especially important in light of a recent Fifth Circuit decision in *Baker v.*

Wade. After the Texas Supreme Court dismissed Danny Hill's lawsuit trying to force the state attorney general to prosecute an appeal, Hill and his DDAA benefactors redoubled their efforts to persuade the Fifth Circuit to recognize their standing to file the appeal. A three-judge panel agreed that Hill was a legitimate representative of the defendant class, and in response, Coleman sought to revitalize the THRF's efforts in Baker's case. "21.06 is important," Coleman stated, "and the outcome of this case is important because it determines if gays are criminals. It would affect child-custody rights, employment, accommodations and discrimination, and it would affect public attitudes toward gays. These all depend on the outcome of 21.06." Coleman pledged the THRF's full resources to winning Baker's case and advancing the cause of queer equality in the courts.[46]

The Fifth Circuit

In April 1984, a three-judge panel composed of Fifth Circuit appellate judges heard Danny Hill's appeal in *Baker v. Wade*. Hill's legal team based their case on four main arguments. First, Hill argued that Baker lacked standing to challenge 21.06 because he had never been arrested or charged with violating the law and countered Baker's assertion that gays and lesbians suffered from widespread discrimination as a result of being singled out by 21.06, dismissing these concerns as "imaginary or speculative." Second, Hill and his attorneys argued that no federal court had ever recognized a constitutional right to engage in same-sex sexual activity. The Supreme Court's landmark rulings on privacy, according to Hill, applied only to marital relationships. Third, the appeal rejected the idea that 21.06 violated guarantees of equal protection since the law applied only to specific conduct and not to status or identity. "The statute in question," Hill asserted, "does not classify persons any more than the Texas penal code governing murder, robbery, rape, [or] child abuse would classify persons. They all apply for any person who engages in the conduct." Finally, Hill argued that even if 21.06 did violate constitutional guarantees of privacy and equal protection, the state of Texas was justified in its action. "The general homosexual community both in Texas and across the nation," Hill argued, "represents a great reservoir of dangerous transmissible diseases," including syphilis, gonorrhea, hepatitis A and B, and AIDS. By prohibiting oral and anal sex between same-sex partners, Hill reasoned, the homosexual conduct law advanced a state interest in promoting public health.[47]

Baker and his legal team struck back in a new set of arguments before the Fifth Circuit panel. On the issue of standing, Baker and his attorneys reminded the court that Dallas County district attorney Henry Wade and Dallas city attorney Lee Holt both stated during the original trial that they vigorously enforced the law. When it came to privacy protections, Baker and his legal team questioned Hill's interpretation of judicial precedent. During oral argument, Barber pointed out that Hill's assertion about privacy rested on his very narrow interpretation of *Griswold v. Connecticut* (1965), in which the Supreme Court found a constitutional right to privacy within a marriage, but ignored the follow-up decision in *Eisenstadt v. Baird* (1972), which extended that right to nonmarried couples. As for equal protection, Baker and his attorneys described Hill's assertion about the alleged neutrality of 21.06 as "nonsense," reminding the Fifth Circuit judges that the homosexual conduct law applied only to sexual activity between two members of the same sex. "Does defendant seriously contend," Baker's attorneys asked in the brief, "that heterosexuals also engage in same-sex conduct? Such a suggestion is a non-sequitur." The real motivation behind the law, according to Barber, was prejudice and discrimination. Baker and his legal team also questioned Hill's assertion that promoting public health was a compelling state interest that justified 21.06. Pointing out that information about AIDS did not exist during the original trial and certainly was not a factor when the legislature approved the new penal code in 1973, Baker and his attorneys suggested that Hill's true motivation was to place in the record outrageous claims about the sex lives of gay men. "It appears that Hill wants to talk about oral/anal sexual contact, 'fisting,' people urinating on one another, and promiscuity," Baker's brief concluded. "Plaintiff cannot understand Hill's apparent fixation on these sexual acts." The worst part, according to Baker's brief, was that Hill based his claims on faulty data in an attempt to make the erroneous argument that 21.06 could halt the spread of sexually transmitted infections. If protecting Texas citizens from diseases such as AIDS was actually Hill's goal, Barber stated during oral argument, then the district attorney should support the repeal of 21.06. "Overwhelmingly the medical experts in the various fields involved with the treatment of AIDS and other sexually transmitted diseases," Barber told the judges, "agree that such a law would have the opposite result from preventing the spread of such diseases."[48]

After hearing oral arguments, the judicial panel declined to rule on the constitutional questions of privacy and equal protection. In September 1984, Judges Alvin B. Rubin, Irving L. Goldberg, and Thomas Reavley reversed the decision of a Fifth Circuit motions panel recognizing Hill's authority to prosecute his appeal. "Having now had the benefit of full briefing, and having more fully considered the matter," Judge Rubin wrote for the panel, "we hold that the aspiring appellant did not have the right to intervene and that the Attorney General of Texas, who chose not to appeal, properly represented the interests of the State." According to Rubin, allowing Hill to advance his appeal was a recipe for chaos at the appellate level. "The State as a sovereign," the Fifth Circuit judge wrote, "speaks in court with a single voice; litigation would be unmanageable were it possible for every district, county, or city attorney who differs with the State's position, as voiced by the Attorney General, to intervene, . . . each asserting perhaps not only a different position but a different legal theory supported by different evidence." This would create an untenable situation, as Rubin saw it, making his dismissal of Hill's appeal necessary to avoid setting an unworkable precedent. With their dismissal of Hill's appeal, the Fifth Circuit panel relieved itself of having to answer the constitutional questions presented in the case. While the decision lacked a positive appellate affirmation, the panel's action was nonetheless a victory for Baker because it preserved Buchmeyer's ruling striking down 21.06.[49]

Baker and his legal team recognized that the panel's ruling could be the final nail in the coffin for 21.06. In a post-decision press release, Baker reminded his supporters that the successful conclusion of his case was a victory not just for Texans but for gays and lesbians across the nation. "It is a signal to them," he wrote, "that an entreaty through the system can be sought and won on our behalf." Hoping to link the effort to rid the Texas penal code of its discriminatory sodomy law with kindred movements for social justice, he placed his case within the context of historic struggles for equality. The panel's dismissal of Danny Hill's appeal, according to Baker, was "a sign that the same system that is making progress in obtaining full and equal rights for Blacks, Hispanics, and women is beginning to know and understand our grievances as well." THRF executive director Tom Coleman echoed Baker's elation a few days later in a status update on the case presented to HGPC members in Houston. There had been a serious rift within the HGPC over whether to endorse Democratic Party candidates in the 1982 election, especially Mark White for governor and Jim Mattox for attorney general, and those divisions continued to plague the organization as the 1984 national election approached. Coleman reiterated his belief in the wisdom of those endorsements and argued that the Fifth Circuit panel's decision was further evidence that the HGPC had followed the right course, especially in its endorsement of Mattox. "As things ultimately turned out," he wrote, "this support paid huge dividends as far as obtaining a fair decision from Attorney General Mattox as to whether or not to continue this appeal. His decision not to appeal the case made it much more difficult for the bigots on the other side to justify its continued prosecution." As Coleman well understood, the lines between judicial decisions and partisan politics could be very thin, and the recent outcome of Baker's case showed just how true this could be.[50]

Baker and Coleman stressed the need to look ahead in the wake of the dismissal of Hill's appeal. "The appeals court decision does not close the book on our struggle for equal rights," Baker warned in his press release, "it merely opens the door." Rather than believing that the court's decision would solve all the problems of queer Texans, Baker reminded his supporters that "we must assess and reassess our goals and objectives and work as intensely as ever." In his update on *Baker v. Wade* to the HGPC, Coleman cited a recent federal circuit court decision in which Judges Robert Bork and Antonin Scalia ruled that constitutional privacy protections did not apply to same-sex relationships. The case, *Dronenburg v. Zech* (1984), involved twenty-seven-year-old naval officer James Dronenburg, who was discharged from the military after admitting to a sexual relationship with a fellow seaman. With assistance from the Lambda Legal Defense and Education Fund, Dronenburg filed suit against the navy, charging them with violating his rights of privacy and equal protection. A California district judge disagreed, and the case wound up on appeal in the Washington, DC, Circuit Court. Judge Bork, writing for the majority that included Judge Scalia, concluded that there was "no constitutional right to engage in homosexual conduct." The panel therefore upheld Dronenburg's military discharge. In his report to the HGPC, Coleman expressed his outrage at the decision. "In layman's terms," he wrote, "what Judge Bork's ruling means is that you and all other gays and lesbians are nothing but common criminals and can be treated accordingly by the government." For Coleman, this judicial development was yet one more sign that the upcoming national election was more important than ever. President Reagan had appointed both Bork and Scalia to the federal bench, and most observers agreed that if elected to a second term, he would send one of the judges to the Supreme Court. "Such a future," Coleman warned HGPC members, "would be catastrophic for the cause of equal legal rights for gays and lesbians. It is a matter of grave concern which cuts across all lines of ideology and party affiliation." Though the odds of denying Reagan a second term seemed remote, Coleman reminded the caucus that a victory in *Baker v. Wade* had also been viewed as far-fetched when activists launched the case, yet three years later, queer Texans had celebrated Buchmeyer's favorable ruling. The Fifth Circuit's dismissal of Danny Hill's appeal, he proclaimed, "has shown that nothing truly valuable can be accomplished without some risk and without some blood, sweat and tears being shed." Rather than being content with their court victory, it was time to charge ahead. "We can celebrate this victory," Coleman concluded, "knowing that there is much more to accomplish, more risks to be taken and, necessarily, more blood, sweat and tears to be shed."[51]

While the Fifth Circuit judges contemplated appeals in *Baker v. Wade*, Houston's queer activists decided to strike while the iron was hot. In June 1984, they persuaded a majority of the city council to protect the employment rights of gay and lesbian municipal employees. Since the state's homosexual conduct statute had been invalidated, many council members presumably believed such protections were on firmer legal ground than when 21.06 was still in effect. They failed to anticipate the groundswell of opposition to their action, however, and early the following year voters overturned the employment protections by a four-to-one margin in a citywide referendum election. Despite Buchmeyer's 1982 ruling and the Fifth Circuit's dismissal of Danny Hill's appeal, this setback in Houston revealed that a more definitive judicial statement invalidating 21.06 might be necessary to advance the cause of queer equality.[52]

Rehearing *En Banc*

At the Fifth Circuit, Danny Hill and his team had a card left to play, albeit one with little chance of success. Emboldened by *Dronenburg v. Zech*, Hill and his attorneys petitioned the court for a rehearing *en banc*. If granted, Hill would be allowed to argue his case again, but this time his audience would be the full sixteen-member Fifth Circuit Court of Appeals. Although the Fifth Circuit rarely granted such a rehearing, Hill remained undeterred. In their legal brief, Hill and his attorneys argued that the three-judge panel had violated Hill's due process rights by refusing to hear his appeal. In February 1985, in a surprising five-to-four ruling, a nine-judge panel of the Fifth Circuit granted Hill's request for a rehearing in front of the full court and allowed the appeal to move forward with the Amarillo attorney general as the recognized appellant. The court agreed that Attorney General

Mattox had insufficiently represented the defendant class by choosing not to pursue an appeal, and the judges concluded that Hill had the right to intervene in the case. Clearly pleased with the ruling, Hill told the *Dallas Times Herald* that he was "much more optimistic this time. . . . It's the kind of issue that should be heard by the whole court, where everybody will take a stand as to where we are on this." Baker's supporters were divided about the fate of the case. "I'm fairly confident," THRF executive director Tom Coleman said, "that after the full panel has the chance to see the case, they'll decide the same way." Jim Barber, however, was not quite as optimistic. "We're certainly not as well off as we were before," he stated to the press.[53]

The following June, all sixteen Fifth Circuit judges heard arguments from both sides in *Baker v. Wade*. While the justifications for preserving 21.06 remained consistent with Hill and DDAA's position, the legal strategy of Baker and his attorneys continued to evolve. In the THRF's new amicus brief submitted to the *en banc* court, Executive Director Tom Coleman argued that gay and lesbian individuals should be considered a suspect class and that the homosexual conduct law should undergo strict scrutiny by the courts. Federal courts had developed three measurements, Coleman told the judges, to test whether a particular group should be considered a suspect class and thus to determine which level of scrutiny a law must pass to withstand a constitutional challenge. First, based on two cases from the 1970s, Coleman asserted that the identifying characteristic that defined the group must be "determined by causes not within the control of the . . . individual, and . . . [have] no relation to the individual's ability to participate in and contribute to society," and Baker's expert witnesses during the original trial had testified that being gay or lesbian was neither a choice an individual makes nor a hindrance to the individual's ability to be a participating member of society. Second, relying on a similar legal precedent established during the 1970s, Coleman asserted that the group in question must have been "subjected to such a history of purposeful unequal treatment, or relegated to such a position of political powerlessness as to command extraordinary protection from the majoritarian political process." Coleman recounted the history of the ways same-sex sexuality had been condemned and punished throughout history, spanning the ancient world to the present. "Thus," Coleman argued, "despite recent gains in the securing of equality under the law by homosexuals, and their increasing political influence, patterns of ignorance and hostility continue to be felt by them." Third, Coleman wrote that a suspect classification required that members be harmed with "unique disabilities on the basis of stereotyped characteristics not truly indicative of their abilities." Coleman argued that gay and lesbian individuals, like racial and ethnic minorities, suffered from an "inferior legal status as criminals and second-class citizens." One need look no further than the recent debates in the Texas Legislature over recriminalizing same-sex sexuality, he pointed out, to get a sense of the animus directed at gays and lesbians in the state. If the court did not recognize gay and lesbian Texans as a suspect class, there was even a legal precedent to recognize them as a quasi-suspect class, which would require a law to undergo an intermediate or heightened level of scrutiny to judge its constitutionality.[54]

Baker's legal team also enlisted the pioneering historian John D'Emilio to strengthen their argument about suspect classification. Then an assistant professor at the University of North Carolina at Greensboro, D'Emilio had recently published his landmark study, *Sexual Politics, Sexual Communities: The Making of a Homosexual Minority in the United States, 1940–1970*. In his affidavit, D'Emilio focused on the achievements of queer individuals throughout history and their oppression in the United States since the nation's founding. From Socrates and Sappho in the ancient world to Walt Whitman and Emily Dickinson in the modern, D'Emilio pointed out that individuals with same-sex attractions had made significant contributions to human history. Yet they had also been "subject to intense oppression — to a wide range of laws, public policies, social customs, extra-legal measures, cultural beliefs, and attitudes that have consigned them to an inferior position in society." D'Emilio traced the earliest laws against sodomy in British North America, illustrating that during the seventeenth and eighteenth centuries, British settlers consistently singled out same-sex sexual contact as a particularly egregious violation of colonial law. During the late nineteenth century, the medical profession added to the widespread condemnation of same-sex relations by labeling same-sex attraction as pathological. These messages, D'Emilio argued, "had a corrosive effect on the self-esteem and self-image of gay people" and worked to "inflict liabilities upon gay men and women." To make matters worse, during the early Cold War of the 1940s and 1950s, the federal government labeled gay and lesbian individuals as threats to national security due to their perceived susceptibility to blackmail. Many queer citizens lost their government jobs or their security clearances because of their sexual orientation. The oppression, however, did not stop at the federal level. Working in partnership with local police departments, the Federal Bureau of Investigation (FBI) encouraged local law enforcement officers to use intrusive surveillance techniques to harass and intimidate gays and lesbians and to use the penal code to secure convictions not only for sodomy but also for disorderly conduct, solicitation, vagrancy, and lewdness. D'Emilio concluded his affidavit by reminding the court that although "the structure of oppression has been somewhat weakened" during the previous two decades, queer Americans still faced systemic and widespread discrimination, condemnation, and harassment. "The survival of laws criminalizing homosexual behavior," D'Emilio told the court, "plays a key role in maintaining this situation."[55]

Bowers v. Hardwick

While Baker and his legal team honed their arguments, a judicial development in Georgia caught their attention. In July 1982, an Atlanta bartender and entertainment designer named Michael Hardwick had just finished a late-night shift redecorating the Cove, a local gay bar, and was heading home. On his way out, he tossed an empty beer bottle into a trash can on the sidewalk. Keith Torick, an Atlanta police officer parked across the street, issued Hardwick a citation for public drinking, even though Hardwick insisted he had finished the beer while still inside the Cove. Although Hardwick promptly paid the $50 fine, an administrative error resulted in a warrant being issued for his arrest. On August 3, Officer Torick arrived at Hardwick's apartment to carry out the warrant. Torick later claimed that when he arrived at Hardwick's residence, the front door was slightly open. Upon entering, a person in the living room indicated that Hardwick was in a back bedroom. As Torick later reported, he made his way down the hallway to the open bedroom door and encountered Hardwick and another man engaged in oral sex. The officer arrested Hardwick and his companion and charged both men with violating Georgia's sodomy law, which made all oral and anal sex a felony punishable with a prison sentence between one and twenty years regardless of the sex of the participants.[56]

ACLU attorneys contacted Hardwick and encouraged him to challenge the constitutionality of Georgia's sodomy law. Hardwick agreed, but Fulton County district attorney Michael Bowers subsequently dropped the sodomy charges, stating he did not think the law should be applied to private consensual sexual activity. Denied the chance to appeal a criminal conviction, Hardwick's attorneys followed the example of Don Baker and filed a lawsuit against Bowers in federal district court. Using language similar to the complaint in *Baker v. Wade*, Hardwick's suit claimed the Georgia law violated the constitutional protections of privacy, free speech, and free association. After a federal judge dismissed the suit in April 1983, Hardwick and his legal team appealed to the Eleventh Circuit Court of Appeals in downtown Atlanta, emphasizing not only a constitutional right to privacy but also a modified claim about the discriminatory way police officers enforced Georgia's law to target gays and lesbians. In May 1985, as the Fifth Circuit weighed the arguments in *Baker v. Wade*, a three-judge panel of the Eleventh Circuit partly agreed with Hardwick's position. In an opinion written by Frank Johnson, the longtime Alabama federal judge who had been instrumental in tearing down the walls of Jim Crow segregation in his home state, the appeals panel ruled that the Georgia sodomy law violated Hardwick's constitutional right to privacy. Because privacy was a fundamental right, Johnson sent the case back down to the federal district court with orders to hold a trial in which Georgia officials would have the opportunity to demonstrate the relationship between the sodomy statute and a state interest. If the state proved unable to do this, Georgia's sodomy law must be declared unconstitutional. When the district attorney appealed the decision to the United States Supreme Court, the case became known as *Bowers v. Hardwick*.[57]

Baker's legal team found grounds for optimism in the Eleventh Circuit's decision. First, the appeals panel determined that Michael Hardwick had standing to challenge the law despite the fact that he, like Baker, had never faced prosecution. Second, in order to recognize Hardwick's right to engage in private sexual conduct with a partner of his choosing, the Eleventh Circuit judges held that *Doe v. Commonwealth's Attorney*, which simply affirmed a lower court's 1975 decision that upheld a Virginia sodomy statute, had not settled the question of the right to privacy. The controlling power of *Doe* was a centerpiece in Hill's argument that the Fifth Circuit was bound by precedent to uphold the Texas sodomy law. If the Eleventh Circuit's decision held up, it would eliminate much of the force of Hill's position on *Doe*. Third, and most important, the Eleventh Circuit ruled that the Georgia sodomy law violated a fundamental right of privacy necessitating that the state demonstrate a compelling interest that justified the intrusion into the private lives of citizens. If the state of Georgia were required to demonstrate this compelling interest to justify its sodomy law, surely the Fifth Circuit judges would require the same of the Texas statute.[58]

Judge Buchmeyer's Decision Overturned

The hopefulness that Baker and his supporters found in *Bowers v. Hardwick* proved to be misplaced. In a nine-to-seven ruling near the end of August, the Fifth Circuit overturned Buchmeyer's 1982 decision and reinstated the homosexual conduct law in Texas. After determining that Hill had the right to intervene in the case, the majority opinion declared that Buchmeyer had inappropriately disregarded *Doe v. Commonwealth's Attorney* and that 21.06 therefore did not represent a violation of Baker's right to privacy or equal protection. According to Fifth Circuit judge Thomas Reavley, the Supreme Court had ruled in *Doe* that the Constitution did not protect same-sex sexual activity. That decision, Reavley wrote, must remain the court's final word "until the Supreme Court itself has issued an unequivocal statement that *Doe* no longer controls." Reavley and the other circuit judges in the majority also refused to concede that gay and lesbian individuals constituted a suspect class. "Because we have held," Reavley wrote, "that engaging in homosexual conduct is not a constitutionally protected liberty interest and because Baker has not cited any cases holding, and we refuse to hold, that homosexuals constitute a suspect or quasi-suspect classification, the standard of review is whether section 21.06 is rationally related to a legitimate state end." The state of Texas simply needed to demonstrate that the statute advanced a permissible goal, and the majority of the Fifth Circuit was satisfied with the state's explanation. "In view of the strong objection to homosexual conduct, which has prevailed in Western culture for the past seven centuries," Reavley wrote, "we cannot say that section 21.06 is 'totally unrelated to the pursuit of'. . . implementing morality, a permissible state goal. Therefore, section 21.06 does not deprive Baker of equal protection of the laws." With the stroke of a pen, the Fifth Circuit resurrected the homosexual conduct law and rendered it fully enforceable in Texas after a nearly three-year hiatus.[59]

Two months later, when the Fifth Circuit denied Baker's petition for a rehearing, the appellate judges used the opportunity to clarify their position and to chide Judge Buchmeyer. The judges asserted that the will of the majority of the citizens of Texas outweighed a decision by any court. "It is not the role or authority of this federal court," their denial of a rehearing stated, "to decide the morality of sexual conduct for the people of the state of Texas. . . . We see ourselves bound by the decision of the lawmakers of the state of Texas and not by the 'finding' of a federal district judge." As for Baker's argument about how 21.06 violated the equal protection clause of the Fourteenth Amendment, the appellate court's denial of a rehearing exhibited the judges' blindness to how the homosexual conduct law operated and their unwillingness to accept current psychological research on the topic. "The statute is directed at certain conduct, not at a class of people," their statement read, and even if "the conduct be the desire of the bisexually or homosexually inclined, there is no necessity that they engage in it. The statute affects only those who choose to act in the manner proscribed." The court also conveyed its acceptance of how 21.06 branded only queer Texans as immoral. "If, as argued, the existence of the statute is a symbolic stigma against homosexually active persons, the stigma is due to the decision of the body politic of Texas that the proscribed conduct is morally wrong." In a final patronizing assertion of the wisdom of their decision, the judges suggested that a ruling against the constitutionality of 21.06 could produce even worse consequences for gays and lesbians. "Were a federal court to decree that the United States Constitution decides the [moral] issue and override the opinion of those of the different view," the judges stated, the "feelings of the losers, perhaps still in the majority, could be elevated by the nature of the fiat, and their frustrations might be vented upon the winners to a degree that increased the burdens of the latter beyond the consequences endured under the invalidated statute." In other words, a backlash against a court decision to overturn 21.06 might be worse than simply living with the law. The message of the Fifth Circuit could not have been clearer: individuals who engaged in same-sex sexual activity were immoral and justly classified as criminals in the state of Texas.[60]

For queer Texans, the news came as a shocking disappointment. "We Are Criminals, Again," read the front page of the *Dallas Voice* a few days later. Baker was troubled that a reinstatement of 21.06 would send a message to gays and lesbians that their rights, and indeed their very lives, were unimportant. "To be denied your dignity," he lamented, "is the worst kind of discrimination you can face." DGA president Bill Nelson also expressed shock at the Fifth Circuit's decision. "I'm appalled at the court's position," he told the *Dallas Morning News*, "one based on ignorance and prejudice. I expected more out of this appeals court." In Houston, the mood was equally somber. HGPC president Sue Lovell said she and many other caucus members simply could not believe their victory could be taken away so easily. "Basically," she said with astonishment, "it means that every gay person in this state becomes a criminal as of tonight." Houston activist Ray Hill was outraged that the decision was a "blatant political ruling. . . . It criminalizes gays as individuals in a degree that we haven't known before." Not one to beat around the bush, Hill wanted people to know the personal impact this ruling would have on gays and lesbians throughout the state. "It means that as my companion and I turn in tonight," he stated, "our relationship will be illegal." Yet Hill also wished to disabuse any observers of the belief that the Fifth Circuit's ruling only applied to same-sex relationships. "What the panel has said," he told the *Houston Post*, "is that the government may delve into anyone's private lives, including their homes, to accomplish whatever arbitrary goals the government may have." THRF president Tom Coleman was not as surprised as many other activists. "There are six Reagan appointees on the [appeals] court," he told the *Houston Post*. "And everybody knows of the administration's anti-gay stance."[61]

After speaking with the media all night, Baker sat down with *Dallas Morning News* reporter Gayle Golden the next morning over breakfast. Golden found Baker weary but determined to carry the battle forward. "Tired of the legal battle," Golden wrote. "Tired of the publicity. Tired of the emotional and psychological burden imposed by his lawsuit." Baker admitted that he had failed to anticipate the emotional toll that would be required of him when he agreed to be the plaintiff in the case and that his quiet life had been upended with the filing of the lawsuit in 1979 and the unrelenting scrutiny he received from the media. "I did begin to feel an incredible amount of responsibility that I don't think I really knew I was getting into," he told Golden. "There was too much attention. . . . I was not quite sure this is what I wanted." While the publicity of his case never threatened his livelihood, he had begun to notice the psychological toll of all the attention. "It's more a mental and emotional than an actual pain. . . . It's just the day-in, day-out realization of being responsible constantly, of being accountable constantly." Despite his weariness, Baker found that the recent setback in the Fifth Circuit served to motivate him to commit all his energies to winning an ultimate victory for gay and lesbian Texans. "It's my responsibility to go on with [the lawsuit], and I will," he affirmed. "It's time to get ready to go one more lap. I have had to mentally and emotionally gear up." When asked why he chose to continue subjecting himself to the pressures of being a public figure in the struggle to overturn 21.06, Baker admitted that he occasionally asked the same question of himself. "Then I go to the grocery store," he said, returning to his characteristic hopefulness, "or I go to the park, or I go to the movies—in Plano, or Garland, or Oak Cliff—and see a lesbian couple or a gay male couple. They are the ones who need protection. They are the ones this [lawsuit] is about."[62]

If Baker was searching for a silver lining among the dark clouds of the court's decision about his case, he could look no further than the dissenting opinions issued by the seven Fifth Circuit judges in the minority. Judge Alvin B. Rubin focused on the error of recognizing Hill's right to intervene in the case after the state attorney general declined to defend 21.06.

"Determined to uphold the constitutionality of a Texas statute whatever obstacles bar the way," Rubin wrote, "the majority opinion tramples every procedural rule it considers." The dissenting judges expressed alarm at the notion that any of Texas's more than one thousand district, county, and city attorneys could overrule the decision of the official class representatives. "The court's judicial sponsorship of Danny Hill as spokesman for the State of Texas," Rubin stated, "is not only unprecedented but ill-advised," opening the door to any local official who wanted to intervene in any case in which they did not agree with the decisions of the proper representatives of their state. Yet even if the Fifth Circuit's action held no precedential value, Rubin argued that allowing the Amarillo district attorney to intervene in this specific case violated Baker's right to equal justice. While Rubin confined his dissent to the question of Danny Hill's standing, Judge Irving Goldberg wrote a concurring dissent in which he commented on the constitutional questions presented in Baker's case. Goldberg disagreed with the majority that the Supreme Court's summary affirmance in *Doe v. Commonwealth's Attorney* bound lower courts on the question of private consensual sexual contact between same-sex partners. "If ever there was a constitutional right to privacy," Goldberg maintained, "Texas has violated it by blatantly intruding into the private sex lives of fully consenting adults." Because the state of Texas offered no persuasive explanation for how the homosexual conduct law was related to a compelling interest of the state, Goldberg concluded that 21.06 was unconstitutional.[63]

The US Supreme Court

Rubin's and Goldberg's dissenting opinions may have seemed like a poor consolation considering how devastating the defeat at the Fifth Circuit had been, but in practical terms, the minority opinion could be helpful in an ongoing appeal. Baker made it clear the day after the Fifth Circuit handed down its decision that he would pursue his case to the US Supreme Court. "I think many gays and lesbians thought this would be an easy trek," he told the *Dallas Morning News*. "It has not been . . . and we are going to continue the fight." Barber thought the Eleventh Circuit's ruling in *Bowers v. Hardwick* would prove useful in persuading the Supreme Court to hear the *Baker* case. "There is now a direct conflict between circuit courts," he told reporters, making it likely that the high court would intervene to settle the dispute. In mid-September, members of the THRF board hired the renowned Harvard Law School professor Laurence Tribe, a constitutional expert who had experience arguing gay and lesbian rights cases before the Supreme Court. "We went for the best constitutional lawyer in the land," Baker stated, "and we got him." THRF members also initiated a fundraising campaign to cover legal costs, and Baker traversed the state giving speeches and shaking hands to persuade donors to give generously. Finally, the THRF board reached out to national gay and lesbian rights organizations to coordinate their efforts, partnering with the Lambda Legal Defense and Education Fund in New York City. Prompted in part by *Baker v. Wade*, Lambda legal director Abby Rubenfeld had recently created a national task force to focus on state-level sodomy law reform and invited THRF executive director Tom Coleman and board member Patrick Wiseman to join it in 1985. By then, the *Baker* and *Bowers* cases dominated the discussions of the task force as members debated the merits of each case and the strategies required to win an ultimate victory in the Supreme Court.[64]

While activists waited for the Supreme Court to decide whether to hear *Bowers v. Hardwick*, Baker and his legal team worked with Tribe to prepare their own appeal to the high court. In November 1985, a series of developments changed their calculations. On November 4, before Baker was able to file his appeal, the Supreme Court granted certiorari in *Bowers v. Hardwick*. Undeterred, Baker and his attorneys believed their case was fundamentally different from *Bowers* and advanced a divergent set of arguments. The Fifth Circuit, according to Baker's petition, "deemed it irrelevant that the statute in this case, unlike that in *Hardwick*, criminalizes acts on a basis expressly dependent upon the *gender* of the actor. Thus, not even a decision by this Court reversing or vacating the Eleventh Circuit's ruling in *Hardwick* on the ground that strict scrutiny is inappropriate would necessarily endorse the extraordinary degree of deference, amounting to virtual abdication of judgment, that the Fifth Circuit accorded the Texas statute in this case." Because Texas's 21.06 applied only to same-sex sexual activity, a final decision upholding Georgia's sodomy law would not answer the equal protection question presented in *Baker v. Wade*. The Supreme Court, therefore, should agree to hear both cases.[65]

Baker and his attorneys thought Tribe and other Lambda task force members agreed with them. During a series of task force meetings held in New York City on November 15 and 16, however, most participants made it clear that *Bowers* would receive top priority and that all other cases would be put on hold. Leading the charge to separate *Baker* from *Bowers*, Tribe admitted that while he had previously supported merging the two cases, he now believed a winning strategy would be to ask the court to consider *Bowers* in isolation. Asking the Supreme Court to rule on the question of privacy alone, according to Tribe, had a higher chance of success than combining privacy with equal protection. "Equality, though perhaps more morally sound," Tribe stated during the meeting, "is a less strong avenue of attack against sodomy statutes. *Baker* is an equality case; it contains an excellent record for consideration of the Equal Protection clause's application to gay people. If, however, the Justices are not persuaded by *Hardwick*'s privacy claim, there is not much hope for *Baker*'s Equal Protection claim." Based on Tribe's calculation, either case would depend on Justice Lewis Powell casting a tie-breaking vote. The way to win Powell, he argued, was to present the case as a narrow question concerning the appropriate level of judicial scrutiny to apply to a law that infringed on the right of privacy rather than on a broader question of civil rights and equal protection for gay and lesbian citizens. "The challenge," he asserted, "is to frame an argument that Powell, who likes to see himself as a Southern gentleman, could conceivably agree to. By focusing on the concrete question of whether the 11th circuit was correct in requiring a harder look, and avoiding abstract questions inviting sweeping gay rights pronouncements, we may be able to win Powell." Tribe admitted that Baker's case raised important constitutional questions and merited a hearing before the Supreme Court, but for the time being he wanted to get the *Bowers* case before the high court as soon as possible and return to *Baker* once the fate of the Georgia law became clear. Members of the task force's Texas delegation disagreed. Barber proclaimed that making the *Baker* case play second fiddle to *Bowers* was "an unspeakable insult to the lesbian and gay movement." Baker stated that to choose not to bring the equal protection argument before the Supreme Court "would be an affront to the gay community. We simply can't sit back and accept our criminal status. We Texans feel we must go on." In the end, Tribe won the argument, and the task force decided to pursue *Bowers* first and to demote *Baker* to a secondary concern.[66]

Against the advice of the task force, Baker and his legal team filed their own petition for certiorari with the Supreme Court in January 1986, hoping that the court's justices would agree to hear their case no matter how they ruled in *Bowers*. Two months later, the nine justices of the Supreme Court heard oral arguments in *Bowers*, and Baker was in the audience to hear the presentation of the case firsthand. Attorneys for the state of Georgia premised their defense on what they viewed as the absence of a constitutional right to engage in homosexual sodomy. Representing the state attorney general's office, lawyer Michael Hobbs argued that his state's sodomy law was not enforced if committed by married couples inside the privacy of their own homes, and he admitted that the statute's constitutionality would be under great suspicion if it were. In the case of same-sex sexual activity, Hobbs asserted that the landmark judicial opinions concerning the right to privacy, such as *Griswold v. Connecticut* (1965) and *Eisenstadt v. Baird* (1972), applied only to procreative sex. Constitutional protections of privacy, therefore, did not apply to same-sex relationships. Tribe countered that judicial precedent extended constitutional protections defined in *Griswold* and *Eisenstadt* to all decisions concerning private sexual conduct no matter the sex of the individuals involved. Several justices openly worried about how far this line of argumentation could be stretched, and they probed Tribe for a limiting principle that would draw the line where privacy rights ended. Drug use, incest, and polygamy, for example, were not protected by a constitutional right to privacy. Tribe responded that the right to privacy did not protect sexual behaviors that were harmful, as incest and polygamy clearly harmed women and children. Private consensual sex between adults, however, harmed no one and should therefore be protected. At the end of oral arguments, Tribe and his team believed they had won the debate and had achieved their objective of convincing Justice Powell to extend the right of privacy to same-sex relationships.[67]

In the end, Tribe and other Lambda task force members were right that Powell would be responsible for breaking a tie vote, but they inaccurately predicted which side he would join. The legal scholar William Eskridge argues that despite Tribe's well-reasoned arguments, Powell was not convinced to extend the constitutional right of privacy as far as the *Bowers* case was asking. "Powell was sympathetic to Tribe's basic point, that applying sodomy laws to private activities between consenting adults was ridiculous," Eskridge writes, "but he felt that Tribe lacked a defensible *constitutional* basis for striking down the statute." For Powell, Tribe had failed to define a reasonable limiting principle, particularly since one could argue that private drug use within the home did not cause harm to other persons. Powell nonetheless agreed that same-sex sexual activity within the home should be decriminalized and searched for an alternative justification for invalidating the law. As it turned out, the comparison between drug use and same-sex sexual activity brought up during oral argument provided the justice with a potential rationale. A gay or lesbian individual, reasoned Powell, could be addicted to sodomy in the same way a user of illegal drugs could be addicted to substances. In 1962, the Supreme Court had ruled in *Robinson v. California* that the Eighth Amendment's prohibition of cruel and unusual punishment protected an individual from being imprisoned simply because he or she was an addict. A prison sentence for a gay or lesbian individual who happened to be addicted to gay or lesbian sex, he thought, might also violate the Eighth Amendment. Yet this line of reasoning had no support among any of the other justices, and Powell quickly dispensed with it. By early April, Powell had agreed to vote to uphold Georgia's sodomy law, admitting that in certain instances a sodomy law might violate the Eighth Amendment but pointing out that it did not apply in this case because Michael Hardwick had never been sentenced to prison for violating the law.[68]

At the end of June, writing for the majority in *Bowers v. Hardwick*, Justice Byron White ignored all of Tribe's arguments about the right to privacy and instead focused on the specific sexual behavior outlawed by the Georgia statute. "The issue presented," White wrote, "is whether the Federal Constitution confers a fundamental right upon homosexuals to engage in sodomy." By making the case solely about the right to engage in specific sexual activity, the majority disconnected *Bowers* from previous cases in which the court upheld the constitutional right to privacy, claiming that those cases dealt specifically with marriage and procreation. "Any claim that these cases nevertheless stand for the proposition that any kind of private sexual conduct between consenting adults is constitutionally insulated from state proscription is unsupportable," White wrote. The court found the idea of extending constitutional protections to same-sex sexual activity particularly abhorrent. "Proscriptions against that conduct," they opined, "have ancient roots," and "to claim that a right to engage in such conduct is 'deeply rooted in this Nation's history and tradition' or 'implicit in the concept of ordered liberty' is, at best, facetious." The Supreme Court, White asserted, remained unwilling to extend the reach of the Constitution to create a new fundamental right. The court's majority was not persuaded by Tribe's attempt to provide a limiting principle for the right of privacy within the home. "Plainly enough," White wrote, "otherwise illegal conduct is not always immunized whenever it occurs in the home. Victimless crimes, such as the possession and use of illegal drugs, do not escape the law where they are committed at home. . . . And if respondent's submission is limited to the voluntary sexual conduct between consenting adults, it would be difficult, except by fiat, to limit the claimed right to homosexual conduct while leaving exposed to prosecution adultery, incest, and other sexual crimes even though they are committed in the home. We are unwilling to start down that road." Since the high court refused to acknowledge a fundamental privacy right at stake in the case, the justices employed the least stringent rational basis test to determine the constitutionality of the Georgia law. White concluded the majority opinion by asserting that the state had clearly shown that its legitimate interest in promoting morality sufficiently justified the statute.[69]

A few days later, the Supreme Court, as expected, denied certiorari in *Baker v. Wade* and allowed the Fifth Circuit's decision upholding the Texas sodomy law to stand. Baker and his supporters were dismayed. As Baker wrote in a letter to Justice Thurgood Marshall, the only judge to vote in support of granting certiorari in *Baker*, "I was hoping that since our case raised similar, but yet different issues (e.g., equal protection and the procedural question), [the other justices who joined Marshall in the *Bowers* dissent] would have wanted to bring our case forward." The fact that 21.06 targeted only queer Texans and the question of whether Danny Hill should be allowed to represent the state of Texas in the appeal suggested to Baker that the Supreme Court might want to hear his case in addition to *Bowers*. Unfortunately, Marshall was the only justice who agreed. THRF executive director Tom Coleman expressed his consternation in a THRF press release. "We are, of course, extremely disappointed," Coleman wrote, "that the Supreme Court did not take the opportunity Don Baker . . . presented to it to restore orderly court procedure and legal equality to all Texans, regardless of sexual orientation." Baker was equally dispirited that his case had ended so unceremoniously. "I laid my life on the line," he wrote to Justice Marshall, "for a cause I deeply believe in. For seven years my people labored with me on this case. It is very difficult to 'just let go' after seeing it end so abruptly." Yet letting go was precisely what Baker realized he needed to do. "A long, adventurous journey has now come to an end," Baker wrote to THRF board member Lee Taft two months later. By the fall of 1986, Baker was exhausted and burned out. As he later acknowledged, "The toll on resources, energies, and emotions was phenomenal. . . . I never dreamed that such an 'adventure' could test my stamina as it did." The most significant chapter in the long struggle to overturn the Texas sodomy law prior to 2003 had ended in disappointment and regret. Battle worn and scarred, Baker and his partner began making plans to move to New England for some much-needed rest.[70]

A Path Forward

While the Supreme Court decision in *Bowers v. Hardwick* and the denial of certiorari in *Baker v. Wade* represented a devastating loss for Baker and his supporters, the case, while a short-term failure, proved to be a critical component in the developing legal strategy in the movement for queer equality. Prior to *Lawrence v. Texas, Baker v. Wade* was the most significant legal challenge to the Texas sodomy law in the state's history. Not only did Judge Buchmeyer's ruling represent the first time a federal district court struck down a state sodomy law based on a gay or lesbian individual's constitutional rights of privacy and equal protection, but the seven-year legal battle also allowed activists to take their movement public and to couch their demands for equality in terms of the Constitution. Although the case ultimately failed to bring about a change in the law, activists were able to use Baker's challenge to lay the groundwork for an impressive series of victories during the following two decades.

Perhaps unintentionally, the Supreme Court's opinion in *Bowers v. Hardwick* suggested a way forward for Texas activists who wanted to eliminate 21.06. Writing for the majority, Justice White made it clear that the case "raises no question about the right or propriety of state legislative decisions to repeal their laws that criminalize homosexual sodomy, or of state court decisions invalidating those laws on state constitutional grounds." As many activists were fuming over the high court's refusal to recognize their constitutional rights, some viewed this particular line in White's opinion as a signal for how to proceed. In a post-decision press release, THRF executive director Tom Coleman echoed White's pronouncement. "Despite the fact that 21.06 remains on the books," he proclaimed, "we have, since the case was filed in 1979, convinced many people that one million otherwise law-abiding and productive gay and lesbian Texans deserve better than the irrational criminal stigma that 21.06 inflicts upon them. Accordingly, we believe that legislative reform or a state court challenge stands a far greater chance of success today than when this effort was first commenced." While legislative repeal of 21.06 remained unlikely, over the next decade, queer activists used the Texas Constitution and the state judicial system in surprising and often ingenious ways in their attempt to rid the legal code of the sodomy law once and for all.[71]

CHAPTER 5

Morales v. Texas and *England v. City of Dallas*, 1986–1994

I'm optimistic that 21.06 can be overturned and that our dreams and goals can be attained. The reward will provide equal protection under the law.

MORALES V. TEXAS PLAINTIFF LINDA MORALES, 1989

Just because I'm gay, I'm not inadequate. It is ignorant for people to think my sexuality will impair me as a police officer. I went to school to study criminal justice, and I'm determined to get a position with the Dallas police.

ENGLAND V. CITY OF DALLAS PLAINTIFF MICA ENGLAND, 1990

On May 14, 1988, John Griffin and Tommy Trimble were enjoying a night out in Oak Lawn, Dallas's gay and lesbian neighborhood. Griffin, a twenty-seven-year-old white man, and Trimble, a thirty-four-year-old Black man, shared the experience of having grown up gay in small towns in West Texas, and the two friends undoubtedly still savored the freedom of living their authentic lives away from the stifling confines of their hometowns. Several miles away in the suburb of Mesquite, Richard Bednarski was also meeting up with friends to plan a night of excitement in Oak Lawn. What the eighteen-year-old North Mesquite High School senior had in mind, however, could not have been more different from Griffin and Trimble's idea of fun. Bednarski and his friends often drove to Oak Lawn to harass, mock, and intimidate gays and lesbians. Yet on this particular night, the stakes proved to be much higher for everyone involved.[1]

As Bednarski and eight friends stood in front of the Village Station nightclub shouting at passersby and attempting to mimic what they interpreted as the stereotypically effeminate mannerisms of gay men, Griffin and Trimble pulled their vehicle near the sidewalk and engaged in small talk, seemingly unaware of the teenagers' intentions. Sensing an opportunity to deceive the two men, Bednarski and one of his companions asked for a ride to Reverchon Park, a popular recreation and cruising location in the neighborhood, so the group could smoke marijuana. There is no evidence that Griffin and Trimble intended to pursue a sexual encounter with Bednarski, but as soon as the four men reached a quiet area of the park, Bednarski ordered the two gay men to remove all their clothing. When Griffin and Trimble refused, Bednarski pulled out a gun and ordered Griffin and Trimble down onto their knees. Bednarski later admitted that he forced his gun into Trimble's mouth and pulled the trigger, killing him almost instantly. As Griffin attempted to flee, Bednarski stepped on his leg to prevent his escape and shot him twice in the back and once in the head. Griffin died from his wounds five days later at Dallas's Parkland Hospital.[2]

Based on information collected from friends and classmates, Mesquite police arrested Bednarski ten days later. After he signed a confession statement admitting to killing Griffin and Trimble, police charged Bednarski with two counts of capital murder, although in June a Dallas County grand jury reduced the charge to simple murder because he had no previous criminal record. The charge of murder nevertheless carried a maximum sentence of two life terms in prison—one for each victim. During his trial the following November, one member of the friend group identified Bednarski as the person responsible for the deaths of Griffin and Trimble. He testified that the group of teens had driven to Oak Lawn that night to "pester the homosexuals" and that they had accepted the ride from Griffin and Trimble with the intention of robbing and beating the two gay men. Bednarski, however, had other plans. Several of Bednarski's classmates at North Mesquite High School testified that Bednarski had bragged about the murders. "I blew those faggots' fucking heads off," one acquaintance remembered him crowing in the days following the double murder. Another classmate testified that Bednarski expressed a desire to go to Parkland Hospital to kill Griffin as he lay dying from his wounds to prevent him from identifying Bednarski as the culprit. After fourteen hours of deliberations, a twelve-member jury unanimously found Bednarski guilty of the two murders. On November 30, 1988, Judge Jack Hampton opted not to enforce the maximum penalty, explaining that the defendant had no prior criminal record, was attending a local community college, and "came from a good family." "I don't think he's going to be a lifetime sociopath," Hampton said. Instead of two life sentences, Judge Hampton sentenced Bednarski to thirty years in prison, although he would be eligible for parole after serving just seven years. The light sentence outraged, but did not surprise, many gays and lesbians in Dallas. "It certainly doesn't speak well for the lives of gay men," Dallas Gay Alliance (DGA) president William Waybourn told the *Dallas Morning News*. "I think it just encourages that type of behavior."[3]

If leaders like Waybourn were unsurprised by the judge's light sentence for the murders of two gay men in cold blood, Hampton's subsequent statements to the press proved more shocking. *Dallas Times Herald* courthouse reporter Lori Montgomery dropped in on Hampton in mid-December to get updates on several recent trials. When the conversation turned to Bednarski's trial, Hampton unleashed a torrent of candid and troubling thoughts about the case, some of which Montgomery published in a front-page story the following day. When Montgomery asked Hampton why he handed down such a light sentence to Bednarski, particularly when the judge had a tough law-and-order reputation, Hampton responded that his judgment of the characters of the victims played a role in his decision. "These two guys that got killed," Hampton said, "wouldn't have been killed if they hadn't been cruising the streets picking up teenage boys. I don't much care for queers cruising the streets picking up teenage boys. . . . These homosexuals, by running around on the weekends picking up teenage boys, they're asking for trouble." If the victims had been "a couple of housewives out shopping, not hurting anybody," Hampton said he would have been more inclined to enforce the maximum penalty on the defendant. Because Griffin and Trimble were gay, according to Hampton, they did not deserve full and equal justice. "I put prostitutes and gays at about the same level," the judge told Montgomery. "If these boys had picked up two prostitutes and taken them to the woods and killed them, I'd consider that a similar case. And I'd be hard put to give somebody life for killing a prostitute."[4]

The DGA and the Texas Human Rights Foundation (THRF), which had been at the forefront of the legal battle against the state's sodomy law since the late 1970s, filed a complaint with the Texas Commission on Judicial Conduct and demanded that Hampton be removed as a state judge. THRF legal director Tom Doyal argued that "Hampton's remarks display a cavalier disregard for the integrity of the judiciary in that he makes plain his belief that punishment for homicide may be conditioned on the identity of the victim rather than on the nature of the criminal conduct. . . . He has created an entirely new class of crime: murder of expendable classes of people." The following day, approximately two hundred activists staged a protest outside the Dallas County Courthouse and vowed to continue with daily demonstrations until authorities removed Judge Hampton from his position. In January 1989, commission members opened an investigation into the matter, and they were so troubled by the judge's behavior that they urged the Texas Supreme Court to hold their own public hearings on Hampton's conduct.[5]

"I put prostitutes and gays at
about the same level. And I'd be
hard put to give somebody life
for killing a prostitute."

Judge Jack Hampton

YOU BE THE JUDGE!

LET OUR GOVERNMENT OFFICIALS KNOW HOW YOU FEEL ABOUT JUDGE JACK HAMPTON.

Robert C. Flowers
State Committee on
Judicial Conduct
P. O. Box 12265
Capitol Station
Austin, TX 78711
512-463-5533

Dallas County
Commissioners Court
411 Elm Street
Dallas, TX 75201

Dallas City Council
City Hall Plaza
1500 Marilla
Dallas, TX 75201

Dallas Morning News
P. O. Box 655237
Dallas, TX 75265

Dallas Times Herald
1101 Pacific Avenue
Dallas, TX 75202

Jack Hampton
3804 Normandy
Dallas, TX 75205
Office   653-6445
Home   528-8616

DALLAS GAY ALLIANCE

Figure 5.1. Dallas Gay Alliance poster protesting Judge Jack Hampton's remarks after his lenient sentencing of Richard Bednarski for the 1988 double murder of John Griffin and Tommy Trimble.

Members of the Texas Supreme Court agreed and opened their hearings in Dallas the following October, nearly one year after the conclusion of Bednarski's trial. Hampton hired former Dallas County district attorney Henry Wade, the defendant in *Baker v. Wade*, who had returned to private practice in 1987, to head up his defense team against the charges of impropriety. "The real complaint of those who seek to oust Judge Hampton," Wade wrote in defense of the judge, "is that he disapproves of the practice of homosexual sodomy." As Wade and Hampton accurately pointed out, 21.06 continued to prohibit certain sexual acts if performed by two or more members of the same sex. Hampton referred to the Fifth Circuit's decision in *Baker v. Wade* and the US Supreme Court's opinion in *Bowers v. Hardwick* to illustrate the standing precedent that individual states could justifiably outlaw same-sex sexual activity in the interest of promoting morality. "Against this historical and legal backdrop," Hampton asked, "can homosexuals truly demand to appear before judges who have no misgivings about their lifestyle?" The judge's answer was that the homosexual conduct law provided a compelling rationale for this blatant partiality and that queer citizens must accept a prejudicial criminal justice system. "To disapprove of deviate sexual behavior condemned as criminal by the people of the State of Texas," Hampton concluded, "cannot serve as the basis for a charge of judicial misconduct."[6]

In late November 1989, the State Commission on Judicial Conduct issued a public censure of Judge Hampton rather than recommend his removal from the bench. Hampton's comments to representatives of the local media "were destructive of public confidence in the integrity and impartiality of the judiciary," commission members concluded. This pleased many gay and lesbian activists, particularly because the censure was "very strongly and harshly worded," as newly appointed THRF legal director David Bryan described it. Yet the commission did not take issue with the logic of Judge Hampton's argument that his public comments were defensible. The fact remained that during the late 1980s, 21.06 still branded all queer Texans as criminals. Judge Hampton simply expressed his belief, which he undoubtedly shared with many judges across the state, that queer citizens were not worthy of equal treatment before the law, even if they were victims of crimes. The homosexual conduct law continued to provide the legal justification for this line of reasoning. In Texas during the late 1980s, the Bednarski trial and Judge Hampton's public comments illustrated that the state sodomy law, in addition to being a rationale for discrimination and injustice, could also become, as it did for John Griffin and Tommy Trimble, a matter of life and death.[7]

The US Supreme Court's 1986 decision in *Bowers v. Hardwick* dealt a shattering blow to queer activists in Texas and across the nation, and their fears about its impact materialized in Judge Hampton's use of the high court's opinion in defense of his lenient sentencing of Richard Bednarski and his inflammatory comments about the trial. Rising from the ruins of the *Bowers* decision, however, as well as from their inability to persuade the Supreme Court to hear their arguments in *Baker v. Wade*, activists in Texas developed new and creative strategies to rid the state of its sodomy law during the late 1980s and 1990s. As the Bednarski trial made clear, it remained critical to eliminate 21.06 before queer Texans would have any semblance of justice or equality before the law. In the wake of the Supreme Court ruling in *Bowers* and the tragic murder of John Griffin and Tommy Trimble, Texas activists focused their attention on two possible routes to eliminate the homosexual conduct law that, ironically, Supreme Court justice Byron White had inadvertently suggested in his written opinion for the majority in *Bowers*. If activists wished to continue their efforts to eradicate state sodomy laws, White seemed to argue, they should focus on either legislative repeal or state constitutional challenges. During the late 1980s and 1990s, Texas activists tried both. The state legislature proved to be a dead end, and activists soon abandoned that option to instead launch legal challenges to the homosexual conduct law based on protections found in the Texas Constitution. Although different in important respects from previous legal confrontations over the state's sodomy law, the two most significant cases activists filed during the immediate post-*Bowers* era—*Morales v. Texas* and *England v. City of Dallas*—shared with previous litigation efforts a profound influence on the ultimate victory over the homosexual conduct law a few years later in *Lawrence v. Texas* (2003). These legal challenges represented the penultimate attack on 21.06 and, together with previous cases, helped pave the way toward a series of critical victories in the movement for queer equality.[8]

The Texas Constitution

In preparation for the legislature's 1987 session, more than sixty representatives of gay and lesbian organizations throughout Texas from major cities like Dallas, Houston, and San Antonio, but also smaller towns like Amarillo and Tyler, pooled their resources to hire a full-time lobbyist with a $100,000 budget to persuade legislators to repeal the homosexual conduct law. Activists soon realized that the legislature would be a more prohibitive obstacle than they had anticipated. During every session since the legislature passed the law in 1973, Houston's Craig Washington had attempted to repeal 21.06, both during his time as a representative between 1973 and 1983 and as a state senator after 1983, but was rebuffed every time by his colleagues. Nevertheless, at the beginning of the 1989 session, Washington introduced another repeal bill, but this time he had an ally in the Texas House who agreed to co-sponsor the bill after meeting with representatives of the Texas Lesbian/Gay Political Caucus and the DGA. Representative David Cain, a Democrat whose district included most of Dallas's Oak Lawn neighborhood, said he was appalled by Judge Hampton's use of the homosexual conduct law as a justification for his lenient sentence of Richard Bednarski in the double murder of Griffin and Trimble. "We need to get away from that kind of thinking," Cain told reporters. "I think the time is past due that this antiquated law be wiped off the books." This latest repeal effort, however, met staunch resistance from many state legislators. "If I knew someone with homosexual tendencies," Republican Senator John Leedom stated in opposition to the repeal bill, "I would say, 'Quit.' It's like discouraging someone from smoking. . . . I think the practice is not a wholesome one for society." Soon Leedom had enough support to defeat this latest effort to repeal 21.06.[9]

As activists saw their efforts frustrated in the legislature, many set their sights on an alternative strategy. In July 1986, ten days after the Supreme Court issued its decision in *Bowers*, members of the Lambda Legal Defense and Education Fund's sodomy law task force discussed potential state-level challenges across the country. Lambda strategist Nan Feyler identified six states that had explicit privacy protections written into their state constitutions and that also retained sodomy laws in their criminal codes. While Feyler left Texas off her list, THRF executive director Tom Coleman believed the Texas Constitution provided a wealth of opportunities to challenge 21.06 on the bases of equal protection and freedom of speech and association. The only significant roadblock was the paucity of legal precedent in Texas courts. Although judges had been willing to recognize that the state constitution guaranteed freedoms beyond the federal constitution, it remained unclear if they would apply these protections to same-sex sexual contact. Coleman admitted that there were "no substantive privacy provisions in the Texas state constitution," and case law indicated that judges often rested their decisions regarding privacy on the Fourteenth Amendment. A more challenging obstacle was the political environment in Texas. As the Republican Party continued to gain ground in the once solidly Democratic state, and because state judges were elected rather than appointed, the composition of the courts reflected the political shift. Texas Democrats did not unfailingly support the elimination of 21.06, as shown in the failed efforts to repeal the law. Yet Republican gains portended an even worse future for queer Texans, as their party platform explicitly called for the increased enforcement of sodomy laws and the quarantine of people with AIDS. As voters elected more Republicans to state courts, the chances of a victory using a state constitutional challenge dwindled.[10]

In October 1987, the Texas Supreme Court handed down a decision that offered some hope by suggesting that state judges might recognize a right to privacy in the state constitution that was broader than the protections found in the federal constitution. In *Texas State Employees Union* [TSEU] *v. Texas Department of Mental Health and Mental Retardation*, the state's highest court ruled that mandatory polygraph tests for state employees unreasonably intruded into their private lives. "While the Texas Constitution contains no express guarantee of a right to privacy," Chief Justice John Hill wrote in the majority opinion, "it contains several provisions similar to those in the United States Constitution that have been recognized as implicitly creating protected 'zones of privacy.'" Hill identified several portions of the state constitution that protected Texans against "arbitrary deprivation of life and liberty," against being "compelled to give evidence against himself," and against "unreasonable intrusion . . . [into] the sanctity of the individual's home and person." "We do not doubt," Hill concluded, "that a right of individual privacy is implicit among those 'general, great, and essential principles of liberty and free government' established by the Texas Bill of Rights." Having recognized this state-level right to privacy, the court concluded that a state agency would be able to infringe on that right "only when the government can demonstrate that an intrusion is reasonably warranted for the achievement of a compelling governmental objective that can be achieved by no less intrusive, more reasonable means."[11]

Although Coleman and his fellow THRF legal strategists contemplated a state constitutional challenge to 21.06 the following year, the main impetus to launch a new litigation effort stemmed from students at two of the state's largest law schools. In November 1988, William Garza, a student at the University of Texas School of Law in Austin, submitted to the THRF board a research paper he had written in one of his law courses. Garza's analysis explored the potential for challenging 21.06 using the state constitution, particularly the Bill of Rights that began the state's document. Of particular interest to Garza was the Equal Rights Amendment (ERA), which Texas voters had approved adding to their state constitution in 1972 by a four-to-one margin. The amendment simply read, "Equality under the law shall not be denied or abridged because of sex, race, color, creed or national origin." He noted that Texas courts had already used the state's ERA to strike down child custody policies based on sex and separate dormitory rules for men and women at the state's colleges and universities. Based on these few cases, Garza reasoned that THRF attorneys could persuade state judges that 21.06 violated the state's ERA because the homosexual conduct law prohibited certain behavior based on the sex of the person involved. "Gays and lesbians are forced by the state," Garza wrote, "to choose their sexual intimates based solely on their" sex. In a related way, Garza argued that 21.06 violated the Texas Constitution's equal protection clauses. Citing two 1985 state supreme court decisions, Garza argued that the classification of Texans as "heterosexual" and "homosexual" required the state to articulate a rational basis for the differentiation of individuals related to the purpose of the statute. Finally, Garza asserted that the right to privacy was perhaps the strongest argument against the homosexual conduct law. Since the Texas Supreme Court recognized a fundamental right to privacy in the Texas Constitution in its 1987 *TSEU* decision, the appropriate standard of review for a law that intrudes upon this right is that the state must show a compelling interest that is furthered by the law and must demonstrate that the interest cannot be advanced by a less intrusive statute. According to Garza, state officials had never articulated a compelling interest that justified the intrusive nature of 21.06. For all these reasons, Garza recommended challenging the law in civil court rather than waiting for an arrest and prosecution in criminal court. While a problem might arise regarding the standing of a civil plaintiff, the experiences of *Baker v. Wade* gave Garza hope that state courts would follow the lead of their federal counterparts. Even though the Fifth Circuit Court of Appeals ultimately ruled against Baker, the court never questioned his right to file his lawsuit and be recognized as a plaintiff. For a new case filed in a state court, however, it would be imperative that a plaintiff demonstrate that the homosexual conduct law inflicted actual harm on queer Texans.[12]

In March 1989, Christopher Wilson, a student at Texas Tech University School of Law in Lubbock, submitted a research paper to the THRF board that he had written for a moot court competition earlier in the year. Wilson was much more pessimistic than Garza about the potential success of a new challenge to the homosexual conduct law. Wilson argued that the most direct way to eliminate 21.06 would be to persuade a court that the law violated both federal and state constitutional guarantees of equal protection. Texas legislators, according to Wilson, had created a suspect classification when they crafted the language of the homosexual conduct law during the late 1960s and early 1970s. Because the statute intentionally targeted gay and lesbian Texans, he argued, 21.06 required judges to apply at least a heightened level of judicial scrutiny. "The equal protection clause does not deny the governmental need to classify individuals and draw distinctions," Wilson wrote, "but it does require that the classifications not be used to arbitrarily burden a class nor does it permit the government to use impermissible criteria in the formulation of a class." In *Bowers v. Hardwick*, as Wilson pointed out, the Supreme Court did not consider whether Georgia's sodomy law created a suspect classification and thus violated the equal protection clause of the Fourteenth Amendment. If a court were to find that the classification of gays and lesbians separately from other citizens was indeed suspect, it would trigger a more robust examination of the intent of 21.06. And unlike the implied right to privacy, the right to equal protection was explicitly stated in both the federal and Texas state constitutions. Wilson also asserted that 21.06, allegedly concerned with conduct, actually operated as a status law. "Homosexuals are defined by the conduct prohibited," Wilson wrote. "The statute has two requirements, a requirement of homosexual status and a conduct requirement," but the law prohibited specific conduct only if the first requirement of homosexual status were met. Although Wilson remained skeptical of the efficacy of convincing a state court to apply heightened scrutiny to 21.06, he believed it was the only possible way, however slim, of eradicating the discriminatory law.[13]

Diverse Plaintiffs

Garza and Wilson convinced the THRF executive committee to initiate a new round of litigation against 21.06, and they hired Austin attorney J. Patrick Wiseman to serve as lead attorney. Wiseman and the THRF board incorporated Garza's and Wilson's perspectives into their state-level litigation strategy, hired Wilson as a summer clerk to assist in the case, and began their search for an acceptable plaintiff. While all agreed that Don Baker had been an excellent plaintiff in *Baker v. Wade*, most wanted a new plaintiff to be more representative of the diversity of the queer community of Texas. In March 1989, board members decided that the most effective way to achieve this diversity was to recruit multiple plaintiffs. That month, Wiseman and the THRF board enlisted Linda Morales, a lesbian woman from Houston, and Tom Doyal, a gay man from Austin. Originally from a small farming community near San Antonio, Morales had been the first Mexican American student body president at her high school. She graduated from the University of Texas at Austin in 1979, where she was active in the campus Chicano movement, and since then she had worked in Houston in the television production industry. In 1988, Morales formed All Mujeres Interested in Getting Active (AMIGA), a Latina lesbian support group and activist community. Doyal was a self-described "fifth generation Texan," originally from Lubbock, who served with distinction in the United States Army during the late 1960s, accepting the Vietnam Service Medal and the Army Commendation Medal before receiving an honorable discharge. He earned a law degree from the University of Texas at Austin in 1975 and worked as an attorney in private practice for several years. During the early 1980s, Doyal, nearly forty years old, came out as a gay man and founded Liberty Books and Liberty Press, a gay and lesbian bookstore and publisher in Austin. For several years he had served on the THRF board, and he was the organization's current legal director.[14]

Later in the month, Wiseman and the THRF board rounded up three additional plaintiffs. Charlotte Taft, originally from Connecticut, earned an undergraduate degree in feminist studies at Brown University and a master's degree in social psychology from Goddard College before moving to Dallas in 1975. Since 1978, Taft had served as director of the Routh Street Women's Clinic in Dallas and was a well-known activist in the movement for both women's rights and the rights of gays and lesbians. She served on the boards of Dallas County's chapter of the National Organization for Women, the Dallas Civil Liberties Union, the Dallas Area Women's Caucus, and Among Friends, a lesbian educational organization. In 1984, Taft was a member of the Democratic Party's national platform committee. Originally from the Pacific Northwest and having grown up in Houston, Patricia Cramer graduated with a degree in nursing from the University of Texas at Austin in 1977 and decided to stay in the state capital. She became a founding member of the Austin Lesbian/Gay Political Caucus in 1979 and two years later became the co-chair of the Lesbian/Gay Rights Lobby of Texas. Finally, John Thomas, originally from Ohio, moved to Dallas in 1980 and for the following two decades worked for various causes related to the gay and lesbian movement for equality. He served as vice president for human resources at the *Dallas Times Herald* until 1988, when he became the executive director of the Gay and Lesbian Community Center and the AIDS Resource Center of Dallas. Wiseman and the THRF board were confident that these five plaintiffs could withstand the pressures of being in the spotlight, demonstrate how the homosexual conduct law inflicted actual harm, and represent the broad diversity of gays and lesbians across the state.[15]

Filing *Morales v. Texas*

On April 12, 1989, Wiseman filed *Morales v. Texas* in the 200th Judicial Court in downtown Austin. In some ways, the suit resembled the one Don Baker had filed a decade earlier. In the petition's factual allegations, for example, the five plaintiffs admitted that they were "practicing homosexuals, who regularly engage in private homosexual acts" with no intention of ceasing in the future. Because of this, they were forced to live with the persistent threat of criminal prosecution under 21.06. "This fear" of prosecution, the plaintiffs stated, "is real and constant." Beyond the immediate criminal and legal threat, the plaintiffs, like Baker, called attention to the social shame associated with being branded criminals because of their intimate relationships. "Section 21.06," they asserted, "encourages discrimination in employment, housing, and other areas of life." The plaintiffs also pointed out that the homosexual conduct law affected the operation of the legal system itself, almost certainly wishing to conjure memories of Judge Jack Hampton's light sentencing of Richard Bednarski for murdering John Griffin and Tommy Trimble the previous year. "Section 21.06," they argued, "even encourages discrimination within our court system, such as in the context of child custody or criminal justice. Section 21.06 encourages police harassment and alienation from law enforcement officials." All these examples, according to the petition, served as evidence of the harmful effects of the statute.[16]

In other important ways, however, this new litigation differed from *Baker v. Wade*. Rejecting a federal constitutional strategy in light of the *Bowers* decision, the petition appealed to the Texas Constitution to challenge the legitimacy of the sodomy law. Section 21.06, the plaintiffs asserted, violated the state constitution's protections of privacy and equal rights. The law "constitutes an unreasonable intrusion into the personal privacy

of Plaintiffs," their brief stated. "This intrusion is not reasonably warranted for the achievement of a compelling governmental objective that can
be achieved by no less intrusive, more reasonable means." The homosexual conduct law, therefore, failed to meet the standards set by the Texas
Supreme Court in its *TSEU* decision. The plaintiffs also argued that 21.06
violated the state's Equal Rights Amendment because it imposed an unwarranted classification based on sex. "Under this statute," the plaintiffs
argued, "a female can engage in 'deviate sexual intercourse' with a male,
but a male, because he is a male, may not. Conversely, a male can engage
in 'deviate sexual intercourse' with a female, but a female, because she is a
female, may not." This, according to the suit, represented an unconstitutional classification based on sex. Section 21.06 also "classifies on the basis
of sexual orientation," the plaintiffs asserted. "'Deviate sexual intercourse'
is illegal under the statute only if engaged in with 'another individual of the
same sex.' The statute thereby treats heterosexuals and homosexuals differently." In the absence of any compelling state interest related to these discriminatory classifications, the plaintiffs argued, the homosexual conduct
law violated these key components of the Texas Constitution.[17]

Wiseman and THRF leaders held a press conference to coincide with
the filing of their new lawsuit where all five plaintiffs had the opportunity to answer questions from reporters. THRF legal director David Bryan
began by reminding his audience that Texas was one of only five states that
continued to prohibit specific sexual acts only when performed by same-sex
couples. "Yet, ironically," Bryan pointed out, "Texas has one of the most
broadly worded Bill of Rights in its constitution, and we Texans have always prided ourselves on a willingness to protect our independence and
our individual rights. You might say that's the Texas spirit." Section 21.06
also inflicted harm on an estimated 700,000 gay and lesbian Texans who
held the status of criminals because of the statute. The homosexual conduct
law, Bryan asserted, "encourages disruption of their family relationships;
it limits their employment opportunities; it encourages discrimination
against them; it encourages hate crimes and violence against them; it subjects them to discrimination in the judicial system (from persons like Judge
Jack Hampton of Dallas, who apparently view gay and lesbian Texans as
second-class citizens); and the law subjects these otherwise contributing
members of our society to emotional stress because of the state-sanctioned
stigma attached to their lives." In a comparison that was notably absent
in *Baker v. Wade*, Bryan cited the Supreme Court's 1967 decision in *Loving v. Virginia*, which struck down state laws banning marriages between

people of different races. The state's claim that 21.06 upheld morality in Texas, according to Bryan, was "the same kind of specious reasoning used in this country until 1967 to outlaw interracial marriages."[18]

The *Morales* plaintiffs supplemented these constitutional arguments with examples of how the homosexual conduct law affected their lives. Linda Morales agreed with the invocation of *Loving v. Virginia* and argued that race, in addition to sexuality, was a significant factor in the current litigation. "Most people who make our laws are straight white males," she asserted. Nevertheless, she expressed hope that justice could be achieved. "I'm optimistic that 21.06 can be overturned and that our dreams and goals can be attained. The reward will provide equal protection under the law." Tom Doyal drew a direct connection between their lawsuit and the historic struggle for African American equality, stating that he was inspired "by the exemplary courage of Rosa Parks and the thousands of others who chose to further the cause of human dignity and justice. . . . In the same way Black Americans chose to challenge voter registration provisions and public accommodation segregation, gays and lesbians have chosen to overturn the so-called 'sodomy statute' as the necessary place to begin our struggle toward the full panoply of civil liberties enjoyed by other Texans." For Charlotte Taft, the issue boiled down to limiting the power of the state to regulate the private lives of citizens. "In the state of Texas," she stated, "nobody wants big government in their bedroom." Proclaiming that he was a registered Republican and a Baptist, John Thomas highlighted the damaging psychological effects of 21.06. "I will do whatever I can for all of the present and future Texans who are gay," he proclaimed, "to reject the sickness of hiding and lying and pretending to be heterosexual." Patricia Cramer expressed most directly what thousands of queer Texans undoubtedly thought about the law. "21.06 makes me angry," she stated. Patrick Wiseman hoped that anger would be enough to sustain a lengthy litigation process, as he predicted the case would take at least two years at the trial court level and potentially even more in appellate courts.[19]

Morales v. Texas presented a dilemma for Texas attorney general Jim Mattox. While he had declined to defend the state's sodomy law during *Baker v. Wade*, he was unsettled when the Fifth Circuit Court of Appeals in New Orleans had allowed Amarillo district attorney Danny Hill to pursue the case in his absence, and many state lawmakers had accused Mattox of shirking his responsibilities as the state's chief legal officer. Mattox intended to run for governor in 1990, turning every decision he made as attorney general into a potential campaign issue. When asked for a statement regarding the new lawsuit, Mattox spokesperson Elna Christopher avoided discussing the wisdom of the law and instead focused on the duties of the attorney general. "It would be a hard option not to defend it," she told the *Dallas Times Herald*. "That is what the attorney general is supposed to do: defend the constitutionality of state laws." The following month, the attorney general's office filed a request for dismissal in *Morales v. Texas*, opting not to defend the constitutionality of 21.06 but rather to assert that the plaintiffs were pursuing their case in the wrong venue. "Because of the dual system of courts in Texas," Mattox stated, "where our civil and criminal laws can be reconciled by no single court with final authority over both, civil courts cannot pass on the constitutionality of a criminal statute." Mattox's argument was not completely unexpected. THRF legal director David Bryan told Dennis Vercher of the *Dallas Voice* that he "anticipated that such a defense might be raised," but he nevertheless would "not deny that it presents a real stumbling block in this litigation." Yet with the legislature unwilling to respond to their pleas and little chance of an arrest that would be as ideal for a constitutional challenge, Bryan remained optimistic that a district judge would recognize a civil lawsuit as the only remaining opportunity to determine the statute's legality.[20]

In August, Wiseman filed an amended petition that attempted to address Mattox's objections. To counter the attorney general's argument that a civil court was an improper forum, the new petition called more attention to how 21.06 threatened the employment prospects and career viability of queer Texans. "Plaintiffs have had to tailor their career and employment choices to avoid discrimination and/or unbearable hostility in employment," the brief stated. This employment discrimination, the plaintiffs argued, represented evidence of measurable financial harm caused by the law. As they phrased it, the law "perpetuates irreparable harm to a vested property right of the plaintiffs." Additionally, Morales and the other plaintiffs pointed out that the mere existence of 21.06 in the criminal code "encourages hate crimes against homosexuals, tacitly condoning what is commonly known as 'queer baiting' or 'fag bashing,' whereby homosexuals are subjected to a spectrum of violence." Yet the statute could cause even more subtle damage, as the law "brands homosexuals as criminals and thus perpetuates irreparable harm to the plaintiffs' good name, reputations and integrity." Because the social stigma caused by being labeled a criminal undoubtedly affected an individual's ability to earn an income, the homosexual conduct law threatened the financial security and property rights of queer Texans.[21]

While awaiting a decision on whether they would get their day in court,

Wiseman, the five plaintiffs, and THRF board members embarked on a statewide publicity and fundraising expedition and continued to educate the public about the harmful effects of 21.06. On April 30, 1989, two weeks after the filing of the *Morales* case, nearly 30,000 people converged on the state capitol in Austin in a demonstration for queer equality. Several state legislators addressed the large crowd, some marveling that this was the most people ever assembled on capitol grounds. Austin area representative Lena Guerrero, only the second Latina elected to the legislature, proclaimed that she was "proud to be with you today. . . . Remember, none of us are free until all of us are free." Senator Craig Washington, who had advocated for legislative repeal of 21.06 since the law's enactment in 1974, continued to situate the struggle for gay and lesbian rights within the context of a much broader movement for equality. "My job is always easy because I read the Constitution," he told the crowd, "which says all people are created equal. It seems very clear to me that rights are indivisible. We are all fighting for the same rights." El Paso representative Nancy McDonald expressed her commitment to the struggle: "There are still some of us in the Texas Legislature who want to end discrimination. I'm proud to be on the front lines of this battle." During a post-march rally, Patricia Cramer had a sharp message for legislators who failed to support the eradication of 21.06. "Who I love has nothing to do with my job performance or how I care for my children," she stated. "It's no business of the state of Texas what we do in our bedrooms. If ignorance were a crime, most of our Texas legislators would be serving a life sentence." John Thomas echoed Cramer's sentiments, pointing out that criminalizing same-sex sexual contact forced gay and lesbian Texans to lie about their most important and intimate relationships. Linda Morales connected their lawsuit to the struggle for justice for people of color across the state and the nation. "It's up to us to leave a legacy for equality for all," she stated. In a show of solidarity, at the end of the rally, organizers gathered hundreds of signatures from attendees who confessed to violating the homosexual conduct law. As *This Week in Texas* (*TWT*) editors summed up the event, "Last Sunday was one of those days which everyone there will never forget—a point in time which gay historians will always harken back to when the statewide gay and lesbian community took a giant step forward."[22]

In late June, THRF board members organized a rally before the Houston Pride parade, and THRF legal director David Bryan joined plaintiffs Linda Morales and Patricia Cramer in a fundraising reception at a Houston restaurant before joining the procession. A few days later, the National Gay

Figure 5.2. Nearly 30,000 people gather in Austin for a demonstration supporting queer equality in April 1989.

and Lesbian Task Force held a "National Day of Mourning for the Right to Privacy" to mark the third anniversary of the Supreme Court decision in *Bowers v. Hardwick*, calling for local activists around the country, particularly in states with discriminatory sodomy laws still on the books, to hold demonstrations at statehouses and in other public spaces. The Central Texas Civil Liberties Union, headquartered in Austin, took the lead in organizing a protest at the state capitol in which plaintiff Tom Doyal addressed the crowd. Plaintiffs Charlotte Taft and John Thomas appeared at a similar event in Dallas. The following month, the United Church of Christ's Coalition for Lesbian and Gay Concerns held a public witness event in Fort Worth to coincide with the church's annual national conference in Fort Worth. During the event, coalition activists presented a petition to state officials denouncing 21.06 and demanding its repeal. For more than a decade, the UCC had been active in supporting the movement to end discrimination against gays and lesbians, and the denomination had passed a resolution in the aftermath of the *Bowers* decision pledging to protest local sodomy laws when they met for their annual conference in states with those statutes still in effect. Bryan and the THRF board worked with the UCC coalition to publicize the event, and plaintiff Charlotte Taft attended the public witness to inform the participants about *Morales v. Texas*. For all these events, the goals of the THRF board and the five plaintiffs included raising money to sustain their legal effort and educating the public about both the damaging effects of 21.06 and their efforts to eradicate it from the criminal code.[23]

The THRF board and the *Morales* plaintiffs also made a concerted effort to explain how 21.06 affected women and people of color. In July 1989, plaintiff Linda Morales penned an essay in *Allgo Pasa*, the newsletter of the Austin Latino/a Lesbian and Gay Organization, in which she continued to advocate for an intersectional analysis of the harmful effects of the sodomy law. "I firmly believe," she wrote, "that our Lesbian/Gay Hispanic/Latino community has a responsibility of informing the straight and non-straight communities of the oppression we face as a people of color." As a lesbian woman of color, Morales believed that her case against 21.06 had the potential not simply to educate nongay Texans about the oppression faced by gays and lesbians but also to reveal the racial discrimination people of color confronted even within the gay and lesbian community and to provoke a bit of self-examination. "While the process may be unpleasant," she concluded, "the reaper[s] of the rewards will be the Tejano Lesbians and Gays." A few months later, plaintiff Charlotte Taft wrote an essay for the Austin-based publication *The Women's Alternative Times* in which she explained how the homosexual conduct law specifically affected women. In the essay titled "21.06—The So-Called 'Sodomy' Law Is Not Just for Those with A Penis!," Taft detailed the precise language of the law, pointing out how it prohibited any oral or anal sexual contact between members of the same sex. "One of the wonderful things about Texas," she proclaimed, "is that it's not subtle. In Texas it is not illegal to have sex with an animal in private, but it is illegal to have sex with an adult of the same gender," a reference to the state legislature's 1973 easing of laws regulating private bestiality while strengthening its prohibition against same-sex sexual activity. Beyond the proscribed sexual behavior, 21.06 justified discrimination against not only gay men but also lesbian women, and Taft made sure her readers understood this point. "The fact is that section 21.06 of the Penal Code provides an excuse for any business, organization, agency, or individual to discriminate against gay men and lesbians in whatever ways they choose." The homosexual conduct law also caused many gays and lesbians to internalize the message that they were criminals unworthy of legal protections. "Almost all of us have, at one time or another, felt afraid and ashamed of who we are," she wrote. "For some of us the shame and fear are ongoing and can be relentless. Laws like 21.06 . . . certainly reinforce both our own internalized self-hatred, and the hatred and fear of others toward us." Taft urged her readers, especially lesbian women, to support the *Morales* plaintiffs because 21.06 affected their lives in significant ways.[24]

Mica England and the Dallas Police Department

While THRF board members and *Morales* plaintiffs traversed the state educating the public about the discriminatory effects of 21.06, an incident involving the Dallas Police Department (DPD) demonstrated how the homosexual conduct law threatened the financial prospects of queer Texans. Mica England, a twenty-five-year-old executive assistant chef in Tulsa, Oklahoma, had long dreamed of becoming a police officer. In March 1989, DPD officials held a recruiting event in Tulsa, which England attended. In response to a question on an initial screening application that asked, "Have you ever committed a deviant sexual act?," England wrote, "I'm gay." England also reiterated that she was a lesbian during a preliminary interview. Officers assured England that the department was so desperate for new officers that hiring officials would not disqualify her simply because she was a lesbian, even if she admitted it on the required polygraph examination. Still a bit skeptical about this assurance, England nonetheless had a burning desire to become a police officer and decided to take a leap of faith. In early July, she used up all her vacation days at her restaurant job and traveled to Dallas for a second round of interviews. This time, however, the same DPD recruiter who had told her in Tulsa that her sexual orientation would not be an impediment informed England that she was automatically disqualified because of her past sexual conduct. To add insult to injury, England later reported that officers attempted to humiliate her during the interview. One officer asked England for the date of her last sexual encounter with a woman and even inquired about the specific sexual acts in which they engaged, seemingly unable to imagine how two women might complete the physical act of sexual intercourse. Another officer told her that she was "too pretty to be a lesbian," a comment England did not interpret as a compliment. "I have never been treated as rudely as they treated me," she said. In the DPD's human resources office, England's dream of becoming a police officer met the reality of the ways the homosexual conduct law justified discrimination against queer Texans.[25]

England's experience was not the first time the police department refused to hire an applicant because of sexual orientation. In addition to innumerable unreported incidences, DPD officials had refused to hire Steve Childers for a position in its evidence storage room in 1974, claiming that as an openly gay man, Childers was a habitual violator of 21.06 and even suggested that he could not be trusted to handle sensitive materials like child pornography. A federal judge agreed in 1981 and ruled that the police department was justified in its refusal to hire Childers. In 1982, after a temporary invalidation of 21.06 in *Baker v. Wade*, plaintiff Don Baker and many of his fellow activists believed that DPD's discriminatory hiring policies should be their next target. The difficulty lay in either finding a current gay or lesbian officer willing to come out and face termination or a member of the gay and lesbian community qualified to become an officer and prepared to submit to the scrutiny of the hiring process. The Fifth Circuit Court of Appeals in New Orleans further complicated the matter when judges reinstated the homosexual conduct law in 1985, thereby reviving the justification for DPD's discriminatory policy. DPD officials had also stonewalled activists by refusing to allow them access to written hiring policies. By the time DPD officials rejected Mica England's application in 1989, activists had filed several federal Freedom of Information Act (FOIA) requests to view the records.[26]

England's response to how DPD officials had treated her generated a new opportunity for local activists to contest the department's discriminatory policies. Furious that DPD recruiters had misled her in Tulsa and upset that they had tried to humiliate her in Dallas, England was determined not to let go of her dream without a fight. Although she did not consider herself an activist, she was aware of the existence of the Dallas Gay Alliance (DGA) and, after searching the local telephone book for the organization's contact number, called to solicit advice on how to proceed. The following day, DGA president William Waybourn accompanied England to the police station to demand an explanation for her disqualification. The department's repeated refrain was that they could not hire a person if he or she admitted to engaging in "deviant sexual conduct" in violation of state law. Undeterred, England showed up at a Dallas City Council meeting the following day. In the lobby of the council chambers she saw a poster on the wall titled "Equal Employment Opportunity Is the Law," and she carried it into the council meeting and waited for her turn to speak. The official topic of discussion was human rights in China, but as England approached the podium, she tearfully recounted how her own human rights had been violated right there in Dallas. Holding up the equal employment poster, she expressed her disbelief that the city's police department had such a tremendous need for new officers yet would turn away qualified applicants because of their private relationships. "I took for granted that in a sophisticated city as large as Dallas that I wouldn't run into this situation," she said. "It came as a total shock." Several council members shared England's surprise, as they were apparently unaware that the police department had a policy against hiring gay and lesbian officers. Council members promised to investigate the matter immediately.[27]

England's encounter with DPD, already covered extensively by the Dallas press, became a national news story the following week. On July 22, she appeared on CNN's *Larry King Live* to discuss her ordeal. King began by asking England why she admitted to being a lesbian in the first place. England responded that "on something like a police test, you just don't lie, and I figured that the department was very professional and would handle it as a professional matter." Much to her surprise, professionalism was hard

Figure 5.3. Mica England holds up an "Equal Employment Opportunity" poster during her remarks to the Dallas City Council in 1989 after being denied a position with the Dallas Police Department because of her sexual orientation.

to come by. Inexplicably, King also invited California Republican congressman Bob Dornan on the show to defend DPD's discriminatory hiring policy, and his sentiments were indicative of the type of opposition England would face over the next few years as she made her complaint public. "Suppose, as a father of five or a grandfather of seven," Dornan stated, "we have a child molestation case, and the police department sends over a male homosexual officer." In the congressman's mind, this gay officer could not be trusted to enforce laws against the sexual assault of children because, as he saw it, most gay men were child molesters themselves. Dornan then turned his attacks toward England, and it was this exchange that showed just how skillfully England could counter harmful stereotypes about gays and lesbians. "I have never met a lesbian, never heard of a prostitute and/or a lesbian in my life, who ever had a true loving father and relationships with males in her family that was [*sic*] normal. There's always some aberration." England responded that she got along perfectly well with her father, particularly on their frequent hunting and fishing trips together. "I don't have a problem with men," she assured the congressman. "I believe that you are very naive when you talk about homosexuals," she continued, highlighting his ignorance. "You need to read up on it." The *Larry King Live* broadcast turned out to be a crash course for England as she honed her skills of public speaking and her ability to weather attacks from opponents. These lessons proved valuable as she forged ahead with a direct challenge not only to DPD's hiring policies but to the constitutionality of the homosexual conduct law itself.[28]

The publicity England generated forced DPD officials to release their official hiring policies, a goal DGA activists had been trying to achieve for some time. "The policy of our department," DPD chief Mack Vines told the *Dallas Morning News* in July, "is we follow the guidelines of the state statutes as they relate to deviant sexual behavior." Captain John Ferguson, supervisor of the DPD personnel office, spelled out the specifics of the policy even more clearly. "Homosexual conduct is against the law," he told the *Dallas Times Herald*. "If somebody admits they engage in homosexual conduct, we're not going to hire them. That's a cut factor. We cannot hire somebody that's violating state law continually." One week later, DPD officials released a copy of their written hiring policy regarding sexual conduct. According to the document, applicants must not admit to "sexual contact with a member of the same sex since age 15" or with "an animal or fowl since age 17." Activists noted that the policy was even more discriminatory than the state law. Section 21.06 criminalized oral and anal sexual contact between members of the same sex, but the statute did not prohibit all sexual contact between same-sex partners. DPD's policy went further to disqualify any applicant who engaged in any sexual contact with a same-sex partner. More appalling, the policy stipulated that if an applicant engaged in sexual contact with a member of the same sex between the ages of fifteen and seventeen, the applicant would be disqualified. If, however, the applicant engaged in sexual contact with an animal between the ages of fifteen and seventeen, but ceased after the age of seventeen, that applicant was acceptable. The conflation of same-sex sexual intimacy between two people with bestiality represented another attempt to humiliate and disparage gays and lesbians, as DPD officers had done to Mica England during her interview. Yet by forcing the police department to release its official policy, England and DGA activists successfully drew attention to the discriminatory nature of DPD personnel decisions.[29]

On July 26, DPD officials issued a final rejection of England's application. In a letter to England, Chief Vines claimed that his hiring officials "were following Departmental guidelines regarding disqualification factors," and he offered to reimburse England for travel and lodging expenses associated with her trip to Dallas. "We apologize for any inconvenience this may have caused you in traveling to Dallas," he concluded. "Again we thank you for your interest and wish you every success in your future endeavors." In late August, Vines again tried to quell the conflict by holding a public event to meet directly with members of the city's gay and lesbian community. In response to a question about long response times when residents called for assistance, Vines lamented that his police force was down about 150 officers from the previous year. DGA president William Waybourn viewed this as an opportune time to ask the chief why, when he had such a desperate need for additional officers, he was refusing to hire qualified gay and lesbian applicants such as Mica England. Once again, the police chief relied on the homosexual conduct law to justify the department's policy. "We don't hire those who break the law," he shot back at Waybourn. "You can't continue to violate the law and be an officer." When Waybourn pressed Vines to explain why a largely unenforced law was such a hindrance to hiring gay and lesbian officers, the police chief refused to say anything more on the matter without his attorney present. At that point, Waybourn and several DGA members walked out of the meeting, determined now more than ever to expose the injustice of DPD's discriminatory hiring policies.[30]

With help from the DGA, England relocated to Dallas and began preparing to take legal action against the police department. Initially, England

Figure 5.4. William Waybourn, president of the Dallas Gay Alliance during the late 1980s, was instrumental in fighting discrimination at the Dallas Police Department.

and her attorney, M. William Nelson, wanted to join with the plaintiffs in *Morales v. Texas.* THRF legal director David Bryan supported this idea because adding England to the list of plaintiffs would help resolve the question of standing that was sure to arise in the *Morales* case. Any challenge to a criminal statute in a Texas civil court without an arrest or a prosecution required that the plaintiff demonstrate how the law in question threatened a vested property interest. In its refusal to consider Mica England's

Figure 5.5. Dallas Gay Alliance members (*from left*) Don Hervey, Daniel Sopko, John Thomas, and B. J. Anderson apply to become Dallas police officers after Mica England was denied a position because of her sexual orientation. John Thomas was also one of the plaintiffs in *Morales v. Texas*.

application to become a police officer because the homosexual conduct law criminalized her intimate relationships, DPD hiring officials provided a lucrative opportunity to show how 21.06 could jeopardize a person's ability to earn an income. By November, however, these plans changed as national gay and lesbian rights organizations took a keen interest in England's case. Attorneys with the Lambda Legal Defense and Education Fund in New York advised England to file her own case against the police department and the city of Dallas. Joining the *Morales* plaintiffs, Lambda attorneys told her, would weaken her case. "These are two separate cases involving two different legal problems," Lambda attorney Evan Wolfson told the *Dallas Voice*. Because England had experienced overt discrimination and economic injury based on 21.06, Wolfson believed she had the best chance of success in Texas courts if she pursued her case on her own.[31]

In May 1990, England filed her suit, now called *England v. City of Dallas, Mack Vines, and the State of Texas*, in Texas's 200th Judicial District Court in Austin, the same district in which the *Morales* case had been filed the previous year. *England*, like *Morales*, relied on the state constitution to challenge the validity of 21.06. The homosexual conduct law, according to England's suit, "constitutes an unreasonable intrusion into the personal privacy of the plaintiff" and "violates the state constitutional guarantee of equality of rights." England and her attorneys also granted interviews to the local press, seeking to explain in straightforward terms the stakes of the case. "This hiring process treats gays differently just because they are gay," Wolfson told the *Dallas Voice*. "That suggests a bias against gays, and that is unconstitutional." While eager to push back against these discriminatory policies, England admitted that being a public figure and an activist was something new in her life. "I always mind my own business, and this has been hard on me," she said. Yet her sense of justice compelled her to take on this more active and public role. "Just because I'm gay, I'm not inadequate," she stated, highlighting the unfairness of the police department's treatment of her. "It is ignorant for people to think my sexuality will impair me as a police officer. I went to school to study criminal justice, and I'm determined to get a position with the Dallas police." By the summer of 1990, for the first time in history, two legal challenges to the homosexual conduct law were pending in the state court system.[32]

Morales Testimony

As Mica England and her legal team continued to develop their own strategy, *Morales v. Texas* attorney J. Patrick Wiseman began collecting testimony from a handful of expert witnesses regarding the harmful effects of 21.06. Judd Marmor, a professor of psychiatry at the University of Southern California Medical School who had testified in *Baker v. Wade*, recounted the history of the American Psychiatric Association's December 1973 decision to remove homosexuality from its list of diagnosable mental disorders. Since that decision, Marmor testified, a majority of the scientific community had come to view homosexuality as a normal variant of the human sexual response and a phenomenon that existed across cultures and nationalities. Continuing to view gay and lesbian individuals as mentally ill, as many proponents of laws like 21.06 often did, inflicted tremendous harm. "Labeling of all homosexuals as ipso facto mentally disordered has lent authoritative weight to the basis on which homosexuals are often subjected to discrimination in employment, discharged from military service without honor, deprived of various legal rights, and sometimes even confined involuntarily in mental institutions," he concluded. Based on his work as a research psychiatrist, Marmor also attempted to counter the myth that gay men were promiscuous sex maniacs. "Most sexual contact between homosexuals takes place in the privacy of their homes," he wrote. "Only a small minority engages in sex in public places." Despite the popular notion that most gay men had hundreds and perhaps thousands of sexual partners, Marmor insisted that many also entered into committed and stable relationships. "Despite the relative ease with which homosexual contacts can be made, not all homosexuals pursue patterns of promiscuity, and perhaps not even most." Like all relationships, the maturity of the partners often determined longevity. "Some homosexual relationships between stable persons go on for many years or even for a lifetime." Another untruth Marmor wanted to shatter was the pernicious image of the gay man as a child predator. "The popular assumption that homosexuals constitute a threat to young children is an unwarranted myth; in fact, the seeking out of children as sexual objects is much less common among homosexuals than among heterosexuals." Laws like 21.06, Marmor argued, often depended on these fallacies to justify their existence in state criminal codes.[33]

University of Houston sociologist William Simon, a veteran researcher who had spent several years at Alfred Kinsey's Institute for Sex Research in Indiana, echoed Marmor's main points. Citing a longitudinal study of gay men and lesbians funded by the National Institutes of Health, Simon insisted that the data he helped collect "amply demonstrates that relatively few homosexual men and women conform to the hideous stereotype most people have of them." Rather than the social misfits and pathological criminals society branded them to be, Simon's research revealed that most gay and lesbian individuals were well-adjusted members of society. If they suffered from any type of mental illness, it was usually caused by the social stigma placed on them because of their sexual orientation, and sodomy laws helped justify and reinforce that stigma. "The continued criminalization of same-gender sexual contacts serves not to only reinforce error-laden stereotypes, but to create conditions that encourage the commission of serious crimes," he concluded. "Criminalizing and, thereby stigmatizing, a substantial portion of the population, creates conditions that foster victimization of these citizens by robbery, assault, and extortion. At a bare minimum, this alienates them from a sense of the fairness of our justice system." Combined with Marmor's testimony, Simon's affidavit showed that in addition to employment discrimination, the homosexual conduct law also encouraged criminal action and even violence against queer individuals.[34]

Two additional expert witnesses provided testimony that focused specifically on how 21.06 hampered efforts to combat the AIDS crisis in Texas. Gregory Herek, a research psychologist at the University of California at Davis, asserted that the homosexual conduct law threatened public health in the state. "The Texas law," Herek testified, "disserves the public health by restricting the effectiveness of educational programs and scientific research designed to reduce the spread of AIDS." According to Herek, the criminalization of same-sex sexual conduct dissuaded many gay and lesbian individuals from informing health care professionals of their sexual orientation, which limited the collection of accurate data in the fight against AIDS. The homosexual conduct law, Herek pointed out, also rendered much of the AIDS education literature illegal. To promote safer sex practices, these materials needed to discuss prohibited activity, such as wearing condoms during oral and anal sex. Section 21.06 made it difficult to convey this necessary information. Ron J. Anderson, president and CEO of Parkland Hospital in Dallas and former chair of the Texas Board of Health, agreed with Herek. Many gay and lesbian individuals were reluctant to submit to testing because they feared criminal prosecution or discrimination. "In this way," he stated, "the sodomy law harms the public health effort to combat AIDS by driving the disease underground where it is more difficult to study and contain. . . . We have seen persons with AIDS lose jobs (hence insurance), apartments, social relationships, etc. when known to be HIV carriers." Anderson acknowledged that many Texans, himself included, had strong reservations about supporting full gay and lesbian equality. Nevertheless, the severity of the AIDS crisis, Anderson argued, demanded that many of those reservations be set aside in order to save lives. "As a Baptist," he testified, "I have a personal belief system that precludes a homosexual lifestyle, but that is between me and God. I believe issues of human sexuality are private matters not for the State, but for consenting individuals to determine. . . . The sodomy statute works against public health funding for HIV education, prevention, and treatment efforts," and therefore should be struck down.[35]

The plaintiffs' testimony in *Morales v. Texas* demonstrated the harmful effects of 21.06. Linda Morales began by asserting that her sexual orientation, just like her ethnicity, was immutable. "I was born a lesbian," she stated. "Just as being Hispanic cannot be changed, my sexual orientation cannot be changed." She recounted how she had known since she was very young that she was romantically attracted to women but had lived in fear of being discovered by her devout Catholic family members. Once she got older, that fear evolved into worries about losing jobs, being ostracized by friends, and confronting violence. At the center of her fear, she stated, was the homosexual conduct law. "When I discovered that my desire for women was considered illegal in Texas," she testified, "I was shocked and hurt. I began to understand that hatred and discrimination toward lesbians and gay men was deeply affirmed and rooted in our legal system." Morales recounted a series of long-term and meaningful romantic relationships with women during her life, but she lamented not being able to share those relationships with certain friends and family members because of her fear of rejection. "To know that intimate conduct taking place in my home is considered criminal hurts me to my core," she testified. Morales maintained that 21.06 justified discrimination in "employment, family issues, housing, criminal justice and other legal issues," as well as encouraged "police harassment against lesbians and gay men." This discrimination was completely unacceptable, according to Morales, because her sexual orientation had nothing to do with her ability to make positive contributions to society. "My work in the health education television medium, my political involvement, and my personal relationships show that I am a good citizen. . . . I pray that this statute will be overturned for the sake of generations and generations of lesbians and gay men." Like Morales, Charlotte Taft had experienced alienation from her family because of her sexual orientation, and she testified that the homosexual conduct law contributed to her fear of revealing herself to anyone. Taft also related a personal experience that illustrated how the discrimination justified by 21.06 affected her life. Through her work with the National Organization for Women (NOW) during the 1970s, Taft had assisted with the legal defense of Mary Jo Risher, a Dallas woman who had lost custody of her children because she was a lesbian. As Taft became a recognizable public figure in Risher's case, many of her opponents threatened to expose her sexual orientation to the public. Because of this, Taft declined several offers to serve on various organizational boards for fear that her being outed could harm those groups. "Section 21.06 proved to be a vehicle for those people opposing such appointments," Taft testified. "They would argue that the appointees could not be trusted to uphold the law if they had violated 21.06." Patricia Cramer also testified to the harmful effects of the homosexual conduct law, stating that she was often afraid to tell anyone about her political activities because they were so closely tied to the movement for gay and lesbian equality.[36]

In October 1990, the attorney general's office responded to the arguments presented in *Morales v. Texas*. Taking a more aggressive tone than

Mattox had used in his initial reaction the previous year, the state's response relied on the testimony of Paul Cameron, a psychologist and chairman of the Family Research Institute who had recently been expelled from the American Psychological Association for ethical violations. Cameron had made a name for himself in the early 1980s by arguing that gay and lesbian individuals exhibited higher incidences of pathological mental illness with violent tendencies and that people with AIDS should be quarantined. In his testimony, Cameron depicted same-sex sexual activity as pathological and took specific aim at the suggestion that gay and lesbian individuals could make positive contributions to society. Contrary to both Simon's and Herek's assertions that for many couples anal sex constituted an important component of their intimate relationships, Cameron continued to insist that this type of sexual behavior was an aberration. "Ejaculate in the rectum," he testified, "appears to be the primary mechanism of sexual spread of the AIDS virus as well as other viruses and germs in the West." Despite Herek's reliance on several social scientific studies showing gay and lesbian individuals were no more inclined to be lawbreakers than anyone else, Cameron cited his own single study to argue the opposite. Gay and lesbian individuals, he testified, had a weakened sense of "social functioning and morality" because of their sexual orientation. Cameron also attacked Marmor's testimony on this issue, citing his own single study to argue that gay and lesbian individuals were more promiscuous, engaged in public sex at higher rates, and were more likely to be child molesters than the rest of the population. Cameron also compared the effectiveness of 21.06 in reducing same-sex sexual contact to the efficacy of laws against child molestation. "From society's standpoint, if a child molester no longer molests, even if he still secretly wants to, the problem is 'solved.' Similarly, . . . if making [homosexual] conduct illegal reduces the numbers of individuals committing such acts or dampens the numbers of acts committed by individuals attracted to such behavior, then the legislation has accomplished its reasonable ends, even if many who might otherwise participate, and who want to participate, fail to do so." While Cameron admitted that Herek's arguments about the AIDS crisis were "mainly true," he insisted that safer sex education would be ineffective in reducing the spread of the virus, stating erroneously that HIV could pass through the barrier of a condom. Cameron also took issue with Anderson's claim that public health officials should refrain from passing judgment on private sexual behavior. According to Cameron, engaging in same-sex sexual behavior was comparable to smoking tobacco or crack cocaine, which carried a set of equally dangerous health risks. Cameron agreed with those who claimed that 21.06 stigmatized an entire group of Texans, but he failed to see this as a problem. "That is part of the function of law," Cameron testified, "to set and codify moral standards." The most apt comparison on this issue, according to Cameron, was to drug abuse. "Were the plaintiffs arguing that they were drug users," he testified, "and that the Texas laws against drug possession disrupts their family relationships, their point would be as valid or invalid." Cameron also dismissed the plaintiffs' complaint that 21.06 hindered their job prospects. "If Plaintiffs wish to be able to advertise that they engage in socially disapproved and illegal activities and not harm their employment chances, they are asking for the impossible," he stated. Similarly, Cameron did not think it such a negative consequence that 21.06 encouraged hate crimes against gay and lesbian Texans. "Homosexual activity is despised by many people in the US and is accepted by only a minority," he testified. "As such, whatever effect 21.06 has, it would no more encourage crimes against those practicing homosexual acts than Texas laws against drug abuse encourage crimes against drug users."[37]

According to the attorney general, Cameron's data successfully controverted all the expert witness testimony the plaintiffs put forward in the *Morales* case. If 21.06 did not actually harm citizens of the state, or if the harm done to gays and lesbians was justified by the need to legislate morality, Mattox argued, the state's sodomy law must be upheld. According to the attorney general, the stigma about which the plaintiffs complained stemmed from the widespread social condemnation of same-sex sexual contact and not from the homosexual conduct law. On the issue of privacy, the attorney general argued that the plaintiffs had failed to demonstrate any ways in which the state constitution protected the right to engage in the sexual conduct prohibited by the law. For the constitutional right of privacy to extend to same-sex sexual contact, according to Mattox, the plaintiffs needed to establish that this type of sexual conduct represented a fundamental right. According to the state's brief, the plaintiffs had failed to accomplish this goal. On the question of equal protection, the state argued that because 21.06 applied to both men and women, the law did not violate the spirit of equal rights found in the state constitution. As the Fifth Circuit Court of Appeals had found in *Baker v. Wade*, the attorney general argued that gays and lesbians did not constitute a suspect or even a quasi-suspect class. The homosexual conduct law, therefore, should not be subject to any more scrutiny than the rational basis test when determining its constitutionality. According to the attorney general, 21.06 was rationally related to public morality, again echoing the appellate court's decision in *Baker*. The sodomy law, therefore, did not violate anyone's state constitutional rights to privacy, equal protection, or due process. For these reasons, the state of Texas urged the court to dismiss the case. After reviewing all the motions and briefs filed on both sides, 200th District judge Paul Davis decided he wanted to hear oral arguments in *Morales v. Texas*.[38]

On December 10, 1990, with four of the plaintiffs present in the Austin courtroom, Wiseman began by quoting Thomas Paine. "In this country, and under our State Constitution, 'political liberties consist in the power of doing what does not injure another,'" he stated. Section 21.06, according to Wiseman, prohibited conduct that hurt no one but caused significant harm to gay and lesbian Texans, violating their state constitutional rights of privacy, equal protection, and due process. Wiseman reiterated that 21.06 labeled them criminals, damaged their family relationships, provoked crimes against them, hampered AIDS education, and justified discrimination in employment and housing. Wiseman reminded Judge Davis that a civil court had jurisdiction to decide the constitutionality of a criminal statute if a property right were at stake. Texas assistant attorney general Harry G. Potter defended 21.06 for the state, disputing the argument that the *Morales* plaintiffs had adequately demonstrated a vested property interest that the law threatened. Potter allowed that the state's sodomy law might cause harm to gay and lesbian Texans, but he maintained that the harm failed to meet the proper threshold for a constitutional challenge in civil court. Even if the plaintiffs were in the proper court, according to Potter, the statute had already withstood a constitutional challenge in *Baker v. Wade*, and the US Supreme Court had refused to recognize a constitutional right to engage in same-sex sexual activity in *Bowers v. Hardwick*. Despite the fact that these earlier cases were based on the federal constitution, according to Potter, the Texas district court should abide by these judicial precedents.[39]

Another Victory

After a five-minute recess in which he met privately with both Wiseman and Potter, Judge Davis issued a verbal ruling from the bench on the constitutionality of 21.06. First, he ruled against the state attorney general's motion to dismiss the case for lack of standing, ruling instead that the plaintiffs had the ability to challenge the constitutionality of a criminal statute in a civil court. Recognizing the validity of the constitutional challenge, Davis promptly struck down 21.06 for violating the plaintiffs' rights of privacy and equal protection. Austin-based freelance writer Thom Prentiss, reporting on the trial for the *Montrose Voice*, wrote that Davis's bench ruling came as a surprise to spectators in the courtroom. When the judge proclaimed his decision, Prentiss remembered, "the attorneys and plaintiffs, and the people sitting in the courtroom's high-backed pew-like seats, were momentarily stunned." Not wanting to disturb the decorum of the courtroom, spectators "were straining to restrain joyous outbursts" as they quietly celebrated this great victory. "The system works," Prentiss remembers someone quietly exclaiming, "it really works!" After Davis dismissed the courtroom and retired to his chambers, "a thunderclap of applause erupted from the courtroom as supporters rushed to embrace the plaintiffs." For the first time, a state district judge had struck down 21.06 based on protections found in the Texas Constitution.[40]

Davis followed up his verbal ruling with a twenty-eight-page written opinion, released on January 2, 1991, that endorsed the analysis of 21.06 offered by Wiseman, the plaintiffs, and their expert witnesses. The Texas Constitution, according to Davis, provided even stronger individual privacy protections than the federal constitution, and the Texas Supreme Court's *TSEU* opinion further clarified the standard of review for any law that trampled upon this fundamental right. "The Texas Constitution," he wrote, "embodies a promise that a certain private sphere of individual liberty will be kept largely beyond the reach of government," especially when a private activity occurred inside the home. Citing *Buchanan v. Batchelor*, Judge Davis reasoned that if a bathroom stall in a department store could be considered private, surely a person's home afforded at least an equal amount of protection. It followed that if the state of Texas were going to enforce a law that intrudes into the privacy of a citizen's home, the state would be required to demonstrate that the statute was "reasonably warranted for the achievement of a compelling governmental objective that can be achieved by no less intrusive, more reasonable means," as the *TSEU* opinion phrased it. Judge Davis concluded that the state's efforts to justify 21.06 based on the promotion of public health or morality had failed. "The State of Texas," Davis asserted, "does not have the right, duty, or burden of deciding who plaintiffs, (or any other citizen of the State), will or should engage in intercourse with, sexual or otherwise." Davis also found that the homosexual conduct law violated state constitutional guarantees of equal rights and equal protection because the law discriminated on the basis of sexual orientation and sex. According to the language of the statute, oral and anal sex were only prohibited if engaged in by same-sex partners. Based on his reading of the state constitution and his interpretation of case law, sexual orientation, like race, represented a suspect classification and therefore triggered a heightened level of judicial scrutiny. At a minimum, according to Davis, the state must demonstrate a compelling objective that was furthered by treating gay and nongay citizens differently. Yet the attorney general's office had failed to do this. Neither had the state demonstrated a compelling objective advanced by classifying on the basis of sex. Because he found 21.06 to be unconstitutional, Judge Davis issued a permanent injunction prohibiting all law enforcement officials in the state from enforcing the statute.[41]

Wiseman, THRF activists, the *Morales* plaintiffs, and thousands of queer Texans celebrated another significant victory on the path to eradicating 21.06. Plaintiff Patricia Cramer told the *Montrose Voice* that she was "astounded" by the ruling. "It means I can be me," she said. Plaintiff and newly appointed DGA executive director John Thomas echoed Cramer's sentiments, rejoicing that the state was now rid of such a "dehumanizing" law. Plaintiff Tom Doyal was equally elated, feeling successful in his effort "to demand, at least in this small corner of the universe, for things to be more just." Wiseman told the *Dallas Morning News* that Davis's ruling was a victory not just for gay and lesbian Texans but for everyone in the state who did not want the government interfering in their private affairs. "I think it's the best ruling for everybody in the state of Texas," he said. "It vindicates everyone's right to privacy." DGA president Bruce Monroe agreed that the ruling was good for all Texans, stating, "We're quite pleased that the judge sees fit to keep government out of people's bedrooms." Closely monitoring the *Morales* case from his new home in Connecticut, Don Baker was also pleased with Judge Davis's decision. "We as a community have been vindicated," he proclaimed. Though perhaps the celebrations following Judge Davis's decision in *Morales v. Texas* did not match the intensity or elation of the "Gayteenth" celebrations in the wake of Judge Buchmeyer's decree in *Baker v. Wade*, most observers nonetheless recognized that the *Morales* ruling was an equally significant milestone on the road to queer equality.[42]

Another State Appeal

By the time Davis issued his opinion in *Morales v. Texas*, the state had sworn in a new attorney general who happened to share a last name with the lead plaintiff in the case. A graduate of Trinity University in San Antonio and

Harvard Law School, Dan Morales worked as a corporate attorney in Houston before serving three terms in the state legislature. In 1990, voters elected the San Antonio Democrat the first Mexican American attorney general in the state's history. Morales attempted to walk a fine line between Mattox's perceived liberalism and the state's rising social conservatism. During a campaign debate in July, he assured voters that he would defend any state law that might be challenged. When Judge Davis issued his verbal ruling in December, Morales remained noncommittal, telling the *Dallas Morning News* that he "would need to wait until I have an opportunity to assume office and review the documentation." After his inauguration in January 1991, he sought a variety of opinions on the constitutionality of 21.06 and the advisability of a state appeal in the *Morales* case, including reaching out to the *Morales* plaintiffs and representatives from the THRF, the DGA, the Houston Gay/Lesbian Political Caucus, and the Lesbian/Gay Rights Lobby.[43]

In March, several members of the THRF board met with Dan Morales and made a request that perhaps surprised the new attorney general. They encouraged him to appeal Davis's decision. This was a different strategy than the one THRF activists employed in *Baker v. Wade*. Since *Baker* was a federal case, Judge Buchmeyer's ruling striking down 21.06 applied to the entire state of Texas. Davis's ruling in *Morales v. Texas*, however, was more limited, and Wiseman remained unsure if other state district courts would agree with Davis's reasoning. Another district or trial court could issue a conflicting ruling, placing Davis's opinion in jeopardy until the matter could be settled by a higher court. For these reasons, Wiseman and THRF board members concluded that an appeal by the attorney general was worth the risk of a potentially adverse ruling if it gave them the opportunity to persuade an appellate court to extend the reach of Davis's opinion. For the new attorney general, this must have been quite a relief, since an appeal would not offend a growing number of gay and lesbian supporters while also allowing him to deliver on his campaign promise to defend all state laws. Republicans in the legislature had already proposed a bill that if passed would have required an appeal, and Morales would have rather avoided a showdown with the legislature this early in his tenure. In response, he promised THRF board members that he would confine the state's arguments to the pertinent legal issues and would not resort to attacking queer Texans. His motivation, he told them, would be to seek clarification of Davis's ruling and not necessarily to defend the wisdom or usefulness of 21.06. THRF board members left the meeting satisfied with the outcome. "[The appeal] won't be all the things the right-wingers would like for it to be," THRF executive director Margaret Tucker stated after the meeting. Compared to Jim Mattox's unpredictability, it must have been reassuring to THRF activists that the new attorney general seemed unwilling to defend the homosexual conduct law if it meant engaging in personal attacks against queer Texans.[44]

In April 1991, Dan Morales filed his appeal in the Third Court of Appeals in Austin, proclaiming that his office had an "obligation to defend the laws of the state when they are challenged." Keeping his promise to the THRF board, he clarified what the tone of his appeal would be. "Our goal," he assured observers, "is [to] seek a determination once and for all on the constitutionality of this particular law." In his brief, the attorney general argued that Judge Davis had erred in allowing the *Morales* plaintiffs to pursue their case in a civil court when they had failed to demonstrate how the homosexual conduct law caused harm to a vested property interest. Morales also argued that Davis erroneously found 21.06 to violate the Texas Constitution. Rather than debate the merits of the sodomy law, the attorney general focused on how to interpret the state constitution, asserting that it offered no more protections of individual rights than the federal constitution. Since the US Supreme Court ruled in *Bowers v. Hardwick* that the federal constitution contained no fundamental right to engage in oral or anal sex, Morales concluded that the Texas Constitution also failed to express such a privacy right. As for equal protection, the attorney general's brief pointed out that the homosexual conduct law applied to both males and females, thereby negating the claim that the law discriminated based on sex. Rather than wade into the weeds of public morality, an issue Morales had promised to avoid, the attorney general simply cited both *Baker v. Wade* and *Bowers v. Hardwick* to show that no court had found that sexual orientation was a suspect classification requiring a heightened level of scrutiny. As courts determined in both of those cases, state sodomy laws were rationally related to morality. For these reasons, the attorney general's office asked the appellate court to overturn Davis's decision and reinstate 21.06.[45]

Despite the attorney general's efforts to defend 21.06 without raising questions of morality or engaging in personal attacks, a group of twenty-eight state legislators managed to inject into the appeal the very language activists wanted to avoid. In January 1992, right before oral arguments were set to begin before a three-judge panel in the Third Court of Appeals, this group of twenty-two Republicans and six Democrats filed an amicus brief condemning all gays and lesbians and impugning their private relationships. Relying on a smattering of controversial data provided by individuals such as the discredited psychologist Paul Cameron and the conservative activist Judith Reisman, the legislators dredged up ugly stereotypes many observers undoubtedly believed had disappeared or at least had gone underground by the early 1990s. To begin with, these legislators wished to revive a two-decades-old debate about the mental health of gay and lesbian individuals. "Contrary to Appellees' 'experts'' allegations," they wrote, "homosexuality *is* a psychiatric psychopathological condition not innate but acquired and a disorder from mental health." The brief explained that the American Psychiatric Association only elected to remove homosexuality as a mental illness in 1973 because of "the relentless intimidation and political pressure applied to the APA by militant homosexual activists." Citing the work of the New York psychiatrist and sex researcher Charles Socarides, who well into the 1990s continued to administer conversion therapy to his gay and lesbian clients, the legislators claimed that "about 70% of the practicing psychiatrists disagree with that delisting and believe homosexuality to be a pathological condition."[46]

Not only were gay and lesbian individuals suffering from a mental illness, according to the group of legislators, but they also threatened public health. The gay and lesbian community, they stated, "represents a great reservoir of dangerous sexually transmitted diseases," which were spread by the very acts prohibited by the homosexual conduct law. "Sanctioning the initial sodomitic acts that precipitate this chain of disease transmission," they asserted, "is a valid and legitimate means of addressing these epidemic STD public health problems." In the minds of these legislators, the decriminalization of same-sex sexual conduct would produce consequences even more dire than the spread of disease. Gay and lesbian individuals, according to the brief, were also more likely to engage in harmful and illegal activities, such as group sex, sex with minors, and violent crime. The legislators were also adamant that state constitutional protections of privacy and due process were relevant only to fundamental rights and did not apply to same-sex sexual activity, just as they did not apply to a range of potentially private activity they found comparable. "If this court were to extend the right of privacy to homosexual sodomy," they wrote, "the same analytical process would require its extension to bigamy, incest, bestiality, necrophilia, and private illicit drug usage." The legislators also discounted the plaintiffs' argument about equal rights and equal protection because, as they saw it, the law outlawed conduct, not status. Section 21.06, according to the brief, prohibited oral and anal sexual contact with a member of the same sex for everyone, not simply one class of citizens. "All persons," they explained, "whether male or female, black, brown, yellow or white, young or old, married or unmarried, employed or unemployed, or of any religion or national origin, are forbidden from engaging in the carefully defined conduct. The statute applies equally to all." Even if the homosexual conduct law discriminated between gay and nongay Texans, the legislators argued, the state had legitimate interests in promoting "morality, decency, health, safety, and welfare of its citizens," all of which justified the law. The legislators concluded by asking the appeals court to reverse Davis's ruling and reinstate 21.06.[47]

During oral arguments, Wiseman reiterated the *Morales* plaintiffs' constitutional challenges to 21.06 and highlighted the law's violation of the rights of privacy and equal protection. The appellate judges indicated early in the hearing that they were inclined to agree with the plaintiffs. During one particularly revealing exchange, Justice Jimmy Carroll, in response to Assistant District Attorney Harry Potter's proclamation that the state had the authority to regulate behavior society deemed to be immoral, asked the assistant attorney general if the state could also regulate sexual relations between married couples. Potter admitted that the state could not. Pressing further, Justice Carroll wanted to know how far the state could extend its power in an effort to regulate public morality. Potter had indicated that the line lay somewhere between same-sex sexual activity and sex between legally married couples. "But what about straight, plain vanilla sex between a man and a woman in the missionary position, on their first date," Carroll asked, "could the state prohibit that?" Potter replied in the affirmative; the state of Texas could legally prohibit sex on a first date between an opposite-sex couple if society deemed that behavior immoral. Sensing the main thrust of the judges' questions, Potter changed direction and emphasized that the plaintiffs lacked standing to challenge the constitutionality of a criminal statute. This was a point the appellate judges seemed more willing to entertain. Nevertheless, the plaintiffs remained optimistic about the outcome after oral arguments ended.[48]

England v. City of Dallas

A few weeks after oral arguments in *Morales v. Texas*, a development in Mica England's ongoing litigation against the Dallas Police Department illustrated just how closely these two cases were related. When Judge Davis issued his ruling against 21.06 in *Morales* in December 1990, England was elated. "I think this is wonderful," she told the *Dallas Morning News* the day after the ruling. "I'm ready for my police job." Yet her hopes for a quick victory based on Davis's ruling were immediately dashed. Dallas assistant city attorney Craig Hopkins made it clear that the decision in the *Morales* case would not affect the police department's hiring policies. "The Police Department's hiring criteria are based on achieving efficient and effective law enforcement and not what may or may not be a violation of state law," he told reporters. "Given the problems that homosexuality has created in other police departments . . . and people's attitudes about homosexuality, the city of Dallas will continue to screen its applicants out on that basis." This assurance pleased many observers in Dallas, including members of an organization called the North Texas Pro-Family Coalition, who based their support for excluding gays and lesbians from the police force on a particularly harsh reading of the Bible. "Homosexuals were not created by God," they proclaimed in a public statement. "In the Old Testament, God required that all homosexuals be publicly executed—without exception. God did not require the executing of anything He created, either race or species. It is heresy to say that God created men and women to practice what He condemned to death." According to this group, the implications for the city of Dallas were clear. "The homosexual lifestyle is not accepted as normal," the group's statement concluded, and allowing gay and lesbian individuals to become police officers "would not only disintegrate public confidence in our police department, but would represent a total denial of the Judeo/Christian ethics that the majority of this country still believes in."[49]

Several Dallas City Council members had been trying to change DPD's hiring policies since England's appearance before them in 1989, but DPD officials continued to resist even after Judge Davis struck down the homosexual conduct law. In January 1992, Bill Rathburn, the new DPD chief, sent a memorandum to the city council clarifying his position on the issue. Citing 21.06, Chief Rathburn insisted that sexual orientation should be used to disqualify some applicants. "While I am aware of no evidence to suggest that gays and lesbians are unable to perform the duties of police officers," he explained, "I do not think that the Dallas Police Department should hire individuals who have a significant history of, or acknowledge an intention to continue, committing deliberate, frequent violations of the law." Despite the chief's proclamation, council member Chris Luna, the first openly gay man ever elected to the council, remained optimistic he could rally enough votes to change the policy. On January 22, 1992, the city council held a public hearing and listened to more than fifty Dallas residents express their opinions on the DPD hiring policy, including several DGA members. At the end of the meeting, the council voted 10–5 to preserve the existing policy.[50]

This latest defeat meant that England and her supporters would have to rely on the courts to achieve their goal, and in the judicial arena, they enjoyed more success. On February 3, nearly two years after England filed her suit, Texas district judge Lawrence Fuller issued a ruling in *England v. City of Dallas* in which he agreed with Judge Davis's opinion in *Morales v. Texas* that 21.06 violated key provisions of the Texas Constitution. Because of the law's unconstitutionality, Fuller ordered DPD to change its hiring practices immediately. England wasted no time celebrating and returned to police headquarters the next day to submit a second application to become an officer. "I want them to know I'm serious," England told the *Dallas Morning News* that morning. "I want this job." This time, instead of disqualifying her immediately, DPD officials announced that they would place England's application on hold until the Dallas City Council had an opportunity to clarify the policy and align it with Judge Fuller's decision. City council members took up the issue the following week but decided to delay any action until all the appeals were exhausted in *Morales v. Texas*.[51]

Victory Affirmed

On March 11, 1992, Judge Jimmy Carroll of the Third Court of Appeals in Austin released the court's decision in *Morales v. Texas*, and it was precisely what both the *Morales* plaintiffs and England had been eagerly anticipating. First, the three-judge appellate panel found that the plaintiffs had standing to challenge 21.06 in a civil court because they had demonstrated that the law inflicted injurious harm on them. While electing not to rule on the question of equal protection, the panel firmly upheld Judge Davis's declaration that the homosexual conduct law violated the privacy protections found in the Texas Constitution. "We can think of nothing more fundamentally private and deserving of protection," Carroll wrote for the panel, "than sexual behavior between consenting adults in private. If consenting adults have a privacy right to engage in sexual behavior, then it cannot be constitutional, absent a compelling state objective, to prohibit lesbians and gay men from engaging in the same conduct in which heterosexuals may legally engage." The appellate panel found none of the state's arguments for a compelling objective that justified 21.06 to be persuasive.[52]

The appellate decision in *Morales v. Texas* could not have come at a better time for Mica England. With her application to become a Dallas police officer on hold, she viewed Judge Carroll's ruling as another step toward fulfilling her dream of becoming a police officer. "The city now has nothing to base its case on," she told the *Dallas Voice* two days after the appellate ruling. "[Section] 21.06 has been ruled unconstitutional twice now. I gave the [city] council the chance to do the right thing without being forced by a judge. With this second judgment, they just look foolish. They should have done the right thing in the first place." Yet many city council members continued to stall. Reluctant to make any serious changes to the police department's hiring policy, Assistant City Attorney Craig Hopkins announced in April that the department would continue to process England's application but would not consider any other applicant who admitted to violating the homosexual conduct law. "If Ms. England is hireable for all other reasons," he told city council members, "we have to hire her. The judge has ruled that the Police Department can continue with its hiring policy [of not hiring gays] while all the appeals are being fought. This applies to anybody else but Ms. England." DPD officials allowed England to take the civil service exam and, if successful, to begin training as a new police officer. Yet there was a significant catch. DPD officials required England to post a $5,000 bond to cover the expenses associated with her training and starting salary in the event that she lost her case against the city. In the meantime, the city of Dallas would continue to appeal Judge Fuller's decision in *England v. City of Dallas*.[53]

The Texas Supreme Court

While the city of Dallas prepared its appeal in the *England* case, the state attorney general's office entered an appeal to the Texas Supreme Court in *Morales v. Texas*, arguing that the plaintiffs lacked standing to challenge the state's sodomy law in a civil court. In January 1993, the Texas Supreme Court agreed to hear the state's appeal in *Morales v. Texas*. To coincide with a hearing that included oral arguments, THRF board members organized a press conference to continue educating the public about the harmful effects of the homosexual conduct law. Plaintiff Charlotte Taft stated that "21.06 is a law whose only function is to create a basis for discrimination." While the state attorney general's office wished to pretend that the law was not un-constitutionally discriminatory, Taft pointed out that the statute prevented gay and lesbian Texans from contributing to society. "The Supreme Court of Texas has an opportunity today," Taft stated, "to move the state of Texas forward into the light, or to remain in the darkness of fear and bigotry." Plaintiff John Thomas hoped that members of the court "will set partisan politics aside and use their full intellectual capacities to do the right thing." Thomas reminded the justices that they did, in fact, know people who were gay or lesbian, even if those individuals had not officially announced their sexual orientation. These individuals were "good, wonderful, productive citizens of Texas, who happen also to be gay," and should not have to hide their identities because of an archaic law. Plaintiff Tom Doyal was a bit more confrontational in his statement on the case, and he had a direct message to anyone—judges, legislators, or regular citizens—who continued to support the type of discrimination that 21.06 justified. "To those who condemn lesbian and gay men, let me say that you are ignorant," he pro-claimed. "Ignorant of psychology, history, art, literature, music, theology, and—most importantly—ignorant of the indwelling dignity of all human beings." All three of the plaintiffs who participated in the press conference urged the Texas Supreme Court to affirm the lower court's ruling and rid the state of the homosexual conduct law once and for all.[54]

During oral arguments before a standing-room-only crowd, both sides in *Morales v. Texas* reiterated their foundational arguments about the constitutionality of 21.06 and the propriety of challenging the law in civil court. All nine state supreme court justices asked questions of Wise-man and Potter, and many of these questions gave the *Morales* plaintiffs cause for optimism. Several justices pressed Potter to explain his statement that the homosexual conduct law was valid because it represented a moral judgment of the state, a query the assistant attorney general was unable to answer. When the justices expressed concern about the credibility of the state's expert witnesses, Potter was forced to admit that it was difficult to find reputable experts to testify that being gay or lesbian was a psycho-logical disorder. Justice Lloyd Doggett wanted to know if 21.06 justified discrimination against gay and lesbian Texans, and Potter admitted that it did. Potter also admitted that the state's sodomy law did nothing to fur-ther public health. To defend the law, Potter finally resorted to an appeal to history. The homosexual conduct law, he argued, was "historically rooted" in the state legal code and reflected society's revulsion at the thought of same-sex sexual activity. Potter also argued that the type of same-sex sexual activity prohibited by 21.06 was not protected by any constitutional provisions because it was not "deeply rooted in the court's history and tradition." Justice Robert Gammage shot back with a question that seemed to get to the heart of the dispute: "Isn't that contrary to the concept that we are a land of liberty?" Trying another tactic, Potter shifted the judges' focus to the standing of the *Morales* plaintiffs. Justice Gammage remained flummoxed. "Is the threat of prosecution not enough to give them standing?" he asked. After the hearing, the *Morales* plaintiffs were optimistic about the substance of their case but worried about the question of standing because it gave the justices an opportunity to reverse the lower court's ruling without having to determine the constitutionality of a state statute. They were right to be worried.[55]

While the Texas Supreme Court prepared a decision in *Morales v. Texas*, Mica England's case against DPD got its own appellate ruling. In February 1993, the Third District Court of Appeals in Austin affirmed Judge Fuller's ruling that the DPD policy against hiring gay and lesbian police officers violated the spirit of the court's ruling in *Morales*, which declared 21.06 to be unconstitutional. Because of *Morales*, DPD could no longer use the state's homosexual conduct law as a justification for the policy. "We've won, and I feel great," England told the *Dallas Voice* after the appellate court announced its decision. "I am so relieved. I have always known I was right in this." It was up to the Dallas City Council to decide whether to appeal to the state supreme court, and England confidently predicted that council members would drop the issue. "If they [city officials] appeal this," she stated, "they are going to look even more ridiculous." Council Member Chris Luna agreed and urged his fellow council members to stop wasting municipal funds on the case. "The appeals court has just re-stated the obvious," he said, "that we need to stop discriminating." Yet Council Member Glenn Box, who had been the most outspoken defender of the current DPD policy, disagreed. "Until we get a definitive ruling from the [Texas] Supreme Court on the sodomy law and this case," he told the *Dallas Morning News*, "we need to uphold the law." Box's perspective eventually won out, as the council voted narrowly to appeal their case to the state supreme court.[56]

The outcome of *England v. City of Dallas* ultimately came down to a technicality. Dallas city attorney Craig Hopkins filed the city's appeal within the thirty-day time limit, but he neglected to complete one important step in the process. According to appellate court rules, an appellant must file a request for a rehearing in the same court in which the decision was rendered before appealing to a higher court for review of the case. In this instance, the city of Dallas was required to ask for a rehearing in the state's Third Court of Appeals, but Hopkins failed to file this necessary request. As a result, the following May, the Texas Supreme Court declined to hear the city's appeal and allowed the appellate court decision to stand, including the ruling that 21.06 violated the Texas Constitution. Two weeks later, the Dallas City Council, in consultation with the city attorney's office and despite opposition from some council members, voted to remove the questions about sexual orientation and past violations of the homosexual conduct law from the police department's initial employment application and from the list of questions administered during the required polygraph examination. More than four years after applying to become a Dallas police officer at the DPD recruitment event in Tulsa, Mica England won her case against the city. Even more significant, there now existed two appellate court decisions that declared the homosexual conduct law unconstitutional and prohibited law enforcement officials in the state from enforcing it. The Texas Supreme Court was the only remaining judicial body that could potentially reverse these successes in the movement for queer equality, and the justices' questions during oral argument in the *Morales* case gave activists hope they would achieve a final victory over 21.06 in the coming weeks.[57]

The favorable judicial rulings also gave activists new hope that the state legislature might finally repeal 21.06, a dream many had all but given up. In October 1991, newly sworn-in Texas governor Ann Richards appointed a commission to review the state penal code and eliminate old laws that were no longer enforced. Activists viewed this as an opportunity to rid the code of 21.06, particularly in light of the recent decision in *Morales v. Texas* declaring the statute unconstitutional. With Governor Richards as an important ally, a handful of gay and lesbian rights lobbyists quietly persuaded the commission to consider removing the homosexual conduct law from the legal code. In November 1992, to the astonishment of many activists, the commissioners approved a revised penal code that did not include 21.06. The following January, the full state legislature began considering the proposed revisions, and there was a surprising absence of voices in support of resurrecting the homosexual conduct law. That silence ended, however, when the *Austin American-Statesman* published a report in April 1993 detailing the proposed penal code revisions and noted that 21.06 would be eliminated. It did not take long for a group of legislators to add the first of many amendments restoring the homosexual conduct law to the legal code. Although state legislators such as Debra Danburg from Houston and Glen Maxey from Austin tried to defeat these amendments, the pro-21.06 advocates ultimately prevailed. Rather than allowing the entire revised penal code to die, in June 1993, Governor Richards signed the amended proposal that retained the homosexual conduct law. The Texas Legislature again failed to repeal the archaic statute, leaving the court system as the only viable option for eliminating 21.06. By the summer of 1993, it all hinged on how the Texas Supreme Court would rule in *Morales v. Texas*.[58]

The Texas Supreme Court issued its final decision in *Morales v. Texas* in January 1994. In his opinion written for the five-to-four majority, Justice John Cornyn asserted that there was only one important question presented in the case, and it had nothing to do with privacy or equal protection. For Cornyn, the issue was judicial jurisdiction. A state civil court, according to the majority opinion, did not have the authority to rule on the constitutionality of a legal statute except under very special circumstances in which a criminal law threatened a vested property right. Cornyn and the majority of his colleagues did not find that these special circumstances existed in the *Morales* case. The justices in the majority remained unpersuaded that the homosexual conduct law threatened the employment prospects of gay and lesbian Texans or that the law might justify hate crimes against them. "We conclude, however," Cornyn wrote, "that neither this court, nor the [district and appellate] courts below, have jurisdiction to enjoin the enforcement of, or issue a declaratory judgment determining the constitutionality of 21.06. Therefore, we reverse the judgment of the court of appeals and remand this case to the trial court with instructions to dismiss." After five years of litigation, the Texas Supreme Court decided that the *Morales* plaintiffs had filed their case in the wrong state court.[59]

Writing the dissenting opinion, Justice Robert Gammage disagreed that the civil court system lacked jurisdiction to rule on the constitutionality of 21.06. The question for Gammage was whether the homosexual conduct law caused irreparable harm to queer citizens regardless of whether that harm threatened a property right. A civil court, according to Gammage, had the authority and even the obligation to determine the constitutionality of a criminal statute, especially if the law in question was rarely or never enforced. "In these infrequent and unusual cases," Gammage wrote, "the fact that there will be no prosecution evidences the lack of an adequate remedy at law because the complaining party is denied an opportunity to argue the unconstitutionality of the statute in the criminal court system." Justice Gammage found the *Morales* plaintiffs' testimony about the personal harm done to them by 21.06 to be credible, noting that their "job choices are limited, that they face discrimination in housing, family, and criminal justice matters, and that they suffer psychological harm to their relationships because they are labeled criminals by the very existence of the statute." What was particularly damaging about the majority ruling, according to Gammage, was that it eliminated the only remaining avenue through which to challenge the law and set a harmful precedent for the future. "Shirking its equitable duty to provide a remedy for a wrong," he wrote, "the court allows the State to insulate its laws from judicial scrutiny. Under the court's analysis, the State may adopt all manner of criminal laws affecting the civil or personal rights of any number of citizens, and by declining to prosecute under them, ensure that no court ever reviews them." The Texas Supreme Court, according to Gammage and the other dissenting justices, had failed both to protect the constitutional rights of queer Texans and to ensure citizens had an opportunity to challenge the legality of unenforced statutes.[60]

In its official press release following the Texas Supreme Court's decision, the THRF board seemed to find a silver lining in defeat. Although they wanted the state's highest tribunal to uphold lower court decisions striking down 21.06, they were nevertheless encouraged by one small piece of the majority opinion in *Morales v. Texas*. While explaining why the state's civil court system lacked jurisdiction to issue a ruling in the case, Justice Cornyn used Mica England's litigation against the Dallas Police Department as an example of when a civil court did have the authority to rule on the constitutionality of a criminal statute. By recognizing the jurisdiction of the Third Court of Appeals in *England v. City of Dallas*, the Texas Supreme Court seemed to affirm the appellate court's opinion that the homosexual conduct law violated the state constitution. "Gays, lesbians and all fair-minded Texans should be outraged at the Texas Supreme Court's dereliction of duty, their failure to defend our rights to privacy while giving ridiculous reasons for not ruling on the case," a THRF press release stated. "Nevertheless, gays and lesbians should celebrate this backhanded victory. [Section] 21.06 is unconstitutional." Uncertainty remained about whether the decision of the Third Court of Appeals in the *England* case applied to the entire state of Texas or simply to that particular judicial district. THRF representatives were confident, however, that the opinion did indeed extend across the state. "The bottom line is that this statute has been declared unconstitutional by the Third District Court of Appeals," THRF executive director Suzy Wagers asserted. "The effect of that ruling is statewide." Yet just a few months later, perhaps after consulting with additional legal experts, members of the THRF board became less certain of this unintentional victory. "Although the *Morales* decision left intact a ruling of unconstitutionality by the Third District Court of Appeals," the board stated in its newsletter later in the spring, "the statute remains on the books and the Third District Court's ruling is not binding on all courts in Texas." At best, it seemed that the homosexual conduct law might be unenforceable, but only within the jurisdiction of the Third District Court around the city of Austin. Elsewhere in Texas, criminal courts could continue to prosecute queer Texans for violating 21.06.[61]

Long-Term Consequences

The results of *Morales v. Texas* and *England v. City of Dallas* were not what the plaintiffs and their supporters had hoped for. Despite winning a favorable ruling at the appellate level, Mica England never realized her dream of becoming a police officer, although her case did open the door for countless other queer applicants to join police forces across the state. By the time the Third Court of Appeals struck down both 21.06 and DPD's hiring policy in 1993, England had been working for several years at upscale restaurants in Dallas and had become an accomplished chef. In September 1994, England settled her lawsuit against the city of Dallas for $73,000 and decided to use the money to open her own restaurant, and a few years later she relocated to Florida to pursue this new career plan. *Morales v. Texas* marked the THRF's final attempt to challenge the state's sodomy law in the court system. After the Texas Supreme Court issued its decision, the THRF's executive director and several board members resigned in the midst of internal divisions over the group's future work. While the THRF board was actively engaged in programs that provided critical legal support to people with AIDS, many THRF activists were dissatisfied with what they saw as a neglect of initiatives to support the struggle for gay and lesbian civil rights. Although the remaining board members restated their commitment to challenging 21.06 and even promised to launch another legal challenge, they found that fundraising became more difficult in the wake of the *Morales* loss as more attention was turned toward alleviating the HIV/AIDS crisis. As a result, a follow-up case to *Morales* never materialized.[62]

The significance of *Morales v. Texas* and *England v. City of Dallas*, like the challenges to Texas sodomy laws preceding them, lay not in their immediate effects on the state criminal code, but rather in their long-term impact on the decades-long struggle for queer equality. Four years later, the arrests of John Lawrence and Tyron Garner near Houston for violating 21.06 indicated that the homosexual conduct law was alive and well in the aftermath of *Morales* and *England*. By 1998, however, queer activists, many of whom had been struggling against state sodomy laws for decades, decided the time had come again to challenge the discriminatory law using the federal court system. Yet this time, activists could rely on a wealth of case history, legal precedent, and organizational momentum in their efforts to rid Texas and the rest of the nation of sodomy laws like 21.06.

Lawrence v. Texas Reconsidered

When Harris County sheriff's deputies arrested John Lawrence and Tyron Garner near Houston in 1998 for violating the state's homosexual conduct law, it is doubtful either man was aware of the battles against such laws that Alvin Buchanan, Don Baker, Linda Morales, Mica England, the Texas Human Rights Foundation, and dozens of additional individuals and organizations across the state had waged for decades. Neither Lawrence nor Garner was involved in gay rights activities and, in fact, "had no interest in them," as the legal scholar Dale Carpenter discovered in his interviews with them. Yet when their arrests thrust the two men into the national spotlight, making them public figures for the rights of gay and lesbian Americans, Lawrence and Garner benefited tremendously from the litany of legal challenges to Texas sodomy laws that preceded theirs. With the creation of the Texas Human Rights Foundation, the Dallas Gay Alliance, the Houston Gay Political Caucus, and others, queer activists raised the necessary funding and provided the essential organizational support to challenge state sodomy laws, which they rightly identified as the primary justification for the harassment, discrimination, and violence they faced. Relying partly on the legal strategy employed by Alvin Buchanan against Article 524, Don Baker and the Texas Human Rights Foundation won a significant victory when a federal district court struck down Section 21.06 of the revised state penal code and simultaneously recognized the privacy and equal protection rights of queer Americans. When that case failed at the appellate level, Linda Morales and her co-plaintiffs, as well as Mica England, picked up where Baker left off and won partial victories against the homosexual conduct law. And all these landmark cases relied on a smattering of smaller court challenges to chart the way forward. As Lawrence, Garner, and their attorneys pursued their case against 21.06 through the Texas court system, the appellate courts, and finally to the US Supreme Court in 2003, they never had to create a legal strategy out of thin air or scramble to find organizations to support their efforts. Activists in Houston, in fact, were instrumental in organizing the *Lawrence* case before handing it off to national organizations. The requisite elements were well established by that time, and Lawrence, Garner, and their legal team had plenty of individuals and organizations to thank for that.[1]

In the US Supreme Court's majority opinion in *Lawrence v. Texas*, Justice Anthony Kennedy quoted the Texas Court of Criminal Appeals' decision in *Morales v. Texas* to remind readers that the Texas sodomy law and those like it in other states served as a basis for a wide range of discrimination against queer citizens. "The effect of Texas' sodomy law is not just limited to the threat of prosecution or consequence of conviction," Kennedy wrote. "Texas' sodomy law brands all homosexuals as criminals, thereby making it more difficult for homosexuals to be treated in the same manner as everyone else. Indeed, Texas itself has previously acknowledged the collateral effects of the law, stipulating in a prior challenge to this action [*Morales*] that the law 'legally sanctions discrimination against [homosexuals] in a variety of ways unrelated to the criminal law,' including in the areas of 'employment, family issues, and housing.'" The plaintiffs in *Morales v. Texas* had borrowed many of these examples from *Baker v. Wade*, and Don Baker and his legal team had used the experiences of queer Texans living under the state sodomy law as evidence of their oppression. Justice Kennedy recognized the validity of these arguments that Texas activists had been making since the 1970s and used them to deliver a final blow to the statute itself.[2]

A new generation of Americans likewise have the pre-*Lawrence* cases documented in this book to credit for the more recent advances in queer equality. Surprisingly, it was Supreme Court justice Antonin Scalia, author of a vicious dissent in *Lawrence v. Texas*, who suggested that the invalidation of the country's remaining sodomy laws could be used as a foundation to challenge a vast array of discrimination against gay and lesbian Americans, a possibility Justice Kennedy did his best to avoid discussing in his majority opinion. While Kennedy hastened to point out that *Lawrence v. Texas* "does not involve whether the government must give formal recognition to any relationship that homosexual persons seek to enter," Scalia responded, "do not believe it." The majority opinion in *Lawrence*, Scalia warned, "dismantles the structure of constitutional law that has permitted a distinction to be made between heterosexual and homosexual unions. . . . This case 'does not involve' the issue of homosexual marriage only if one entertains the belief that principle and logic have nothing to do with the decisions of this Court." For Scalia, the Supreme Court's decision in *Lawrence* would inevitably lead to nationwide marriage equality because for the first time the majority of the high court explicitly acknowledged that gay and lesbian

Americans enjoyed constitutional rights and protections that the law must respect and that the courts must uphold.[3]

Yet Scalia's fears about the consequences of the Supreme Court's decision in *Lawrence v. Texas* extended beyond the prospect of same-sex marriage. "Today's opinion is the product of a Court," he wrote, "that has largely signed on to the so-called homosexual agenda . . . [and] has taken sides in the culture war, departing from its role of assuring, as neutral observer, that the democratic rules of engagement are observed." Scalia noted that there were plenty of Americans who did not want to work alongside gay and lesbian individuals in their places of employment or to interact with them in places of public accommodation or to have their children taught by them in schools or to see them serve in the military or to allow them to be seen as role models in society, and he thought this kind of discrimination was perfectly legal if the people of a state believed it would safeguard "themselves and their families from a lifestyle that they believe to be immoral and destructive." Scalia pointed out that Congress repeatedly rejected claims that Title VII of the Civil Rights Act of 1964 protected gay, lesbian, or transgender individuals from employment discrimination, that the federal government actually required discrimination against queer Americans who wished to join the US military, and that sometimes discrimination was a constitutionally protected right, as the Supreme Court had ruled in a 2000 case involving the Boy Scouts of America. Scalia's apprehension stemmed from his concern that the Supreme Court's decision in *Lawrence v. Texas* would undermine the basis for this type of legal discrimination.[4]

As it turned out, Scalia accurately predicted the consequences of the *Lawrence* ruling. The invalidation of the Texas homosexual conduct law and all remaining state sodomy laws represented a long step toward eliminating the legal basis for discrimination against queer Americans. In 2010, the US Congress repealed Don't Ask, Don't Tell, a policy signed by President Bill Clinton in 1993 that allowed gay and lesbian individuals to serve in the armed forces only if they remained closeted about their sexual orientation. During its first ten years of existence, Don't Ask, Don't Tell resulted in the discharge of almost 10,000 queer service members, prompting several to pursue litigation against the policy itself. This strategy hit a dead end as federal courts relied on the Supreme Court's 1986 decision in *Bowers v. Hardwick*, which affirmed the constitutionality of Georgia's sodomy law, to uphold the discriminatory military policy. By overturning the *Bowers* decision in *Lawrence* in 2003, the high court removed the controlling power of their earlier opinion and cleared the way for challenges to policies that relied on it. In the aftermath of *Lawrence*, several gay and lesbian members of the military began using federal courts to challenge Don't Ask, Don't Tell, while national gay and lesbian rights organizations put pressure on Congress to issue a legislative repeal. In December 2010, Congress responded; the House voted 250 to 175 in favor of repeal and the Senate followed suit three days later with a 65-to-31 vote, despite Arizona senator John McCain's last-minute efforts to rally his fellow Republicans to kill the bill. Less than one week later, President Barack Obama signed the repeal bill into law and effectively ended decades of discrimination against gay and lesbian Americans who wanted to serve in the armed forces, although military officials pursued a gradual implementation plan that lasted most of the following year. By the fall of 2011, however, queer Americans could serve openly in the US military, an outcome hardly conceivable as long as they were still deemed criminals in more than a dozen states. The years of activism against Texas sodomy laws leading up to the Supreme Court's decision in *Lawrence v. Texas* helped make possible this victory in the quest for queer equality.[5]

In 2013, the US Supreme Court struck down a portion of the Defense of Marriage Act (DOMA), a federal law passed in 1996 that defined marriage as between one man and one woman and asserted the right of individual states to refuse to recognize same-sex marriages performed in other states. Because a wide range of federal benefits were tied to marriage, DOMA effectively prohibited legally married same-sex spouses from receiving Social Security survivor payments and federal spousal insurance coverage, filing joint tax returns, or securing a number of additional benefits most married Americans took for granted. Married couples like Edith Windsor and Thea Spyer felt these discriminatory regulations acutely. In 1963, Windsor, a thirty-four-year-old divorcee, met Spyer in an Italian restaurant in New York City's Greenwich Village, and the couple hit it off immediately. Four years later, the two women promised to marry each other, although it took four decades to make that vow a reality. Windsor and Spyer finally got married in Ontario, Canada, in 2007, and when they returned to their home in New York, the state agreed to recognize the marriage. By that time, Spyer had been diagnosed with multiple sclerosis and suffered from declining health, and in 2009 she died. Because DOMA stipulated that the federal government could not recognize the marriage of two women, Windsor faced a hefty inheritance tax bill that was more than $350,000 higher than it would have been if "Thea had been Theo," as Windsor phrased it. Because DOMA denied federal tax benefits to same-sex spouses, Windsor could not enjoy the same exemption from the federal estate tax that opposite-sex spouses received, regardless of the fact that the state of New York recognized her marriage to Spyer. Windsor sued the federal government the following year and argued that DOMA violated the Constitution. A federal district court in New York agreed and ruled that the portion of DOMA that defined marriage as between one man and one woman and withheld federal marriage benefits to same-sex spouses violated the equal protection guarantees found in the Fifth Amendment. Although the Department of Justice declined to defend DOMA in court, a group in the House of Representatives known as the Bipartisan Legal Advisory Group (BLAG) stepped in to argue the case. After an appellate court upheld the district court's ruling, the US Supreme Court agreed to review the decision, delivering its final opinion in June 2013. Citing *Lawrence v. Texas*, Justice Anthony Kennedy recognized that some states were attempting to extend the logic of the *Lawrence* opinion to protect the marriage rights of gay and lesbian Americans, an extension he now supported. "Private, consensual, sexual intimacy between two adult persons of the same sex may not be punished by the State," he wrote, and it followed that those states could also recognize that sexual intimacy "can form 'but one element in a personal bond that is more enduring,'" directly quoting from his majority opinion in *Lawrence*. New York was one such state that attempted to extend the right to pursue a private sexual relationship with a member of the same sex to the right to marry. "For same-sex couples who wished to be married," Kennedy wrote, "the State [of New York] acted to give their lawful conduct a lawful status," reflecting "the community's considered perspective on the historical roots of the institution of marriage and its evolving understanding of the meaning of equality." Because DOMA interfered with New York's efforts to grant all the rights and privileges of marriage to same-sex couples, the federal law violated constitutional guarantees of due process and equal protection. "DOMA writes inequality into the entire United States Code," Kennedy concluded. With its reliance on the high court's decision in *Lawrence v. Texas*, Kennedy's opinion in *United States v. Windsor* again demonstrated the fruits of the long grassroots struggle to overturn the Texas sodomy law.[6]

As he had done in *Lawrence*, Justice Scalia offered a dissent in *United States v. Windsor* that predicted the Supreme Court's landmark marriage equality ruling two years later. While the *Windsor* decision robbed the federal government of the right to discriminate against legally married same-sex couples, according to Scalia, it was only a matter of time before the Supreme Court would be asked to require individual states to recognize same-sex marriages performed in other states. "As far as this Court is concerned," he wrote in his dissenting opinion, "no one should be fooled; it is just a matter of listening and waiting for the other shoe." In the aftermath of *United States v. Windsor*, an assortment of federal district courts did just that by ordering states to recognize same-sex marriages performed in other states. One of these judicial rulings involved James Obergefell and John Arthur, who had entered into a long-term relationship with each other during the 1990s. In 2011, doctors diagnosed Arthur with terminal amyotrophic lateral sclerosis (ALS), and the two men wanted to get married before Arthur died. Since their home state of Ohio did not recognize same-sex marriages, the couple traveled to Maryland to tie the knot in 2013. A few months later, Arthur died, but because the state of Ohio refused to recognize their marriage, public officials in the county where the two men lived would not allow Obergefell to be listed as the surviving spouse on Arthur's death certificate. Obergefell sued and received a favorable ruling in a federal district court in Ohio. Predictably, the state of Ohio appealed. In 2015, Obergefell's case reached the US Supreme Court, bundled together with more than a dozen similar cases from three other states. In a decision announced in June, Justice Anthony Kennedy reached back to the high court's 2003 decision in *Lawrence v. Texas* to defend another major victory for queer equality. "As this Court held in *Lawrence*," Kennedy wrote, "same-sex couples have the same right as opposite-sex couples to enjoy intimate association. . . . But while *Lawrence* confirmed a dimension of freedom that allows individuals to engage in intimate association without criminal liability, it does not follow that freedom stops there. Outlaw to outcast may be a step forward, but it does not achieve the full promise of liberty." It was no longer sufficient, Kennedy believed, to recognize that the Constitution protected gay and lesbian Americans in their choice of sexual partners and to stop there. The time had come to acknowledge that individual states that refused to treat same-sex couples with the same dignity and respect as opposite-sex couples also acted against constitutional principles, particularly the due process and equal protection clauses found in the Fourteenth Amendment. Kennedy and the high court's majority ruled not only that individual states must recognize the legal status of same-sex couples married in other states but also that states must certify the marriages of all same-sex couples who wed within each state. The legal challenges to Texas sodomy laws that produced the Supreme Court decision in *Lawrence v. Texas* helped make possible the victory for nationwide marriage equality in *Obergefell v. Hodges* twelve years later. It is simply beyond reason to believe that the Supreme Court would have ordered officials in all fifty states to honor the marriages of same-sex couples had the romantic relationships of queer individuals still been criminalized in more than a dozen states.[7]

In the wake of the victory celebrations for marriage equality, some observers noted that millions of queer Americans across the country still suffered from discrimination in their daily lives, particularly in their places of employment or prospective employment. In many states, it remained legal to fire an employee because of his or her sexual orientation or gender identity even after the victories in *Lawrence, Windsor,* and *Obergefell.* In 2013, Atlanta resident Gerald Bostock, who worked for the child welfare services department of Clayton County, Georgia, just south of the city, discovered the reality of this continuing discrimination when he joined an amateur gay softball league. Despite a stellar ten-year record with the county, upon learning of Bostock's association with the softball league, county officials terminated his employment for "conduct unbecoming of a county employee." Bostock sued the county, arguing that Title VII of the Civil Rights Act of 1964 protected gay and lesbian employees from being discriminated against because of their sexual orientation. A federal district court and an appellate court both disagreed and ruled against Bostock, asserting that the law's prohibition on sex discrimination did not extend to discrimination based on sexual orientation. When Bostock appealed to the US Supreme Court, his case was combined with two similar court challenges. One case involved a New York skydiving business known as Altitude Express, whose owner fired skydiving instructor Donald Zarda in 2010 after a customer complained that Zarda had proclaimed that he was "100% gay" before a tandem jump. The other case involved the owner of a Michigan funeral home who terminated the employment of Aimee Stephens in 2013 after she notified her colleagues that she would be transitioning to live full-time as a woman. Both Zarda and Stephens had received favorable district and appellate court rulings based on Title VII protections, however, setting the stage for the Supreme Court to settle the dispute. Unfortunately, both Zarda and Stephens had died by the time the Supreme Court heard the cases in 2020, but that did not diminish the legal impact of the high court's ruling. The question before the court was whether Title VII of the Civil Rights Act of 1964, which made it "unlawful . . . for any employer to fail or refuse to hire or to discharge any individual, or otherwise to discriminate against any individual with respect to his compensation, terms, conditions, or privileges of employment, because of such individual's race, color, sex, or national origin," protected the employment rights of gay, lesbian, and transgender workers. All three plaintiffs argued that their employers wrongfully terminated their employment because of sex. Gerald Bostock and Donald Zarda, for example, were men who were romantically attracted to other men, and their employers fired them for that reason. If they had been women who were romantically attracted to men, Bostock and Zarda argued, they would still have their jobs. This, according to the two men, was sex discrimination. Similarly, Aimee Stephens had been assigned the sex of male at birth and identified as female as an adult. If she had been assigned the sex of female at birth and identified as female as an adult, Stephens argued, her employer would not have terminated her employment. She argued that this was also a case of sex discrimination. A majority of the Supreme Court agreed. Announcing the six-to-three decision, Justice Neil Gorsuch wrote that the matter before the high court was simple: whether employers could fire employees because of their sexual orientation or gender identity. For Gorsuch and the court's majority, the answer was also simple. "An employer who fires an individual for being homosexual or transgender," Gorsuch wrote, "fires that person for traits or actions it would not have questioned in members of a different sex. Sex plays a necessary and undisguisable role in the decision, exactly what Title VII forbids." Because "it is impossible to discriminate against a person for being homosexual or transgender without discriminating against that individual based on sex," Gorsuch and the court's majority concluded that "an employer who fires an individual merely for being gay or transgender defies the law." As was the case with the repeal of Don't Ask, Don't Tell and the court decisions invalidating the Defense of Marriage Act and state bans on same-sex marriage, *Bostock v. Clayton County, Georgia* emerged partly as a result of the agitation against the Texas sodomy law that led to *Lawrence v. Texas* in 2003. As long as multiple states continued to label queer citizens criminals, it seemed doubtful that a majority of US Supreme Court justices would have interpreted the Civil Rights Act of 1964 in a way that protected their employment rights.[8]

The recent victories in the movement for queer equality are unmistakable, and in large part they are the products of decades of grassroots activism aimed at ridding the nation of its discriminatory sodomy laws that reduced queer Americans to the status of second-class citizens at best and criminals at worst. The efforts of Texans who began challenging the constitutionality of the state's sodomy laws during the late 1960s were critical to making *Lawrence v. Texas* possible in 2003, a landmark Supreme Court decision that set the stage for further gains for the country's queer citizens. Yet as most gay, lesbian, and transgender Americans are aware, the struggle for full equality remains unfinished. A prominent legal question today is whether private businesses or individuals can discriminate against queer people because of their religious beliefs. Can owners of a bakery or flower shop in a state that protects its queer citizens from discrimination in public accommodations, for example, refuse to bake a cake or provide flowers for a same-sex wedding because they believe marriage should only be between a man and a woman? Can these business owners similarly refuse to provide their services for a gender reveal party for a transgender individual? Despite hearing such a case in 2018 in *Masterpiece Cake Shop v. Colorado Civil Rights Commission*, the Supreme Court has not yet issued any definitive answers to these questions. There have also been several attempts to roll back federal protections for transgender Americans during the past few years. Upon taking office in 2017, President Donald Trump quickly ended Obama-era policies that protected transgender schoolchildren by allowing them to use the restroom that matched their gender identity, and members of the Trump administration vowed to eliminate all transgender personnel from the US military. Trump also enacted new federal rules that allowed single-sex homeless shelters to turn away transgender individuals, medical professionals to refuse to treat transgender patients, and private insurance companies to deny benefits for certain health care procedures sought by some transgender patients. President Joe Biden reversed some of these Trump-era changes after taking office in 2021, but the fact that these basic rights are subject to the whim of the sitting president is a sign that there is much work left to do. Similarly, queer people of color, and particularly transgender people of color, continue to face blatant discrimination and outright violence. According to the Human Rights Campaign, forty-four gender-nonconforming Americans lost their lives to violence in 2020—up from twenty-seven the previous year—and most of them were transgender women of color. To stop the attacks on the rights and lives of queer Americans and potentially bring about an even broader expansion of equality, individuals and organizations must take the initiative to fight back, and litigation in the court system should be a significant part of the overall strategy.[9]

Although few people today realize it, the fundamental right of marriage, presumably so firmly established for same-sex couples as a result of *Obergefell v. Hodges*, seems to have an uncertain future. When the US Supreme Court handed down its marriage equality ruling in 2015, county clerk Kim

Davis from Kentucky's Rowan County refused to issue any marriage licenses at all, arguing that the high court's opinion failed to change her religious view that same-sex marriages were immoral. Two couples who were unable to obtain marriage licenses from Davis's office—David Ermold and David Moore, and James Yates and Will Smith—sued Davis for violating their constitutionally protected right to marriage. A federal district court ruled against Davis, concluding that her actions violated the *Obergefell* decision and that her religious objection to same-sex marriage was an insufficient defense. The Sixth Circuit Court of Appeals agreed in 2019, prompting Davis to appeal her case to the US Supreme Court. The high court's justices refused to hear the case in October 2020, but Justices Samuel Alito and Clarence Thomas used the opportunity to advance their criticisms of the *Obergefell* decision and perhaps to signal a path to dismantle it. "As a result of this Court's alteration of the Constitution [in *Obergefell*]," Alito and Thomas wrote in their appended statement that accompanied the court's decision not to hear the case, "Davis found herself faced with a choice between her religious beliefs and her job." The two justices believed that Davis's case failed to present the constitutional question clearly, but they noted that the issues she raised were legitimate. "Davis may have been one of the first victims of this Court's cavalier treatment of religion in its *Obergefell* decision," they wrote, "but she will not be the last." Alito and Thomas looked forward to the day when the Supreme Court would hear a more compelling case against its marriage equality ruling. "By choosing to privilege a novel constitutional right over the religious liberty interests explicitly protected in the First Amendment," they concluded, "and by doing so undemocratically, the Court has created a problem only it can fix." Alito and Thomas's statement provides a stark warning to supporters of nationwide marriage equality that even the fate of this recent victory for gay and lesbian rights, seemingly so anchored in the firm terrain of judicial precedent, remains unresolved.[10]

Even the Supreme Court decision in *Lawrence v. Texas* might not be as secure as it once seemed. In June 2022, the US Supreme Court issued its decision in *Dobbs v. Jackson Women's Health Organization*, which overturned *Roe v. Wade* (1973) and *Planned Parenthood v. Casey* (1992). In the radically originalist majority opinion, Justice Alito wrote that the Constitution contained no right to an abortion and that "*Roe* was egregiously wrong from the start." While Alito attempted to limit the decision solely to abortion, it nevertheless remains probable that *Dobbs* will be used in ongoing efforts to roll back judicial victories for queer Americans. Justice

Thomas stated as much in his concurring opinion, arguing that *Lawrence* and *Obergefell* should be reconsidered in light of *Dobbs*. Thomas's pronouncement certainly pleased members of the anti-abortion group Texas Right to Life, who submitted an amicus brief in *Dobbs* that argued that both *Lawrence* and *Obergefell* rest on the same faulty constitutional reasoning as *Roe*. "These 'rights,'" they wrote, "like the right to an abortion from *Roe*, are judicial concoctions, and there is no other source of law that can be invoked to salvage their existence. . . . *Lawrence* and *Obergefell* . . . are as lawless as *Roe*." It remains to be seen if the Supreme Court will overturn *Roe* and what effect their action will have on decisions that rely on a similar understanding of privacy and equality, but supporters of reviving discriminatory sodomy laws are beginning to explore the connections.[11]

The decades of grassroots organizing and agitating necessary for challenging the Texas sodomy law are relevant to the continuing struggle for equality, as a similar commitment will be required not only to bring about new victories but also to preserve what activists have already achieved. As the legal scholar and activist David Cole has shown, the US Constitution is only a living document if citizen activists breathe life into it. "If constitutional law were a sentence," Cole has written, "the Supreme Court's decision would be the period at the end of the sentence—maybe sometimes an exclamation point—but the words of the sentence would reflect the work of citizens engaged in advocacy outside the Supreme Court altogether." Meaningful constitutional change that protects freedom, expands equality, enhances democracy, and empowers citizens must originate from grassroots activists willing to take risks and devote the time and energy necessary to bring about a new way of thinking about how to apply the nation's founding documents to our current era. This kind of change is often slow to come about due to the sheer amount of labor required of any grassroots movement wanting to interpret the Constitution in a new way. To view the Supreme Court's 2003 decision in *Lawrence v. Texas* as revolutionary, therefore, is to miss all the words in, and indeed the very meaning of, a lengthy sentence by solely paying attention to the period at the end. To remove the central obstacle to expanding equality for queer Americans by persuading the federal court system that state sodomy laws like the one in Texas violated the Constitution, grassroots activists had to begin waging the battle decades before their followers achieved the victory in the early twenty-first century. Every major success of the queer rights movement since then has hinged on the *Lawrence* decision, as it is inconceivable that the expansion of equality could have occurred had millions of queer citizens still been considered criminals.[12]

The victories achieved for queer Americans since 2003 owe a tremendous debt to the activists who waged a long battle against the Texas sodomy law, which made *Lawrence v. Texas* possible, and many of those activists recognized that they were part of a long struggle for freedom and equality. "I am very aware of the fact that we may lose the decision," Don Baker said in 1986 as he awaited news from the Supreme Court on whether justices would hear his appeal in *Baker v. Wade*. "Long after the debate and arguments of this case, I hope to say we brought something to Texas and a better understanding of gay people. You have to look at the long term, not the short term in this case." Baker could hardly have foretold that it would take another seventeen years to overturn the Texas sodomy law or that unfortunately his goal would be achieved after his death from cancer in December 2000. Baker understood, however, that the struggle for equality waged by queer Americans would be a long one and would not end with a revolutionary decision by a court of law. He and other activists recognized that to protect the gains of the past and chart a course for the future, they must not become complacent, defeated, or hopeless, but instead they should remain vigilant in their quest to be treated as first-class citizens and as human beings. These are lessons today's activists should take to heart.[13]

Acknowledgments

Appropriately enough, the idea for this book came to me on Constitution Day in 2015 when my colleague Tom Cox asked me to deliver a lecture on the meaning of *Lawrence v. Texas*. I did not know at the time that the questions raised during that event would come to dominate my thoughts for the next seven years, but I am glad they did. Researching and writing this book has led me on a remarkable journey, and it is a pleasure to thank those who have helped me along the way.

This book would not have been possible without generous financial support from a Special Collections Research Fellowship from the University of North Texas Libraries, multiple writing grants from UNT's College of Liberal Arts and Social Sciences, and travel funding from the history departments at UNT and Sam Houston State University and from SHSU's College of Liberal Arts and Social Sciences. In particular, Tamara Brown, Steve Cobb, Brian Domitrovic, and Jennifer Jensen Wallach helped ensure I had the resources to complete this project.

Many archivists and librarians helped me navigate the voluminous legal and organizational records that exist from this period in history. Morgan Gieringer and Courtney Johnson in the Special Collections department at the University of North Texas Libraries provided valuable insights into their massive LGBT collection, and Meagan May helped make it possible to access the collection digitally after the COVID-19 pandemic closed the reading room. The entire staff at the Briscoe Center for American History at the University of Texas at Austin was helpful, and it was sifting through the Texas Human Rights Foundation Records in their reading room that I first came across the fascinating history of *Baker v. Wade*. I would also like to thank Alexandra Dzienkowski at the Legislative Reference Library of Texas, Mike Miller at the Austin History Center, Javier Garza at MD Anderson's Research Medical Library, Larry Criscione at the Botts Collection in Houston, Evelina Stulgaityte at the Tarleton Law Library at the University of Texas at Austin, Michael Jackson at the Cushing Memorial Library and Archives at Texas A&M University, and Gene Elder at the Happy Foundation Archives in San Antonio. I also greatly benefited from the assistance of archivists at the Houston Metropolitan Research Center at the Houston Public Library and the Texas State Library and Archives. I wrote chapter 2 during the pandemic lockdowns of summer 2020, and this would not have been possible without J. D. Doyle's efforts to digitize historical gay and lesbian publications from across Texas at the J. D. Doyle Archives (http://www.jddoylearchives.org/).

Many individuals read portions of the manuscript and provided helpful feedback, including Dale Carpenter, Robert Emery, Yvonne Frear, Kerry Goldmann, Luke Harlow, Rusty Hawkins, David Johnson, Allison Madar, J. Gordon Melton, Clark Pomerleau, Audrey Thorstad, and Chris Todd. Conversations with Gene Alviar, Dale Carpenter, Eric Coleman, Tom Cox, Charles Ford, Jeff Littlejohn, Ervin Malakaj, Todd Moye, Bernadette Pruitt, Brian Riedel, Mark Stanley, Andrew Torget, and Karen Wisely helped me think through my arguments and improved the final product significantly. I am also thankful to Mike Anglin, Jim Barber, Michael Cline, Mica England, Dick Peeples, Maggie Watt, and William Waybourn for taking the time to share their memories with me. At the University of Texas Press, Robert Devens and Dawn Durante have been steadfast supporters of this project, and Lynne Ferguson and Nancy Warrington smoothed the rough edges of the manuscript and rendered this book more readable. I will be forever grateful for their enthusiasm and expert guidance.

My brother and brother-in-law, Paul Phelps and Tim Norwood, are two of the many beneficiaries of the activism I narrate in this book. When I proudly served as best man in their wedding in Dallas a few months after the *Obergefell* decision, I was often overcome with the weight of all they had to endure to reach that milestone in their lives. It was a joyous occasion filled with flashes of historical awareness and a recognition of just how momentous it all was, but a sense of past injustice occasionally crept into my thoughts. It seemed to me that marriage equality had arrived so suddenly and yet so late. Too late, in fact, for my friend Terry Beavers, who died from complications of AIDS in 2002. Terry would have marveled at the pace of change in the years immediately following his death, and I continue to lament the unfairness of this loss every time I see an old antique store or a Stetson cowboy hat, two of his favorite things. Although I never got the chance to tell him when he was alive, Terry's wise words and gentle compassion meant the world to me when I was trying to figure out my own identity. I often thought about Paul, Tim, and Terry while writing this book, and I am grateful that my life is so enriched by these three outstanding men who lived through much of the history I document in these pages.

It is not an overstatement to say that completing this book has been a family effort. In 2018, Devon Phelps accompanied me on a research trip to the University of North Texas in Denton, little knowing that the following year we would begin building a life there after I joined the UNT history department. During that trip we met Maggie Watt, Don Baker's sister, who gave us a glimpse of the real, in-the-flesh person behind the federal lawsuit I had been researching. Watching my life partner's passions stirred by these stories further confirmed for me that this history would appeal not just to historians but to anyone interested in social justice, as she certainly is. Devon graciously served as a sounding board from that point forward, and I am deeply thankful for the many times she encouraged me to forge ahead with the project during periods of doubt and frustration. In many ways, our daughter, Jordan, is growing up in a world radically different from the one reflected in these pages. This became apparent during the Covid-19 lockdown summer of 2020 when she worked as my research assistant and was shocked and appalled by the discriminatory ways many queer Texans were treated in court documents. Not only was her work immensely helpful for completing this project, but her perspective was a valuable reminder of the significant obstacles that activists faced in their quest for freedom and equality, making their achievements even more notable. I continue to count myself lucky to spend my life with these two amazing women, and it is to them that I dedicate this book.

Notes

Introduction. Before *Lawrence v. Texas*

1. *Lawrence v. Texas*, 539 U.S. 558 (2003), quotations on 578; *Bowers v. Hardwick*, 478 U.S. 186 (1986).

2. *United States v. Windsor*, 570 U.S. 744 (2013); *Obergefell v. Hodges*, 576 U.S. 644 (2015); *Bostock v. Clayton County, Georgia*, 590 U.S. ___ (2020). Works skeptical of the movement's progress include Marc Stein, *Rethinking the Gay and Lesbian Movement* (New York: Routledge, 2012); Christina Hanhardt, *Safe Space: Gay Neighborhood History and the Politics of Violence* (Durham, NC: Duke University Press, 2013); Nayan Shah, *Stranger Intimacy: Contesting Race, Sexuality, and the Law in the North American West* (Berkeley: University of California Press, 2012); Eithne Luibhéid, *Entry Denied: Controlling Sexuality at the Border* (Minneapolis: University of Minnesota Press, 2002); Genny Beemyn, *A Queer Capital: A History of Gay Life in Washington, D.C.* (New York: Routledge, 2015); Holly Anne Wade, "Discrimination, Sexuality and People with Significant Disabilities: Issues of Access and the Right to Sexual Expression in the United States," *Disability Studies Quarterly* 22, no. 4 (Fall 2002): 9–27; David Rayside, *Queer Inclusions, Continental Divisions: Public Recognition of Sexual Diversity in Canada and the United States* (Toronto: University of Toronto Press, 2008); and Wesley G. Phelps, "The Politics of Queer Disidentification and the Limits of Neoliberalism in the Struggle for Gay and Lesbian Equality in Houston," *Journal of Southern History* 84, no. 2 (May 2018): 311–348. For a concise overview of this debate over progress, see Marc Stein, "Law and Politics: 'Crooked and Perverse' Narratives of LGBT Progress," in *The Routledge History of Queer America*, ed. Don Romesburg (New York: Routledge, 2018), 315–330. With regard to sodomy law reform, the historian Timothy Stewart-Winter argues that the repeal of Illinois's sodomy statute in 1961 had no measurable effect on police harassment in Chicago or on the queer rights movement in the city. See Stewart-Winter, *Queer Clout: Chicago and the Rise of Gay Politics* (Philadelphia: University of Pennsylvania Press, 2016), 43–45. The historian Scott De Orio is particularly critical of many activists' reliance on constitutional protections of privacy in their struggles against sodomy laws, and he takes specific aim at Texas activists like those involved in *Buchanan v. Batchelor*. See De Orio, "The Invention of Bad Gay Sex: Texas and the Creation of a Criminal Underclass of Gay People," *Journal of the History of Sexuality* 26, no. 1 (January 2017): 53–87.

3. The details of *Lawrence v. Texas* are well known. See Dale Carpenter, *Flagrant Conduct: The Story of* Lawrence v. Texas (New York: W. W. Norton, 2012), quotation on 109; William N. Eskridge Jr., *Dishonorable Passions: Sodomy Laws in America, 1861–2003* (New York: Viking, 2008), 299–330; Lillian Faderman, *The Gay Revolution: The Story of the Struggle* (New York: Simon and Schuster, 2015), 546–550; Carlos A. Ball, *From the Closet to the Courtroom: Five LGBT Rights Lawsuits That Have Changed Our Nation* (Boston: Beacon Press, 2010), 199–247.

4. Historians are beginning to pay attention to the evolution of state sodomy laws and some pre-*Lawrence* challenges. See De Orio, "The Invention of Bad Gay Sex"; Brock Thompson, *The Un-Natural State: Arkansas and the Queer South* (Fayetteville: University of Arkansas Press, 2010), 63–97; Faderman, *The Gay Revolution*, 537–551; Eskridge, *Dishonorable Passions;* Joyce Murdoch and Deb Price, *Courting Justice: Gay Men and Lesbians v. the Supreme Court* (New York: Basic Books, 2001), 159–161; Stein, *Rethinking the Gay and Lesbian Movement*, 102–192; and Stephen Robertson, "Shifting the Scene of the Crime: Sodomy and the American History of Sexual Violence," *Journal of the History of Sexuality* 19, no. 2 (May 2010): 223–242.

5. David Cole, *Engines of Liberty: The Power of Citizen Activists to Make Constitutional Law* (New York: Basic Books, 2016), quotation on 9. For the methodology of social history, see Peter N. Stearns, "Social History Present and Future," *Journal of Social History* 37, no. 1 (Autumn 2003): 9–19, as well as the additional essays assessing the state of the field in the special Autumn 2003 issue. Since the 1980s, many legal historians have followed Robert W. Gordon's plea to apply historicism to studies of the law. Most of those works, however, focus on the eighteenth and nineteenth centuries. See Robert W. Gordon, "Critical Legal Histories," *Stanford Law Review* 36, no. 1–2 (January 1984): 57–125, and the symposium on Gordon's classic essay published in the Winter 2012 edition of *Law and Social Inquiry*. For excellent examples of what is often called the social history of the law, or legal culture, or sociolegal studies, see Laura F. Edwards, *The People and Their Peace: Legal Culture and the Transformation of Inequality in the Post-Revolutionary South* (Chapel Hill: University of North Carolina Press, 2009); Hendrik Hartog, *Man and Wife in America: A History* (Cambridge, MA: Harvard University Press, 2002); Dylan C. Penningroth, *The Claims of Kinfolk: African American Property and Community in the Nineteenth-Century South* (Chapel Hill: University of North Carolina Press, 2003); and Barbara Young Welke, *Recasting American Liberty: Gender, Race, Law, and the Railroad Revolution, 1865–1920* (New York: Cambridge University Press, 2001). For a call to apply this methodology to the twentieth century, see Stephen Robertson, "What's Law Got to Do with It? Legal Records and Sexual Histories," *Journal of the History of Sexuality* 14, no. 1–2 (January–April 2015): 161–185. This book attempts to extend some of these insights about law and society into the twentieth century. As the historian John D'Emilio has argued, during the twentieth century, gay and lesbian activists posed "the strongest attack on the status quo . . . in the realm of law." See D'Emilio,

Sexual Politics, Sexual Communities: The Making of a Homosexual Minority in the United States, 1940–1970 (Chicago: University of Chicago Press, 1983), 211.

6. James Woods Harris, Oliver Cromwell Hartley, and James Willie, *The Penal Code of the State of Texas* (Galveston, TX: The News Office, 1857). For the early legal history of Texas, see Michael Ariens, *Lone Star Law: A Legal History of Texas* (Lubbock: Texas Tech University Press, 2016), esp. 211–236. For earlier histories of sodomy laws in North America, see Richard Godbeer, *Sexual Revolution in Early America* (Baltimore, MD: Johns Hopkins University Press, 2002); Thomas Foster, *Sex and the Eighteenth-Century Man: Massachusetts and the History of Sexuality in America* (Boston: Beacon Press, 2006); Jen Manion, *Liberty's Prisoners: Carceral Culture in Early America* (Philadelphia: University of Pennsylvania Press, 2015); Eskridge, *Dishonorable Passions*; Doron S. Ben-Atar and Richard D. Brown, *Taming Lust: Crimes Against Nature in the Early Republic* (Philadelphia: University of Pennsylvania Press, 2014).

7. *Fennell v. State*, 32 Tex. 378 (1869), first and second quotations on 379; *Frazier v. State*, 39 Tex. 390 (1873), third quotation on 390.

8. *The Penal Code of the State of Texas*, 1879, Texas State Law Library, https://www.sll.texas.gov/assets/pdf/historical-statutes/1879/1879-4-penal-code-of-the-state-of-texas.pdf; *Ex parte Bergen*, 14 Tex. Ct. App. 52 (1883), 56–57.

9. *Medis v. State*, 27 Tex. Ct. App. 194 (1889), 194.

10. *Prindle v. State*, 21 S.W. 360 (1893), 361.

11. *Lewis v. State*, 35 S.W. 372 (1896), 372.

12. *Mitchell v. State*, 95 S.W. 500 (1906); *Harvey v. State*, 55 Tex. Crim. 199 (1909), first and second quotations on 200. Florida's sodomy statute similarly omitted specific reference to oral sex before the 1920s, although the law itself was rarely enforced before the 1940s. See Julio Capó Jr., *Welcome to Fairyland: Queer Miami Before 1940* (Chapel Hill: University of North Carolina Press, 2017), 38–39.

13. *The Penal Code of the State of Texas*, 1911, Texas State Law Library, https://www.sll.texas.gov/assets/pdf/historical-statutes/1911/1911-3-penal-code-of-the-state-of-texas.pdf; *The Penal Code of the State of Texas*, 1925, Texas State Law Library, https://www.sll.texas.gov/assets/pdf/historical-statutes/1925/1925-3-penal-code-of-the-state-of-texas.pdf; *Munoz v. State*, 103 Tex. Crim. 439 (1926), quotations on 440.

14. *Vernon's Texas Statutes: 1943 Supplement* (Kansas City, MO: Vernon Law Book, 1943), Texas State Law Library, https://www.sll.texas.gov/assets/pdf/historical-statutes/1943/1943-supplement-to-1936-vernons-texas-statutes.pdf, 471.

15. *Furstonburg v. State*, 148 Tex. Crim. 638 (1945), first, second, and third quotations on 639; *Medrano v. State*, 205 S.W. 2d 588 (1947), fourth quotation on 588.

16. *Blankenship v. State*, 163 Tex. Crim. 94 (1956); *Jones v. State*, 165 Tex. Crim. 472 (1957), quotation on 473.

17. *Sinclair v. State*, 166 Tex. Crim. 167 (1958), first quotation on 169; *Shipp v. State*, 170 Tex. Crim. 615 (1961), second, third, fourth, and fifth quotations on 617.

18. Pippa Holloway and Elizabeth Catte, "Rural," in *The Routledge History of Queer America*, ed. Don Romesburg (New York: Routledge, 2018), 175–186, quotation on 179. See also Colin R. Johnson, *Just Queer Folks: Gender and Sexuality in Rural America* (Philadelphia: Temple University Press, 2013).

Chapter 1. *Buchanan v. Batchelor* **and the Evolution of the Texas Sodomy Statute, 1965–1974**

The first chapter epigraph is from Ralph G. Langley to John F. Onion Jr., August 17, 1966, quoted in W. Page Keeton and William G. Reid, "Proposed Revision of the Texas Penal Code," *Texas Law Review* 45, no. 3 (February 1967): 399–412, quotation on 402. The second chapter epigraph is from Rob Cole, "Appeal to Supreme Court on Sodomy Law to Include Gays," *Advocate*, May 13–26, 1970, 3.

1. Texas Legislature, Senate, Senate Jurisprudence Committee, Subcommittee on Criminal Matters, Regular Session, February 20, 1973, Tape 0518, side 2, Texas State Library and Archives Commission, Austin, Texas (hereafter cited as TSLAC); Texas Legislature, Senate, Senate Jurisprudence Committee, Subcommittee on Criminal Matters, Regular Session, February 20, 1973, Tape 0519, side 1, TSLAC, quotations.

2. A question that has been central to the study of queer history is how same-sex sexuality evolved from specific acts in which anyone might engage to becoming the basis of an identity. The theorist Michel Foucault located the turning point in this evolution in the late nineteenth century when, as he wrote in volume 1 of his *History of Sexuality*, "the nineteenth-century homosexual became a personage." Subsequent scholars have refined Foucault's argument. Eve Kosofsky Sedgwick, for example, has argued that at various times throughout history competing frameworks for understanding sexuality have operated simultaneously. Debates in the Texas legislature and among members of the state's penal code revision committee during the 1960s and 1970s reveal that older models focusing on same-sex acts intermingled with newer paradigms of mental disorders and identities based on sexual object choice. See Foucault, *The History of Sexuality: Volume 1, An Introduction*, trans. Robert Hurley (New York: Pantheon Books, 1978), quotation on 43; Sedgwick, *Epistemology of the Closet* (Berkeley: University of California Press, 2008); David M. Halperin, *How to*

Do the History of Homosexuality (Chicago: University of Chicago Press, 2002), 24–47; Andrew E. Clark-Huckstep, "The History of Sexuality and Historical Methodology," *Cultural History* 5, no. 2 (October 2016): 179–199; Umberto Grassi, "Acts or Identities? Rethinking Foucault on Homosexuality," *Cultural History* 5, no. 2 (October 2016): 200–221.

3. Alfred C. Kinsey, Wardell Baxter Pomeroy, and Clyde Eugene Martin, *Sexual Behavior in the Human Male* (Philadelphia: W. B. Saunders, 1948); Alfred C. Kinsey, Wardell B. Pomeroy, Clyde E. Martin, and Paul H. Gebhard, *Sexual Behavior in the Human Female* (Philadelphia: W. B. Saunders, 1953). For the life of Alfred Kinsey, see James H. Jones, *Alfred C. Kinsey: A Public/Private Life* (New York: W. W. Norton, 1997), and Jonathan Gathorne-Hardy, *Sex the Measure of All Things: A Life of Alfred C. Kinsey* (Bloomington: Indiana University Press, 1998).

4. American Law Institute, *Model Penal Code: Official Draft and Explanatory Notes: Complete Text of Model Penal Code as Adopted at the 1962 Annual Meeting of the American Law Institute of Washington, D.C., May 24, 1962* (Philadelphia: The Institute, 1985), 142–151, quotation on 145.

5. Louis B. Schwartz, "Morals Offenses and the Model Penal Code," *Columbia Law Review* 63, no. 4 (April 1963): 669–686, first quotation on 673–674, second and third quotations on 675–676. For the public/private distinction in Kinsey's work and how it affected the Model Penal Code, see David Allyn, "Private Acts/Public Policy: Alfred Kinsey, the American Law Institute and the Privatization of American Sexual Morality," *Journal of American Studies* 30, no. 3 (December 1996): 405–428. For the relationship between queer Americans and the mental health profession, see Jack Drescher and Joseph P. Merlino, eds., *American Psychiatry and Homosexuality: An Oral History* (New York: Harrington Park Press, 2007). For the connections between mid-century debates about sexual psychopath laws and sodomy law reform, see Marie-Amelie George, "The Harmless Psychopath: Legal Debates Promoting the Decriminalization of Sodomy in the United States," *Journal of the History of Sexuality* 24, no. 2 (May 2015): 225–261.

6. Keeton and Reid, "Proposed Revision"; Page Keeton and Seth S. Searcy III, "A New Penal Code for Texas," *Texas Bar Journal*, December 22, 1970, 982–984, quotation on 982; Mike Engelman, "Wilson: A Code of Punishment," *Dallas Morning News*, January 20, 1966, 2D.

7. State Bar of Texas, Committee on Revision of the Penal Code, "Outline: Review of Progress," B600.8 P371M, Legislative Reference Library of Texas, Austin, Texas (hereafter cited as LRLT), first quotation on 404; Engelman, "Wilson: A Code of Punishment," second quotation on 2D; State Bar of Texas, Committee on Revision of the Penal Code, "Revision of Texas Penal Code for Committee Meeting of April 28, 1967, Prelim. Draft," 1967, B600.8 P371WR, LRLT, third quotation on 2.

8. Keeton and Reid, "Proposed Revision," 399–412; Minutes of the State Bar of Texas, Committee on Revision of the Penal Code, April 28–29, 1967, B600.8 P371M, LRLT, quotations.

9. Page Keeton and Michael T. Johnson, "Report on Sex Offenses," May 17, 1968, Box 5, Folder 1, Frank Maloney Papers, Tarlton Law Library, University of Texas, Austin, Texas (hereafter cited as TLL), quotations on 29–31; Circle of Friends, newsletter, October 1967, Box 65, Folder 13, Resource Center LGBT Collection of the UNT Libraries, University of North Texas, Denton, Texas. For the origins of the Circle of Friends in Dallas, see James T. Sears, *Rebels, Rubyfruit, and Rhinestones: Queering Space in the Stonewall South* (New Brunswick, NJ: Rutgers University Press, 2001), 55–56.

10. State Bar of Texas, Committee on Revision of the Penal Code, "Proposed Texas Penal Code Working Papers," 1970, B600.8 P371W V. 6, LRLT, first quotation on 13; Keeton and Johnson, "Report on Sex Offenses," second, third, and fourth quotations on 30–31, fifth quotation on 29.

11. Minutes of the State Bar of Texas, Committee on Revision of the Penal Code, June 21, 1968, B600.8 P371M, LRLT, quotations on 30; Randy Von Beitel, "The Criminalization of Private Homosexual Acts: A Jurisprudential Case Study of a Decision by the Texas Bar Penal Code Revision Committee," *Human Rights* 6 (1976–1977): 23–73. In neighboring Arkansas, state legislators removed their sodomy statute in 1976, only to replace it with a new one the following year. See Brock Thompson, *The Un-Natural State: Arkansas and the Queer South* (Fayetteville: University of Arkansas Press, 2010), 78–88.

12. Minutes of the State Bar of Texas, Committee on Revision of the Penal Code, June 21, 1968, B600.8 P371M, LRLT, 31–32.

13. Minutes of the State Bar of Texas, Committee on Revision of the Penal Code, June 21, 1968, B600.8 P371M, LRLT, first quotation on 32; Carpenter, *Flagrant Conduct*, second quotation on 12; emphasis in original.

14. Von Beitel, "The Criminalization of Private Homosexual Acts," 45–46. For more on the phenomenon of reprivatizing sexual identity, see Wesley G. Phelps, "The Politics of Queer Disidentification and the Limits of Neoliberalism in the Struggle for Gay and Lesbian Equality in Houston," *Journal of Southern History* 84, no. 2 (May 2018): 311–348.

15. Von Beitel, "The Criminalization of Private Homosexual Acts," 50.

16. *Buchanan v. Batchelor*, 308 F. Supp. 729 (N.D. Tex. 1970); John Geddie, "Gossett Blisters Judges for Sodomy Law Ruling," *Dallas Morning News*, February 6, 1970, 1D.

17. David J. Garrow, *Liberty and Sexuality: The Right to Privacy and the Making of Roe v. Wade* (Berkeley: University of California Press, 1994), 398–404; Joshua Prager, "The Accidental Activist," *Vanity Fair*, February 2013, 112–113.

18. Garrow, *Liberty and Sexuality*, 398–404; Prager, "The Accidental Activist"; "Suit Filed Against Vice Unit," *Dallas Morning News*, May 29, 1969, 3D, quotation; *Griswold v. Connecticut*, 381 U.S. 479 (1965).

19. *Buchanan v. Batchelor*, 308 F. Supp. 729 (N.D. Tex. 1970); "Panel to Rule on Legality of Homosexual Law," *Dallas Morning News*, June 14, 1969, 9B.

20. "U.S. Court Hears Plea to Change Sodomy Law," *Dallas Morning News*, November 15, 1969, 3A.

21. *Buchanan v. Batchelor*, 308 F. Supp. 729 (N.D. Tex. 1970).

22. *Buchanan v. Batchelor*, 308 F. Supp. 729 (N.D. Tex. 1970), first and second quotations on 733, third and fourth quotations on 735; Earl Golz, "Sodomy Law Ruled Void by 3-Judge Court," *Dallas Morning News*, January 22, 1970, 1D.

23. "Homosexuals and the Law," *Dallas Morning News*, January 23, 1970, 2D.

24. "Council Enacts Law Against Public Sodomy," *Dallas Morning News*, January 27, 1970, 1D; "Dallas Plugs Hole with Own Sodomy Law," *Los Angeles Advocate*, April 1970, 5, first quotation; "Golman Urges Smith to Call Special Session," *Dallas Morning News*, February 20, 1970, 10A; "Golman's Bills Get Support," *Dallas Morning News*, March 9, 1971, 3, second quotation; De Orio, "The Invention of Bad Gay Sex," 53–87, esp. 66–67.

25. Geddie, "Gossett Blisters Judges," quotations on 1D; "Buchanan Still in Jail Despite 'Victory,'" *Los Angeles Advocate*, April 1970, 5.

26. A. R. Ovard, "Bouquets to Gossett," *Dallas Morning News*, February 12, 1970, 2D, first quotation; James B. Caudle, "Owes Debt to Gossett," *Dallas Morning News*, February 12, 1970, 2D, second quotation; Mrs. B. R. Tilford, "Three Cheers," *Dallas Morning News*, February 15, 1970, 2D, third and fourth quotations; Wes Drawbaugh, "Criminals' Rights," *Dallas Morning News*, February 26, 1970, 2D, fifth quotation; Larry W. Campbell, "Should Liberalize Views," *Dallas Morning News*, February 15, 1970, 2D, sixth quotation.

27. Earl Golz, "Federal Panel Stands Pat on Sodomy Law Voidance," *Dallas Morning News*, February 21, 1970, 1D; "Ruling on Sodomy Appealed," *Dallas Morning News*, April 22, 1970, 4A.

28. "Sodomy Ruling Appealed by Wade to High Court," *Dallas Morning News*, August 6, 1970, 1D.

29. Golz, "Federal Panel Stands Pat"; "Buchanan Writes from Jail," *Los Angeles Advocate*, April 29–May 12, 1970, 5, all quotations; "Buchanan Still in Jail."

30. "Buchanan Writes from Jail," quotations on 5; "Circle of Friends Did Support Buchanan, President Replies," *Advocate*, May 13–26, 1970, 3. For more on Frank Kameny, see David K. Johnson, *The Lavender Scare: The Cold War Persecution of Gays and Lesbians in the Federal Government* (Chicago: University of

Chicago Press, 2004), esp. 179–208; and Eric Cervini, *The Deviant's War: The Homosexual vs. The United States of America* (New York: Farrar, Straus, and Giroux, 2020).

31. Cole, "Appeal to Supreme Court."

32. "Circle of Friends Did Support Buchanan"; "Dallas Sodomy Case Is Now Most Important One Ever," *Advocate*, May 13–26, 1970, 3, all quotations.

33. *Younger v. Harris*, 401 U.S. 37 (1971), first quotation on 401; Saralee Tiede, "Lower Courts Ordered to Reconsider Rulings," *Dallas Morning News*, March 30, 1971, 13A, second quotation.

34. "Dallas DA Goes All Out on Traffic in Public Toilets," *Advocate*, August 18–31, 1971, 5, all quotations; "Sodomy Prosecutions Have Been Renewed," *Dallas Morning News*, July 12, 1971, 3D.

35. *Buchanan v. State*, 471 S.W. 2d 401 (1971), quotations on 404; "Court Takes Action on Two Morals Cases," *Dallas Morning News*, July 15, 1971, 10A.

36. *Buchanan v. Batchelor*, 308 F. Supp. 729 (N.D. Tex. 1970); Page Keeton, "Report on Violation of Privacy," March 16, 1970, B600.8 P371R, Texas Penal Code Revision Project, LRLT, quotation on 13.

37. "Homosexual to Be Topic of Meeting," *Dallas Morning News*, April 9, 1970, 15AA, first quotation; Martha Man, "Little Change Seen in Texas Law on Sodomy," *Dallas Times Herald*, April 19, 1970, 39, 45, second and third quotations on 39.

38. Roland A. Brinkley Jr., John C. Watkins, Donald J. Weisenhorn, and George G. Killinger, "The Laws Against Homosexuality," *Criminal Justice Monograph*, Vol. 2, no. 4 (1970), Institute of Contemporary Corrections and the Behavioral Sciences, Sam Houston State University, Huntsville, Texas, Z S205.7 C868, LRLT, first quotation on 2, second quotation on 62, third quotation on 64.

39. Page Keeton, Texas Penal Code Revision Project, "Offenses Against the Person," October 26, 1970, B600.8 P371OF, LRLT, quotation on 4; Keeton and Searcy, "A New Penal Code for Texas"; "Texas Penal Code Faces Revisions," *Dallas Morning News*, November 8, 1970, 12A.

40. "Penal Code Revision Gets Chamber Praise," *Dallas Morning News*, January 16, 1971, 4D, first quotation; "Wade Asks More Time," *Dallas Morning News*, February 10, 1971, 2D; John Geddie, "Revision of Code Step Away," *Dallas Morning News*, February 21, 1971, 20A, second quotation.

41. Henry Tatum, "Police Chiefs Oppose Change in Penal Code," *Dallas Morning News*, February 6, 1971, 1D, first quotation; "City Council Supports Delay of State Penal Code Revision," *Dallas Morning News*, February 18, 1971, 3D, second quotation; "Law Dean Raps Penal Code Critics," *Dallas Morning News*, March 16, 1971, 4B, third quotation.

42. John Geddie, "Searcy Defends New Penal Code," *Dallas Morning News*, February 23, 1971, 5A, first and second quotations; State Bar of Texas, Committee on Revision of Penal Code, "The Proposed Texas Penal Code: A Reply to Its Critics I," March 1, 1971, B600.8 P371C, LRLT, third, fourth, fifth, and sixth quotations.

43. Carol S. Vance, "Prepared Remarks Concerning the Revision of the Texas Penal Code," March 1, 1971, B600.8 P371V, LRLT.

44. "Law Dean Raps," first quotation on 4B; John Geddie, "Wade, Legislators Continue Hassle," *Dallas Morning News*, March 21, 1971, 37A, second, third, fourth, and fifth quotations; John Geddie, "Argument Continues Over Revised Code," *Dallas Morning News*, March 21, 1971, 10A.

45. "Texas Reform: Better Than Nothing?," *Advocate*, April 14–27, 1971, 8, 14, quotations on 8.

46. A. R. Stout, "The Proposed Keeton Code Et Al Should Be Defeated," April 16, 1971, 345 ST77, LRLT, first and second quotations on 1, third quotation on 2, fourth and fifth quotations on 4, sixth quotation on 20.

47. Robert Heard, "Wade Big Influence on Code Decision," *Dallas Morning News*, May 16, 1971, 32A, first quotation; "Penal Reform Dies in Senate," *Dallas Morning News*, May 28, 1971, 3D, second quotation.

48. *Everette v. State*, 465 S.W. 2d 162 (1971), quotation on 162. Although *Pruett v. State* involved forcible rape, state judges used the case as another opportunity to comment on both Judge Hughes's opinion in *Buchanan v. Batchelor* and the constitutionality of Article 524. The privacy precedent established by the US Supreme Court in *Griswold*, according to Judge P. J. Woodley, could not be applied outside the bounds of marriage, and he refused to abide by Judge Hughes's *Buchanan* ruling. See *Pruett v. State*, 463 S.W. 2d 191 (1970).

49. *Dawson v. Vance*, 329 F. Supp. 1320 (1971).

50. *Dawson v. Vance*, 329 F. Supp. 1320 (1971); Allan Turner, "Ben Levy, Founder of Local ACLU Made His Mark," *Houston Chronicle*, April 11, 2004, https://www.chron.com/news/houston-texas/article/Ben-Levy-founder-of-local-ACLU-made-his-mark-1962119.php.

51. *Dawson v. Vance*, 329 F. Supp. 1320 (1971), first and second quotations on 1322, third quotation on 1327.

52. *Turner v. State*, 497 S.W. 2d 593 (1973); *Lee v. State*, 505 S.W. 2d 816 (1974); Terry Kliewer, "Penal Code Plan Up for Revision," *Dallas Morning News*, February 18, 1972, 3D; "Penal Code Progress," *Dallas Morning News*, May 24, 1972, 2D; State Bar Committee on Revision of the Texas Penal Code, "Texas Penal Code: A Proposed Revision, Final Draft," October 1972, LRLT.

53. State Bar Committee on Revision of the Texas Penal Code, "Texas Penal

Code"; Stewart Davis, "State Bar Group Releases Newly-Revised Penal Code," *Dallas Morning News*, January 4, 1973, 13A, quotation.

54. Texas Legislature, Senate, Senate Jurisprudence Committee, Subcommittee on Criminal Matters, Regular Session, February 20, 1973, Tape 0518, side 1, TSLAC; Texas Criminal Defense Lawyers Association, "Provisions of Proposed Penal Code (S.B. 34 by Herring) Objectionable to Texas Criminal Defense Lawyers Association," February 21, 1973, 345 T312, LRLT, first and second quotations; Texas Legislature, Senate, Senate Jurisprudence Committee, Subcommittee on Criminal Matters, Regular Session, February 20, 1973, Tape 0518, side 2, TSLAC, third quotation.

55. Texas Legislature, Senate, Senate Jurisprudence Committee, Subcommittee on Criminal Matters, Regular Session, February 20, 1973, Tape 0518, side 2, TSLAC; Texas Legislature, Senate, Senate Jurisprudence Committee, Subcommittee on Criminal Matters, Regular Session, February 20, 1973, Tape 0519, side 1, TSLAC, quotations. For more on Stokes, Milam, and the movement for gay and lesbian equality at the University of Texas and in the city of Austin, see Eric Jason Ganther, "From Closet to Crusade: The Struggle for Lesbian-Gay Civil Rights in Austin, Texas, 1970–1982," master's thesis, University of Texas at Austin, 1990, esp. 51–52.

56. Texas Legislature, Senate, Senate Jurisprudence Committee, Subcommittee on Criminal Matters, Regular Session, February 20, 1973, Tape 0519, side 1, TSLAC.

57. Dotty Griffith, "Lower Penalties Seen in Victimless Crimes," *Dallas Morning News*, March 12, 1973, 21A; David Morris, "Revise Sodomy Law," *Texas Observer*, March 16, 1973, 19, newspaper clipping, National Organization for the Reform of Sodomy Laws, Assorted Documents, 1972–1973, David Morris Papers, Box 1, Folder 5, Austin History Center, Austin, Texas, quotations.

58. "SB 34: The Penal Code of Texas, Passed by the 63rd Regular Session of the Legislature, Signed by Governor Dolph Briscoe," June 14, 1973, L1800.8 P371, LRLT; "Penal Code Progress"; "Toward a New Penal Code," *Dallas Morning News*, May 18, 1973, 2D; Sam Kinch Jr., "Penal Code Given Boost," *Dallas Morning News*, May 22, 1973, 11B; Carl Freund, "Crime Is Changing," *Dallas Morning News*, December 25, 1973, 9.

Chapter 2. The Texas Homosexual Conduct Law in Action, 1974–1982

The first chapter epigraph is from Randy Von Beitel, "Gay Law: Section 21.06 Has to Go!," *Community News: Gay Paper of North Texas*, December 1974, 4. The second chapter epigraph is from "Fort Worth Gay Fights and Wins Job Discrimination Issue," *Community News*, August 1975, 1.

1. Don Mason, "'More at Ease,' Young Risher Says," *Dallas Morning News*, December 19, 1975, 30, quotations; Don Mason, "Custody Undecided," *Dallas*

Morning News, December 23, 1975, 5; Amelia De Luna-Owsley, "Risher v. Risher," *Handbook of Texas Online,* https://www.tshaonline.org/handbook /entries/risher-v-risher. For a broader history of the challenges facing gay and lesbian parents, see Daniel Winunwe Rivers, *Radical Relations: Lesbian Mothers, Gay Fathers, and Their Children in the United States since World War II* (Chapel Hill: University of North Carolina Press, 2013); and Carlos A. Ball, *Same Sex Marriage and Children: A Tale of History, Social Science, and Law* (New York: Oxford University Press, 2014).

2. "Jury Seated in Lesbian Child Custody Case," *Dallas Morning News,* December 17, 1975, 41; Don Mason, "Lesbian Involved in Child Custody Case," *Dallas Morning News,* December 18, 1975, 59, first quotation; Mason, "Custody Undecided," second quotation; "2 Experts Say Risher Boy Stable with Lesbian Mother," *Dallas Morning News,* December 20, 1975, 24.

3. Don Mason, "Jury Awards Custody of 9-Year-Old to Father Rather Than Lesbian Mother," *Dallas Morning News,* December 24, 1975, 1, quotation; "Lesbian, in a Texas Trial, Loses Son to Ex-Husband," *New York Times,* December 24, 1975, 42; "Anthony Fred 'Tony' Liscio, 1940–2017," obituary, *Dallas Morning News,* June 21, 2017, https://obits.dallasnews.com/obituaries/dallasmorningnews /obituary.aspx?n=anthony-fred-liscio-tony&pid=185866565&fhid=11533.

4. The historian Stephen Robertson has urged social historians of the twentieth century to pay particular attention to the ways criminal statutes operated in the lives of those they targeted. In this chapter, I seek to understand how 21.06 affected queer Texans, even those who were never arrested for violations. This chapter relies primarily on gay and lesbian publications to reveal how 21.06 affected the everyday lives of queer Texans. As the historian Jim Downs has argued, these publications were critical to the establishment of gay and lesbian communities because they "allowed people to communicate across regional and often national boundaries," particularly by providing a forum, among other things, "to report on the violence and crimes committed against gay people." See Stephen Robertson, "What's Law Got to Do with It?," *Journal of the History of Sexuality* 14, no. 2 (January–April 2005): 161–185, and Jim Downs, *Stand by Me: The Forgotten History of Gay Liberation* (New York: Basic Books, 2016), 113–141, quotation on 118.

5. Robert Finklea, "4 Investigators Hired for City Vice Squad," *Dallas Morning News,* August 29, 1974, 8, quotation; "Dallas Bartender Beaten in Police Raid," *Contact,* April 16, 1975, 40; "Police Beating Sparks Dallas Political Plans," *Contact,* May 28, 1975, 29. For police harassment in other cities, see Marc Stein, *City of Sisterly and Brotherly Loves: Lesbian and Gay Philadelphia, 1945–1972* (Philadelphia: Temple University Press, 2004), 78–79, 155–161, 179–184, 274–277; Elizabeth Lapovsky Kennedy and Madeline D. Davis, *Boots of Leather, Slippers of Gold: The History of a Lesbian Community* (New York: Routledge, 2014), 55, 64, 74, 92, 145–147, 189; Esther Newton, *Cherry Grove, Fire Island: Sixty Years in America's First Gay and Lesbian Town* (Boston: Beacon

Press, 1993), 187–201; George Chauncey, *Gay New York: Gender, Urban Culture, and the Making of the Gay Male World, 1890–1940* (New York: Basic Books, 1994), 146–149, 210–217, 249–250, 331–332, 337–349; D'Emilio, *Sexual Politics, Sexual Communities,* 110–111, 182–184, 187–188, 206–207; Johnson, *The Lavender Scare,* 60–63, 153–154, 175–178, 191–192; John Howard, *Men Like That: A Southern Queer History* (Chicago: University of Chicago Press, 2001), 142–173; Nan Alamilla Boyd, *Wide-Open Town: A History of Queer San Francisco to 1965* (Berkeley: University of California Press, 2003), 110–121, 214–218, 233–236; Peter Boag, *Same-Sex Affairs: Constructing and Controlling Homosexuality in the Pacific Northwest* (Berkeley: University of California Press, 2003), 54–55, 150; Stewart-Winter, *Queer Clout,* 78–80, 87, 93–94, and "Queer Law and Order: Sex, Criminality, and Policing in the Late Twentieth-Century United States," *Journal of American History* 102, no. 1 (June 2015): 61–72; Joey L. Mogul, Andrea J. Ritchie, and Kay Whitlock, *Queer (In)Justice: The Criminalization of LGBT People in the United States* (Boston: Beacon Press, 2011), 45–68.

6. "Police Stage Raid on Dallas Baths," *Contact,* October 8, 1975, 6; Henry Tatum, "Homosexual Club Issue Viewed at State Level," *Dallas Morning News,* November 3, 1976, 1D, first and second quotations; "Dallas Police Begin Bar Raids," *Advocate,* December 15, 1976, 10, third quotation; "Police Become Bored with Real Crime," *This Week in Texas,* May 14, 1977, 7, 9; King T. Solomon, "Comment," *This Week in Texas,* August 12–18, 1978, 21, 23. For a longer history of bathhouses in queer communities, see Chauncey, *Gay New York,* 207–225; and Allan Bérubé, "The History of Gay Bathhouses," *Journal of Homosexuality* 44, no. 3–4 (2003): 33–53.

7. Hardy K. Haberman, "Police Harassment," letter to the editor, *This Week in Texas,* February 8–14, 1980, 21, 23, quotation; "DGPC Update on Violence," *This Week in Texas,* May 16–22, 1980, 11–12; "Village Station vs. Dallas Police," *This Week in Texas,* November 2–8, 1979, 7; Michael Cline, interview by Morgan Gieringer and Wesley G. Phelps, January 8, 2021, video available at https://texashistory.unt.edu/ark:/67531/metadc1750935. For a longer history of the discriminatory enforcement of public lewdness and disorderly conduct statutes, see Chauncey, *Gay New York,* 171–173.

8. "GPC Documents Harassment," *This Week in Texas,* January 25–31, 1980, 8–9, first quotation; "DPD Officer Under Investigation," *This Week in Texas,* March 21–27, 1980, 12; "DGPC Intervenes on Famous Case," *This Week in Texas,* March 28–April 3, 1980, 7, 9; "Dallas Police Raid Bars," *This Week in Texas,* February 1–7, 1980, 7, 9; "Successful Police Harassment Forum," *This Week in Texas,* February 15–21, 1980, 7, 9, second quotation on 9; "DGPC Update on Violence"; "DAIR Fund-Raising," *This Week in Texas,* May 23–29, 1980, 19–20.

9. M. R. Williams, "Gays, Straights, Cops and Violence," letter to the editor, *This Week in Texas,* July 13–19, 1979, 15.

10. "The Trial in Galveston," *This Week in Texas*, August 7–13, 1976, 14–15, first quotation on 14, second quotation on 14–15; "July 4th Raid," *This Week in Texas*, July 10–16, 1976, 7; "40 Men Busted at Texas Bath," *Advocate*, September 8, 1976, 10; "Dancers Arrested," *This Week in Texas*, July 24–30, 1976, 16.

11. "Police Accused of Harassing Gay Bars and Bookstores," *Montrose Star*, July 23–29, 1976, 1; "Police Harassment Beginning," *Nuntius*, July 23, 1976, 1, quotations. For the significance of restaurants and cafeterias in queer communities, see Chauncey, *Gay New York*, 163–168.

12. Ray Hill, "Comment," *This Week in Texas*, November 6–12, 1976, 21–22, 25, first and second quotations on 21; Ray Hill, "Comment," *This Week in Texas*, March 19–25, 1977, 47–50, third and fourth quotations on 50.

13. Bob Jones, "Dear Residents and Visitors to the Montrose Area," *This Week in Texas*, August 20–26, 1977, 7–13, quotations on 7.

14. "Police Go Mad, Bust Gay Bars," *Star*, January 13, 1978, 7–9, first quotation on 8; "The Locker Raid," *LXIX*, January 25–31, 1978, 4–6, second quotation on 4; "Bar Raid," *This Week in Texas*, March 18–24, 1978, 49, third quotation.

15. A Montrose Citizen, "Apathetic Gays and Helpful Gays," letter to the editor, *This Week in Texas*, June 22–28, 1979, 27; "Houston Arson Rampage," *This Week in Texas*, August 24–30, 1979, 7, quotation; "Violence in Gay Montrose," *This Week in Texas*, August 31–September 6, 1979, 7; "Ten Montrose Murders Unsolved," *This Week in Texas*, October 5–11, 1979, 9.

16. "Mary's vs. Houston Police," *This Week in Texas*, November 2–8, 1979, 7; Mike Catrett, "HPD Still Won't Let Up," letter to the editor, *This Week in Texas*, November 9–15, 1979, 15; "Houston Police Raid Bars," *This Week in Texas*, February 1–7, 1980, 7; Jone Devlin, "Mary's Tradition Continues Under New Ownership," *Texas Triangle*, January 3, 2003, 1, quotation.

17. "61 Arrested at Mary's," *This Week in Texas*, June 27–July 3, 1980, 9–11, first quotation on 9; Art Tomaszewski, "61 Feted in 3rd Annual Mary's Bust," *Upfront America*, July 4, 1980, 7, second quotation; "Owner and Manager in Jail Overnight," *This Week in Texas*, June 27–July 3, 1980, 11–12, third quotation; Paul J. Theall, "Proud to Be . . . in Jail," letter to the editor, *This Week in Texas*, June 27–July 3, 1980, 23–24; Carl James, "Harassment in Houston," *This Week in Texas*, July 25–31, 1980, 33–39; "Last Two 'Mary's Fairies' Win Their Court Appeals," *Montrose Voice*, February 26, 1982, 3; "Police Official Counters Gays' Denouncing Raid," *Houston Chronicle*, June 21, 1980, newspaper clipping, Newspaper Clipping Files, Folder GPC Houston 1980, Botts Collection of Lesbian, Gay, Bisexual, and Transgender History, Kindred Montrose, Houston, Texas.

18. "GPC Secretary Fred Paez Shot and Killed," *This Week in Texas*, July 4–10, 1980, 10–11, 13.

19. "Investigation Probes Paez Death," *This Week in Texas*, July 4–10, 1980,

13–14; Barbara Canetti, "Gun That Killed Paez Couldn't Have Discharged Accidentally, Expert Says," *Houston Post*, July 2, 1980; Fred King and Barbara Canetti, "Source Says Officer was Drinking Before Shooting," *Houston Post*, July 8, 1980; Debra Danburg, "Task Force Tackles Paez Killing," *Upfront America*, August 29, 1980, 1, 14; "Cop Indicted in Paez Killing," *Upfront America*, October 24, 1980, 3; "Jury Finds McCoy Not Guilty," *This Week in Texas*, September 11–17, 1981, 9.

20. David and Cheree, "We Were Nearly Killed," letter to the editor, *This Week in Texas*, October 3–9, 1980, 19, first, second, third, and fifth quotations; "HPD Beats Up Unlucky Dozen," *This Week in Texas*, October 3–9, 1980, 9, fourth quotation.

21. Happy Foundation, "Oral History of Harassment of San Antonio Gay Bars," November 22, 1993, Texas Archive of the Moving Image, https://texasarchive .org/2018_03978. For histories of military policies regarding sexual orientation, see Allan Bérubé, *Coming Out Under Fire: The History of Gay Men and Women in World War Two* (New York: Free Press, 1990); Leisa Meyer, *Creating GI Jane: Sexuality and Power in the Women's Army Corps during World War II* (New York: Columbia University Press, 1996); and Margot Canaday, *The Straight State: Sexuality and Citizenship in Twentieth-Century America* (Princeton, NJ: Princeton University Press, 2009), 55–90, 174–213. For the ways the military's off-limits policy operated in San Francisco, see Boyd, *Wide-Open Town*, 114–117.

22. "Military Madness Meets the Gays," *Together Gay*, April 1974, 3; Happy Foundation, "Oral History of Harassment."

23. "Top Story of 1980: Harassment and Violence," *This Week in Texas*, December 26, 1980–January 1, 1981, 9–11, quotation on 9.

24. Downs, *Stand by Me*, 17–40; Sears, *Rebels, Rubyfruit, and Rhinestones*, 100–103. See also Robert W. Fieseler, *Tinderbox: The Untold Story of the Up Stairs Lounge Fire and the Rise of Gay Liberation* (New York: Norton, 2018).

25. "Farmhouse Destroyed," *Contact*, April 1974, 1–3; "Arsonist(s) Burn Farmhouse Club," *Nuntius*, April 1974, 1; "Farmhouse Offers $5000 Reward," *Contact*, May 1974, 1; "Arson Suspect in Houston Fire," *Contact*, August 13, 1975, 8, quotation.

26. "Second Sun Fire," *This Week in Texas*, October 9–15, 1976, 11; "Arson Suspected in Bullet Blaze," *This Week in Texas*, October 15–21, 1977, 7; "Bullet Burned by Arsonist," *Star*, February 17, 1978, 3; "Fire Hits Bullet," *LXIX*, February 23–March 1, 1978, 15–18, first quotation on 15; "Houston Arson," *This Week in Texas*, March 10–16, 1979, 46; "Fire Hits Mary's," *LXIX*, March 11–18, 1978, 15–18; "Gay Fires: Topic of Discussion," *LXIX*, April 1–7, 1978, 14–20, second quotation on 14, third quotation on 20.

27. "Gay Bar Burns," *LXIX*, May 26–June 1, 1978, 36; "Arson Strikes Again," *This Week in Texas*, January 6–12, 1979, 35; "Silver Phoenix Fire," *This Week in Texas*, June 15–21, 1979, 58; "Houston Arson Rampage."

28. "Sampling Texas," *This Week in Texas,* January 24–30, 1976, 7; David Bauer, "Lords of an Underground Empire," *D Magazine,* June 1, 1979, https://www.dmagazine.com/publications/d-magazine/1979/june/lords-of-an-underground-empire/; "Coping with Charred Chiffon," *This Week in Texas,* November 5–11, 1977, 7; "Dallas Restaurant Target of Arsonist," *This Week in Texas,* October 12–18, 1979, 10.

29. "Fort Worth Gay Fights and Wins," first quotation on 1; "Complaint Filed Over Dismissal," *Dallas Morning News,* May 24, 1975, 8; Henry Tatum, "Board Rejects Claims," *Dallas Morning News,* July 2, 1975, 7; "Civil Service Board Denies Discrimination Against Gay Dallas City Employee," *Community News,* July 1975, 10; "Up Front," *This Week in Texas,* November 26–December 2, 1977, 9, second quotation. For more on Gary Van Ooteghem, see Phelps, "The Politics of Queer Disidentification," 311–348, esp. 322–323.

30. Charles Maples to William H. Nelson, September 21, 1979, Box 1, Folder 37, William H. "Bill" Nelson Jr. and Jean Nelson Collection (*The Dallas Way*), 1970–2011, University of North Texas Special Collections, Denton, Texas; "Dallas School Teacher to Fight for Job," *This Week in Texas,* October 5–11, 1979, 9–10; Mike Anglin, "William H. 'Bill' Nelson," May 10, 2015, *The Dallas Way,* http://www.thedallasway.org/stories/written/written-stories/2015/5/10/william-h-bill-nelson; "Texas Teacher Gets Job Back," *This Week in Texas,* October 19–25, 1979, 10, quotation; "Counselor Faces Lewdness Charge," *Mesquite Daily News,* October 17, 1979, 1; "Mesquite High School Counselor Commits Suicide: Newspaper Blamed," *This Week in Texas,* November 9–15, 1979, 9–11; "Up Front," *This Week in Texas,* January 20–26, 1979, 7.

31. "Houston's Law Leaves Gays Out," *Contact,* March 19, 1975, 3, first quotation; Ganther, "From Closet to Crusade," 176–179, second quotation on 178.

32. Gene Leggett, "A Food Stamp Odyssey—or—Faggots Need Food, Too," *Together Gay,* September 1974, 7–10, quotations; "Leggett Loses Reinstatement Try," *Community News,* July 1975, 6.

33. "UT-Austin Told to Accept," *Contact,* May 1974, 5; *Gay Student Services v. Texas A&M University,* 737 F. 2d 1317 (5th Cir. 1984), quotations; Sherri Skinner, interview by Kevin Bailey, December 9, 1984, Box 1, Folder 1, Kevin Bailey Collection, 1976–1990, LGBTQ Archive, Cushing Memorial Library and Archives, Texas A&M University, College Station, Texas.

34. Minutes of the Southern Region Caucus of the Texas Gay Task Force, September 28, 1977, Texas Gay Conference Materials, June 1978, J. D. Doyle Collection, houstonlgbthistory.org/misc-tgc.html, quotation; "TGTF Outlines Plans for Fighting Discrimination," *Star,* October 21–27, 1977, 7.

35. Canaday, *The Straight State,* 214–247, quotation on 247. See also Marc Stein, *Sexual Injustice: Supreme Court Decisions from Griswold to Roe* (Chapel Hill: University of North Carolina Press, 2010), 57–93; and Luibhéid, *Entry Denied.*

36. Richard Longstaff, interview by Karen Wisely, August 4, 2013, OH 1817,

UNT Oral Histories, University of North Texas, Denton, Texas, 3–10; Richard Longstaff, interview by Mike Anglin, March 31, 2014, *The Dallas Way*, thedallasway.org/stories/written/2017/12/8/richard-longstaff.

37. Richard Longstaff, interview by Karen Wisely, August 4, 2013, OH 1817, UNT Oral Histories, University of North Texas, Denton, Texas, 22–26; Richard Longstaff, interview by Mike Anglin, March 31, 2014, *The Dallas Way*, thedallasway .org/stories/written/2017/12/8/richard-longstaff, first, second, and third quotations; Longstaff v. INS, Brief of Appellee, n.d. (1979), Box 62, Folder Record of Richard John Longstaff v. INS, Resource Center LGBT Collection of the UNT Libraries, 1940–2011, University of North Texas, Denton, Texas (hereafter cited as Resource Center LGBT Collection); Ann Zimmerman, "A Gay's American Dream," *Dallas Times Herald*, February 20, 1983, 1H, 3H–4H, fourth quotation.

38. Richard Longstaff, interview by Karen Wisely, August 4, 2013, OH 1817, UNT Oral Histories, University of North Texas, Denton, Texas, 27, third, fourth, fifth, and sixth quotations; Richard Longstaff, interview by Mike Anglin, March 31, 2014, *The Dallas Way*, thedallasway.org/stories/written/2017/12/8 /richard-longstaff, first and second quotations; Longstaff v. INS, Brief of Appellee, n.d. (1979), Box 62, Folder Record of Richard John Longstaff v. INS, Resource Center LGBT Collection, seventh quotation.

39. "'P' or 'H,'" *This Week in Texas*, February 5–11, 1977, 8, first quotation; Elizabeth Kastor, "It's a Wrap: Dallas Kills Film Board," *Washington Post*, August 13, 1993, https://www.washingtonpost.com/archive/lifestyle/1993 /08/13/its-a-wrap-dallas-kills-film-board/9e1f623b-d2c0-419d-a82c -4070bd3307b6/, second quotation; "Fort Worth Newspaper Labels Gays Child Molesters," *This Week in Texas*, February 26–March 4, 1977, 7; Louise Young and Campbell B. Read to Roger Bearwolf, April 26, 1979, Box 494, Folder Don Baker Correspondence, Resource Center LGBT Collection.

40. "TWT Labeled Pornographic," *This Week in Texas*, December 18–24, 1976, 7, quotation; "A Censor Is Someone Telling You That You Are Not Capable of Deciding for Yourself What You Like or Dislike," *This Week in Texas*, February 26–March 4, 1977, 37; "Up Front," *This Week in Texas*, January 20–26, 1979, 7; "This Week," *This Week in Texas*, March 24–30, 1979, 7; "Austin Hotel Found Guilty," *This Week in Texas*, July 20–27, 1979, 7; "Austin Straight Disco Fined for Not Allowing Same-Sex Dancing," *Montrose Star*, July 20, 1979, 1.

Chapter 3. Resisting the Effects of the Texas Homosexual Conduct Law, 1974–1982

The first chapter epigraph is from Gifford Guy Gibson and Mary Jo Risher, *By Her Own Admission: A Lesbian Mother's Fight to Keep Her Son* (New York: Doubleday, 1977), 151, 276. The second chapter epigraph is from "TWIT Visits Police Headquarters," *This Week in Texas*, August 7–13, 1976, 6.

1. Randy Von Beitel, "Gay Law: Section 21.06 Has to Go!," *Community News*, December 1974, 4.

2. "Texas Gay Conference, 1974," Texas Gay Conference Materials, June 1974, J. D. Doyle Collection, http://houstonlgbthistory.org/misc-tgc.html; Galveston Gay Society to *This Week in Texas*, July 31–August 6, 1976, 23; "Military Madness Meets the Gays!," *Together Gay*, April 1974, 3, quotations; Happy Foundation, "Oral History of Harassment of San Antonio Gay Bars," November 22, 1993, Texas Archive of the Moving Image, https://texasarchive.org /2018_03978.

3. M. Robert Schwab, Journal, n.d., Box 1, Folder 1, M. Robert Schwab Collection, MSS 344, Houston Metropolitan Research Center, Houston Public Library, Houston, Texas (hereafter cited as Schwab Collection), quotation; M. Robert Schwab, resume, n.d., Box 1, Folder 3, Schwab Collection; Don Hrachovy, Jim Cagle, and Gary J. Van Ooteghem, "Gay Political Caucus," press release, September 7, 1977, Box 1, Folder 22, Schwab Collection. For the history of the Houston Gay Political Caucus, see John Goins, "Forging a Community: The Rise of Gay Political Activism in Houston," *Houston History* 7, no. 2 (Spring 2010): 38–42; Phelps, "The Politics of Queer Disidentification," 311–348; and Sears, *Rebels, Rubyfruit, and Rhinestones*, 216–223.

4. "Sampling Texas," *This Week in Texas*, January 24–30, 1976, 6; "Sampling Texas," *This Week in Texas*, February 7–13, 1976, 6; "TWIT Visits Police Headquarters," first and second quotations on 6; Ray Hill, "We've Come a Long Way, Baby," *This Week in Texas*, August 21–27, 1976, 31, 38, 42, third and fourth quotations; Mort Schwab, "Accomplishments of the GPC," *This Week in Texas*, August 28–September 3, 1976, 25, 38; "Mayor's Assistant Holds Meeting with Gay Activist," *Montrose Star*, January 28–February 3, 1977, 2; "Human Rights League Formed," *This Week in Texas*, May 28–June 3, 1977, 7.

5. Joe Pouncy, "Gays Protest Police Enforcement," *Dallas Morning News*, November 7, 1976, 38A, first quotation; "Gay Rally Urges Fight of Discriminatory Laws," *Dallas Morning News*, November 9, 1976, 4D; "DAIR to Be Seen and Heard!," *This Week in Texas*, November 13–19, 1976, 6–7, second quotation on 7; "Dallas Won't 'Cower,'" *Advocate*, December 29, 1976, 7; King T. Solomon, "Comment," *This Week in Texas*, August 12–18, 1978, 21, 23; Norma Wade Adams, "Homosexual Club Charges Police with Harassment," *Dallas Morning News*, December 14, 1979, 59; "DAIR Endorsements," *This Week in Texas*, April 2–8, 1977, 7; Sears, *Rebels, Rubyfruit, and Rhinestones*, 55–56; Karen S. Wisely, "The 'Dallas Way' in the Gayborhood: The Creation of a Lesbian, Gay, Bisexual, and Transgender Community in Dallas, Texas, 1965–1986" (master's thesis, University of North Texas, 2011), 31–48; "Chronological History of the Dallas Gay Political Caucus," November 1978, Box 1, Folder 3, Donald F. Baker Collection, University of North Texas Special Collections, Denton, Texas (hereafter cited as Baker Collection); Dallas Gay Political Caucus, "Goals of the Dallas Gay Political Caucus," n.d., Box

1, Folder 3, Baker Collection; Texas Gay Task Force, "Texas Gay Conference III," June 18–20, 1976, J. D. Doyle Collection, "Houston LGBT History," http://www.houstonlgbthistory.org/misc-tgc.html.

6. "Gay Political Caucus Operation: Documentation," *This Week in Texas*, February 17–23, 1979, 7, 54; "A Spring Rally," *This Week in Texas*, April 6–12, 1979, 7; "Leaders Hope for Large Turnout for Tuesday Gay Rally at City Hall," *Montrose Star*, April 9, 1979, 1; "This Week," *This Week in Texas*, April 13–19, 1979, 7; "Shifflet Subpoenaed," *This Week in Texas*, June 6–14, 1979, 7; "Operation Documentation," *This Week in Texas*, June 15–21, 1979, 7, quotation; "Gay Lawyer Named," *This Week in Texas*, September 7–13, 1979, 8; "Operation Documentation Comes to Dallas," *This Week in Texas*, May 18–24, 1979, 7; "Dallas Operation Documentation," *This Week in Texas*, August 17–23, 1979, 7; "GPC Documents Harassment," *This Week in Texas*, January 25–31, 1980, 8–9.

7. "First-Hand Report on Houston Police Arrogance," *Montrose Star*, June 7, 1979, 10, quotations; "Star Publisher Arrested by Houston Cops," *Montrose Star*, June 7, 1979, 3; "Montrose Star vs. Houston Police," *Montrose Star*, July 27, 1979, 8.

8. "First-Hand Report"; "Star Publisher Arrested"; "Montrose Star vs. Houston Police," quotation on 8; Henry McClurg, "Important Legal Events Occurred Recently," *Montrose Star*, August 23, 1979, 10; "One of Mary's Twelve Found Guilty," *This Week in Texas*, September 19–25, 1980, 9.

9. "Village Station vs Dallas Police," *This Week in Texas*, November 2–8, 1979, 7; "Lewdness Trial Lasts Two Days," *This Week in Texas*, March 21–27, 1980, 9, 11; Christi Harlan, "Hearing to Study County Charges of Judicial Bias," *Dallas Morning News*, May 2, 1980; Christi Harlan, "Wade Inquiry Sought," *Dallas Morning News*, August 2, 1980; "Dallas D.A. Admits Forum-Shopping," *This Week in Texas*, August 22–28, 1980, 12–13; Don Maison, interview by Karen Wisely, July 30, 2013, OH 1796, Special Collections of the UNT Libraries, University of North Texas, Denton, Texas, 24–26; Michael Cline, interview by Morgan Gieringer and Wesley G. Phelps, January 8, 2021, video available at https://texashistory.unt.edu/ark:/67531/metadc1750935.

10. Richard Craig Schwiderski, personal information and arrest affidavit, October 26, 1979, The Portal to Texas History, https://texashistory.unt.edu/ark:/67531/metadc1752742/?q=Schwiderski, first quotation; *State of Texas v. Richard Craig Schwiderski*, "Memorandum in Support of Defendant's Motion to Quash Information," June 11, 1980, The Portal to Texas History, https://texashistory.unt.edu/ark:/67531/metadc965297/?q=schwiderski%20motion%20to%20quash; *Richard Craig Schwiderski v. the State of Texas*, "Brief for the Appellee: Richard Craig [Schwiderski] v. the State of Texas," June 22, 1981, The Portal to Texas History, https://texashistory.unt.edu/ark:/67531/metadc965388/?q=schwiderski%20brief%20from%20the%20appellee; Christi Harlan, "Bible-Toters Watch 'Parade of Perverts,'" *Dallas*

Morning News, August 29, 1980, 1A, 11A, second and third quotations; "Disco Dance Demo in Lewdness Trial," *This Week in Texas,* September 19–25, 1980, 9–10; "Lewdness Conviction Ends Cases," *Dallas Morning News,* November 1, 1980; "Village Station Cases Closed," *This Week in Texas,* November 7–13, 1980, 11.

11. "Sunset Blvd vs. San Antonio Police," *This Week in Texas,* June 6–12, 1980, 16.

12. *Donoho v. State,* 628 S.W. 2d 483 (1982), first quotation on 484, second and third quotations on 485. For sexual contact, see *Resnick v. State,* 574 S.W. 2d 558 (1978). Interestingly, a three-judge appellate panel overturned John Herring's public lewdness conviction in 1982 on the grounds that Herring had only allowed his genitals to be touched by another man in public. Herring "cannot be guilty of the offense charged," the panel concluded, "because 'allowing' is not an act (and therefore not conduct as defined in the Penal Code)." *Herring v. State,* 633 S.W. 2d 905 (1982), quotation on 909. The opinion seemed not to have enjoyed much precedential effect, as courts continued to convict gay men for "allowing" certain acts to be performed on them.

13. Elaine Bonilla, "Montrose Patrol," *This Week in Texas,* February 8–14, 1980, 23–24; " 'Bang Bang, Queer' 7 Arrested in 28 Minutes," *This Week in Texas,* October 5–11, 1979, 9, quotations; "Montrose Patrol Restructures," *This Week in Texas,* May 23–29, 1980, 9.

14. "Complaint Filed Over Dismissal," *Dallas Morning News,* May 24, 1975, 8; "Ft. Worth Gay Fights and Wins Job Discrimination Issue," *Community News,* August 1975, 1; "Up Front," *This Week in Texas,* December 16–22, 1978, 7; "Texas Teacher Gets Job Back," *This Week in Texas,* October 19–25, 1979, 10.

15. Ganther, "From Closet to Crusade," 180–194; "Council Majority Supports Fair Housing," ALGPC Newsletter, August 1981, 1–2, qtd. in Ganther, "From Closet to Crusade," 182.

16. "Austin Hotel Found Guilty," *This Week in Texas,* July 20–27, 1979, 7, quotation; "Austin Straight Disco Fined for Not Allowing Same-Sex Dancing," *Montrose Star,* July 20, 1979, 1.

17. Gene Leggett, "A Food Stamp Odyssey—or—Faggots Need Food, too," *Together Gay,* September 1974, 7–10, quotation on 10.

18. "Ft. Worth Newspaper Labels Gays Child Molesters," *This Week in Texas,* February 26–March 4, 1977, 7; Bruce Buursma, "Anti-Gay Evangelist Taken Off TV," *Dallas Times Herald,* August 3, 1979, first quotation; "Dallas TV Station Sides with Gay Group, Cancels Homophobic Preacher," *Montrose Star,* March 9, 1979, 1, second quotation; Campbell Read, "Robison: The True Story," *Dialog: Newsletter of the Dallas Gay Political Caucus,* May 1979, 1, 3, Box 2, Folder 4, Tom & Tom Collection, Texas A&M Cushing Library and Archives, College Station, Texas (hereafter cited as Tom & Tom Collection); Arthur L.

Ginsburg to Campbell B. Read, June 18, 1979, Box 494, Folder 44, Resource Center LGBT Collection of the UNT Libraries, University of North Texas, Denton, Texas (hereafter cited as Resource Center LGBT Collection); "Robison Returns to WFAA-TV," *This Week in Texas*, July 6–12, 1979, 7.

19. "This Week," *This Week in Texas*, February 24–March 2, 1979, 7, first quotation; "Legislature Adjourns," *This Week in Texas*, June 8–14, 1979, 7; "Texas Gay Lobby Victories," *This Week in Texas*, June 22–28, 1979, 7, 10, third and fourth quotations on 7; "First Gay Lobby Considered a Political Success," *Montrose Star*, July 27, 1979, 3–4, second quotation on 4.

20. "Kenneth A. Cyr," obituary, *Fort Worth Star Telegram*, January 9, 1993, 21; "Fort Worth to Be Site of Texas Gay Conference," *Community News*, May 1974, 1; "Texas Gay Conference," program, June 21–23, 1974, J. D. Doyle Collection, http://www.houstonlgbthistory.org/Houston80s/Assorted%20Pubs/Texas %20Gay%20Conference/TGC-ONE-74.pdf; "Police Actions Held Legal in License Plate Listings," *Fort Worth Star Telegram*, June 27, 1974; Ken Cyr to T. S. Walls, August 25, 1974, J. D. Doyle Collection, http://www.houston lgbthistory.org/Houston80s/Assorted%20Pubs/Texas%20Gay%20Conference /TGC-ONE-74.pdf; Awareness, Unity and Research Association, press release, August 26, 1974, J. D. Doyle Collection, http://www.houstonlgbthistory .org/Houston80s/Assorted%20Pubs/Texas%20Gay%20Conference/TGC -ONE-74.pdf; "Gay Confab Pulls Crowd," *Contact*, July 31, 1974, 1, 5; "Fort Worth Harassment," *Contact*, August 28, 1974, 18.

21. "Cyr Sues Police, Is Fired at TCU," *Contact*, April 16, 1975, 12; "Suit Filed Against Fort Worth Police," *Community News*, March–April 1975, 1, 9; "Rumors," *Montrose Star*, November 19–25, 1976, 1, 13, quotation on 1; *Cyr v. Walls*, 439 F. Supp. 697 (N.D. Tex, October 31, 1977); Richard Burkhart, "The Gay Archives of Texas," letter to the editor, *This Week in Texas*, October 26–November 1, 1979, 22.

22. *Cyr v. Walls*, Agreed Judgment, March 8, 1978, Box 80, Folder Ken Cyr, Resource Center LGBT Collection; *Cyr v. Walls*, 439 F. Supp. 697 (N.D. Tex, 1977); "Ruling Stymies Surveillance of Homosexuals by Officers," *Dallas Morning News*, March 16, 1978.

23. *Gay Student Services v. Texas A&M University*, 737 F. 2d 1317 (5th Cir. 1984), quotation; *Gay Student Services v. Texas A&M University*, "Appeal from the United States District Court for the Southern District of Texas: Brief for Appellant," March 1978, Box 3, Folder 12, Tom & Tom Collection; *Gay Student Services v. Texas A&M University*, "Defendants' Original Answer, April 21, 1977, Box 3, Folder 11, Tom & Tom Collection; "Gay A&M Aggies File Federal Suit," *Montrose Star*, March 4–10, 1977, 3.

24. *Gay Student Services v. Texas A&M University*, 737 F. 2d 1317 (5th Cir. 1984).

25. Henry Tatum, "Board Rejects Claims," *Dallas Morning News*, July 2, 1975, 7;

"Civil Service Board Denies Discrimination Against Gay Dallas City Employee," *Community News*, July 1975, 10.

26. Tatum, "Board Rejects Claims," first quotation on 7; Randy Nordhem, "Gay Files Suit Against City Alleging Job Discrimination," *Dallas Morning News*, April 4, 1976, 14; Norma Adams Wade, "Homosexual Says Police Ignored His Qualifications," *Dallas Morning News*, March 20, 1980, second quotation; *Childers v. Dallas Police Department*, 513 F. Supp. 134 (N.D. Tex. 1981), third quotation on 138; "Steve Childers Sues Dallas Police," *This Week in Texas*, April 4–10, 1980, 7–8, fourth quotation on 7; "Childers's Case Undue Hardship," *This Week in Texas*, April 11–17, 1980, 8–9.

27. *Childers v. Dallas Police Department*, 513 F. Supp. 134 (N.D. Tex. 1981), first quotation on 137, second quotation on 142.

28. Don Mason, "Battle Lines Drawn on Significance of Lesbian's Child Custody Case," *Dallas Morning News*, December 21, 1975, 33, quotations; "Sampling Texas," *This Week in Texas*, January 24–30, 1976, 6; Judi Klemesrud, "Lesbian Fights to Get Son Back; Seeks Funds Here for an Appeal," *New York Times*, January 31, 1976, 45; "A Texas Mother Loses Custody of Her 9-Year-Old Son Because She Is a Lesbian," *People*, January 19, 1976, https://people.com/archive/a-texas-mother-loses-custody-of-her-9-year-old-son-because-she-is-a-lesbian-vol-5-no-2/; "Father Given Child Custody," *Breakthrough*, January 1976, 1; Laura Allen, "Lesbian Couple's Openness Cost Them Privacy," *Dallas Morning News*, May 24, 1976, 6.

29. Don Mason, "Lesbian Who Lost Custody Called Prejudice Victim," *Dallas Morning News*, December 3, 1976, 28, quotation; "Lesbian Plans Appeal," *Dallas Morning News*, January 8, 1977, 8; "Mary Jo Risher Seeks Aid," *Montrose Star*, April 1–7, 1977, 19; "Bid Denied to Reduce Lesbian's Time with Son," *Dallas Morning News*, May 28, 1977, 8; Amelia De Luna-Owsley, "Risher v. Risher," *Handbook of Texas Online*, https://www.tshaonline.org/handbook/entries/risher-v-risher; "Anne Foreman and Mary Jo Risher Discuss the Book *By Her Own Admission*," June 25, 1977, Studs Terkel Radio Archive, Chicago History Museum, studsterkel.wfmt.com/programs/anne-foreman-and-mary-jo-risher-discuss-book-her-own-admission.

30. In Re Petition of Naturalization of Richard John Longstaff, "Brief of Appellee," n.d., Box 62, Folder Record of Richard John Longstaff v. INS, Resource Center LGBT Collection, first and second quotations on 5; In Re Petition of Naturalization of Richard John Longstaff, "Appellant's Reply Brief," September 6, 1979, Box 62, Folder Longstaff v. INS Appellants Reply Brief, Resource Center LGBT Collection; *In Re Longstaff*, 631 F. 2d 731 (Fifth Cir. 1980).

31. Minutes of the Texas Human Rights Foundation Board of Directors, November 15, 1980, Box 4B39, Folder THRF Retired Minutes and Correspondence, Texas Human Rights Foundation Records, 1978–1992, Dolph Briscoe Center for American History, University of Texas, Austin, Texas (hereafter cited as

THRF Collection); In Re Longstaff, "Petitioner's Response to Findings of Fact, Conclusions of Law, and Recommendation of Designated Naturalization Examiner," March 12, 1982, Box 4B52, Folder Petition for Naturalization of Richard Longstaff, THRF Collection; In Re Petition for Naturalization of Richard John Longstaff, "Memorandum of Decision," March 23, 1982, Box 4B31, Folder Longstaff Case, THRF Collection; *In Re Longstaff*, 538 F. Supp. 589 (N.D. Tex. 1982); "Court Again Hears Appeal from Union Jack Owner," *Dallas Gay News*, February 11, 1983, 3; *Longstaff v. INS*, "Petition for a Writ of Certiorari to the United States Court of Appeals for the Fifth Circuit," October 1983, Box 4B37, Folder Immigration, THRF Collection; "Denial of Citizenship to Gay Upheld," *Houston Chronicle*, May 30, 1984, 8; William J. Choyke and Christy Hoppe, "Homosexual Loses Bid for Citizenship," *Dallas Morning News*, May 4, 1984, 1A, 7A; Richard Fly and Renee Tawa, "Dallas Gay Faces Deportation Proceedings," *Dallas Times Herald*, May 30, 1984; "Homosexual, a U.S. Resident 19 Years, Faces Deportation," *New York Times*, June 3, 1984, 17; Richard Longstaff, interview by Mike Anglin, March 31, 2014, *The Dallas Way*, thedallasway.org/stories/written/2017/12/8/richard-longstaff.

Chapter 4. *Baker v. Wade*, 1975–1986

The first chapter epigraph is from Don Baker, "News Release," August 17, 1982, Box 4B33, Folder Press Releases *Baker v. Wade*, Texas Human Rights Foundation Records, 1978–1992, Dolph Briscoe Center for American History, The University of Texas at Austin (hereafter cited as THRF Collection). The second chapter epigraph is from Lucia Valeska, "Statement Re: Baker v. Wade," August 17, 1982, Box 494, Folder Don Baker, *Baker v. Wade*, Resource Center LGBT Collection of the UNT Libraries, University of North Texas, Denton, Texas (hereafter cited as Resource Center LGBT Collection).

1. *Baker v. Wade*, 563 F. Supp. 1121 (N.D. Tex. 1982), rev'd 769 F. 2d 289 (5th Cir. 1985), *cert. denied*, 478 U.S. 1022 (1986); *Baker v. Wade*, "Record Excerpts for Appellant's Brief," July 6, 1983, Box 4B33, THRF Collection, first quotation; Maggie Watt, interview by the author, July 10, 2018, Denton, Texas, second quotation; Don Baker, speech draft, n.d., Box 494, Folder Don Baker Notes and Speeches, Resource Center LGBT Collection, third, fourth, and fifth quotations; Michele Weldon, "Don Baker's Battle: Striving to Return Humanity to the Fight for Gay Rights," *Dallas Times Herald*, January 21, 1986, B1, 8, 9; Holly Warren, "Pioneering Dallas Gay-Rights Activist Donald Baker Dies," *Dallas Morning News*, December 2, 2000, 35.

2. *Baker v. Wade*, "Record Excerpts for Appellant's Brief," July 6, 1983, Box 4B33, THRF Collection; Weldon, "Don Baker's Battle," quotations on 8; Watt interview.

3. *Baker v. Wade*, "Record Excerpts for Appellant's Brief," July 6, 1983, Box 4B33, THRF Collection, quotations; Texas Human Rights Foundation, press release,

n.d., Box 1, Folder 6, M. Robert Schwab Collection, MSS 344, Houston Metropolitan Research Center, Houston Public Library, Houston, Texas (hereafter cited as Schwab Collection).

4. *Baker v. Wade*, "Record Excerpts for Appellant's Brief," July 6, 1983, Box 4B33, THRF Collection, first, second, and fourth quotations; Don Baker, speech draft, n.d., Box 494, Folder Don Baker Notes and Speeches, Resource Center LGBT Collection, fifth quotation; Weldon, "Don Baker's Battle," third quotation on 8; Watt interview. For a history of gay and lesbian teachers, see Jackie M. Blount, *Fit to Teach: Same-Sex Desire, Gender, and School Work in the Twentieth Century* (Albany: State University of New York Press, 2004).

5. Weldon, "Don Baker's Battle," quotation on B9.

6. Mort Schwab, "Commentary," September 7, 1977, Box 1, Folder 22, Schwab Collection; "Baker v. Wade Timeline," n.d., Box 4B32, Folder THRF Correspondence 1985–1986, part 2, THRF Collection; Houston Human Rights Defense Foundation, "I.R.S. Grants Foundation Tax Exempt Status," press release, May 4, 1978, Box 4B33, Folder Correspondence 1979, THRF Collection; Mike Anglin, interview by Karen Wisely, October 24, 2015, OH 1851, Special Collections of the UNT Libraries, University of North Texas, Denton, Texas, 16–18; Dick Peeples, "Outrageous Oral," lecture, *The Dallas Way*, Dallas, Texas, January 28, 2016, available at http://www.thedallasway .org/stories/videos/2016/6/20/outrageous-oral-01-28-16-dick-peeples; Mort Schwab to Trustees of THRF, August 10, 1978, Box 4B33, Folder Correspondence 1979, THRF Collection; Mort Schwab to Ted Hoyt, June 1, 1978, Box 4B31, Folder HHRDF, THRF Collection; Mike Anglin, interview by the author, July 19, 2018, Dallas, Texas; Dick Peeples, interview by the author, July 15, 2018, Dallas, Texas.

7. J. Patrick Wiseman to Mort Schwab, February 20, 1978, Box 4B33, Folder Correspondence 1979, THRF Collection, quotations; *Roe v. Wade*, 410 U.S. 113 (1973); *Doe v. Commonwealth's Attorney*, 425 U.S. 901 (1976); *Eisenstadt v. Baird*, 405 U.S. 438 (1972); *Griswold v. Connecticut*, 381 U.S. 479 (1965); *Carey v. Population Services International*, 431 U.S. 678 (1977); *Buchanan v. Batchelor*, 308 F. Supp. 729 (N.D. Tex. 1970).

8. James C. Barber to Mort Schwab, August 7, 1978, Box 4B33, Folder Correspondence 1979, THRF Collection; Jim Barber, interview by the author, July 17, 2018, Dallas, Texas; Mike Anglin, interview by the author, July 19, 2018, Dallas, Texas; Dick Peeples, interview by the author, July 15, 2018, Dallas, Texas. For more on suspect classification, see Marcy Strauss, "Reevaluating Suspect Classification," *Seattle University Law Review* 35 (2011): 135–174; and Sharon E. Rush, "Whither Sexual Orientation Analysis? The Proper Methodology When Due Process and Equal Protection Intersect," *William and Mary Bill of Rights Journal* 16, no. 3 (March 2008): 685–745. In 1982, federal courts carved out a middle space when a law disproportionately affects a quasi-suspect class, requiring intermediate or heightened scrutiny. In

this situation, a state must demonstrate that the law in question is, according to Strauss, "substantially related to an important government purpose" (137). See *Plyler v. Doe*, 457 U.S. 202, 215–221 (1982).

9. Mort Schwab to James Barber, September 12, 1978, Box 4B33, Folder Correspondence 1979, THRF Collection; Mort Schwab to Patrick Wiseman, September 12, 1978, Box 4B33, Folder Correspondence 1979, THRF Collection; Mike Anglin, interview by Karen Wisely, October 24, 2015, OH 1851, Special Collections of the UNT Libraries, University of North Texas, Denton, Texas, 19; James C. Barber to Mort Schwab, September 13, 1978, Box 4B33, Folder Correspondence 1979, THRF Collection, first quotation; Minutes of the Texas Human Rights Foundation Board of Directors, July 7, 1979, Box 4B39, Folder THRF Retired Minutes and Correspondence, THRF Collection; James C. Barber to Dick Peeples, July 25, 1979, Box 4B33, Folder Correspondence 1979, THRF Collection; Richard H. Peeples to James C. Barber, August 3, 1979, Box 4B33, Folder Correspondence 1979, THRF Collection, second quotation; Mike Anglin, interview by the author, July 19, 2018, Dallas, Texas; Jim Barber, interview by the author, July 17, 2018, Dallas, Texas; Dick Peeples, interview by the author, July 15, 2018, Dallas, Texas.

10. "Most Officials Oppose Texas Gay Teachers," *Dallas Morning News*, October 9, 1977, 22, first quotation; Eric Miller, "DISD Ban on Gays Told," *Dallas Morning News*, October 7, 1977, 1, second quotation; Don Baker, "Making the Grade: Dallas and Its Schools Have Come a Long Way in Dealing with Gay Issues," *This Week in Texas*, May 10–16, 1996, third quotation; Eric Miller, "Gay Estimates 10% of City Teachers are Homosexual," *Dallas Morning News*, October 9, 1977, 35, fourth quotation; "Chronological History of the Dallas Gay Political Caucus," November 1978, Box 1, Folder 3, Donald F. Baker Collection, University of North Texas Special Collections, Denton, Texas (hereafter cited as Baker Collection).

11. Baker, "Making the Grade"; Harryette Ehrhardt, interview by Karen Wisely, July 9, 2013, 8–13, OH 1843, Special Collections of the UNT Libraries, University of North Texas, Denton, Texas; Harryette Ehrhardt, "Outrageous Oral, Volume 6," lecture, *The Dallas Way*, Dallas Texas, June 27, 2013, quotation, http://www.thedallasway.org/stories/videos/2016/6/21/outrageous -oral-volume-6-harryette-ehrhardt; Jaime Dunaway-Seale, "How Former State Rep. Harryette Ehrhardt Became the 'Fairy Godmother' of the LGBTQ Community," *Advocate: Lakewood/East Dallas*, May 23, 2019, https://lakewood .advocatemag.com/harryette-ehrhardt/.

12. Baker, "Making the Grade," first quotation; Harryette Ehrhardt, interview by Karen Wisely, July 9, 2013, 8–13, interview OH 1843, Special Collections of the UNT Libraries, University of North Texas, Denton, Texas, second quotation; Ehrhardt, "Outrageous Oral."

13. Ehrhardt, "Outrageous Oral," first quotation; Baker, "Making the Grade," second quotation.

14. Roger Oglesby, "Gay Man Says He's 'Typical,'" *Dallas Times Herald*, June 16, 1981, 1, 2, quotation; *Baker v. Wade*, 563 F. Supp. 1121 (N.D. Tex. 1982), rev'd 769 F. 2d 289 (5th Cir. 1985), *cert. denied*, 478 U.S. 1022 (1986); Barbara Canetti, "SMU Grad Student Suing to Overturn Homosexuality Laws," *Houston Post*, undated newspaper clipping, Box 4B49, THRF Collection. For Baker's use of his middle name, Floyd, see Dotty Griffith, "Gays Coming Out of Political Closet," *Dallas Morning News*, July 10, 1977, 34.

15. *Baker v. Wade*, 563 F. Supp. 1121 (N.D. Tex. 1982), rev'd 769 F. 2d 289 (5th Cir. 1985), *cert. denied*, 478 U.S. 1022 (1986); Mike Anglin, interview by Karen Wisely, October 24, 2015, interview OH 1851, Special Collections of the UNT Libraries, University of North Texas, Denton, Texas, 23–24, quotations on 24; Mike Anglin, interview by the author, July 19, 2018, Dallas, Texas.

16. *Baker v. Wade*, "Plaintiff's Original Complaint—Defendants' Class Action," Box 4B33, Folder Pre-Trial Pleadings 1979–1981, THRF Collection, quotations; "Gay Challenges Sex Conduct Statute," *Dallas Times Herald*, November 20, 1979, Box 494, Folder Don Baker Newspaper Clippings, Resource Center LGBT Collection; Norma Adams Wade, "Teacher Files Suit Against Homosexual Conduct Law," *Dallas Morning News*, November 20, 1979, 44; "Curb on Homosexuality in Texas Is Challenged in Suit by Teacher," *New York Times*, November 25, 1979, 66.

17. Mary Barrineau, "Homosexual Says State Law Produces 'Chilling' Effect," *Dallas Times Herald*, November 21, 1979, newspaper clipping, Box 494, Folder Don Baker Newspaper Clippings, Resource Center LGBT Collection, first, second, third, and fifth quotations; Steve Blow, "'The Perfect Plaintiff' Hits the Legal Trail for Homosexuals," *Dallas Morning News*, November 21, 1979, 43, fourth quotation; Texas Human Rights Foundation, "Press Advisory," November 20, 1979, Box 1, Folder 6, Schwab Collection.

18. "Jerry Buchmeyer: Newest Federal Judge Winning Praise," *Dallas Downtown News*, July 6–12, 1981, newspaper clipping, Box 495, Folder Don Baker Newspaper Clippings, Resource Center LGBT Collection; Dennis Holder, "Buchmeyer vs. Dallas," *D Magazine*, June 1, 1991, available at http://www.dmagazine.com/publications/d-magazine/1991/june/buchmeyer-vs-dallas/; *Baker v. Wade*, 563 F. Supp. 1121 (N.D. Tex. 1982), rev'd 769 F. 2d 289 (5th Cir. 1985), *cert. denied*, 478 U.S. 1022 (1986); Barber interview, first quotation; Oglesby, "Gay Man Says He's 'Typical,'" second quotation.

19. Doug Nogami, "Homosexuality 'Victimless Crime,' Sociologist Testifies at Statute Trial," *Dallas Morning News*, June 16, 1981, 14, first, second, third, fourth, and sixth quotations; Victor P. Furnish, "Replies to Interrogatories," n.d., Box 495, Folder Victor Furnish, Resource Center LGBT Collection, fifth quotation; Texas Human Rights Foundation, "Witnesses in *Baker v. Wade*, et al.," press release, n.d., Box 1, Folder 6, Schwab Collection; James C. Barber to Victor Furnish, September 25, 1980, Box 4B33, Folder Correspondence

1980–1984, THRF Collection; Victor Paul Furnish, *The Moral Teaching of Paul* (Nashville: Abingdon Press, 1979); Barber interview.

20. *Baker v. Wade*, 563 F. Supp. 1121 (N.D. Tex. 1982), rev'd 769 F. 2d 289 (5th Cir. 1985), *cert. denied*, 478 U.S. 1022 (1986); *Baker v. Wade*, In the United States District Court of Texas, Dallas Division, "Answers and Deposition of Henry Wade," Box 4B33, Folder Depositions, THRF Collection, quotations; *Baker v. Wade*, In the United States District Court of Texas, Dallas Division, "Answers and Deposition of Lee Holt," Box 4B33, Folder Depositions, THRF Collection; *Griswold v. Connecticut*, 381 U.S. 479 (1965); *Roe v. Wade*, 410 U.S. 113 (1973); *People v. Onofre*, 51 N.Y. 2d 476, 415 N.E. 2d 936, 434 N.Y.S. 2d 947 (1980).

21. *Baker v. Wade*, 563 F. Supp. 1121 (N.D. Tex. 1982), rev'd 769 F. 2d 289 (5th Cir. 1985), *cert. denied*, 478 U.S. 1022 (1986); *Baker v. Wade*, In the United States District Court of Texas, Dallas Division, "Answers and Deposition of Lee Holt," Box 4B33, Folder Depositions, THRF Collection, quotations.

22. Roger Oglesby, "Grigson: Gays Suffer from Pathological Illness," *Dallas Times Herald*, June 17, 1981, Metro 1, 4.

23. Oglesby, "Grigson," first and second quotation on 1; Doug Nogami, "Grigson Classifies Homosexuality as an 'Illness,'" *Dallas Morning News*, June 17, 1981, 23, third, fourth, and fifth quotations; Texas Human Rights Foundation, "Federal Court Hears Baker v. Wade Testimony," press release, June 18, 1981, Box 1, Folder 6, Schwab Collection; Watt interview.

24. *Baker v. Wade*, "Post-Trial Brief of Henry Wade," June 14, 1981, Box 4B43, Folder Baker v. Wade Early Documents, THRF Collection, first quotation on 27; *Baker v. Wade*, "Defendant Holt's Post-Trial Brief," July 17, 1981, Box 4B43, Folder Baker v. Wade Early Documents, THRF Collection, second quotation on 2; *Baker v. Wade*, "Plaintiff's Post-Trial Brief," August 7, 1981, Box 4B43, Folder Baker v. Wade Early Documents, THRF Collection; Texas Human Rights Foundation, "Defendants File Post Trial Briefs," press release, August 5, 1981, Box 1, Folder 6, Schwab Collection; Texas Human Rights Foundation, "For Immediate Release," press release, August 30, 1981, Box 1, Folder 6, Schwab Collection; Texas Human Rights Foundation, "Additional Post Trial Briefs Filed in Baker v. Wade," press release, February 12, 1982, Box 1, Folder 6, Schwab Collection.

25. *Baker v. Wade*, 563 F. Supp. 1121 (N.D. Tex. 1982), rev'd 769 F. 2d 289 (5th Cir. 1985), *cert. denied*, 478 U.S. 1022 (1986).

26. *Baker v. Wade*, 563 F. Supp. 1121 (N.D. Tex. 1982), rev'd 769 F. 2d 289 (5th Cir. 1985), *cert. denied*, 478 U.S. 1022 (1986).

27. "Gayteenth: Aug. 17, 1982," Box 2, Folder 3, Baker Collection; Don Baker, "News Release," August 17, 1982, Box 4B33, Folder Press Releases Baker v.

Wade, THRF Collection, first quotation; Esther M. Bauer, "Gay Activists Say Ruling May Start Nationwide Effort," *Dallas Morning News*, August 18, 1982, 17, 18, second quotation on 17, third quotation on 18; Doug Nogami, "Judge Voids Texas Ban on Gay Sex Acts," *Dallas Morning News*, August 18, 1982, B1, fourth quotation; Texas Human Rights Foundation, "Federal Court Rules Texas Homosexual Conduct Law Unconstitutional," press release, August 17, 1982, Box 1, Folder 6, Schwab Collection, fifth quotation; Jack Booth, "U.S. Judge Rules State Anti-Gay Law Unconstitutional," *Dallas Times Herald*, August 18, 1982, 1, 7, sixth quotation on 7; "Texas Ban on Homosexual Conduct Struck Down," *New York Times*, August 18, 1982, A8. For a brief history of Juneteenth, see Teresa Palomo Acosta, "Juneteenth," *Handbook of Texas Online*, http://www.tshaonline.org/handbook/online/articles/lkj01.

28. "21.06 Unconstitutional," *Dialog: Newsletter of the Dallas Gay Alliance*, vol. 6, no. 9, September 1982, 1, first quotation; Wade Moore to Don Baker, November 20, 1979, Box 495, Folder Congratulating Don Baker, Resource Center LGBT Collection; Steve Engwall to Don Baker, November 22, 1979, Box 495, Folder Congratulating Don Baker, Resource Center LGBT Collection; Steve Parker to Don Baker, August 19, 1982, Box 495, Folder Congratulating Don Baker, Resource Center LGBT Collection; Ric Huett and Tim Martin to Don Baker, August 18, 1982, Box 495, Folder Congratulating Don Baker, Resource Center LGBT Collection; Charles B. Woodard to Don Baker, July 8, 1986, Box 2, Folder 5, Baker Collection; Sonny and Gary to Don Baker, telegram, August 17, 1982, Box 495, Folder Congratulating Don Baker, Resource Center LGBT Collection.

29. Abby R. Rubenfeld to Robert Schwab, August 25, 1982, Box 4B40, THRF Collection, first quotation; Lucia Valeska, "Statement Re: Baker v. Wade," August 17, 1982, Box 494, Folder Don Baker, Baker v. Wade, Resource Center LGBT Collection; Bauer, "Gay Activists," second quotation on 17.

30. Don Baker, "News Release," August 17, 1982, Box 4B33, Folder Press Releases Baker v. Wade, THRF Collection, first quotation; "21.06 Appeal Unlikely," *This Week in Texas*, August 27–September 2, 1982, 15; "Homosexual Law: Wrong Decision," *Dallas Morning News*, August 21, 1982, 26, second quotation.

31. Robert Hyde, "Lord Mac: In the Winter of His Years," *Montrose Voice*, May 18, 1984, 1–3; Linda Wyche, " 'Lord Mac' Dies of AIDS—But Some Good Things Never End," *Montrose Voice*, October 26, 1984, 1; Jonathan C. Heath, "Strength in Numbers: Houston's Gay Community and the AIDS Crisis, 1977–1989" (master's thesis, University of Houston, 2006), 37–38; Molly Ellen Bundschuh, "Cowboys, 'Queers,' and Community: The AIDS Crisis in Houston and Dallas, 1981–1996" (master's thesis, University of North Texas, 2014), 26–28; Ray Hill, interview by Renee Tappe, September 29, 2016, Houston, Texas, OH018, The OH Project: Oral Histories of HIV/AIDS in Houston, Harris County, and Southeast Texas, Woodson Research Center,

Rice University, Houston, Texas, 12–15. In the interview, Hill inaccurately remembered his interaction with McAdory occurring in 1979, but multiple sources confirm this occurred in 1981.

32. James S. Olson, "Disease, Dollars, and Death: The Rise and Fall of the Institute for Immunological and Infectious Disorders, Houston, Texas, 1984–1987," *Journal of South Texas* 23, no. 1 (Spring 2010): 30–45; Bundschuh, "Cowboys," 27; Jonathan Engel, *The Epidemic: A Global History of AIDS* (New York: Smithsonian Books, 2006), 5–10; "Epidemic of Gay Diseases," *This Week in Texas*, February 5–11, 1982, 9; Guy R. Newell, M.D., "Kaposi's Sarcoma and Opportunistic Infections," *This Week in Texas*, February 5–11, 1982, 21–23; "Clint Moncrief Dies," *Montrose Voice*, March 12, 1982, 5; "Clint Moncrief," *This Week in Texas*, March 12–18, 1982, 65; "AIDS Epidemic Sweeps Texas," *This Week in Texas*, December 31, 1982, 13; Peter W. A. Mansell and Sue Cooper, interview by Lesley Williams Brunet, February 28, 2003, Making Cancer History Voices Oral History Collection, Historical Resources Center, Research Medical Library, University of Texas MD Anderson Cancer Center, Houston, Texas; Peter Mansell and Earl Shelp, interview by Sue Cooper, September 20, 2004, Making Cancer History Voices Oral History Collection, Historical Resources Center, Research Medical Library, University of Texas MD Anderson Cancer Center, Houston, Texas. For the beginning of the AIDS crisis, see Jennifer Brier, *Infectious Ideas: U.S. Political Responses to the AIDS Crisis* (Chapel Hill: University of North Carolina Press, 2009); Tamar W. Carroll, *Mobilizing New York: AIDS, Antipoverty, and Feminist Activism* (Chapel Hill: University of North Carolina Press, 2015); and David France, *How to Survive a Plague: The Inside Story of How Citizens and Science Tamed AIDS* (New York: Vintage, 2016).

33. Randolph B. Campbell, *Gone to Texas: A History of the Lone Star State* (New York: Oxford University Press, 2003), 447–451, quotation on 450.

34. Ira Perry, "White's Appeal of Case Has Gays in Quandary," *Houston Post*, November 17, 1982, 2A; Ira Perry and Bill Hensel, "White Tells Gays Here Why He Appealed Ruling," *Houston Post*, November 18, 1982, 8A; Ira Perry, "White Makes Peace with Gays on Appeal of Ruling," *Houston Post*, November 19, 1982, 4A.

35. "Danny Hill," Legislative Reference Library of Texas, https://lrl.texas.gov/legeleaders/members/memberdisplay.cfm?memberID=577#bio; Eric Quitugua, "Reaching Out," State Bar of Texas, https://www.texasbar.com/AM/Template.cfm?Section=articles&Template=/CM/HTMLDisplay.cfm&ContentID=46991; Terrence Stutz, "DA Ready for Battle," *Dallas Morning News*, August 28, 1985, 21A, quotation.

36. David R. Richards to Gilbert F. Ganucheau, March 9, 1983, Box 4B38, Folder HB 2138, THRF Collection; Ira Perry, "Private Homosexuality Decriminalized," *Houston Post*, March 12, 1983, 1, 27, first and second quotations on 27, fourth quotation on 1; Rick Abrams, "Mattox Won't Fight for Sodomy Law," *Dallas Morning News*, March 13, 1983, 1, 40, third quotation on 1.

37. Glenna Whitley, "Group Seeks Reinstatement of Law in Effort to Fight AIDS," *Dallas Morning News*, February 25, 1983, first quotation; "Articles of Incorporation of Dallas Doctors Against A.I.D.S., Inc.," Box 4B38, Folder HB 2138, THRF Collection; James C. Barber to Roger W. Enlow, Peter Mansell, James Wheeler, Marcus Conant, Ronald R. Stegman, William H. McBeath, and F. Kevin Murphy, March 15, 1983, Box 4B40, THRF Collection; Texas Human Rights Foundation, "Appeal of Baker vs. Wade Continues," press release, March 16, 1983, Box 4B43, Folder Motion for Leave to File Amicus Brief by DDAA, THRF Collection; *Hill v. Mattox*, "Motion for Leave to File Petition for Writ of Mandamus," March 21, 1983, Box 4B33, Folder Various Baker v. Wade Materials, 1980–1985, THRF Collection; Linda Little, "Supporters Press Fight for Homosexuality Law," *Dallas Times Herald*, March 15, 1983, C1–C2, second quotation on C1; Hollis Hood, "Attorney General Drops 21.06 Appeal, but 'Doctors' Pursue Anti-Gay Legislation," *Dallas Fort Worth Gay News*, March 18, 1983, 1.

38. James C. Barber to Don Baker, February 23, 1983, Box 4B43, Folder Motion for Leave to File Amicus Brief by DDAA, THRF Collection, first quotation; *Baker v. Wade*, "Opposition of Appellee, Donald F. Baker, to Motion for Leave to File Amicus Curiae Brief and for Leave for Later Filing or for Enlargement of Time of Dallas Doctors Against AIDS, Inc.," Box 4B43, Folder Motion for Leave to File Amicus Brief by DDAA, THRF Collection, second and third quotations; THRF, "Appeal of Baker vs. Wade Continues," press release, March 16, 1983, 4B43, Folder Motion for Leave to File Amicus Brief by DDAA, THRF Collection; Little, "Supporters Press Fight," fourth and fifth quotations on C2; Hood, "Attorney General," sixth quotation on 1.

39. Bill Ceverha, "House Bill 2138," Box 4B38, Folder HB 2138, THRF Collection, quotations; *Baker v. Wade*, "Supplemental Opinion," April 3, 1984, Box 4B33, Folder Various Baker v. Wade Materials 1980–1985, THRF Collection; Don Ritz, "Dallas Attorney Lobbying for Anti-Gay Legislation," *Dallas Fort Worth Gay News*, March 18, 1983, 6.

40. Jackie Calmes, "Legislator Says Homosexuals Pose Health Threat," *Dallas Morning News*, April 20, 1983, 16, first quotation; Mike Thomas, "Homosexual Conduct and Activity in Dallas, Texas," Box 4B38, Folder HB 2138, THRF Collection, second, third, fourth, fifth, and sixth quotations; "Committee Hears Sodomy Law Testimony," *Dallas Fort Worth Gay News*, April 22, 1983, 1.

41. Don Baker, "Statement," n.d., Box 4B38, Folder HB 2138, THRF Collection, quotations; "Statement of James C. Barber, Attorney, in Opposition to H.B. 2138," n.d., Box 4B38, Folder HB 2138, THRF Collection; Texas Civil Liberties Union, "Testimony of John B. Duncan, Executive Director, Texas Civil Liberties Union, Against HB 2138 before the House Criminal Jurisprudence Committee," April 19, 1983, Box 4B38, Folder HB 2138, THRF Collection; "Committee Hears Sodomy Law Testimony"; Carl Allen, "Lobby Austin Immediately, Warns Activist," *Dallas Fort Worth Gay News*, April 29, 1983, 1.

42. Ruth Miller Fitzgibbons, "Out of the Closet and Into City Hall: Will Dallas Gays Change the Face of City Politics?," *D Magazine*, July 1983, 130–134, 144–147; Allen, "Lobby Austin Immediately," quotations on 8; *Baker v. Wade*, "Supplemental Opinion," April 3, 1984, Box 4B33, Folder Various Baker v. Wade Materials 1980–1985, THRF Collection.

43. Don Ritz, "365 Days of Freedom," *Dallas Fort Worth Gay News*, August 26, 1983, 3, 6, first, second, and third quotations on 3; fourth, fifth, sixth, and seventh quotations on 6.

44. William Marberry and Hollis Hood, "Activist Attorney Robert Schwab Is AIDS Victim," *Dallas Fort Worth Gay News*, May 20, 1983, 1, 6, quotation on 1.

45. Clifford Pugh, "Living With AIDS," *Houston Post*, September 20, 1983, 1F, 4F, first quotation on 1F; "Gay Rights Activist Dies of AIDS," *Houston Post*, December 16, 1983, 14A; Ann Zimmerman, "The Final Battle," *Dallas Times Herald*, December 24, 1983, 1F, 3F; Hollis Hood, "Crowd Gathers to Honor Gay Rights Activist Robert Schwab at Houston Memorial Service," *Dallas Fort Worth Gay News*, January 13, 1984, 1, 6, second and third quotations on 1, fourth and fifth quotations on 6; Texas Human Rights Foundation, "M. Robert Schwab, National Gay Leader, Succumbs to AIDS," press release, December 15, 1983, Box 1, Folder 3, Schwab Collection; Minutes of the Texas Human Rights Foundation, November 19, 1983, Box 4B39, Folder THRF Retired Minutes and Correspondence, THRF Collection.

46. Hollis Hood, "'We Have to Keep It Going,' Tom Coleman Says of THRF," *Dallas Fort Worth Gay News*, January 20, 1984, 1, quotations; *Hill v. Mattox*, "Respondent's Reply to Motion for Leave to File Petition for Writ of Mandamus," March 28, 1983, Box 4B33, Folder Various Baker v. Wade Materials, 1980–1985, THRF Collection; Hollis Hood, "State High Court Says It Won't Force Mattox to Fight Repeal of 21.06," *Dallas Fort Worth Gay News*, April 8, 1983, 1; *Baker v. Wade and Hill*, "Appeal from the United States District Court for the Northern District of Texas," June 6, 1983, Box 4B40, THRF Collection; James C. Barber to Don Baker, June 9, 1983, Box 4B40, THRF Collection; *Baker v. Wade*, Appeal from the United States District Court for the Northern District of Texas, "Brief for Appellant," July 6, 1983, Box 4B33, THRF Collection.

47. *Baker v. Wade*, "Brief for Appellant," July 6, 1983, Box 4B33, THRF Collection, first quotation on 10, third quotation on 36; *Baker v. Wade*, "Transcript of Oral Argument Before Judge Alvin B. Rubin, Irving L. Goldberg, Judge Thomas Reauleg [*sic*], Taken in the Fifth Judicial Circuit Court of Appeals, New Orleans, Louisiana," April 17, 1984, Box 4B33, THRF Collection, second quotation on 25.

48. *Baker v. Wade*, "Appellee's Response to Reply Brief of Appellant," November 21, 1983, 6–9, Box 4B39, THRF Collection, first and second quotations on 8; *Baker v. Wade*, "Plaintiff's Reply Brief to Opposition to Danny Hill's

Motion to Set Aside Judgment and Reopen the Evidence," July 12, 1983, 1–13, Box 4B33, Folder Appeal Pleadings 1983, THRF Collection, third quotation on 12; *Baker v. Wade*, "Transcript of Oral Argument Before Judge Alvin B. Rubin, Irving L. Goldberg, Judge Thomas Reauleg [*sic*], Taken in the Fifth Judicial Circuit Court of Appeals, New Orleans, Louisiana," April 17, 1984, 32–43, Box 4B33, THRF Collection, fourth quotation on 47.

49. *Baker v. Wade*, "Appellee's Response to Reply Brief of Appellant," November 21, 1983, 1–6, Box 4B39, THRF Collection; *Baker v. Wade*, "Transcript of Oral Argument Before Judge Alvin B. Rubin, Irving L. Goldberg, Judge Thomas Reauleg [*sic*], Taken in the Fifth Judicial Circuit Court of Appeals, New Orleans, Louisiana," April 17, 1984, 33, Box 4B33, THRF Collection; *Baker v. Wade*, Federal Reporter, United States Court of Appeals Fifth Circuit, September 21, 1984, 236–244, Box 4B33, Folder Post Trial Readings, THRF Collection, first quotation on 237, third quotation on 242–243; Charlotte-Anne Lucas, "Appellate Court Refuses to Revive State Anti-Gay Law," *Dallas Times Herald*, September 22, 1984; W. R. Deener III, "Federal Ruling Apparently Kills Texas Law Against Homosexual Acts," *Dallas Morning News*, September 22, 1984, 40A.

50. Don Baker, "Statement by Don Baker, Plaintiff in the Case," September 21, 1984, Box 494, Folder Don Baker Newspaper Clippings, Resource Center LGBT Collection, first and second quotations; Thomas J. Coleman Jr., "Status Report on *Baker v. Wade*," n.d., Box 4B42, Folder GPC, THRF Collection, third quotation.

51. Don Baker, "Statement by Don Baker, Plaintiff in the Case," September 21, 1984, Box 494, Folder Don Baker Newspaper Clippings, Resource Center LGBT Collection, first and second quotations; *Dronenburg v. Zech*, 741 F. 2d 1388 (DC Cir.), rehearing denied, 746 F. 2d 1579 (DC Cir. 1984), third quotation on 1397; Thomas J. Coleman Jr., "Status Report on *Baker v. Wade*," n.d., Box 4B42, Folder GPC, THRF Collection, fourth, fifth, sixth, and seventh quotations; Stuart Taylor Jr., "Discharge of a Homosexual," *New York Times*, August 18, 1984, 1; David G. Savage, "Gay Rights Case a Window to Ginsburg Centrist Views," *Los Angeles Times*, June 17, 1993, https://www.latimes.com/archives/la-xpm-1993-06-17-mn-3918-story.html.

52. For the history of the 1984–1985 battle over Houston's nondiscrimination ordinance, see Phelps, "The Politics of Queer Disidentification," 311–348; and Carpenter, *Flagrant Conduct*, 28–37.

53. *Baker v. Wade*, Appellant's Supplemental Brief on Rehearing En Banc, March 13, 1985, Box 4B33, THRF Collection; *Baker v. Wade*, Federal Supplement, Box 4B33, THRF Collection; Charlotte-Anne Lucas, "Full Appeals Court to Hear Texas Anti-Gay Law Case," *Dallas Times Herald*, February 2, 1985, 28A, quotations; Minutes of the Texas Human Rights Foundation, April 20, 1985, Box 4B32 Folder THRF Correspondence 1985–1986, part 2, THRF Collection; Howie Dare et al. to Community Leader, May 5, 1985, Box 1, Folder 10, Baker Collection.

54. *Baker v. Wade*, Appellee's Supplemental Brief on Rehearing En Banc, April 11, 1985, Box 4B33, THRF Collection; Thomas J. Coleman to James C. Barber, April 4, 1984, Box 4B43, Folder Baker v. Wade THRF Amicus, THRF Collection; Nan D. Hunter to Thomas Coleman, August 8, 1983, Box 4B40, Folder Summary Affirmance, THRF Collection; Thomas J. Coleman Jr. to James C. Barber, April 4, 1984, Box 4B43, Folder Baker v. Wade THRF Amicus, THRF Collection; *Baker v. Wade*, Amicus Curiae Brief on Behalf of the Texas Human Rights Foundation, n.d., Box 4B33, Folder Various Baker v. Wade Materials 1980–1985, THRF Collection, first quotation on 41, second quotation on 42, third quotation on 44, fourth and fifth quotations on 45. For "quasi-suspect class" and "intermediate scrutiny," see *Plyler v. Doe*, 457 U.S. 202, 215–221 (1982) and *City of Cleburne, Texas v. Cleburne Living Center, Inc.*, 473 U.S. 432 (1985).

55. *Baker v. Wade*, Affidavit of John D'Emilio, PhD, April 5, 1985, Box 4B33, THRF Collection, first quotation on 15, second quotation on 29, third quotation on 37, fourth quotation on 38; Don Baker to James C. Barber, March 17, 1985, Box 2, Folder 5, Baker Collection; D'Emilio, *Sexual Politics, Sexual Communities*; John Boswell, *Christianity, Social Tolerance, and Homosexuality: Gay People in Western Europe from the Beginning of the Christian Era to the Fourteenth Century* (Chicago: University of Chicago Press, 1980).

56. Eskridge, *Dishonorable Passions*, 231–233.

57. Eskridge, *Dishonorable Passions*, 233–236; William J. Choyke, "Supreme Court Agrees to Review Georgia's Sodomy Law," *Dallas Morning News*, November 5, 1985, H2.

58. David A. Bryan to the Board of Trustees of the Texas Human Rights Foundation, May 24, 1985, Box 4B32, Folder THRF Correspondence 1985–1986, part 2, THRF Collection.

59. *Baker v. Wade*, 563 F. Supp. 1121 (N.D. Tex 1982), rev'd 769 F. 2nd 289 (5th Cir. 1985), cert. denied 478 U.S. 1022 (1986).

60. *Baker v. Wade*, "Appellee's Petition for Rehearing En Banc," September 9, 1985, Box 4B33, Folder Various Baker v. Wade Materials 1980–1985, THRF Collection, first quotation on 9; *Baker v. Wade*, "On Petition for Rehearing En Banc," October 23, 1985, Box 4B33, Folder Various Baker v. Wade Materials 1980–1985, THRF Collection, second quotation on 3, third and fourth quotations on 4, fifth quotation on 5.

61. Don Ritz, "We Are Criminals, Again," *Dallas Voice*, August 30, 1985, 1, 14, first quotation on 1, second quotation on 14; Laurie Paternoster, "Court Upholds Texas Ban on Homosexual Act," *Dallas Morning News*, August 27, 1985, 16A, third quotation; Eduardo Paz Martinez, "Federal Court Rules Against Homosexuals," *Houston Post*, August 27, 1985, 1A, 6A, fourth quotation on 6A, fifth and sixth quotations on 1A, seventh and eighth quotations on 6A; Jim Barber, interview by the author, July 17, 2018.

62. Gayle Golden, "Gay Activist Determined," *Dallas Morning News*, August 28, 1985, 1A, 24A, first quotation on 1A; second, third, fourth, and fifth quotations on 24A.

63. *Baker v. Wade*, 563 F. Supp. 1121 (N.D. Tex 1982), rev'd 769 F. 2nd 289 (5th Cir. 1985), cert. denied 478 U.S. 1022 (1986).

64. Gayle Golden, "Battle Lines Drawn," *Dallas Morning News*, August 28, 1985, 24A, first and second quotations; Texas Human Rights Foundation, press release, n.d., Box 1, Folder 10, Baker Collection, third quotation; David A. Bryan to the Board of Trustees of the Texas Human Rights Foundation, September 15, 1985, Box 4B32, Folder THRF Correspondence 1985–1986, part 2, THRF Collection; Eugene Harrington to Board Members of the Texas Human Rights Foundation, memorandum, September 20, 1985, Box 4B32, Folder THRF Correspondence 1985–1986, part 2, THRF Collection; Minutes of the Texas Human Rights Foundation, September 21, 1985, Box 4B32, Folder THRF Correspondence 1985–1986, part 2, THRF Collection; Gene Harrington to Dick Peeples, memorandum, September 24, 1985, Box 4B32, Folder THRF Correspondence 1985–1986, part 2, THRF Collection; Don Baker to James C. Barber, October 17, 1985, Box 2, Folder 6, Baker Collection; Don Baker, draft of speech, n.d., Box 1, Folder 10, Baker Collection; Eskridge, *Dishonorable Passions*, 234–235; Gene Harrington to Dick Peeples, memorandum, September 24, 1985, Box 4B32, Folder THRF Correspondence 1985–1986, part 2, THRF Collection; Abby R. Rubenfeld to Robert Schwab, August 25, 1982, Box 4B40, THRF Collection; Jim Barber, interview by the author, July 17, 2018.

65. *Baker v. Wade*, "Petition for Certiorari," January 18, 1986, Box 4B32, THRF Collection, quotations; Eskridge, *Dishonorable Passions*, 236–237; Richard S. Dunham, "High Court to Review Georgia Sodomy Law," *Dallas Times Herald*, November 5, 1985.

66. Minutes of Lambda Legal Defense and Education Fund Ad Hoc Task Force to Challenge Sodomy Laws, November 15, 1985, Box 1, Folder 8, Baker Collection; Minutes of Lambda Legal Defense and Education Fund Ad Hoc Task Force to Challenge Sodomy Laws, November 16, 1985, Box 2, Folder 7, Baker Collection, quotations; Minutes of the Texas Human Rights Foundation, November 17, 1985, Box 4B32, Folder THRF Correspondence 1985–1986, part 2, THRF Collection; Jim Barber, interview by the author, July 17, 2018.

67. *Baker v. Wade*, "Petition for Certiorari," January 18, 1986, Box 4B32, THRF Collection; Eskridge, *Dishonorable Passions*, 238–242.

68. Eskridge, *Dishonorable Passions*, 243–247, quotation on 243.

69. *Bowers v. Hardwick*, 478 U.S. 186 (1986).

70. *Bowers v. Hardwick*, 478 U.S. 186 (1986), Donald F. Baker to Thurgood Marshall, July 10, 1986, Box 2, Folder 6, Baker Collection, first and third quotations; Texas Human Rights Foundation, "Supreme Court Denies Appeal of

21.06 Case," press release, n.d., Box 4B32, Folder THRF Correspondence 1985–1986, part 1, THRF Collection, second quotation; Don Baker to Lee Taft, September 12, 1986, Box 2, Folder 6, Baker Collection, fourth quotation; Don Baker, "The Challenge to Statute 21.06," Box 1, Folder 10, Baker Collection, fifth quotation; Watt interview.

71. *Bowers v. Hardwick*, 478 U.S. 186 (1986), first quotation; Texas Human Rights Foundation, "Supreme Court Denies Appeal of 21.06 Case," press release, n.d., Box 4B32, Folder THRF Correspondence 1985–1986, part 1, THRF Collection, second quotation.

Chapter 5. *Morales v. Texas* and *England v. City of Dallas*, 1986–1994

The first chapter epigraph is from Chuck Patrick, "New 21.06 Challenge," *This Week in Texas*, April 21–27, 1989, 26, 27, 29, quotation on 27, 29. The second chapter epigraph is from Catalina Camia, "Woman Sues City Over Police Job," *Dallas Morning News*, May 23, 1990, 1A, 6A.

1. Lori Montgomery, "Why Judge Was Easy on Gays' Killer," *Dallas Times Herald*, December 16, 1988, A1, A16; Lori Montgomery and Jeff Collins, "Prejudice and Presumption: Views of Victims' Lifestyle Blur Truth in Gay-Bashing Case," *Dallas Times Herald*, January 8, 1989, A1, A16–A17.

2. "1 Killed, 1 Wounded by Gunman in Reverchon Park," *Dallas Morning News*, May 16, 1988, 20A; Montgomery, "Why Judge Was Easy"; Montgomery and Collins, "Prejudice and Presumption."

3. Anne Belli and Lori Stahl, "Mesquite Junior, 18, Arrested in 2 Slayings," *Dallas Morning News*, May 26, 1988, 29A; "Mesquite Teen Faces 2 Murder Charges in Park Slayings," *Dallas Morning News*, May 27, 1988, 31A; "Metro Report," *Dallas Morning News*, June 8, 1988, 22A; David Jackson, "Ex-Classmate Says He Saw Teen Carrying Gun," *Dallas Morning News*, November 16, 1988, 27A, first quotation; Montgomery and Collins, "Prejudice and Presumption," second quotation on A17; Craig Flournoy, "Teen-Ager Convicted in 2 Deaths—Defense Vows Appeal Alleging Misconduct," *Dallas Morning News*, November 19, 1988, 33A; David Jackson, "Teen Gets 30 Years in Slayings—Defense Says It Will Appeal Verdict," *Dallas Morning News*, November 30, 1988, 29A, third, fourth, and fifth quotations; Christopher Haight, "The Silence Is Killing Us: Hate Crimes, Criminal Justice, and the Gay Rights Movement in Texas, 1990–1995," *Southwestern Historical Quarterly* 120, no. 1 (July 2016): 21–40.

4. Montgomery, "Why Judge Was Easy," first and second quotations on A1, third quotation on A16; William Waybourn, interview by the author, January 5, 2021, Denton, Texas.

5. "The Texas Human Rights Foundation Filed a Complaint Friday," United Press International, December 16, 1988, https://www.upi.com/Archives

/1988/12/16/The-Texas-Human-Rights-Foundation-filed-a-complaint
-Friday/3829598251600/; "Gay Alliance Seeks Ouster of State Judge,"
Dallas Morning News, December 19, 1988, 17A; Kelley Shannon, "Protesters Call Judge's Ruling Biased," *Houston Chronicle*, December 20, 1988,
19A; "Judicial Inquiry Begins on Judge After Light Sentence on Gays' Killer," *Austin American Statesman*, January 14, 1989, B3; Siva Vaidhyanathan,
"Panel Wants Hampton Complaints Heard—Texas Supreme Court Asked to
Appoint Master," *Dallas Morning News*, February 28, 1989, 21A; Waybourn
interview.

6. Anne Belli, "Hearing Starts Monday on Hampton's Remarks," *Dallas Morning
News*, October 15, 1989, 31A; In Re: Hampton, Jack, in the Supreme Court of
Texas, "Brief in Support of Motion to Quash, Motion to Dismiss, Exceptions
and Objections and Answer Subject Thereto with Plea in Abatement," April 19,
1989, Box 4B49, Texas Human Rights Foundation Records, 1978–1992, Dolph
Briscoe Center for American History, University of Texas, Austin, Texas (hereafter cited as THRF Collection), quotations on 13–14.

7. Robert C. Flowers, "Order of Public Censure of Morris Jackson Hampton,
Judge, 238th Judicial District Court, Dallas, Texas," November 27, 1989, Box
4B49, THRF Collection, first quotation; Dennis Vercher, "THRF 'Extremely
Pleased' with Action Against Judge," *Dallas Voice*, December 1, 1989, 1, 3, 5,
7, second quotation on 1.

8. *Bowers v. Hardwick*, 478 U.S. 186 (1986).

9. Bennett Roth, "Sodomy Law Repeal Sought," *Dallas Times Herald*, January
24, 1989, first and third quotations; "Sodomy Law Repeal Sought," *Dallas
Morning News*, January 24, 1989, 6A, second quotation; Craig C. McDaniel,
"Texans Spearhead Gay Rights Plan," *New York Native*, September 8, 1986, 8,
newspaper clipping, Box 4B49, THRF Collection; Mike Anglin, interview by
the author, July 19, 2018, Dallas, Texas.

10. Nan Feyler to Members of the Ad Hoc Task Force, memorandum, July 10,
1986, Box 4B31, Folder 21.06 State Constitutional Challenge, THRF Collection; Thomas J. Coleman Jr., to Ad Hoc Task Force, memo, July 15, 1986,
Box 4B31, Folder 21.06 State Constitutional Challenge, THRF Collection,
quotations.

11. *Texas State Employees Union v. Texas Department of Mental Health and Mental
Retardation*, 746 S.W. 2d 203 (Tex. 1987), quotations on 205; Dennis Vercher, "THRF Will File Challenge to 21.06 in State Court," *Dallas Voice*, March
31, 1989, 3, 19.

12. William Garza, "Strategies for Analyzing and Litigating a Texas Constitutional
Challenge to Texas' Homosexual Conduct Law," Box 4A458, Folder Research
Papers by William Garza (UT Law School) and Christopher T. Wilson (Texas
Tech), THRF Collection.

13. Christopher T. Wilson, "An Equal Protection Analysis of Texas Penal Code

21.06: The Texas Homosexual Conduct Statute," Box 4A458, Folder Research Papers by William Garza (UT Law School) and Christopher T. Wilson (Texas Tech), THRF Collection, quotations; Christopher T. Wilson to David A. Bryan, March 30, 1989, Box 4A458, Folder 21.06 Correspondence 1989–1990, THRF Collection.

14. David A. Bryan to J. Patrick Wiseman, April 26, 1989, Box 4A458, Folder 21.06 Correspondence 1989–1990, THRF Collection; David A. Bryan to 21.06 Plaintiffs, May 25, 1989, Box 4A458, Folder 21.06 Correspondence 1989–1990, THRF Collection; Minutes of the Texas Human Rights Foundation Executive Committee, November 20, 1988, Box 1, Folder Board of Trustees Meeting Minutes 1988–1990, Texas Human Rights Foundation Records Collection (The Dallas Way), University of North Texas Special Collections, Denton, Texas (hereafter cited as UNT THRF Collection); Minutes of the Texas Human Rights Foundation Board of Directors, January 21, 1989, Box 1, Folder Board of Trustees Meeting Minutes 1988–1990, UNT THRF Collection; "Attorney Profile: J. Patrick Wiseman of Austin," Box 4A458, Folder Press Releases (21.06) 1989–1992, THRF Collection; David A. Bryan to J. Patrick Wiseman, March 15, 1989, Box 4A458, Folder 21.06 Correspondence 1989–1990, THRF Collection; David A. Bryan to Linda Morales, March 20, 1989, Box 4A458, Folder 21.06 Correspondence 1989–1990, THRF Collection; "Plaintiff Profile: Linda Morales of Houston," Box 4A458, Folder Press Releases (21.06) 1989–1992, THRF Collection; "Plaintiff Profile: Tom Doyal of Austin," Box 4A458, Folder Press Releases (21.06) 1989–1992, THRF Collection; Linda Morales, interview by Samantha Rodriguez and Sandra Enriquez, July 7, 2016, Houston, Texas, Civil Rights in Black and Brown Oral History Project, The Portal to Texas History, https://texashistory.unt.edu/ark:/67531/metapth987519/m1/; Mike Anglin, interview by the author, July 19, 2018, Dallas, Texas; Dick Peeples, interview by the author, July 15, 2018, Dallas, Texas.

15. David A. Bryan to Charlotte Taft, March 24, 1989, Box 4A458, Folder 21.06 Correspondence 1989–1990, THRF Collection; "Plaintiff Profile: Charlotte Taft of Dallas," Box 4A458, Folder Press Releases (21.06) 1989–1992, THRF Collection; "Plaintiff Profile: Patricia Cramer of Austin," Box 4A458, Folder Press Releases (21.06) 1989–1992, THRF Collection; "Plaintiff Profile: John Thomas of Dallas," Box 4A458, Folder Press Releases (21.06) 1989–1992, THRF Collection; Dennis Vercher, "AIDS Activist Instrumental, Passionate about Making a Difference," *Houston Voice*, January 22, 1999, 6, 8.

16. *Morales v. Texas*, "Plaintiffs' Original Petition," April 7, 1989, Box 507, Folder 21.06 Morales v. Morales, Resource Center LGBT Collection of the UNT Libraries, 1940–2011, University of North Texas, Denton, Texas (hereafter cited as Resource Center LGBT Collection), quotations.

17. *Morales v. Texas*, "Plaintiffs' Original Petition," April 7, 1989, Box 507, Folder 21.06 Morales v. Morales, Resource Center LGBT Collection, quotations; Tex. Const. art. I, sec. 3a.

18. David Bryan, "Text of April 12, 1989, press conference statement announcing the filing of Morales vs. The State of Texas," Box 4A458, Folder Press Releases (21.06) 1989–1992, THRF Collection, quotations; Texas Human Rights Foundation, "Morales et al. vs. The State of Texas," press release, April 11, 1989, Box 4A458, Folder Press Releases (21.06) 1989–1992, THRF Collection; Texas Human Rights Foundation, "Morales et al. vs. The State of Texas," press release, April 12, 1989, Box 4B51, Folder Morales, THRF Collection.

19. Patrick, "New 21.06 Challenge," first and second quotations on 27, 29, sixth quotation on 27; Tom Doyal, "Statement to the Press," April 12, 1989, Box 4A458, Folder Press Releases (21.06) 1989–1992, THRF Collection, third quotation; Bennett Roth, "Gay Advocates Challenge Sodomy Law in State Court," *Dallas Times Herald*, April 13, 1989, B1–B2, fourth and fifth quotations on B1; "Rights Group Files Suit over Gay-Relations Law," *Dallas Morning News*, April 13, 1989, 27A; "Activists Challenge Sexual Contact Law," *Houston Post*, April 13, 1989, A8; Bruce Hight, "Homosexuals File Suit Challenging Texas Sex Law," *Austin American Statesman*, April 13, 1989, B3; "Five Homosexuals Sue to Change Texas Law," *San Antonio Express-News*, April 13, 1989, 8A; "Suit Seeks Decriminalization of Homosexual Conduct in Texas," *Montrose Voice*, April 14, 1989, 1; Dennis Vercher, "Suit Filed in Austin to Overturn 21.06," *Dallas Voice*, April 14, 1989, 1; Robin Kane, "Suit Filed Against Sodomy Law," *Washington Blade*, May 5, 1989, 16–17; "Morales et al. vs. The State of Texas," AMIGA de Houston Newsletter, Spring 1989, Box 4A458, Folder FNC (21.06) 1989–1992, THRF Collection; Morales interview.

20. Hight, "Homosexuals File Suit"; Roth, "Gay Advocates," first quotation on B1; *Morales v. Texas*, "Defendant's Plea to Jurisdiction," n.d., Box 507, Folder 21.06 Morales v. Morales, Resource Center LGBT Collection, second quotation; David A. Bryan to Pat Cramer, Tom Doyal, Linda Morales, Charlotte Taft, and John Thomas, June 8, 1989, Box 507, Folder 21.06 Morales v. Morales, Resource Center LGBT Collection; David A. Bryan to Dennis Vercher, June 11, 1989, Box 4A458, Folder 21.06 Correspondence 1989–1990, THRF Collection, third quotation; David A. Bryan to Sherry Darbonne, June 22, 1989, Box 4A458, Folder 21.06 Correspondence 1989–1990, THRF Collection.

21. *Morales v. Texas*, "Plaintiffs' First Amended Petition," Box 4A458, Folder State of TX v. Morales Court Documents 1989–1993, THRF Collection.

22. "Thousands March on Texas State Capitol," *This Week in Texas*, May 5–11, 1989, 19–21, quotations on 20–21; David A. Bryan to Sue Hyde, May 10, 1989, Box 4A458, Folder 21.06 Correspondence 1989–1990, THRF Collection.

23. Texas Human Rights Foundation, "Arriba," flyer, June 25, 1989, Box 4A458, Folder 21.06 Correspondence 1989–1990, THRF Collection; David A. Bryan to Pat Cramer, Tom Doyal, Linda Morales, Charlotte Taft, and John Thomas,

May 25, 1989, Box 4A458, Folder 21.06 Correspondence 1989–1990, THRF Collection; David A. Bryan to Sherry Darbonne, June 22, 1989, Box 4A458, Folder 21.06 Correspondence 1989–1990, THRF Collection; Sheri Cohen Darbonne, "Texas Activists Focus on Pending 'Right to Privacy' Suit," *Montrose Voice*, June 30, 1989, 6; National Gay and Lesbian Task Force, "National Day of Mourning for the Right to Privacy," June 30, 1989, Box 4A458, Folder Press Releases (21.06) 1989–1992, THRF Collection; Central Texas Civil Liberties Union, "Central Texas Civil Liberties Union Summer Events," postcard, n.d., Box 4A458, Folder Press Releases (21.06) 1989–1992, THRF Collection; David A. Bryan to Jan Griesinger, May 9, 1989, Box 4A458, Folder 21.06 Correspondence 1989–1990, THRF Collection; United Church Coalition for Lesbian and Gay Concerns, press release, June 2, 1989, Box 4A458, Folder 21.06 Correspondence 1989–1990, THRF Collection; David A. Bryan to Jan Griesinger, June 10, 1989, Box 4A458, Folder 21.06 Correspondence 1989–1990, THRF Collection.

24. Linda Morales, "Fighting Texas Law," *Allgo Pasa*, July 1989, newspaper clipping, Box 4A458, Folder News Clippings (21.06) 1989–1992, THRF Collection, first and second quotations; Charlotte Taft, "21.06—The So-Called 'Sodomy' Law Is Not Just for Those with a Penis!," *The Women's Alternative Times*, December 1989, newspaper clipping, Box 4A458, Folder News Clippings (21.06) 1989–1992, THRF Collection, third, fourth, and fifth quotations.

25. *England v. State of Texas, et al.*, "Oral Deposition of Mica England," October 23, 1990, Box 62, Folder Oral Deposition of Mica England, Resource Center LGBT Collection; Lorraine Ianello, "Lesbian Asks City Council for Backing," *Dallas Times Herald*, July 13, 1989, B3, first and second quotations; Todd J. Gillman, "Gay Recruit Is Rejected by Police," *Dallas Morning News*, July 13, 1989, 21A, 24A; Tammye Nash, "Lesbian Squares Off to Fight DPD Discrimination," *Dallas Voice*, July 14, 1989, 3–4, third quotation; Waybourn interview.

26. Minutes of the Texas Human Rights Foundation, November 11, 1982, Box 4B39, Folder THRF Retired Minutes and Correspondence, THRF Collection; Bill Nelson to Tom Coleman, February 9, 1983, Box 4B39, Folder THRF Retired Minutes and Correspondence, THRF Collection; Jack Booth, "U.S. Judge Rules State Anti-Gay Law Unconstitutional," *Dallas Times Herald*, August 18, 1982, 1, 7; Waybourn interview.

27. *England v. State of Texas, et al.*, "Oral Deposition of Mica England," October 23, 1990, Box 62, Folder Oral Deposition of Mica England, Resource Center LGBT Collection; Steve Blow, "Quest for Job Turns into Local Crusade," *Dallas Morning News*, July 14, 1989; Ianello, "Lesbian Asks City," quotation; Gillman, "Gay Recruit"; Nash, "Lesbian Squares Off"; Waybourn interview.

28. Mica England on *Larry King Live*, video, July 22, 1989, Mica England Collection (*The Dallas Way*), University of North Texas Special Collections, Denton, Texas, https://digital.library.unt.edu/ark:/67531/metadc1634452/m1/; Waybourn interview.

29. Gillman, "Gay Recruit," first quotation on 24A; Ianello, "Lesbian Asks City," second quotation; Todd J. Gillman, "Police Reject Homosexual Job Seekers," *Dallas Morning News*, July 19, 1989, 27A, 29A, third quotation on 29A; Todd J. Gillman, "Not All Texas Police Hiring Policies Reject Gays," *Dallas Morning News*, July 14, 1989, 21A, 24A; "Big Flap in Big D over Police Policy," *This Week in Texas*, August 4–10, 1989, 19.

30. Mack M. Vines to Mica England, July 26, 1989, Box 62, Folder Oral Deposition of Mica England, Resource Center LGBT Collection, first and second quotations; "Meeting with Police," *Dallas Voice*, August 18, 1989, 3; Tammye Nash, "Vines Enrages Lesbians, Gays at Citizens' Meeting," *Dallas Voice*, August 25, 1989, 3, 24; "Gays Walk Out on Vines," *Dallas Times Herald*, August 25, 1989, A18; "Dallas Police Meet with Gays," *This Week in Texas*, September 1–7, 1989, 21, third quotation; Waybourn interview.

31. David A. Bryan to J. Patrick Wiseman, October 17, 1989, Box 4A458, Folder 21.06 Correspondence 1989–1990, THRF Collection; David A. Bryan to Mica England, October 17, 1989, Box 4A458, Folder 21.06 Correspondence 1989–1990, THRF Collection; Tammye Nash, "England's Case Is Headed for Court," *Dallas Voice*, November 3, 1989, 17; Tammye Nash, "Lawyers Preparing England's Lawsuit," *Dallas Voice*, December 15, 1989, 3, 11, quotation.

32. Camia, "Woman Sues City," first and second quotations on 6A, sixth quotation on 1A–6A; Nash, "Lawyers Preparing," third quotation; Karen Reed, "England Gives Up Quiet Life to Test Her Rights," *Dallas Times Herald*, May 23, 1990, A22, fourth and fifth quotations.

33. David A. Bryan to Banks Tarver, February 1, 1990, Box 4A458, Folder 21.06 Correspondence 1989–1990, THRF Collection; Banks Tarver to William Simon, April 25, 1990, Box 35, Folder Morales v. State of Texas, Resource Center LGBT Collection; Banks Tarver to Judd Marmor, April 25, 1990, Box 35, Folder Morales v. State of Texas, Resource Center LGBT Collection; *Morales v. Texas*, "Affidavit of Judd Marmor in Support of Plaintiffs' Motion for Summary Judgment," Box 4A458, Folder State of TX v. Morales Court Documents 1989–1993, THRF Collection, quotations.

34. *Morales v. Texas*, "Affidavit of William Simon in Support of Plaintiffs' Motion for Summary Judgment," Box 4A458, Folder State of TX v. Morales Court Documents 1989–1993, THRF Collection.

35. *Morales v. Texas*, "Affidavit of Gregory M. Herek in Support of Plaintiffs' Motion for Summary Judgment," July 6, 1990, Box 4A458, Folder State of TX v. Morales Court Documents 1989–1993, THRF Collection, first quotation; *Morales v. Texas*, "Affidavit of Dr. Ron J. Anderson in Support of Plaintiffs' Motion for Summary Judgment," July 2, 1990, Box 4A458, Folder State of TX v. Morales Court Documents 1989–1993, THRF Collection, second and third quotations.

36. Banks Tarver to Tom Doyal, Linda Morales, Charlotte Taft, and John Thomas, April 25, 1990, Box 35, Folder Morales v. State of Texas, Resource Center

LGBT Collection; *Morales v. Texas*, "Affidavit of Linda Morales in Support of Plaintiffs' Motion for Summary Judgment," June 29, 1990, Box 4A458, Folder State of TX v. Morales Court Documents 1989–1993, THRF Collection, first, second, third, fourth, and fifth quotations; *Morales v. Texas*, "Affidavit of Charlotte Taft in Support of Plaintiffs' Motion for Summary Judgment," June 29, 1990, Box 4A458, Folder State of TX v. Morales Court Documents 1989–1993, THRF Collection, sixth quotation; *Morales v. Texas*, "Affidavit of Patricia Cramer in Support of Plaintiffs' Motion for Summary Judgment," n.d., Box 4A458, Folder State of TX v. Morales Court Documents 1989–1993, THRF Collection.

37. Texas Human Rights Foundation, "Sodomy Law Shown to Promote Anti-Gay Violence and Hinder Efforts at AIDS Education and Prevention," press release, July 19, 1990, Box 4A458, Folder Press Releases (21.06) 1989–1992, THRF Collection; *Morales v. Texas*, "Plaintiffs' Response to Defendant's Plea to Jurisdiction," August 27, 1990, Box 4B35, Folder Pre and Post Trial Communications, THRF Collection; *Morales v. Texas*, "Response to Plaintiffs' Motion for Summary Judgment," October 1, 1990, Box 4A458, Folder State of TX v. Morales Court Documents 1989–1993, THRF Collection; *Morales v. Texas*, "Affidavit of Dr. Paul Cameron," September 28, 1990, Box 4A458, Folder State of TX v. Morales Court Documents 1989–1993, THRF Collection, quotations.

38. *Morales v. Texas*, "Response to Plaintiffs' Motion for Summary Judgment," October 1, 1990, Box 4A458, Folder State of TX v. Morales Court Documents 1989–1993, THRF Collection.

39. Minutes of the Texas Human Rights Foundation Trustees, October 27, 1990, Box 1, Folder Board of Trustees Meeting Minutes 1988–1990, UNT THRF Collection; *Morales v. Texas*, "Statement of Facts," December 10, 1990, Box 4A458, Folder State of TX v. Morales Court Documents 1989–1993, THRF Collection, quotation.

40. *Morales v. Texas*, "Statement of Facts," December 10, 1990, Box 4A458, Folder State of TX v. Morales Court Documents 1989–1993, THRF Collection; Thom Prentiss, "Judge Expected to Issue Written Ruling on 21.06 Decision Wednesday," *Montrose Voice*, December 28, 1990, 1–2, quotations on 1.

41. *Morales v. Texas*, "Findings of Fact and Conclusions of Law," January 2, 1991, Box 2, Folder Litigation Morales, UNT THRF Collection.

42. Minutes of the Texas Human Rights Foundation Trustees, February 3, 1991, Box 1, Folder Board of Trustees Meeting Minutes 1991–1995, UNT THRF Collection; Texas Human Rights Foundation, "Texas Judge Officially Enters Decision Declaring 21.06 Unconstitutional," press release, March 18, 1991, Box 2, Folder Litigation Morales, UNT THRF Collection; Prentiss, "Judge Expected," first and third quotations on 2, second quotation on 3; Christy Hoppe, "Judge Rules Against Texas Sodomy Law," *Dallas Morning News*, December 11, 1990, 1A, fourth quotation; Catalina Camia, "Local, National Gay

Rights Groups Hail Court," *Dallas Morning News*, December 11, 1990, 16A, fifth and sixth quotations.

43. Robert Draper, "State Politics: Dan Morales," *Texas Monthly*, September 1996, https://www.texasmonthly.com/politics/state-politics-%e2%80%a2-dan -morales/; Bill Lodge, "Attorney General Hopefuls Debate," *Dallas Morning News*, July 19, 1990, 16A; "Morales to Wait to Assess Appeal in Sodomy Case," *Dallas Morning News*, December 12, 1990, 24A, quotation; Lee Taft to Will Pryor, February 5, 1991, Box 35, Folder Morales v. State of Texas, Resource Center LGBT Collection.

44. Sheri Cohen Darbonne, "THRF Expects 21.06 Ruling to be Appealed by Attorney General," *The New Voice*, March 29–April 4, 1991, 3, quotation; "Sodomy Law Under Fire," *Christian Informer*, April 4, 1991, 3; Morales interview.

45. *Morales v. Texas*, "Brief of the Appellant, State of Texas," June 10, 1991, Box 4A458, Folder State of TX v. Morales Court Documents 1989–1993, THRF Collection; Minutes of the Texas Human Rights Foundation Trustees, April 21, 1991, Box 1, Folder Board of Trustees Meeting Minutes 1991–1995, UNT THRF Collection; "Texas Officials Appeal Judge's Ruling on Sodomy," *Dallas Morning News*, April 6, 1991, 29A, quotations; "Attorney General Morales Appeals Ruling on 21.06," *Dimensions*, May 1991, 8.

46. *Morales v. Texas*, "Brief Amici Curiae of Certain Texas Legislators," January 21, 1992, Box 4A458, Folder State of TX v. Morales Court Documents 1989–1993, THRF Collection, quotations; "Court Brief from 29 State Lawmakers Expresses Support for Ban on Sodomy," *Houston Chronicle*, January 22, 1992, 2. The twenty-eight Texas legislators who signed the amicus brief were Senators Chris Harris, John Leedom, and David Sibley, and Representatives Kevin Brady, Bill Blackwood, Ben Campbell, John J. Carona, Warren Chisum, John R. Cook, Tom Craddick, John Culberson, Dianne W. Delisi, Toby Goodman, Kent Grusendorf, Will Hartnett, Talmadge Heflin, Fred Hill, Mike Jackson, Ted Kamel, Dan Kubiak, August R. (Augie) Ovard, Lyndon P. (Pete) Patterson, Randy Pennington, Glenn Repp, Curtis Soileau, David Swinford, Robert Turner, and Gerald V. Yost.

47. *Morales v. Texas*, "Brief Amici Curiae of Certain Texas Legislators," January 21, 1992, Box 4A458, Folder State of TX v. Morales Court Documents 1989–1993, THRF Collection.

48. Texas Human Rights Foundation, "Texas Human Rights Foundation Case Heard at Appellate Level," press release, January 29, 1992, Box 4A458, Folder Press Releases (21.06) 1989–1992, THRF Collection; Chris Luther, "State's Case on 21.06 Constitutionality Weak, says THRF Attorney," *The New Voice*, February 3–17, 1992, newspaper clipping, Box 4A458, Folder News Clippings (21.06) 1989–1992, THRF Collection, quotations; Suzy Wagers, "Texas Human Rights Foundation's Case Challenging 21.06 Heard Before Court of Appeals," *This Week in Texas*, February 7–13, 1992, 22, 31.

49. Camia, "Local, National," first and second quotations; North Texas Pro-Family Coalition, "Statement," January 15, 1992, Box 35, Folder Morales v. State of Texas, Resource Center LGBT Collection, third and fourth quotations.

50. Catalina Camia, "Chief Clarifies Hiring Stance," *Dallas Morning News*, January 19, 1992, 31A, 34A, quotation on 31A; Dallas City Council, "Citizen Appearances," January 22, 1992, Box 35, Folder Morales v. State of Texas, Resource Center LGBT Collection; "Court Brief from 29 State Lawmakers"; Al Brumley, "Woman Reapplies to Police after Ruling," *Dallas Morning News*, February 5, 1992, 21A, 26A.

51. *Dallas v. England*, 846 S.W. 2d 957 (1993); Brumley, "Woman Reapplies," quotation; Clay Robison, "Morales Says State's High Court Should Rule on Anti-Sodomy Law," *Houston Chronicle*, March 12, 1992, 1A, 10A.

52. *Morales v. Texas*, "Appeal Decision," March 11, 1992, Box 4A458, Folder State of TX v. Morales Court Documents 1989–1993, THRF Collection, quotations; *Morales v. Texas*, "Final Judgment," March 11, 1992, Box 4A458, Folder State of TX v. Morales Court Documents 1989–1993, THRF Collection; Texas Human Rights Foundation, "Texas Human Rights Foundation Wins Favorable Decision," March 11, 1992, Box 4A458, Folder Press Releases (21.06) 1989–1992, THRF Collection; Dennis Vercher, "State Appeals Panel Upholds District Court's 1990 Decision That Sodomy Statute Violates Privacy Rights," *Dallas Voice*, March 13, 1992, 1, 7.

53. Vercher, "State Appeals Panel," first quotation; Mark McDonald, "Judge's Ruling Puts England Nearer Goal," *Dallas Morning News*, April 12, 1992, 6F, second quotation.

54. *Morales v. Texas*, Petition for Discretionary Review," May 8, 1992, Box 4A458, Folder State of TX v. Morales Court Documents 1989–1993, THRF Collection; Texas Human Rights Foundation, "State Appeals Texas Human Rights Foundation's Case Against 21.06 to Both the Texas Supreme Court and the Court of Criminal Appeals," press release, May 8, 1992, Box 2, Folder Publications-News Releases 1989–2000, UNT THRF Collection; Christy Hoppe, "Texas Justices to Weigh Sodomy Law's Repeal Today," *Dallas Morning News*, January 5, 1993, 11A, 18A; Charlotte Taft, "Statement on the Supreme Court Consideration of 21.06," January 3, 1993, Box 35, Folder Morales v. State of Texas, Resource Center LGBT Collection, first and second quotations; John Thomas, "Statement to the Press," n.d., Box 35, Folder Morales v. State of Texas, Resource Center LGBT Collection, third and fourth quotations; Tom Doyal, "Statement to the Press," January 4, 1993, Box 35, Folder Morales v. State of Texas, Resource Center LGBT Collection, fifth quotation.

55. Ross Ramsey, "Court Hears Challenge to Sodomy Law," *Houston Chronicle*, January 6, 1993, 15A, 21A, first quotation on 15A; William A. Scott, "High Court Hears Arguments on State Law Against Sodomy," *Fort Worth Star Telegram*, January 6, 1993, 15, second, third, and fourth quotations; Rick Brown,

"Texas Supreme Court Hears 21.06 Case," *Texas Triangle*, January 7, 1993, 1, 5; "Texas Supreme Court Hears Oral Arguments in Texas Human Rights Foundation's Law Suit Challenging 21.06," THRF News, March–April 1993, 1, Box 4A458, Folder State of TX v. Morales Court Documents 1989–1993, THRF Collection, fifth quotation. For more on the legal and political career of Robert Gammage, see John C. Domino, *Texas Supreme Court Justice Robert Gammage: A Jurisprudence of Rights and Liberties* (Lanham, MD: Lexington Books, 2019).

56. *England v. City of Dallas*, "Appellate Decision," February 10, 1993, Box 2, Folder Litigation England, UNT THRF Collection; Lambda Legal Defense and Education Fund, Inc., "Texas Appellate Court Upholds Right of Lesbian Denied Employment by Dallas Police Department, Strikes Down 'Sodomy' Law," press release, February 11, 1993, Box 35, Folder Morales v. State of Texas, Resource Center LGBT Collection; Tammye Nash, "Justices Rule Police Policy Excluding Lesbians and Gays Is Unconstitutional," *Dallas Voice*, February 12, 1993, 1, 11, first and third quotations on 11; Anne Belli, "City Loses Ruling over Gay Officers," *Dallas Morning News*, February 11, 1993, 33A, 40A, second quotation on 33A, fourth quotation on 33A–40A.

57. Lori Stahl, "Lesbian Still Wants to Be Police Officer after Long Legal Fight," *Dallas Morning News*, May 8, 1993, 37A; Rick Brown, "Court Refuses to Hear Appeal in Police Discrimination Case," *Texas Triangle*, May 13, 1993, 11; John R. Selig, "England Brings Changes to Hiring Process at Dallas Police Department with Lawsuit," *Texas Triangle*, June 16, 1993, 10.

58. Rick Brown, "Gov. Says 21.06 Kept Alive by Fear," *Texas Triangle*, June 2, 1993, 1, 10.

59. Rick Brown, "Sodomy Law Challenge Still Pending," *Texas Triangle*, June 21, 1993, 8; Cyndi Drolet, "21.06 Overthrow Looks Hopeful," *Alliance News*, July 1993, 4, Box 2, Folder Publications-Articles-Academic Journals and Magazines 1989–1996, UNT THRF Collection; *Morales v. Texas*, "On Application for Writ of Error to the Court of Appeals for the Third District of Texas," n.d., Box 23, Folder Legal Aspects, Resource Center LGBT Collection, quotations.

60. *Morales v. Texas*, "On Application for Writ of Error to the Court of Appeals for the Third District of Texas," n.d., Box 23, Folder Legal Aspects, Resource Center LGBT Collection.

61. Texas Human Rights Foundation, "Texas Human Rights Foundation Calls Today's Outcome in 21.06 Case a 'Backhanded Victory,'" press release, January 12, 1994, Box 1, Folder Correspondence January–April 1994, UNT THRF Collection, first and second quotations; "Texas v. Morales Decided," THRF News, Second Quarter, 1994, Box 2, Folder Publications-Newsletters 1989–1994, UNT THRF Collection, third quotation; Michael Garbarino to Alan Levi, memorandum, February 13, 1995, Box 2, Folder Litigation-Meetings, UNT THRF Collection.

62. "Lesbian Settles Suit for Bias in Dallas," *New York Times*, September 16, 1994, A24; Eugene Sepulveda to All THRF Trustees, memorandum, January 26, 1994, Box 1, Folder Correspondence January–April 1994, UNT THRF Collection; "Staff Changes, Morales Outcome Set the Stage for a New Era at THRF," THRF News, Second Quarter, 1994, Box 2, Folder Publications-Newsletters 1989–1994, UNT THRF Collection; Dick Peeples, interview by the author, July 15, 2018, Dallas, Texas.

Conclusion. *Lawrence v. Texas* Reconsidered

1. Carpenter, *Flagrant Conduct*, 90.

2. *Lawrence v. Texas*, 539 U.S. 558 (2003), quotation on 581–582.

3. *Lawrence v. Texas*, 539 U.S. 558 (2003), quotations on 604–605.

4. *Lawrence v. Texas*, 539 U.S. 558 (2003), quotations on 602; *Boy Scouts of America v. Dale*, 530 U.S. 640 (2000).

5. Pamela Glazner, "Constitutional Law Doctrine Meets Reality: Don't Ask, Don't Tell in Light of *Lawrence v. Texas*," *Santa Clara Law Review* 46 (2006): 635–676; Gavin W. Scott Jr., "Queer Eye for the Military Guy: Will 'Don't Ask, Don't Tell' Survive in the Wake of *Lawrence v. Texas*?," *St. John's Law Review* 78 (2004): 897–932; Jennifer Steinhauer, "House Votes to Repeal 'Don't Ask, Don't Tell,'" *New York Times*, December 15, 2010, A27; Carl Hulse, "Senate Ends Military Ban on Gays Serving Openly," *New York Times*, December 19, 2010, A1.

6. David W. Dunlap, "A Marriage Born Where Tables for Two Women Were Common," *New York Times*, March 26, 2013, A18; Jeremy W. Peters, "Plaintiff, 83, Is Calm Center in a Legal and Political Storm," *New York Times*, March 28, 2013, A19, quotations on 769–771; Chris Palmer, "City Backing Widow's Suit over U.S. Law on Marriage," *New York Times*, June 21, 2012, A21; *United States v. Windsor*, 570 U.S. 744 (2013). Many judges and legal scholars agree that there exists in the Fifth Amendment's due process clause a guarantee of equal protection similar to that found in the Fourteenth Amendment. See Kenneth L. Karst, "The Fifth Amendment's Guarantee of Equal Protection," *North Carolina Law Review* 55, no. 3 (March 1977): 541–562.

7. *United States v. Windsor*, 570 U.S. 744 (2013), first quotation on 800; *Obergefell v. Hodges*, 576 U.S. 644 (2015), second quotation on 667.

8. Samantha Schmidt, "Fired After Joining Gay Softball League, Gerald Bostock Wins Landmark Case," *Washington Post*, June 16, 2020, 6, first quotation; Alan Feuer and Benjamin Weiser, "Civil Rights Act Offers Shield for Gay Workers, Court Rules," *New York Times*, February 27, 2018, A1, second quotation; Monica Hesse, "Supreme Court's LGBTQ Ruling Is an Ode to Aimee Stephens," *Washington Post*, June 16, 2020, 6; *Bostock v. Clayton County*, 590 U.S. ___ (2020), third, fourth, and fifth quotations.

9. *Masterpiece Cake Shop, Ltd. v. Colorado Civil Rights Commission*, 584 U.S. ___ (2018); Chris Cameron, "Trump Presses Limits on Transgender Rights over Supreme Court Ruling," *New York Times*, June 24, 2020, A16; Samantha Schmidt, "Federal Judge Blocks Trump Administration from Ending Transgender Health-Care Protections," *Washington Post*, August 17, 2020, https://www.washingtonpost.com/dc-md-va/2020/08/17/federal-judge -blocks-trump-administration-ending-transgender-healthcare-protections/; Human Rights Campaign, "Violence Against the Transgender and Gender Non-Conforming Community in 2020," https://www.hrc.org/resources /violence-against-the-trans-and-gender-non-conforming-community-in-2020.

10. *Ermold v. Davis*, 936 F. 3d 429 (Sixth Cir., 2019); *Davis v. Ermold*, 2020 U.S. LEXIS 3709, S.C., October 5, 2020, 1–5, quotations on 2–4; Nina Totenberg, "Justices Thomas, Alito Blast Supreme Court Decision on Same-Sex Marriage Rights," October 5, 2020, National Public Radio, https://www.npr .org/2020/10/05/920416357/justices-thomas-alito-blast-supreme-court -decision-on-gay-marriage-rights.

11. *Dobbs v. Jackson Women's Health Organization*, 597 U.S. ___ (2022); *Dobbs v. Jackson Women's Health Organization*, "Brief of Texas Right to Life as Amicus Curiae in Support of the Petitioners," https://www.supremecourt .gov/DocketPDF/19/19-1392/185344/20210729162610813_Dobbs%20 Amicus%20FINAL%20PDFA.pdf, quotation on 24–25; *Roe v. Wade*, 410 U.S. 113 (1973); *Planned Parenthood v. Casey*, 505 U.S. 833 (1992).

12. Cole, *Engines of Liberty*, 8.

13. Michele Weldon, "Don Baker's Battle: Striving to Return Humanity to the Fight for Gay Rights," *Dallas Times Herald*, January 21, 1986, B1, B8–B9, quotation on B9; Maggie Watt, interview by the author, July 10, 2018, Denton, Texas.

Photo Credits

p. 31 Box 1904, Folder 5, Judge Sarah T. Hughes Collection, University of North Texas Archives and Rare Books, Denton, Texas.

p. 57 Image used by permission from the Associated Press.

p. 62 The Dallas Gay Alliance, brick wall with graffiti: "Stop police harassment," photograph, https://texashistory.unt.edu/ark: /67531/metadc965363/, University of North Texas Libraries, The Portal to Texas History, courtesy of UNT Libraries Special Collections.

p. 67 RGD0006N-1980-1997, Houston Post Photographic Collection, Houston Metropolitan Research Center, Houston Public Library. Used by permission from the Houston Public Library.

p. 78 Bill Nelson and Richard Longstaff, photograph, undated, https://texashistory.unt.edu/ark:/67531/metadc823027/, University of North Texas Libraries, The Portal to Texas History, courtesy of UNT Libraries Special Collections.

p. 86 RGD0006N-1978-2010-03, Houston Post Photographic Collection, Houston Metropolitan Research Center, Houston Public Library. Used by permission from the Houston Public Library.

p. 87 1977 DGPC retreat, photograph, June 11, 1977, https:// texashistory.unt.edu/ark:/67531/metadc1787487/m1/2/, University of North Texas Libraries, The Portal to Texas History, courtesy of UNT Libraries Special Collections.

p. 88 Dallas Gay Political Caucus, Dallas Gay Political Caucus flyer, poster, 1977, https://digital.library.unt.edu/ark:/67531 /metadc304793/, University of North Texas Libraries, UNT Digital Library, courtesy of UNT Libraries Special Collections.

p. 92   Smiling man handling money in front of a counter, photograph, https://digital.library.unt.edu/ark:/67531/metadc965354/, University of North Texas Libraries, UNT Digital Library, courtesy of UNT Libraries Special Collections.

p. 113   http://www.thedallasway.org/stories/written/2017/11/23 /baker-vs-wade. Image courtesy of *The Dallas Way.*

p. 119   Don Baker holding a sign at the 1979 March on Washington, photograph, October 14, 1979, https://digital.library.unt .edu/ark:/67531/metadc276210/, University of North Texas Libraries, UNT Digital Library, courtesy of UNT Libraries Special Collections.

p. 129   Gayteenth: Texas homosexual conduct law ruled unconstitutional, poster, August 17, 1982, https://texashistory .unt.edu/ark:/67531/metadc947732/, University of North Texas Libraries, The Portal to Texas History, courtesy of UNT Libraries Special Collections.

p. 131   Dallas Gay Alliance, 21.06 bar flyer, poster, 1982, https:// digital.library.unt.edu/ark:/67531/metadc304803/, University of North Texas Libraries, UNT Digital Library, courtesy of UNT Libraries Special Collections.

p. 166   Dallas Gay Alliance, poster: Dallas Gay Alliance advertise for public reaction against Judge Jack Hampton, https:// texashistory.unt.edu/ark:/67531/metadc916032/, University of North Texas Libraries, The Portal to Texas History, courtesy of UNT Libraries Special Collections.

p. 179   Photograph of the gay rights march in Austin, Texas, https:// texashistory.unt.edu/ark:/67531/metadc1608531/m1/1/, University of North Texas Libraries, The Portal to Texas History, courtesy of UNT Libraries Special Collections.

p. 183   Mica England holds up Equal Employment Opportunity poster, photograph, July 12, 1989, https://digital.library.unt.edu/ark: /67531/metadc1634426/, University of North Texas Libraries, UNT Digital Library, courtesy of UNT Libraries Special Collections.

p. 186   William Waybourn Portrait, photograph, https://digital.library .unt.edu/ark:/67531/metadc276241/, University of North

Texas Libraries, UNT Digital Library, courtesy of UNT Libraries Special Collections.

p. 187   Dallas Gay Alliance members Don Hervey, Daniel Sopko, John Thomas, and B. J. Anderson, photograph by Rodger Mallison, Fort Worth Star-Telegram Collection, courtesy of the University of Texas at Arlington Libraries.

Index

abortion. See *Roe v. Wade*
ACLU. *See* American Civil Liberties Union
acquired immune deficiency syndrome. *See* AIDS
activism, 17–18, 50–52, 89, 218; Baker on, 222; grassroots, 4, 15; long-term approach of, 221–222. *See also* Dallas Gay Alliance; Dallas Gay Political Caucus; Houston Gay Political Caucus; Texas Human Rights Foundation
Adamson, Ollie, 73, 96
AIDS (acquired immune deficiency syndrome), 133; *Baker v. Wade* appeal invoking, 143, 144; Schwab diagnosis announcement of, 141
AIDS crisis, 12; arrival of, 132–133; Cameron on, 192; DDAA on, 137; Schwab on, 141–142; Section 21.06 exacerbating, 190
ALGPC. *See* Austin Lesbian and Gay Political Caucus
ALI. *See* American Law Institute
Alito, Samuel, 220
Allgo Pasa, 180
All Mujeres Interested in Getting Active (AMIGA), 173
Altitude Express, 217
American Civil Liberties Union (ACLU), 47, 84, 103
American Law Institute (ALI), 11, 18–23
American Psychiatric Association (APA), 20, 122; Cameron expelled

from, 192; Grigson censured by, 125; homosexuality mental illness delisting from, 188
AMIGA. *See* All Mujeres Interested in Getting Active
anal sex, sodomy laws on, 7, 8–9
Anderson, Ron J., 190
Anglin, Mike, 118–119
APA. *See* American Psychiatric Association
arson, 70–72
Arthur, John, 216
Article 524, 17, 18; *Buchanan v. Batchelor* regarding, 27, 28–30, 36–37; Court of Criminal Appeals rulings on, 9–11; *Dallas Morning News* on, 33; *Dawson v. Vance* regarding, 47–48; Everette legal challenge to, 46–47; Gossett on, 32; Keeton on, 26; language of, 8–9; married couple private sexual activity regarding, 33, 47–48; nonheteronormative persons influenced by, 14; ordinance replacing, 30, 32; police arrests and prosecutions on, 37; reclassification of, 39; replacement of discussed, 32–33; sexual behaviors prohibited by, 29; Sexual Offenses subcommittee on, 21–22; State Bar Committee on Revision of the Penal Code on, 23–25; unconstitutionality of, 29–30; US Constitution regarding, 11–12, 29–30; US Supreme Court on, 44; Vance, Carol, on, 44